Popular Conservatism and the Culture of National Government in Inter-War Britain

This radical new reading of British Conservatives' fortunes between the wars explores how the party adapted to the challenges of mass democracy after 1918. Geraint Thomas offers a fresh perspective on the relationship between local and national Conservatives' political strategies for electoral survival, which ensured that Conservative activists, despite their suspicion of coalitions, emerged as champions of the cross-party National Government from 1931 to 1940. By analysing the role of local campaigning in the age of mass broadcasting, Thomas recasts inter-war Conservatism. Popular Conservatism thus emerges less as the didactic product of Stanley Baldwin's consensual public image, and more concerned with the everyday material interests of the electorate. Exploring the contributions of key Conservative figures in the National Government, including Neville Chamberlain, Walter Elliot, Oliver Stanley and Kingsley Wood, this study reveals how their pursuit of the 'politics of recovery' enabled the Conservatives to foster a culture of programmatic, activist government that would become prevalent in Britain after the Second World War.

Geraint Thomas is Fellow and Director of Studies in History at Peterhouse, University of Cambridge. He has previously held positions at the Universities of Oxford and York. His research publications have focused on the politics of inter-war Britain and include, as co-editor, *Brave New World: Imperial and Democratic Nation-building in Britain between the Wars* (2012).

Popular Conservatism and the Culture of National Government in Inter-War Britain

Geraint Thomas
Peterhouse, Cambridge

CAMBRIDGE
UNIVERSITY PRESS

University Printing House, Cambridge CB2 8BS, United Kingdom

One Liberty Plaza, 20th Floor, New York, NY 10006, USA

477 Williamstown Road, Port Melbourne, VIC 3207, Australia

314–321, 3rd Floor, Plot 3, Splendor Forum, Jasola District Centre,
New Delhi – 110025, India

79 Anson Road, #05–04/06, Singapore 079906

Cambridge University Press is part of the University of Cambridge.

It furthers the University's mission by disseminating knowledge in the pursuit of
education, learning, and research at the highest international levels of excellence.

www.cambridge.org
Information on this title: www.cambridge.org/9781108483124
DOI: 10.1017/9781108672849

© Geraint Thomas 2020

This publication is in copyright. Subject to statutory exception
and to the provisions of relevant collective licensing agreements,
no reproduction of any part may take place without the written
permission of Cambridge University Press.

First published 2020

A catalogue record for this publication is available from the British Library.

Library of Congress Cataloging-in-Publication Data
Names: Thomas, Geraint, 1983– author.
Title: Popular conservatism and the culture of national government in inter-war
Britain / Geraint Thomas.
Description: Cambridge, United Kingdom ; New York, NY : Cambridge
University Press, 2020. | Includes bibliographical references and index.
Identifiers: LCCN 2020019830 | ISBN 9781108483124 (hardback) | ISBN
9781108672849 (ebook)
Subjects: LCSH: Great Britain – Politics and government – 1910–1936. | Great
Britain – Politics and government – 1936–1945. | Conservatism – Great Britain –
History – 20th century. | Conservative Party (Great Britain) – History – 20th
century.
Classification: LCC DA578 .T448 2020 | DDC 324.2410409/043–dc23
LC record available at https://lccn.loc.gov/2020019830

ISBN 978-1-108-48312-4 Hardback

Cambridge University Press has no responsibility for the persistence or accuracy of
URLs for external or third-party internet websites referred to in this publication
and does not guarantee that any content on such websites is, or will remain,
accurate or appropriate.

Contents

List of Figures and Table		*page* vii
Acknowledgements		viii
List of Abbreviations		xi
1	The National Government and Interwar Conservatism: The Historical Task	1

Part I Rethinking Interwar Conservatism

2	Local Politics and the Limits of Baldwinite Conservatism, 1918–1931	25
3	Conservatives and the Politics of National Recovery, 1931–1937	64

Part II Popular Conservatism and the National Government

4	Anti-Socialism and Working-Class Conservatism in the Industrial North	103
5	The Politics of Anti-Socialism in the Suburbs	134
6	Modernity and Paternalism in Rural Politics	165
7	National Conservatism in Scotland and Wales	197

Part III Reputations of Government

8	The Unravelling of National Anti-Socialism?	233
	Conclusion	258

vi   Contents

Appendix Parties' Share of the Vote in the Constituency
             Case-Study Areas, 1918–1945   269
Bibliography   312
Index   343

Figures and Table

Figures

3.1 'The Great Achievements of the National Government',
ILN, 28 April 1934 *page* 78

3.2 'I got the job – help me to keep it', National government
poster, general election 1935 80

5.1 'Unity and Security', National government poster, general
election 1931 139

5.2 'England Expects', National government poster, general
election 1931 139

6.1 'Back to the Plough', National government poster, general
election 1931 177

6.2 'Milk at school', *The Times*, 27 September 1934 185

6.3 'Not worth the picking', National government poster,
general election 1931 192

Table

1.1 Average share of the national vote by party, 1918–1935 13

Acknowledgements

'Writing a book is a horrible, exhausting struggle, like a long bout of some painful illness.' So said George Orwell. I don't know about him, but my task would have been a good deal trickier without the patient help and support of many individuals. That I am not much of a networker I hope makes my gratitude to them all the more sincere.

First, I would like to thank the many students I have taught at Cambridge, Oxford, and York since 2009. Little do they realise just how much our weekly discussions have shaped this study. To witness and benefit from their enthusiasm, good humour, and at times 'solidarity' has been one of the greatest privileges of my early career. The other has been the cooperation and friendship of colleagues: Michael Broers, Ambrogio Caiani, Allan Doig, George Garnett, Clive Holmes, Dame Frances Lannon, Gillian Peele, and Grant Tapsell during my time in Oxford; Julie Barrau, Larry Klein, David Maxwell, Dame Fiona Reynolds, and Elisabeth van Houts in Emmanuel College, Cambridge; and Lawrence Black, Simon Ditchfield, Tom Johnson, and Mark Roodhouse in York. It seems fitting that the final touches to this book on Conservatism should be applied during my first year as a Fellow of Peterhouse, where friendship, loyalty, and good cheer abound. Most especially I would like to thank Stephen Hampton, Saskia Murk Jansen, Mari Jones, Sam Kennerley, Andrew Lever, Scott Mandelbrote, James Carleton Paget, Magnus Ryan, Brendan Simms, Sir John Meurig Thomas, and András Zsák, for the warmth and conviviality of their welcome. To all colleagues: your unstinting support has not gone unnoticed.

Before the book came the thesis, and the person to whom fell the unenviable task of coaxing an unpolished graduate student towards completion was Jon Lawrence. Working with one of the great living historians of modern Britain was and continues to be a source of pride. If at times this pleasure was also daunting, it was always provocatively so, and for that – and much more – I owe him an enormous debt of gratitude. David Jarvis, whose work has done so much to shape our understanding of

Acknowledgements

interwar Conservatism, remained a source of advice and support long after I completed my MPhil under his supervision. Ross McKibbin, unrivalled as the chief interpreter of early twentieth-century Britain, was most generous with his time and did more than he probably realises to gee me up when necessary. As the external examiner, Andrew Thorpe brought insight and humour to proceedings, and I remain grateful to him for his careful reading of the thesis and his ready advice on the early stages of the book. Last but not least is Jon Parry, to whom I owe an incalculable debt. For his example as a scholar, mentor, and colleague, I offer my sincerest gratitude.

For friendship forged during the course of our PhDs, and many other favours besides, I thank the following: Gareth Atkins, David Beckingham, Rachel Hewitt, Gary Love, Tom Murgatroyd, Peter Newbon, Ed Sanders, David Thackeray, and above all Christopher Cotton, who despite his defection from academic history has found time to read several drafts of what follows.

My archival research took me to the British Library; the Manuscripts Reading Room in the University Library, Cambridge; the Churchill Archives Centre, Cambridge; the London School of Economics library archive; the Conservative Party Archive and the Department of Special Collections in the Bodleian Library, Oxford; the Parliamentary Archives; the National Library of Scotland; the National Library of Wales; Birmingham City Archives; Birmingham University Library; the University of Dundee Archive Services; Durham Record Office; West Glamorgan Archive Service; Liverpool Record Office; Norfolk Record Office; Northumberland Archives; Pembrokeshire Archives; Redbridge Local History Centre; West Yorkshire Archive Service; and Wiltshire and Swindon Archives. I am grateful to the staff in each of these, for many hours of patient and professional assistance, and to the copyright holders for permission to quote from the papers consulted. Some material in Chapter 7 draws upon my article in the *English Historical Review* – 'The Conservative party and Welsh politics in the inter-war years', vol. 128 (2013), 877–913 – and I am grateful to Oxford University Press for permission to use it. To Lord Hurd of Westwell, I offer my deepest thanks for generously granting me the private loan of the papers of his grandfather, Sir Percy Hurd.

At Cambridge University Press, Liz Friend-Smith has been a tremendously supportive and understanding editor. The two anonymous readers, in very different ways, offered invaluable comments and suggestions. I would also like to thank Stuart Ball for reading the entire draft; his encyclopaedic knowledge of interwar politics saved me from several embarrassing errors. Any errors that remain I managed all by myself.

And so to those who have been closest to me, yet farthest from my research. For candidness and kindness, I can count on my sisters and their families: Llinos, Gareth, and Tomos, and Meleri and Caio; while for steadfast support, no one measures up to my parents, Windsor and Glynwen. *Diolch.*

Abbreviations

ACC Association of Conservative Clubs
CA Conservative Association (or Constitutional Association)
CAJ *Conservative Agents' Journal*
CUA Conservative & Unionist Association
GPO General Post Office
IDL India Defence League
ILN *Illustrated London News*
LCC London County Council
LNU League of Nations Union
MMB Milk Marketing Board
NCSS National Council of Social Service
NPB National Publicity Bureau
PAC Public Assistance Committee
STCO Stockton & Thornaby Constitutional Organisation
UAB Unemployment Assistance Board
UBI Union of Britain and India

Journal Titles
AHR *Agricultural History Review*
CSH *Cultural and Social History*
EcHR *Economic History Review*
EHR *English Historical Review*
HJ *Historical Journal*
HWJ *History Workshop Journal*
JBS *Journal of British Studies*
JCH *Journal of Contemporary History*
JSH *Journal of Social History*
LHR *Labour History Review*
MH *Midland History*
P&P *Past and Present*
RH *Rural History*

xii   List of Abbreviations

SHR   *Scottish Historical Review*
TCBH   *Twentieth Century British History*
TRHS   *Transactions of the Royal Historical Society*
UH   *Urban History*
WHR   *Welsh History Review*

1 The National Government and Interwar Conservatism: The Historical Task

Frankly, he had no use for the National Government. He feared the Conservative Party had been led astray by strange gods and had departed from its old ideals.

This was how the *Norfolk Chronicle* summed up the speech of Colonel Thomas Purdy to a gathering of the North Norfolk Conservative Association in January 1935.[1] The colonel was well known in the county. He had served as an officer in the Norfolk Regiment during the Great War, including as a company major with the men of the king's Sandringham estate who met their fate in Gallipoli. A lifelong Conservative and party activist, he had railed against the cross-party National government's 'un-Conservative' policies since the formation of that administration in 1931. Continued membership, he warned, amounted to self-destruction. He had most emphatically not become a Conservative in order to support a coalition government, much less so one led since 1931 by a Labour prime minister. Ramsay MacDonald was a peace campaigner during the war and a socialist whose policies now included far-reaching reforms to the Indian constitution, a particular bugbear for Purdy.

Such partisanship was rooted in more than instinct and ideology. It was shaped by the Conservative party's unhappy experience of the post-war coalition led by Lloyd George, whose toppling by Conservative MPs in 1922 was attributed in large part to grassroots dissatisfaction.[2] However, whereas the post-war coalition was condemned by a majority of activists (except in large parts of Scotland), by 1935 Colonel Purdy cut an increasingly lonesome and eccentric figure in his hostility to the MacDonald coalition – as he himself acknowledged in his speech to his local association. Similarly in the House of Commons, whereas 187 Conservative

---

[1] *Norfolk Chronicle*, 18 Jan. 1935.
[2] K. Morgan, *Consensus and disunity: the Lloyd George coalition government, 1918–1922* (Oxford, 1979), ch.14.

2   Introduction

MPs voted to leave the first coalition in 1922, in 1934 a hundred of them signed a letter to *The Times* calling for the establishment of a National Party that would make the National government 'for all practical purposes, a permanent ideal in British politics'. The following year, virtually all Conservatives campaigned to renew the government at the general election.[3]

The National government was formed in August 1931, following the collapse of the Labour government, and lasted until 1940. It comprised the Conservative party, led first by Stanley Baldwin, followed by Neville Chamberlain from May 1937; a rump of the Labour party loyal to MacDonald, known as National Labour; and two Liberal contingents, the Liberal Nationals led by John Simon and the National Liberals led by Herbert Samuel. With the exception of the Samuelite Liberals, whose ministers resigned in 1932 in protest at the introduction of tariffs, the government remained intact until May 1940. Up until Chamberlain's resignation as prime minister and Winston Churchill's decision to invite the mainstream Labour party into the wartime coalition, thereby creating a genuine all-party coalition government, Labour was locked out of power. It is therefore unsurprising that the opportunity to control a broad anti-socialist alliance, one that commanded much Liberal and 'moderate' support, is commonly cited as the reason for continued Conservative membership of the National government.[4] According to this view, the Conservatives used the crisis of 1931 to exploit patriotic feeling in the country and thereby secure for themselves a 'national' mandate to force through partisan priorities, including protection and budgetary cuts.[5]

This caricature of a Tory administration in thin disguise has long been discredited, with historians arguing that the government pursued more centrist policies than a purely Conservative administration would have done.[6] Even so, the relationship between the National government and the culture of popular Conservatism in the country has remained surprisingly under-examined. Our understanding of Conservative involvement in the National government comes from historians' attempts to explain the party's electoral dominance of the interwar period as a whole. Thus it

[3] *The Times*, 14 Jun. 1934.

[4] E.g., P. Williamson, 'The Conservative party, 1900–1939: from crisis to ascendancy', in C. Wrigley (ed.), *A companion to early twentieth-century Britain* (Oxford, 2003), 3–22, 19.

[5] For a classic statement, see R. Miliband, *Parliamentary socialism: a study in the politics of Labour* (London, 1961; 2nd edn, 1973), 169–92.

[6] J. Stevenson & C. Cook, *The slump: society and politics during the depression* (London, 1977); J. Ramsden, *The age of Balfour and Baldwin, 1902–1940* (London, 1978), ch.14; N. Smart, *The national government, 1931–40* (Basingstoke, 1999); G. Fry, *The politics of crisis: an interpretation of British politics, 1931–1945* (Basingstoke, 2001).

The National Government and Interwar Conservatism 3

is tempting to interpret the National government as the ultimate embodiment of Baldwin's strategy, starting in the 1920s, to position the party as the only reliable repository of 'national' values, as an appeal to men and women across the social, political, and religious divides through a disarmingly common-sense commitment to national instead of party interests.[7] Or it can be interpreted as the apotheosis of a powerful coalition of voters known as 'the public', which – in Ross McKibbin's famous argument – relied on anti-socialist propaganda to compel many working-class voters to coalesce around middle-class opinion, served by Conservative policy but cast in the form of 'conventional wisdom'.[8] In this way, the National government appears as little more than an adjunct to the party's electoral designs of the 1920s. Indeed, Conservatives like Purdy, who rejected the National government, are commonly presented as opponents of Baldwinite Conservatism, misfits in the whole project of moderate Conservatism between the wars.[9]

Moreover, our understanding of the National government is distinctly national in perspective. Accounts of its formation have focused on high-level politicking, reflecting the fact that after 1922 the idea of party cooperation at the level of central government was almost entirely confined to high political circles.[10] Accounts of the government's life have tended to focus on foreign policy, while research on the domestic politics of the 1930s has preoccupied itself with tracing the rise of the planned economy, primarily by the left in reaction to the National government.[11] This, in turn, reflects the relative neglect of the local dimension in analyses of the decade. Several historians of interwar Conservatism have turned to local party records, but none as the basis of sustained

---

[7] Ramsden, *Age of Balfour and Baldwin*, 330–1; P. Williamson, *Stanley Baldwin: Conservative leadership and national values* (Cambridge, 1999).

[8] R. McKibbin, 'Class and conventional wisdom: the Conservative party and the "public" in inter-war Britain', in *The ideologies of class: social relations in Britain, 1880–1950* (Oxford, 1990), 259–93.

[9] E.g., R. Self, *The evolution of the British party system, 1885–1940* (Harlow, 2014), 187; M. Pugh, *'Hurrah for the Blackshirts!' Fascists and fascism in Britain between the wars* (London, 2006), 123–4.

[10] S. Ball, 'The Conservative party and the formation of the National government: August 1931', *HJ*, 29 (1986), 159–82; P. Williamson, *National crisis and national government: British politics, the economy and empire, 1926–1932* (Cambridge, 1992); G. Searle, *Country before party: coalition and the idea of 'national government' in modern Britain, 1885–1987* (London, 1995), ch.7.

[11] M. Cowling, *The impact of Hitler: British politics and British policy, 1933–1940* (Cambridge, 1975); N. Crowson, *Facing fascism: the Conservative party and the European dictators, 1935–40* (London, 1997); D. Ritschel, *The politics of planning: the debate on economic planning in Britain in the 1930s* (Oxford, 1997); R. Toye, *The Labour party and the planned economy, 1931–1951* (Woodbridge, 2003).

4   Introduction

examination of National Conservatism.[12] Furthermore, these works stand in contrast to work on Victorian and Edwardian popular Conservatism, which embeds local parties in the wider and grittier world of community politics.[13] Only with the same focus on local communities can the implications of the National government for popular Conservatism on the ground, and the reasons for grassroots support for the coalition, be understood.

This book offers the first detailed study of why local Conservatives, up and down the country and across a range of constituency types, supported the National government. While the landslide election victory of 1931 and the introduction of tariffs in 1932 obviously played an important part, these initial advantages hardly explain why Conservatives continued to forfeit the prospect of single-party rule for so many years after. Writing to Baldwin in 1932, the party chairman, Lord Stonehaven, expressed grave doubts about the grassroots' commitment to the government and predicted that its break-up was 'only a question of time'.[14] This book delves beneath existing accounts of the National government to explore why local Conservative activists, contrary to Stonehaven's fears, supported the new government up to a second general election in 1935 and beyond. Given that their experience of the Lloyd George coalition was instrumental in forcing Conservative withdrawal in 1922, their experience of the 1930s is key to understanding the party's enduring commitment to the National government in the face of the undoubted costs of coalition – to the career prospects of Conservative MPs competing for ministerial jobs; to party morale, at least in constituencies where the 'national' ticket was held by the Liberal Nationals or National Labour; and to the integrity of party opinion on the empire and much else. In 1934, the County Durham MP Cuthbert Headlam confided to his diary that the government's record on employment looked insufficient to impress working-class voters in the depressed north. He also described how many of his colleagues in the region, desperate to

---

[12] S. Ball, *Baldwin and the Conservative party: the crisis of 1929–31* (London, 1988); Crowson, *Facing fascism*; N. McCrillis, *The British Conservative party in the age of universal suffrage: popular Conservatism, 1918–1929* (Columbus, OH, 1998); S. Ball, *Portrait of a party: the Conservative party in Britain, 1918–1945* (Oxford, 2013).

[13] E.g., J. Lawrence, *Speaking for the people: party, language and popular politics in England, 1867–1914* (Cambridge, 1998); M. Brodie, *The politics of the poor: the East End of London, 1885–1914* (Oxford, 2004); T. Cooper, 'London-over-the-border: politics in suburban Walthamstow, 1870–1914', in M. Cragoe & A. Taylor (eds.), *London politics, 1760–1914* (Basingstoke, 2005), 211–32; M. Roberts, '"Villa Toryism" and popular Conservatism in Leeds, 1885–1902', *HJ*, 49 (2006), 217–46; A. Windscheffel, *Popular Conservatism in imperial London, 1868–1906* (Woodbridge, 2007).

[14] Memorandum by Stonehaven, n.d. 1932, Cambridge University Library, Baldwin papers, 46/47–58.

The National Government and Interwar Conservatism   5

retain their seats, were becoming 'more Socialist than the Socialists'.[15] Meanwhile in the prosperous south, a leading activist, Sir James Hawkey, had fewer doubts about the anti-socialist instincts of his fellow voters in suburban Essex, which made the 'socialistic tendencies of the Government' all the more puzzling.[16] Such could be the topsy-turvy world of cross-party government for many Conservatives. Yet up and down the country the party grassroots supported the government regardless. Why?

It was not just senior Conservatives in Westminster who exploited the crisis of 1931; party activists in the constituencies did so too. The book builds on Ross McKibbin's interpretation of 1931 as a pivotal 'accident' that recalibrated British politics amid the parties' ongoing attempts to adapt to the challenging new conditions of mass democracy ushered in with the armistice.[17] This was something that local Conservatives themselves came to realise and act upon in the months and years that followed. For while the new government brought its own challenges, it also set in train a range of opportunities for local parties to forge new narratives, reconsider priorities, and formulate new appeals – which, after their fraught experience of adapting to mass politics since the war, party activists were glad to embrace. In short, the book investigates how Conservative activists responded to the National government over time; how they shaped the government's appeals in the country, with what objectives and results; and with what consequences for the party itself and British political culture more widely.

Party Activists and Local Politics

To bring the focus of analysis closer to the party grassroots and their relationship with the voters they sought to mobilise, the arguments presented here draw upon evidence from a range of constituencies. This case-study approach has important advantages. It allows for clear and systematic analysis of a range of different constituency types – urban, suburban, and rural; metropolitan and provincial; agricultural, industrial, and professional; northern and southern; 'working-class' and 'middle-class'; English, Scottish, and Welsh. It also facilitates a depth of historical contextualisation that is all but impossible to ensure when analysing a larger sample of constituencies. As many works of microhistory tell us, the conclusions drawn have relevance beyond the case studies

---

[15] *Parliament and politics in the age of Baldwin and MacDonald: the Headlam diaries, 1923–1935*, ed. S. Ball (London, 1992), 301–2 (24, 30 Apr. 1934).
[16] Hawkey to W. Churchill, 27 Nov. 1934, Churchill Archives Centre, Churchill papers, CHAR 7/12B (232).
[17] R. McKibbin, *Parties and people: England, 1914–1951* (Oxford, 2010).

6   Introduction

themselves.[18] The aim of this book is to illuminate, by example, phenomena that had a crucial bearing on the nature of popular Conservatism between the wars – and through this to explore what drove the wider party's attachment to the National government.

The case-study approach also permits a deeper exploration of the enduring role that locality played in shaping political discourse after 1918. Because no area can be defined by an exact set of socio-economic interests to which all residents unanimously subscribe, a locality is best understood as a community of converging interests. 'Interests do not have to be identical to form a community', explains the sociologist Graham Day, 'but they do have to converge with one another around matters of mutual concern'.[19] These communities were rarely static. Many of them changed dramatically in the interwar period as a consequence of suburbanisation, broadcast media, mass consumerism, and long-term unemployment.[20] So did the actions of local Conservatives as they responded to the changing shape of community interests, and also as they mediated the relationship between voters and a national political establishment now able to transmit its message with unprecedented reach and directness. In this way, the constituency case studies bring to the fore the local itself, but also the lived experience of those inhabiting it.

This in turn highlights the considerable degree of agency that local political culture continued to wield in the early decades of mass democracy. By the 1990s an interpretative trend had emerged among historians of modern British politics that rejected structuralist explanations of political behaviour and instead laid stress on the role that national politicians themselves played in constructing public appeals.[21] However, this approach has too often marginalised the question of how these appeals were received by voters and activists. Undoubtedly there are methodological challenges involved in isolating and interrogating multiple processes of reception. Studying the reception of political ideas by 'ordinary' voters, for instance, rarely involves those voters' own individual commentaries or responses except where Mass Observation records exist. Before the introduction of opinion polling in 1937, politicians relied on a contextualised conception of 'public opinion' drawn from the intersecting worlds of the press, parliament, and the public platform.[22] Similarly

[18] For a discussion of these microhistories and their legacies, see S. Magnússon & I. Szijártó, *What is microhistory? Theory and practice* (Abingdon, 2013), esp. 1–11, 39–61.
[19] G. Day, *Community and everyday life* (Abingdon, 2006), 117.
[20] R. McKibbin, *Classes and cultures: England, 1918–1951* (Oxford, 1998).
[21] See the contributions in J. Lawrence & M. Taylor (eds.), *Party, state and society: electoral behaviour in Britain since 1820* (Aldershot, 1997); Williamson, *Stanley Baldwin.*
[22] J. Thompson, *British political culture and the idea of 'public opinion', 1867–1914* (Cambridge, 2013).

The National Government and Interwar Conservatism

for the historian, interpretation of voters' response to political messages is informed by analysis of political appeals in tandem with broad contemporaneous evidence concerning social identity, economic conditions, and social and historical circumstances.

The sources through which activists' reception of political messages can be gleaned are more accessible. Activist voices are heard in local party records and personal correspondence, as well as in party forums and the local press. Yet these currently contend with a somewhat deterministic assumption that places the technological advances of the 1920s and 1930s, which enabled the direct transmission of political appeals across the electorate, as the more important determinant of a party's performance. As a result, not only is the popular reception of political appeals in interwar Britain poorly understood, but the story of their construction is all too often told through the actions of national political leaders. The case studies redress this imbalance. They highlight the fact that the construction of effective appeals was equally a preoccupation of activists in the constituencies. These activists operated at a geographic and temporal remove from their national leaders, for whom the new media represented a means to better *manage* public opinion. In the constituencies, however, the imperative to be seen to *represent* voters was a constant factor in ensuring that political language played a reflective and not just a constitutive role.[23] Appeals were designed according to powerful assumptions about how to address the local electorate – by its class, gender, occupational, denominational, or regional interest; by policy appeal, social events, or philanthropy; through personality, press, or auxiliary organisations. These inherited assumptions also determined how grassroots members mediated the party's national appeals in the constituency. In this way, the case studies extend analytical awareness of the deep contexts of Victorian and Edwardian traditions of popular politics into post-First World War political culture.

Like all methodologies, the case-study approach adopted here reflects particular choices in historical reconstruction, and therefore has its disadvantages. Twelve constituencies cannot be fully representative of 600. However, in recognising that no constituency is hermetically sealed from its neighbours, we can incorporate insights from neighbouring seats. Such a framework, involving a dozen primary constituency case studies each in contact with an orbit of secondary constituency case studies, shows how each constituency was shaped by powerful regional forces in addition to

---

[23] G. Thomas, 'Political modernity and "government" in the construction of inter-war democracy: local and national encounters', in L. Beers & G. Thomas (eds.), *Brave new world: imperial and democratic nation-building in Britain between the wars* (London, 2011), 39–65.

8   Introduction

local factors. It also ensures that consideration is given to those seats where the Conservatives gave way to National Labour or the Liberal Nationals, whereas the Conservatives held the National ticket in all but one of the primary case studies.

The Constituency Case Studies

The case studies selected here cover five broad categories of constituency in the 1930s: industrial, old suburban, new suburban, rural, and Celtic. Stockton-on-Tees and Leeds West represent industrial, typically 'working-class' areas where families suffered the threat of long-term unemployment and Conservatives suffered the threat of Labour. They possessed historical industries of their own – shipbuilding and increasingly chemical works in the former, and clothes manufacturing in the latter – but were nevertheless steeped in the coalmining and textile-industry politics of County Durham and the West Riding respectively. Harold Macmillan represented Stockton for most of the period, while Vyvyan Adams, a 'centrist' Conservative and leading light in the League of Nations Union, represented Leeds West from 1931 to 1945.[24] Both were prominent anti-appeasers in the late 1930s, though neither lost the support of his local association.

Representing the 'middle-class' sensibilities of old suburbia are Birmingham Moseley and Liverpool East Toxteth. These cannot be separated from their main cities, and therefore offer a glimpse of how the civic culture of the great centres of Victorian caucus politics impacted on the Conservatives' electoral strategies after 1918. The former was the seat of Patrick Hannon, a figure whose close association with Joseph Chamberlain and Lord Beaverbrook, and involvement in self-styled patriotic organisations such as the Navy League and British Commonwealth Union, has seen him classified as a Conservative of the far right.[25] Liverpool East Toxteth, by contrast, passed between several Conservative MPs during the period under consideration.[26]

---

[24] The social, economic, and political features of the case studies are outlined in greater detail in the historiographical discussion at the head of each chapter. For a general orientation of politics in these two regions, see K. Nicholas, *The social effects of unemployment on Teesside, 1919–39* (Manchester, 1986) and J. Reynolds & K. Laybourn, *Labour heartland: the history of the Labour party in West Yorkshire during the inter-war years, 1918–1939* (Bradford, 1987).

[25] T. Linehan, *British fascism, 1918–1939: parties, ideology and culture* (Manchester, 2000), 43–4.

[26] There is, remarkably, no modern volume on Birmingham politics in this period, only the rather dated A. Briggs, *History of Birmingham, vol. 2: borough and city, 1865–1938* (London, 1952). On Liverpool, see P. Waller, *Democracy and sectarianism: a political and social history of Liverpool, 1868–1939* (Liverpool, 1981) and S. Davies, *Liverpool*

The National Government and Interwar Conservatism 9

Suburban expansion, the proliferation of housing estates, and the consequent clash of 'new' and 'old' middle classes was a particular feature of the interwar years. New suburbia is therefore examined through the examples of Ilford and Epping, both in Essex. The former was a fast-growing London dormitory town, adjoined by the Becontree estate, and birthplace of the famous Peace Ballot initiative of 1934–5. Nearby Epping was a more mixed rural-urban area and experienced limited social change in these years. Held by Winston Churchill throughout his 'wilderness years', Epping is of particular interest in bringing to this analysis a Conservative tradition commonly thought to be opposed to the National government.[27]

Norfolk North and the Wiltshire constituency of Devizes represent two different categories of rural seat. The former was a bastion of the early agricultural trade union movement in East Anglia and one of Labour's great hopes in the countryside between the wars. In Devizes, by comparison a relatively safe Tory seat, the party had to contend with the enduring strength of West Country Liberalism.[28] The same was true of much of Wales. The constituencies of Pembrokeshire and Gower form the basis of the study of Wales – a region where the Conservatives failed to prosper under the National government. The former was a mixed constituency, with a Welsh-speaking, nonconformist population in the rural north of the county, distinct from a mostly anglicised population in the industrial and maritime south. Gower was also mixed although mainly industrial, reliant on tinplate and coal mining, and remained a Labour stronghold throughout the period.[29]

Scottish Conservatives – or Unionists, as they continued to call themselves – derived more electoral advantage from the National government compared to their Welsh counterparts, as the examples of Dunbartonshire and Dundee reveal. The former was a mixed constituency encompassing Highland country in the north; industry including textiles, shipbuilding, and coal mining on and around the Clyde in the south; and a portion of suburban Glasgow. Up to the First World War, according to Henry Pelling, 'this was a marginal constituency, saved from

---

Labour: social and political influences on the development of the Labour party in Liverpool, 1900–1939 (Keele, 1996).

[27] See A. Olechnowicz, *Working-class housing in England between the wars: Becontree estate* (Oxford, 1997) and D. Thomas, *Churchill: the member for Woodford* (London, 1994).

[28] See A. Howkins, *Poor labouring men: rural radicalism in Norfolk, 1872–1923* (London, 1985) and G. Tregidga, *The Liberal party in south-west Britain since 1918: political decline, dormancy and rebirth* (Exeter, 2000).

[29] See D. W. Howell (ed.), *Pembrokeshire county history, vol. iv: modern Pembrokeshire, 1815–1974* (Haverfordwest, 1993) and C. Williams, *Capitalism, community and conflict: the South Wales coalfield, 1898–1947* (Cardiff, 1998).

10 Introduction

being Conservative ... by the growth of the industrial population and by the strength of feeling in favour of Free Trade'. By the 1920s its Vale of Leven district, one of interwar Britain's 'Little Moscows', simultaneously posed the ultimate threat to the Conservative world view and a counterpoint to Conservative claims of moderation.[30] Further east, Dundee, despite a tradition of working-class Unionism allied with Irish Protestantism, remained a working-class Liberal stronghold up to the 1920s, at which stage it looked set to become a Labour city. Its politics bore three main characteristics: first, the dominance of the jute industry and therefore the city's exposure to global trade; second, the high proportion of women employed in the industry as weavers, which carried implications for the nature of political citizenship in the city, the form of trade-union activities, and the demands of protest movements; and third, the amalgam of radical traditions and campaigns that underpinned pre-war popular Liberalism, including Scottish home rule, prohibitionism, trade unionism, Lib-Labism, municipal welfarism, and women's rights.[31]

The primary source base for each constituency comprises divisional and area Conservative party records, the local or regional press, and wherever possible the papers of parliamentary candidates and MPs, including in some instances those of Labour and Liberal opponents. None of these constituencies was self-contained. Voters shared material and political interests with people in surrounding seats, either electively or circumstantially. This manifested itself across divisional boundaries, most obviously within established urban centres like Birmingham, Leeds, and Liverpool, but also in more diverse areas like the eastern suburbs of London, where rural Essex met the metropolitan East End, and the semi-rural central south, where market towns like Devizes neighboured regional centres of the growing consumer and service economy like Reading. For some, such as the residents of Dundee, perceptions of regional interests involved distinctly global considerations. While the regional unit continued to shape the political imaginary in fundamental ways, a more intricate awareness of other communities and interests further afield was fostered by the growth of radio, cinema, and the popular national press, and indeed the growing market for popular social surveys like J. B. Priestley's *English Journey* (1934). This book uses developments in the documentary movement as a means of accessing these important regional and national hinterlands.

[30] H. Pelling, *Social geography of British elections, 1885–1910* (London, 1967), 406–7; S. Macintyre, *Little Moscows: Communism and working-class militancy in inter-war Britain* (London, 1980).

[31] J. Tomlinson, *Dundee and the empire: 'Juteopolis', 1850–1939* (Edinburgh, 2014).

Nor were local Conservatives themselves parochial. Although based in the constituency and tasked primarily with organising routine activities and masterminding local election plans, Conservative agents were professionals. They belonged to a national network of agents, received instruction in the latest methods of electioneering, and often sought advancement to a more lucrative or promising position in another seat.[32] Neither MPs nor candidates viewed themselves as belonging solely to the local political landscape. Those with ministerial duties had little choice but to spend more time in London, and so also, for professional, commercial, and social reasons, did many backbench MPs and candidates. Detachment from the constituency often seemed greater for those with a prominent public profile and a 'safe' seat, like Churchill in Epping, and arguably imposed greater demands of public duty on leading officials within the association. Meanwhile for those on the make, like Macmillan, it was imperative to maintain a presence in the constituency as well as to forge a reputation in Westminster. But gone were the days when MPs might treat the constituency as a means simply to enter parliament and thereafter absent themselves. For Oliver Stanley, standing as a parliamentary candidate in Liverpool Edge Hill in 1923, such was the need to integrate with the local party that he requested a photo album of party workers 'with their names underneath and a line or two of information about them'.[33] The growing practice of holding constituency surgeries, although not commonplace until after 1945, reflected the growing involvement of MPs in case work and the publicity value of deeds done on behalf of voters and their families. In an interview with the press, the MP for Ilford, Sir Frederic Wise, stressed that Fridays were spent in the constituency.[34] Despite the advent of mass communication and new recreational attractions like the cinema, all of which threatened to divert public attention away from local politics, the focus of MPs and activists on the local scene remained undiminished.

Rethinking Conservative Electoral 'Dominance'

The interwar years are commonly described as a period of Conservative electoral 'dominance', or 'hegemony'. This refers to the fact that the party

---

[32] Ball, *Portrait of a party*, 174–6.
[33] S. Salvidge, *Salvidge of Liverpool: behind the political scene, 1890–1928* (London, 1934), 254–5.
[34] Cutting from *The Evening News*, 25 Sep. 1925, Redbridge Local Studies & Archives, Ilford CA, 90/61/25/1. See also M. Rush, *The role of the member of parliament since 1868* (Oxford, 2001), 205–11; J. Lawrence, *Electing our masters: the hustings from Hogarth to Blair* (Oxford, 2009), 118–19.

12   Introduction

occupied government for seventeen of those years, a remarkable record in any democracy and one that stands in marked contrast to the party's Edwardian 'crisis' and its more chequered performance after 1945.[35] But such chronological categorisations make sense only with hindsight. In order to contextualise the subjectivities inherent in the electoral readings undertaken by local Conservatives, it is important to analyse the extent to which, in psephological terms, the Conservative party really did 'dominate' the electoral landscape between the wars, and crucially to ask when, if at all, was this apparent to Conservatives themselves. Developments in national, regional, and local voting patterns were integral to how activists evaluated their own and their leaders' performances and enabled direct comparisons to be drawn with historical performance. As this book shows, these evaluative processes shaped the logic with which local Conservatives embraced the National government as and when they did. For despite never having willed the cross-party government, they quickly identified compelling reasons to support it. The key to understanding why lies in their experience and interpretation of electoral politics since 1918, which Chapter 2 explores in detail. But first it is important to outline this study's alternative perspective on the Conservatives' electoral trajectory between the wars. This will bring to the fore important trends that have been lost in national readings of interwar Conservatism, yet which proved formative for activists at the time.

Compared with 46 per cent at the general elections of 1910, the Conservative party secured 36 per cent of the national vote in 1918 and settled on about 38 per cent at each of the general elections in the 1920s. The exception was 1924, when it won 48 per cent. It was not until 1931 and 1935 that the Conservative vote soared to anything like a position of sustained dominance, to 55 and 48 per cent respectively. Meanwhile, Labour registered more than 22 per cent of the vote in 1918, up from 7 per cent in 1910, and thereafter never fell much below 30 per cent.[36] By comparing the average percentage share of the vote won across the seven general elections between 1918 and 1935, it becomes clear that the Conservatives did indeed enjoy a lead over their Labour and Liberal opponents (see Table 1.1). However, if we compare the average percentage share of the vote in the 1920s with that of the 1930s, the Conservatives performed considerably better under the National government. In this way, a distinction exists between Conservative electoral success under the

---

[35] E.g., D. Jarvis, 'The shaping of the Conservative electoral hegemony, 1918–1939', in Lawrence & Taylor (eds.), *Party, state and society*, 131–52; M. Pugh, *The making of modern British politics, 1867–1945* (3rd edn, Oxford, 2002), ch.11.

[36] Labour's share of the national vote was 29.5 per cent in 1922, 30.5 in 1923, 33 in 1924, 37.1 in 1929, 30.6 in 1931, and 37.9 in 1935.

The National Government and Interwar Conservatism

Table 1.1 *Average share of the national vote by party, 1918–1935 (%)*

	1918–1935	1918–1929	1931–1935
Conservative	43.1	39.8	51.5
Labour	31.8	30.8	34.3
Liberal	20.3	25.1	8.3

Note: These calculations combine the Coalition/National and non-prefixed vote for each party (in 1918, 1922, and 1931), except in the case of Labour's share of the vote in 1931–5, which does not include National Labour.

primarily party-government system of the 1920s and more assured success in the cross-party government of the following decade.

The distinction would have been perceptible to local Conservatives in each of the constituencies studied here, since, as the electoral data in the Appendix shows, their own shares of the vote demonstrated a similar pattern. The same applies to almost all the other seats which the party contested regularly throughout the period. Of the 421 constituencies contested at least twice between 1918 and 1930 (including by-elections) and at both 1931 and 1935 general elections, only in 23 did the Conservative party of the 1920s outperform the 'National' Conservative party of 1931–40.[37]

This pattern can be explained in part by the shift away from the three-party system of the 1920s to the two-party system of the 1930s. McKibbin interprets 1931 as a game-changing 'accident' in British politics which swept away most of the remaining precepts of Edwardian Lib-Lab pro-gressivism and gave way to a duopolistic party system that reflected the fundamental distinction between 'middle-class' and 'working-class' interests.[38] One factor accounting for this transformation was the reduced number of seats fought by the Liberal party: 153 in 1931 (41 Simonite Liberal Nationals, 112 Samuelite Liberals) and 161 in 1935, compared to more than 400 in all but one (1924) of the general elections since the war. Added to this, an electoral partnership between the Conservatives, Liberals, and National Labour materialised in 371 con-stituencies, with the Conservative party holding the National candidature in a straight contest against Labour in 313 of these. In this way the party could claim outright control of the anti-socialist vote in a majority of seats.

[37] These calculations exclude university and two-member constituencies and are based on data in F. W. S. Craig, *British parliamentary election results, 1918–1949* (Glasgow, 1969).
[38] McKibbin, *Parties and people*, 87–8, 177–80.

14   Introduction

Sir Edward Cadogan, MP for Finchley, articulated the basis of many Conservative victories when he wrote to Baldwin, 'Whereas in the last Parliament I owed my seat to a split vote and I was not in a majority over the opposition, I have in this Parliament a clear majority of 27 thousand!'[39]

Yet it does not follow axiomatically that non-Conservative anti-socialists, once deprived of the opportunity to vote Liberal, transferred their vote to the Conservatives. That many did so, as the outcome of the 1931 election on a high turnout strongly suggests,[40] signals the increased purchase of anti-socialist ideas in the specific context of 1931. Moreover, the Conservatives' electoral surge in the 1930s is apparent in seats where the party system remained stable across the two decades. This was the case in Ilford, where three-way contests remained the norm up to 1935 despite the diminishing unity of local Liberals; and in Devizes, where Conservatives competed in straight fights with the Liberals in all interwar elections except 1929 and the prospect of anti-socialist unity under the 'National' label was therefore undermined by the decidedly anti-Tory politics of local Liberalism.[41]

Thus, structural factors alone do not explain why the Conservative vote peaked dramatically in the 1930s. Instead, the answer lies in how the crisis of 1931 and then membership of the National government enabled the party to construct a more effective set of popular appeals. While the idea of a national government circulated among senior figures in Whitehall and Westminster by the late 1920s, it was impossible for activists to anticipate the events of 1931 and virtually inconceivable that they should seek electoral salvation through membership of a cross-party coalition, especially one headed by a Labour prime minister. Even so, it is possible to explore activists' experiences of the 1920s and thereby reconstruct the mindset with which they approached the opportunities presented by the 'National' politics of the 1930s. Critical to this story is the fact that for many Conservatives the 1920s felt like a decade of electoral struggle, not just from the vantage point of 1931 or 1935 but also in their lived experiences of politics since the war. As Chapter 2 argues, fear of stagnation or even decline developed in response to the perceived atrophying of established means of political organisation and communal political culture.

Two electoral processes in particular reinforced activists' perception of relative decline in the 1920s. One was the decline in the Conservative

---

[39] Cadogan to Baldwin, 30 Oct. 1931, Baldwin papers, 45/147–8.
[40] See A. Thorpe, *The British general election of 1931* (Oxford, 1991), 264 (table 11.4).
[41] For further statistical evidence in support of this point, see Thorpe, *General election of 1931*, 263–6.

The National Government and Interwar Conservatism 15

share of the vote from pre-war levels. Analysis of the electoral swing in each case study area reveals that the party's vote declined, or at best flatlined, between the elections of 1885–1910 and those of 1918–1929 (see Appendix). According to these calculations, the steepest swings away from Conservatism occurred in English urban, suburban, and industrial areas (Ilford area -12.6 per cent, Birmingham -9.6, Epping -8.4, Stockton -9.0, Leeds -5.2, Liverpool -6.8), whereas the less significant changes were confined to English rural and Scottish areas (Norfolk -2.7, Devizes -0.2, Dundee +0.5, Dunbartonshire -1.7). While some individual constituencies witnessed a positive swing, in each of the case study areas such instances were too isolated or too modest to counter the decline or flatlining of the Conservative share of the vote. If not for the coupon election of 1918, at which many coalition Conservatives commanded Liberal votes, the negative swing would have been steeper.

A great many of the activists who populate this book were in a position to compare and contrast pre- and post-war politics at first hand. Almost regardless of how much their constituency boundary was redrawn by the Redistribution Act of 1918 – which was minimal in areas with stable populations, like North Norfolk and Devizes but very considerable in growing urban centres like Birmingham, Liverpool, and some London suburbs – local party organisers inhabited the same geographic spaces as before and therefore spoke to established ideas of community interests. Notwithstanding the routine imperative to adapt to local demographic and economic changes, which in fast-growing areas like Ilford proved to be acute in the early twentieth century, the Conservative activist of the 1920s was especially attuned to continuities with pre-war political culture – and arguably more so than many of their Liberal or Labour counterparts, for whom the formal breakdown of the progressive alliance in itself represented a major disjuncture. This can be seen in how Conservatives drew upon pre-war practices to confront the challenges brought about by adult suffrage. For despite the profound policy debates that so destabilised the intellectual coherence and electoral prospects of Edwardian Conservatism, it was possible to look admiringly to the example set by social organisations like the Primrose League and pressure groups like the Tariff Reform League, both of which worked energetically to bring working-class and female supporters into the fold – and thus to reimagine the pre-war period as the heyday of Conservative popular activism.[42] As many local studies have shown, the

---

[42] See E. H. H. Green, *The crisis of Conservatism: the politics, economics and ideology of the British Conservative party, 1880–1914* (London, 1995); M. Pugh, *The Tories and the people, 1880–1935* (Oxford, 1985); D. Thackeray, *Conservatism for the democratic age:*

16   Introduction

vibrancy of urban Conservatism rested on some combination of working-men's clubs, thinly veiled treating of voters and non-voters in the form of sponsorship, deference to 'masculinist' leadership, and displays of civic patriotism. The vibrancy of rural Conservatism similarly relied on displays of local patriotism, together with the effective sponsorship of recreational life, and a measure of social deference as negotiated between landowners, tenants, and workers.[43] As Chapter 2 discusses, these methods proved difficult to recreate after the war, and were increasingly susceptible to both contestation by opponents and undermining by the new – typically national – methods of communication employed by the Conservative leadership. Therefore, although in government for most of the 1920s, Conservative activists did indeed experience what the polls told them, namely that their command of local voters and of local political culture had weakened since the war. There were few areas akin to Wales, whose Conservatives – for years excluded by the disestablishment debate – could take encouragement from the retreat of Edwardian politics.[44]

But there, as elsewhere, a second process fatally impinged on grassroots confidence. While the nature of the Labour threat continued to vary by region, the 'rise of Labour' became increasingly ubiquitous as it spread to new electoral battlegrounds. In parts of South Wales, County Durham, and central Scotland, as well as pockets of London's East End, Labour consolidated its pre-war position and mobilised significant proportions of the newly enfranchised electorate to create lasting anti-Conservative strongholds. But this surge was not simply the result of the 'franchise factor' in 1918, as figures showing the general trend of pro-Labour swings *after* 1918 reveal (see Appendix). A similar swing occurred in Birmingham, Leeds, Liverpool, and Ilford. Whereas before the war Labour contested few parliamentary seats in these areas, focusing its energies more on obtaining representation at the municipal level, during the 1920s almost all the constituencies came to be contested on a regular basis, generating an average of more than 40 per cent of the vote in the

---

Conservative cultures and the challenge of mass politics in early twentieth-century England (Manchester, 2013).

[43] Waller, *Democracy and sectarianism* on Liverpool; J. Lawrence, 'Class and gender in the making of urban Toryism, 1880–1914', *EHR*, 108 (1993), 629–52 on Wolverhampton; Brodie, *The politics of the poor* and Windscheffel, *Popular Conservatism* on London; Roberts, 'Villa Toryism' on Leeds; M. Cragoe, *An Anglican aristocracy: the moral economy of the landed estate in Carmarthenshire, 1832–1895* (Oxford, 1996); N. Mansfield, *English farmworkers and local patriotism, 1900–1930* (Aldershot, 2001) on Shropshire.

[44] G. Thomas, 'The Conservative party and Welsh politics in the inter-war years', *EHR*, 128 (2013), 877–913.

The National Government and Interwar Conservatism 17

wider Leeds and Ilford areas and more than 35 per cent in Birmingham. Labour continued to grow even in 1924, despite the famous anti-socialist campaign of that year and the pro-Conservative swing among erstwhile Liberal voters. By 1929, Labour candidates could poll close to half the vote in these areas, not far behind their colleagues in the industrial heartlands.

Where Labour's presence remained patchy or yielded limited results, the threat to Conservatism was often experienced vicariously by activists as they observed the challenge in neighbouring seats. Conservatives in suburban Ilford and semi-rural Epping, for instance, saw how Labour cultivated a following through the discourse of relief in the slum areas of east London and through aspirational appeals to working-class commuters in Romford, Tottenham, and Walthamstow, where formerly the Conservatives had held their own.[45] Only once between the wars, in 1929, did Labour trouble to contest Devizes, yet Labour's ascent in neighbouring Swindon and nearby Frome, where Percy Hurd was unseated in 1923, meant that despite the Conservative-Liberal duopoly that remained formally in place locally, the local Conservative party could hardly discount the possibility of a Labour challenger at each next election.[46] Nationally, given that the 1924 election was fought as a three-way contest, the Conservative share of the vote (48 per cent) was undoubtedly impressive. However, as Chapter 2 demonstrates, the fact that many party activists assessed matters less positively highlights the importance of perceived, and not only actual, electoral performance. Overall, the 1920s saw the party's share of the vote shrink in many constituencies. A sense of stagnation and even decline, and the election defeats of 1923 and 1929, therefore loomed larger in many Conservative minds than the victory of 1924. It was in this context that activists encountered the opportunities presented by membership of the National government.

Cultures of Government and Popular Politics in the 1930s

The more familiar history of the Conservative party in the 1920s lays stress on the creation and projection of new Conservative appeals from

---

[45] For Labour in West Ham, see J. Marriott, *The culture of Labourism: the East End between the wars* (Edinburgh, 1991). On working-class suburbs, see Cooper, 'London-over-the-border', and Pelling, *Social geography*, 65–6.

[46] The association minutes reveal that a Labour candidate was active in Devizes from 1933 but resigned in April 1935, which offers a cautionary note to attempts to measure the spread of Labour through electoral data alone. Executive committee, 5 May 1933, 24 Oct. 1935, Devizes CA.

18   Introduction

the centre. It highlights developments in the party's electoral strategy and self-presentation, technological innovation and pioneering use of political communication, as well as institutional and financial strengths.[47] This is an important perspective and identifies some of the factors that under-pinned organisational efforts and shaped activists' experiences in the constituencies. But, as with accounts of the party's dominance, the con-tribution of such factors to electoral outcomes became clear only with hindsight. This begs the question whether, and how, their effect was understood in real time by activists who mostly operated outside or on the margins of the professional party hierarchy and in accordance with their own, often parochial, assumptions about how to engage voters. Local activists often responded ambivalently to the methods favoured by party professionals. As Chapter 2 argues, they sought a culture of Conservative government that reinforced local appeals. What they fre-quently experienced, by contrast, was a culture of national politics that disrupted the norms of local political life. As Duncan Tanner's work has shown in the case of Labour, party expansion and voter mobilisation in this period could still be pursued along routine lines that were highly localised, often slow, even primitive, in comparison with the mass-media alternatives being developed.[48] The fact that local activists had very definite expectations of government is therefore also crucial to under-standing how and why they negotiated the transition from party to cross-party government.

The political crisis of 1931 proved a valuable lesson in how to exploit historical accidents. The fact that the Conservatives were lucky to have lost power in 1929, as some of them privately acknowledged at the time,[49] did not deter them from presenting the financial and political crises that followed as products of Labour's unfitness to govern. Throughout the decade, on posters, in pamphlets, and in speeches, '1931' remained a potent reminder to voters of the devastating consequences of socialist rule. Stripped of – and now openly condemnatory of – MacDonald's leadership, the Labour party in opposition lacked the 'gradualist' script

---

[47] E.g., T. J. Hollins, 'The Conservative party and film history between the wars', *EHR*, XCVI (1981), 359–69; D. Jarvis, 'British Conservatism and class politics in the 1920s', *EHR*, 111 (1996), 59–84; S. Nicholas, 'The construction of a national identity: Stanley Baldwin, "Englishness" and the mass media in inter-war Britain', in M. Francis & I. Zweiniger-Bargielowska (eds.), *The Conservative party and British society, 1880–1990* (Cardiff, 1996), 127–46; Williamson, *Stanley Baldwin*; Ball, *Portrait of a party*.

[48] D. Tanner, 'Gender, civic culture and politics in South Wales: explaining Labour municipal policy, 1918–1939', in M. Worley (ed.), *Labour's grass roots: essays on the activities and experiences of local Labour parties and members, 1918–1945* (Aldershot, 2005), 170–93; also Tanner, 'Elections, statistics and the rise of the Labour party, 1906–1931', *HJ*, 34 (1991), 893–908.

[49] H. Macmillan to D. Malcolm, 6 Jun. 1929, Bodleian Library, Macmillan papers, c.65/29.

The National Government and Interwar Conservatism 19

that had guided its response to such attacks in the 1920s.[50] Led between 1932 and 1935 by George Lansbury, forever associated with the party's past use of discredited 'direct action' methods, and with Stafford Cripps and the Socialist League agitating for a drastic socialist programme, the Labour party was poorly placed to deflect anti-socialist claims. In this sense, anti-socialism worked broadly as planned for the Conservatives in the 1930s. As an electoral mechanism it consolidated anti-Labour forces enough to keep Labour out of government and at the same time eased the transfer of erstwhile Liberal votes to the Conservatives. This remained the case up until May 1940, when the demands of total war compelled Winston Churchill as the incoming prime minister to create an all-party government – a genuinely 'National' government. It is not unreasonable, then, to view the 1931 and 1935 elections as belonging to the same strategy as the 1924 election.[51]

In addition, the key attraction of the anti-socialist discourse wrought in 1931 was that it evolved thereafter in tandem with the government's pursuit of national economic recovery. As Chapter 3 explores, the National government's objective of economic recovery called for a carefully crafted culture of government, which Neville Chamberlain as chancellor was largely responsible for coordinating. It argues that its focus on recovery in trade, employment, and wages, as well as new schemes of relief to assist those for whom the recovery proved elusive, suggests a concerted government effort according to the standards of the time. Alongside the dreaded means test and the public displays of fiscal orthodoxy, there were ambitious and innovative schemes to encourage economic development and support welfare provision. These included slum clearance and housing reform, infrastructure projects including the expansion of the road network, and pioneering regional policy that channelled grants to the distressed areas. Such policies gained added coherence thanks to the government's publicity drive, which reflected the government's willingness to embrace new trends emanating from the documentary movement normally associated with the political left of the period. The argument here is not that these policies proved especially effective – that is a debate for economic historians[52] – but that they contributed to a *politics* of recovery that carried far-reaching consequences

---

[50] See R. MacDonald, *Parliament and revolution* (1919) and *Parliament and democracy* (1920), reproduced in B. Barker (ed.), *Ramsay MacDonald's political writings* (London, 1972).
[51] E.g., McKibbin, *Parties and people*, 87.
[52] See B. Eichengreen, 'The British economy between the wars', R. C. Floud & P. A. Johnson (eds.), *The Cambridge economic history of modern Britain, vol. 2: economic maturity, 1860–1939* (Cambridge, 2004), 314–43.

20   Introduction

and to this day remains at odds with most commonly held assumptions about the decade.

Local Conservatives quickly identified in the politics of national economic recovery a route to restoring an effective relationship between central government and local popular politics. The same economic crisis that triggered the government's formation also ensured that, over time, regional interests were brought firmly to the fore in popular political discourse, as some communities adapted to recovery, marked by the arrival of new industries and the expansion of the suburbs, and others struggled to survive the ordeals of unemployment. Part II of the book comprises a chapter each on industrial, rural, suburban, and 'Celtic' constituencies and offers a detailed exploration of how the national politics of recovery chimed with political and social conditions on the ground. It highlights a central paradox that is fundamental to understanding grassroots attitudes towards the government: the cross-party 'National' government, far from homogenising political culture, created conditions that enabled Conservatives to forge distinctly localised, differentiated political appeals.

Conservatives found themselves in a position to rehabilitate aspects of the late-Victorian and Edwardian politics of place that they had feared lost amid the disruptive consequences of adult suffrage and the perceived homogenising effect of national broadcast communication. Both the narrative of recovery and the relief work contributed to this. In industrial and urban areas, Conservatives revived plebeian appeals that centred on the material well-being as well as the recreational life of the working man. Where economic recovery was limited, the scope for relief work opened up valuable opportunities to cultivate a place for the party in the community's survival strategies. But this was no anachronistic return to some lost world. Like British society itself, Conservatives at all levels of the party were all too aware of the social changes, together with attendant shifts in political sensibilities, wrought by the mass experience of the war.[53] Moreover, such was the scale of electoral success in 1931 that the pre-war methods of 'doing' popular politics no longer provided the only blueprint. In rural areas, Conservatives cultivated a traditional paternalistic appeal in pursuit of the deferential vote, but also celebrated the modernisation of agriculture itself under the guiding hand of the National government's reforms. In this way, National government

---

[53] A. Gregory, *The last Great War: British society and the First World War* (Cambridge, 2008); J. Lawrence, 'The transformation of British public politics after the First World War', *P&P*, 190 (2006), 185–216; R. Carr, *Veteran MPs and Conservative politics in the aftermath of the Great War: the memory of all that* (Farnham, 2013).

The National Government and Interwar Conservatism 21

ushered in the last great flowering of localist politics in Britain before the advent of televised politics altered British political culture irretrievably.

Together, the politics of recovery and the rehabilitation of popular Conservatisms underpinned the local associations' support for the National government. Conservatives in Epping, for example, backed the government despite the controversy over India. In urban, suburban, and rural seats alike, where the introduction of tariffs looked certain to alienate Liberal opinion, the party hardly ever questioned the wisdom of membership. Support remained likewise constant in the distressed areas, where unemployment remained unpropitiously high for any government. The National government was embraced even in those areas where the party failed to make progress in 1931. It fought and lost Pembrokeshire, but its share of the vote improved sufficiently to convince local activists that their chances of recapturing the seat were still enhanced by membership. There were more than 100 seats not fought by the party in 1931, where a Liberal or a MacDonaldite stood as the National candidate. Yet area records show grassroots support for the government even in these regions, including County Durham, Teesside, Tyneside, and South Wales. Discontent was more likely to arise from inter-party rivalry over who should hold the 'National' designation than in response to the government itself.

Of course, all political constructs are contestable and the National government was no exception. Just as the Conservatives found new opportunities in the politics of the 1930s, so did their opponents. Albeit a monumental setback with far-reaching consequences for Labour, the 1931 election was followed in due course by a degree of electoral recovery, and a process of intellectual and organisational reappraisal that some have interpreted as the wellspring of the party's famous victory in 1945.[54] Perhaps the most striking indication of Labour's comeback was its victory in the London County Council elections of 1934. By the time of the 1935 general election the party was back to its 1929 level in the national poll, commanding 8.3 million votes and more than 37 per cent of the vote. This secured the recovery of more than 100 constituencies, most of them in the industrial heartlands, but the party also reaped success elsewhere, including in the expanding suburbs of east London. Some of the biggest swings to Labour occurred in urban and suburban centres where the candidates – although not elected, such was the magnitude of Conservative majorities to be undone – commanded a larger proportion of the vote than in 1929. In opposition from 1933, the Liberal party

---

[54] G. Fry, 'A reconsideration of the general election of 1935 and the electoral revolution of 1945', *History*, 76 (1991), 43–55; M. Pugh, '*The Daily Mirror* and the revival of Labour, 1935–1945', *TCBH*, 9 (1998), 420–38; Toye, *The Labour party and the planned economy*.

22 Introduction

(excluding the Liberal Nationals, who remained in the government throughout) failed to match Labour's electoral achievements, but proved equally capable of constructing a radical response to the government, especially in suburban and rural seats.

Nor did the National government's reputation last in the longer term. Because of the actual pattern of recovery, which occurred mainly in the Midlands and South, and was conspicuous by its absence in the old industrial areas, the theme of recovery – and especially state-led recovery – is now rarely associated with the National government years. Falling as it does between two periods of paradigmatic reform, of the New Liberals and Attlee, and given also the failure of reconstruction after the First World War, the interwar period is taken by comparison to reflect the barren reformist capabilities of a succession of Conservative-dominated governments. Often attributed to non-party groupings, intellectual and policy developments that foreshadowed the reforms of the 1940s, such as economic planning, are most commonly understood to have occurred despite, and in criticism of, the National government.[55] This view of the 1930s is by no means unique to Britain.[56] But, as Chapter 8 argues, Labour was to prove instrumental in defining Britain's particular memory of the decade. The party began to write its version of the National government's legacy in earnest during the late 1930s, giving the north-south divide – that twentieth-century totem of inequality – greater shape in the public imagination, ready for whenever an election next came.

Yet opinion polls from the period had the government on course for a historic third victory when the war intervened.[57] Whatever the outcome might have been, few Conservatives would have had reason to question the proven advantages of membership of the National government. Long after the government's formation, Conservatives successfully invoked the very fact of a National government to remind voters of the calamitous consequences of a Labour government. The cross-party nature of the government enabled Conservatives to seek to neutralise Labour and especially Liberal threats in the constituencies, by pledging common cause with those of their leaders who shared in the national crusade for recovery. And all the while, the National government enabled the Conservatives to rehabilitate their own traditions of popular politics.

---

[55] See A. Marwick, 'Middle opinion in the thirties: planning, progress and political "agreement"', *EHR*, 79 (1964), 285–98; Ritschel, *The politics of planning*, esp. ch.8.

[56] As Barry Eichengreen has recently argued, policymakers across the western world sought to learn lessons from the 'mistakes' of their predecessors in the 1930s in an attempt to respond to the 'great recession' of 2008 (B. Eichengreen, *Hall of mirrors: the great depression, the great recession, and the uses – and misuses – of history* (Oxford, 2015)).

[57] McKibbin, *Parties and people*, 104.

Part I

Rethinking Interwar Conservatism

2 Local Politics and the Limits of Baldwinite Conservatism, 1918–1931

When Conservatives surveyed the political landscape of November 1918, two challenges stood out above all others. The first was an electorate tripled in size since the last general election, now containing working men and, for the first time, women, whose new enfranchisement seemed certain to destabilise established patterns of popular allegiance. The second was the threat posed by Labour – a burgeoning force, now committed to socialism. As these two challenges compounded each other, no small number of activists feared the Conservatives' eventual, even if not imminent, demise. Meanwhile, few could foretell how the environment in which they themselves operated would change, often dramatically, in the years ahead. Developments in broadcasting and media technology transformed the way in which national leaders communicated with voters, enabling them in effect to bypass party volunteers on the ground. Meanwhile, key events like the formation of the first Labour government in 1924, the general strike in 1926, and the fall of the second Labour government provoked additional unpredictability for party workers. So too did choices taken by the party leadership, such as Baldwin's decision to call an election in 1923 and to join the National government in 1931. Yet the Conservative party survived and at times thrived.

Explanations of Conservative survival and success between the wars draw heavily on Stanley Baldwin's leadership in the 1920s. Baldwin initially set the scene for interwar Conservatism in 1922, when he led the party's withdrawal from the post-war coalition with a warning against the destructive careerism of Lloyd George, who was then without a party of his own to lead. From then on, the Conservative party was free to fight for monopoly of the anti-socialist vote. He further set the tone of interwar Conservatism during the 1924 general election campaign. Reflecting lessons learnt from the party's election campaign the previous year, which misfired and ushered in the Labour government, the campaign is held up as the perfect manifestation of 'Baldwinite Conservatism': evidence of Baldwin's aptitude for communicating with the masses,

26   Rethinking Interwar Conservatism

testimony to his moderate anti-socialism that nevertheless accommodated Labour, and proof of the appeal of his non-partisan rhetoric among former Liberal voters and the so-called silent majority. As a result, many historians have come to interpret the Conservative victory of 1924, so long considered a key moment in the realignment of British politics and the establishment of the modern two-party system, as something of a personal triumph for Baldwin.[1] Thus Baldwin has emerged as the trusted anti-hero, a reassuring foil to the machinations and bravura of Lloyd George and Winston Churchill, and the guiding hand of a party otherwise ill-equipped to adapt to the times.

Baldwin the indispensable electoral asset has taken his place in current understandings of interwar politics despite the misgivings of many contemporary Conservatives. The relentless disapproval of the right-wing Rothermere and Beaverbrook press for his accommodating style of anti-socialism and failure to champion a protectionist programme after 1923 is well known. Among cabinet colleagues he remained a curious enigma, especially to the likes of Neville Chamberlain and Leo Amery who, despite witnessing Baldwin's effectiveness as a communicator, held true to the world view that a party's popularity really hinged on its ability to match voter interests with policy initiatives.[2] Nor was such despair at Baldwin's apparent detachment from policy by the late 1920s confined to the upper echelons of the party, as close reading of the annual conference proceedings or constituency association minutes reveals. Stuart Ball, although he considers Baldwin an 'asset', concludes that the Conservatives' strength ultimately rested on a number of factors ranging from a 'basic consensus on principles' to superior organisational resources, such that they 'would probably have done nearly as well if they had followed the same course under some other personality'.[3]

What Baldwin's detractors failed to recognise was how much his unique style of leadership was carefully crafted by design. In his influential rehabilitation of the Conservative leader's reputation, Philip Williamson argues that Baldwin drew on 'resources of method, ideas, and will' to fashion an inclusive brand of Conservatism that eluded alternative leaders in the party and proved uniquely resonant among

---

[1] On realignment, see M. Cowling, *The impact of Labour, 1920–1924: the beginning of modern British politics* (Cambridge, 1971), and C. Cook, *The age of alignment: electoral politics in England, 1922–1929* (London, 1975). On Baldwin's role, see K. Middlemas & J. Barnes, *Baldwin: a biography* (London, 1969), 274–6; P. Williamson, *Stanley Baldwin: Conservative leadership and national values* (Cambridge, 1999), 83–4; R. McKibbin, *Parties and people: England, 1914–1951* (Oxford, 2010), 61–5.

[2] Williamson, *Stanley Baldwin*, ch.2.

[3] S. Ball, *Portrait of a party: the Conservative party in Britain, 1918–1945* (Oxford, 2013), 518–22.

Local Politics and the Limits of Baldwinism 27

voters.[4] But to what extent did Conservatives in the country feel the benefit of Baldwinite Conservatism? This chapter takes up the story of how local Conservative parties related to a powerful public appeal that was created in their party's name but which they often found at odds with their own conception of popular Conservatism. Like Baldwin, activists sought to shape their policy appeals, choice of language, and public identity according to design, and drew on their own 'resources of method, ideas, and will' from local political traditions and according to the perceived interests of the local electorate. Such asymmetry of design, while arguably an unavoidable and timeless feature of democratic politics, was especially significant in light of the particular historical circumstances of the 1920s.[5] That the two co-existed uneasily within the Conservative party in the years after 1918 – a period of perceptible electoral stagnancy for the party in some regions – highlights the mixed reception and doubts about the effectiveness of Baldwinite Conservatism in its 1920s guise. Crucially, it also brings to the fore the attitudes with which Conservative activists approached the formation of the National government in 1931.

Reclaiming the Local Politics of Place and Class, 1918–1924

Around the time of the armistice, Conservatives took stock of their local party organisations in a concerted effort to rehabilitate what Jon Lawrence has termed the 'politics of place'.[6] This happened not least because of the redistribution bill accompanying the Fourth Reform Act, which, in the name of 'equalisation', created new seats (like Ilford), altered the constellation of seats in large urban centres such as Birmingham, and, in some instances, changed constituency names, often in defiance of local sensitivities, as in the case of East Wiltshire, which became Devizes.[7] More than that, however, it mirrored the intention of the grassroots to reconstruct a politics that unmistakably locked

---

[4] Williamson, *Stanley Baldwin*, 63 and passim; also B. Schwarz, 'The language of constitutionalism: Baldwinite Conservatism', in Schwarz & M. Langan (eds.), *Formations of nation and people* (London, 1984), 1–18.

[5] G. Thomas, 'Political modernity and "government" in the construction of inter-war democracy: local and national encounters', in L. Beers & G. Thomas (eds.), *Brave new world: imperial and democratic nation-building in Britain between the wars* (London, 2011), 39–65.

[6] See J. Lawrence, *Speaking for the people: party, language and popular politics in England, 1867–1914* (Cambridge, 1998) and 'The politics of place and the politics of nation', *TCBH*, 11 (2000), 83–94.

[7] M. Kinnear, *The British voter: an atlas and survey since 1885* (London, 1968), 70, 142–5; *CAJ*, Jan. 1918, 18; executive committee, 28 Jun., 9 Aug. 1917, Wiltshire and Swindon History Centre, Devizes CA, 2305/1.

28   Rethinking Interwar Conservatism

party into the local community. In 1918, for instance, all but one of the Birmingham seats came together to form the Birmingham Conservative and Unionist Association, a central organisation charged with coordinating Unionist activity in the city. Modelled on the old Birmingham 'caucus' and with Neville Chamberlain as its ambitious architect, the organisation clearly anticipated the continuation of a resonant communitarian culture. It was not long before activists in the city referred to it somewhat presumptuously as 'the Birmingham scheme' of party organisation. Above all, its aims were to reaffirm the party's ubiquity in all facets of municipal life, and to achieve a level of self-sufficiency in matters of propaganda and activist training.[8]

The confidence that activists placed in the popular purchase of local political cultures after the war is an underlying theme of this book. For this reason, it is worth stressing the depth of their confidence in a politics of place at the outset of this period. As Sam Davies and Bob Morley show in their analysis of interwar municipal elections, the Labour party scored its first notable advance in many boroughs in 1919.[9] The BCUA responded to the Labour breakthrough in Birmingham by augmenting the distinctly parochial tone of its public language. It did so, to begin with, by establishing a limited company charged with publishing a Unionist monthly, called the *Straightforward*, in response to Labour's *Town Crier*.[10] This Unionist magazine had originally been a short-lived project of the party in West Birmingham in 1914. But in 1920, convinced that the 'ordinary literature obtainable from the Central Office was not sufficiently effective to be worth the trouble of distribution', the *Straightforward* was now revived as the form of political literature most

---

[8] Special meeting, 1 Jul. 1918, Birmingham Central Library, Birmingham CUA, AQ329.94249; *The Neville Chamberlain diary letters, vol. 1: the making of a politician, 1915–1920*, ed. R. Self (Aldershot, 2000), 281–2 (to Hilda, 3 Aug. 1918). After standing aloof in 1918, the party association in the Erdington division entered the central organisation in 1920 (management committee, 20 Jan. 1920, Birmingham CUA). For a brief outline of the renewal of the Working Men's Conservative Association in Liverpool, headed by Sir Archibald Salvidge, see P. Waller, *Democracy and sectarianism: a political and social history of Liverpool, 1868–1939* (Liverpool, 1981), 280–1.

[9] S. Davies & B. Morley, 'Electoral turnout in county borough elections, 1919–1938', *LHR*, 71 (2006), 167–86, and their *County borough elections in England and Wales, 1919–1938: a comparative analysis, Volume 1: Barnsley – Bournemouth* (Aldershot, 1999), 645, and *volume 3: Chester – East Ham* (Aldershot, 2006), 639. The Labour victories of 1919 occurred despite the fact that most of the new and unpropertied male voters traditionally associated with the party could still not vote in municipal elections. See D. Tanner, 'Elections, statistics, and the rise of the Labour party, 1906–1931', *HJ*, 34 (1991), 893–908, at 906.

[10] P. Drake, '*The Town Crier*: Birmingham's Labour weekly, 1919–1951', in R. Shackleton & A. Wright (eds.), *Worlds of Labour: essays in Birmingham Labour history* (Birmingham, 1983), 103–26.

likely to 'find its way into the houses of the people'. Its brief was to be 'as local as possible', although not without the odd 'trenchant' article on national affairs.[11] It was run at a loss over four years, always in preference to the standardised literature available from Central Office and until evidence amassed of the 'cordial support' of the daily press in the city.[12] In addition to this, a body called the Unionist Propaganda Society was formed. Since 1918 Conservatives in the city had been struck by the apathy of voters and activists. The Propaganda Society therefore assumed an important advisory role, reporting to the BCUA Management Committee on the state of local opinion while also recruiting and educating working-class speakers with the aim of encouraging 'open-air meetings in the streets'.[13]

Advocating the 'politics of place' did not always entail continuity in local strategy – nor, indeed, a grassroots world view impervious to new challenges. In fact, in constituencies like Ilford the Conservatives had no choice but to face entirely new conditions. This constituency was one of four new seats carved out of the old county seat of Romford in 1918. Not only was it a new parliamentary seat, it was also a new town, having expanded from a rural Essex village with a population of just 11,000 in 1891 to a desirable outer-London suburb of more than 85,000 by 1921. The population would grow larger still with the building of the London County Council's Becontree estate, part of which lay in the division.[14] Constructing and then appropriating a 'politics of place' in an area experiencing such transition – in a town which had not yet arrived at a concrete sense of 'place' – would not be easy. Whereas the reassertion of the 'civic gospel' in Birmingham appeared a feasible plan given the party's historic connections, Conservatives in Ilford lacked historic civic institutions and had few other continuities upon which to draw. Yet the local party responded by forging its own politics of place. It did so by celebrating Ilford as a model of modern urban growth and championing the cause of amenities for residents. This echoed the pre-war initiatives of several civic leaders, except that now it became acutely partisan as the Conservatives tried to wrestle the mantle of civic leadership from the socialist Reverend Herbert Dunnico. Although an MP for Consett in

---

[11] Management committee, 15 Mar. 1920, sub-committee, 31 Mar., 12 Apr. 1920, Birmingham CUA.

[12] E.g., management committee, 14 Jul. 1922, 9 Feb. 1923, 19 Sep. 1924, Birmingham CUA.

[13] *The Austen Chamberlain diary letters: the correspondence of Sir Austen Chamberlain with his sisters Hilda and Ida, 1916–1937*, ed. R. Self (Cambridge, 1995), 99–100 (to Ida, 8 Dec. 1918). Management committee, 9 Jul. 1920, Birmingham CUA.

[14] See A. Olechnowicz, *Working-class housing in England between the wars: Becontree estate* (Oxford, 1997).

30 Rethinking Interwar Conservatism

County Durham, Dunnico was a popular resident of Ilford, a councillor and magistrate as well as president of the Ilford Football Club, while his wife Harriet took a leading role in public health campaigns as founder of the Ilford Maternity and Child Welfare Association. Following the 1924 election victory, the Ilford Conservative party launched *The Ilford Monthly*, which became a self-appointed publicity organ for the campaign to grant Ilford borough status and a persistent challenger of Dunnico's right to speak for such a 'pronouncedly Conservative' town.[15] In the process the party helped to position Frederic Wise, the Conservative MP, as the rightful advocate of Ilford society, a claim well publicised when, amid much pomp and in the presence of the Duke of York, he became Charter Mayor upon the town's incorporation in 1926.[16]

The challenge facing Stockton Conservatives was rather different, but again required the party to break with pre-war practices if they were to assert their presence. The town had a clear sense of its civic identity but the Conservatives' unspectacular electoral record on Teesside made it difficult for them to lay claim to a partisan ownership of Stockton's public life after 1918. In this regard, the war had already offered something of an opportunity. In keeping with the wartime truce and with the party's membership of the coalition government, Conservatives in Stockton had, since 1917, supported the sitting Liberal MP, Bertrand Watson. The Conservative-Liberal alliances forged in several urban centres and throughout Scotland during this period, both municipal and parliamentary, are commonly understood to represent, as one historian has put it, 'one purpose – to keep labour out of office'.[17] But such an alliance also enabled the Conservatives in Stockton to gain a place in the public consciousness through a process of stealth. By associating closely with

---

[15] *Ilford Monthly*, Jan., Feb. 1925; M. Heller, 'Suburbia, marketing and stakeholders: developing Ilford, Essex, 1880–1914', *UH*, 41 (2014), 62–80.

[16] For Ilford's Charter Day celebrations, see *The Times* and *Ilford Recorder*, 22 Oct. 1926.

[17] J. Smyth, 'Resisting Labour: Unionists, Liberals, and moderates in Glasgow between the wars', *HJ*, 42 (2003), 375–401, at 377; E. H. H. Green, 'Conservatism, anti-socialism, and the end of the Lloyd George coalition', in Green, *Ideologies of Conservatism: Conservative political ideas in the twentieth century* (Oxford, 2002), 114–34, 131; Davies & Morley, 'Electoral turnout', 169; H. Mathers, 'The city of Sheffield, 1893–1926', in C. Binfield, et al. (eds.), *The history of the city of Sheffield, 1843–1993, vol. 1: politics* (Sheffield, 1993), 53–83, at 75–7. In Bristol, the Conservative and Liberal organisations had cooperated closely since 1918 and continued to do so during the 1923 general election despite their conflicting response to Baldwin's protectionist policy (*The Times*, 5 Dec. 1923). However, such pacts were not available to Conservatives everywhere. Many Liberal organisations declined Conservative partnership for the same reasons as they had rejected the progressive alliance with Labour before the war. See G. Bernstein, 'Liberalism and the Progressive Alliance in the constituencies, 1900–1914: three case studies', *HJ*, 26 (1983), 617–40; B. Doyle, 'Urban Liberalism and the "lost generation": politics and middle class culture in Norwich, 1900–1935', *HJ*, 38 (1995), 617–34.

Watson, a strong supporter of Lloyd George's reform agenda, Conservatives in Stockton hoped their party would be advantageously placed to appeal to the working-class electorate.[18] They established a joint coalition committee in the town, to which Liberal officials were invited, and together they staged a Coalition Demonstration. By 1922 efforts were being made to secure Watson as the official Conservative candidate. Though he declined, Conservatives were nevertheless glad to renew their support for him as a National Liberal. In a working-class constituency which, as Harold Macmillan later noted, required 'positive policies', the Conservatives had little to gain from direct identification with their own leader's pledge of 'Tranquillity'.[19] Additionally, their close association with Watson in due course helped many of his personal followers to switch to the Conservative party, becoming active propagandists in the slum areas and industrial works of nearby Billingham.[20]

In these various ways, Conservatives after 1918 were active in shaping their organisations in ways that would help to build and sustain distinctly local strains of popular Conservatism. Much of this work met the rudimentary purposes of any constituency association: fundraising, oversight of the electoral register, maintenance of the subscription list, selection of officers and delegates, and the establishment of women's branches.[21] It also saw activists respond to the peculiarities of Lloyd George's coalition by aligning themselves with particular coalition policies and therefore with particular interest groups within the community. As general secretary of the British Commonwealth Union and later Conservative candidate in Birmingham, Patrick Hannon found himself in contact with a range of local activists. His correspondence with Frank Sheppard, a prominent Coalition Labour figure in Bristol, discloses 'the housing question' as the focus of the government's reconstruction policy for the 'wage-earning community'. 'The conditions of life for our working people in the large centres of industry in this country are the scandal of civilisation'.[22] Backing Lloyd George's promise of 'homes fit for heroes' was a way of reasserting the Conservative commitment to improving the health and happiness of the worker and prolonging the popular legacies of

---

[18] Special committee, 16 Sep. 1918, executive committee, 22 Nov. 1918, Durham County Record Office, Stockton CA, D/X 322/2.

[19] Finance & advisory committee, 27 Oct. 1922, Stockton CA, D/X 322/3; H. Macmillan, *Winds of change, 1914–1939* (London, 1966), 146. For Law's speech, see *The Times*, 8 Nov. 1922.

[20] Adoption Meeting, 13 Oct. 1924, Stockton CA, D/X 332/4.

[21] For more, see Ball, *Portrait of a party*, ch.3.

[22] Hannon to F. Sheppard, 9 Dec. 1918, 11 Feb. 1919, Parliamentary Archives, Hannon Papers, HNN 11/4.

32   Rethinking Interwar Conservatism

Disraeli and Joe Chamberlain.[23] When Hannon later fought the by-election at which he was elected MP for Moseley, a Birmingham suburb, he pledged himself to safeguard the interests of ex-servicemen 'of all classes', including wage earners, but above all stood for economy, low taxation, and against 'government waste'. The same 'middle-class' interests marked the Conservative message in Ilford in 1920.[24] Conservatives in many urban and especially suburban areas increasingly withdrew support for the coalition as it became inconsistent with the anti-waste concerns of property-owners and businesses, while in large parts of rural England activists turned against the coalition in protest at its removal of wartime price guarantees.[25]

The way activists understood voters and their interests was typically based on occupation. In Norfolk North and Devizes, where 44 and 40 per cent respectively of adult males worked in agriculture in 1921, the target voter was the 'working-class' farm labourer; while in Ilford and Epping, where 49 and 37 per cent respectively of adult males worked in commerce, public administration, the professions, or clerical positions, the target voter was the broadly 'middle-class' commuter.[26] When officials in a newly formed branch association in the Epping division were offered the services of a 'working man speaker' to address voters, they noted that 'as we are not what you can call a "working class district", the Committee thought no good purpose would be served in having an open-air meeting'.[27] In areas with more mixed economies, like Pembrokeshire or Dunbartonshire, and in those with unstable economies either as a result of declining trade (Dundee) or the displacement of traditional industries (Stockton), the social and economic nuances of the electorate were typically collapsed to create a simplified working-class or middle-class voter who would, Conservatives hoped, respond to their appeal to composite representations of the stereotypical 'industrial worker', 'farm labourer', 'property owner', or 'professional'. Such labels were not arbitrary but deeply rooted in activists' experience of mobilising working-class and middle-class votes in the pre-war polity.

The Conservative party as a whole took a deterministic view of class. That Conservatives fundamentally believed in what they most feared –

---

[23] E.g., election address to the electors of the Kingswinford Division from A. E. Beck, Conservative candidate, 30 Nov. 1918, Hannon Papers, HNN 11/3.

[24] By-election address to the electors of Birmingham Moseley, Mar. 1921, Hannon Papers, HNN 62/3; by-election address to the electors of Ilford from Frederic Wise, Conservative candidate, Sep. 1920, LSE Archives, Wise Papers, WISE C/12.

[25] Green, 'Conservatism, anti-socialism'.

[26] 1921 census data in Kinnear, *The British voter*, 119, 122.

[27] Branch committee, 8 May 1924, Redbridge Local Studies & Archives, Epping CA, Aldersbrook branch, Acc.A6853.

the workers' instinctively materialistic engagement with politics – was a measure of their fatalism. However, the arrival of Labour as a major force, independent of the Liberals and still capable of electoral advance (winning almost 30 per cent of the national vote in 1922), elicited different responses from national and local Conservatives. For the growing band of educated professionals who took charge of the party organisation and advised the parliamentary leadership, and whose education had introduced them to Marxist thought, the Labour movement's most formidable asset was a deep ownership of the language of class that no competitor could hope to share or dislodge. According to this, the precepts of late-Victorian popular Toryism, including gendered social politics and populist local and imperial patriotism, seemed consigned to a Labour-less past, never to return; so, too, did the Conservatives' Edwardian tradition of appealing to working-class interests on a programmatic platform, especially following the failure of the protectionist policy to return a Conservative government at the 1923 general election. Conservative appeals from the centre were therefore forged along broad and encompassing lines ('the public', 'the nation'), so as more or less to circumvent class. Agents and delegates from the constituencies were encouraged to attend the party's training college in order to be educated in this latest 'professional' thinking.[28] Yet local Conservatives did not break with the class politics of the past. Not only were they far removed from the intellectual case for doing so (as remained most of those who attended the Philip Stott College and later Ashridge College), but instinctively it would have meant the dislocation of their own political habitat. They had no good reason to abandon the familiar rhetorical framework that had built up around class and which would continue to provide them with the necessary field of reference to gauge voter interests. For these Conservatives, the best way to confront Labour – and indeed the Liberals – was to turn the tables on them and outbid them with social reform policies of their own.

It was in this context that many Conservatives, especially in areas of mounting unemployment and slowing trade, enthusiastically embraced Baldwin's policy of protection at the 1923 general election. Macmillan later suggested that the election proved to be one of Baldwin's better moments as leader, since the national leadership's position on that occasion was 'easy to explain', clearly aligned with the electoral needs of the grassroots in the industrial areas, and helped Stockton Conservatives to

---

[28] D. Jarvis, 'British Conservatism and class politics in the 1920s', *EHR*, 111 (1996), 59–84; C. Berthezène, 'Creating Conservative Fabians: the Conservative party, political education and the founding of Ashridge College', *P&P*, 182 (2004), 211–40.

34   Rethinking Interwar Conservatism

come within just seventy-three votes of their first victory since 1906. 'It was a policy for which we could canvass by day, talk in the schoolrooms by night, or preach in the afternoon from the Market Cross in Stockton ... to an audience mostly out of work themselves'.[29] Forty-seven Conservative candidates were fielded in the traditionally free-trade divisions of Yorkshire and *The Times* correspondent in Leeds remarked on the 'changed attitude' among voters: 'The one thing which has clearly emerged is that the attitude of the electors towards tariff reform is not the attitude of 1906 and 1910'.[30] Instead of import taxes, the protection of agriculture would take the form of a direct government subsidy to farmers. This proved popular among Conservatives in agricultural seats since, as well as boosting farmers' incomes, it also guaranteed farm labourers a minimum wage of 30s a week and thereby promised to undercut the growing influence of the agricultural unions.[31] In Devizes, the agent attributed the narrow defeat of the sitting Conservative not to the policy of protection – which was endorsed with enthusiasm at the adoption meeting and later criticised for failing to cover additional agricultural sectors – but the local party's practical failure to compete with the Liberals, who drafted in professional speakers.[32]

Conservative losses in 1923 were soon commonly blamed on the 'dear food cry', resurrected by the reunited Liberal party and mobilised by both Liberals and Labour in a bid to target the 'housewife' and, through her, the male vote.[33] While tariffs specifically were liable to provoke such set-piece clashes, the experience of the 1923 election did not erode local Conservatives' belief in the necessity of a programmatic platform policy. Many of these activists identified party organisation, not the tariff policy,

[29] Macmillan, *Winds of change*, 146. Despite their defeat, local activists shared his enthusiasm about the nature of the campaign: meeting of polling district officers, 4 Jan. 1924, Stockton CA, D/X 322/4.

[30] *The Times*, 29 Nov. 1923. In Lancashire, Lord Derby devised a formula ('Exceptional measures for abnormal times') that enabled the party to support Baldwin while still protecting the historic interests of Unionist free traders in the region. *The Times*, 19 Nov. 1923. For an insider account of the election campaign in Lancashire, see *Salvidge of Liverpool: behind the political scene, 1890–1928*, ed. S. Salvidge (London, 1934), 252–6 (diary notes, Nov., Dec. 1923).

[31] See overviews of the rural contest in the West Country and in Norfolk, *The Times*, 22 Nov., 3 Dec. 1923.

[32] *Wiltshire Gazette*, 22 Nov. 1923; executive committee, 22 Dec. 1923, Devizes CA, 2305/2. Similarly, representatives drawn from Conservative associations in East Anglia agreed unanimously that 'Tariff reform be retained as an integral part of the policy of the Conservative party'. Executive committee, 8 Jan. 1924 and AGM, 2 May 1924, Bodleian Library, Eastern Area, ARE 7/1/6.

[33] 'Unionist losses in Lancashire', *The Times*, 8 Dec. 1923; *Real old Tory politics: the political diaries of Robert Sanders, Lord Bayford, 1910–1935*, ed. J. Ramsden (London, 1984), 211 (12 Dec. 1923).

Local Politics and the Limits of Baldwinism 35

as the deficient factor. As a result, by 1924 many constituency associations were seeking Central Office assistance in the form of literature and speakers; there was also a perceptible interest in attending 'training' courses.[34] Such developments were symptomatic of a focus on organisational problems, and here too social assumptions played an important part.

Alongside local Conservatives' appeals to particular classes ran their insistence on the public participation of certain classes in the construction of local party appeal. The most important of such groups in urban areas was a body of supporters commonly described in local party records as 'known Conservatives'. These were normally men of private if often modest means, businessmen, and professionals, whose public spirit and party allegiance had always been evident in their public speaking, involvement in local government, and social work. These were the 'Villa Tories' of the late Victorian era, drafted into the party organisation by the landed aristocrats in order to shape the urban electorate. Though not necessarily involved in the party organisation on a permanent basis, by dint of tradition and self-interest they could be relied upon to adopt the party label and represent the party in municipal affairs.[35] To understand something of the declinist mentality of 1920s Conservatism, we must look at what implications the growing apathy of this group had on party morale.

The apathy of 'known Conservatives' became a source of growing anxiety for the party in urban and suburban seats. In Epping, party officials kept a list of 'known supporters' whose active participation they sought, in part to compensate for men who had resigned from committee work in order to concentrate on their business interests.[36] But it was in large urban centres like Birmingham that such apathy trespassed most damagingly on the Conservatives' municipal traditions. Despite Labour's early post-war advance, it did not obtain a majority on the Birmingham City Council until 1946 – a fact later presented as testament to a special tradition of labour relations rooted in low trade-union membership and

---

[34] E.g., *The Duff Cooper diaries, 1915–1951*, ed. J. J. Norwich (London, 2005), 205 (10 Oct. 1924); central committee, 24 Jul., 22 Nov. 1924, Devizes CA, 2305/2; education and literature committee, 17 Sep. 1924, Stockton CA, D/X/ 322/4; executive committee, 16 Jun. 1924, Eastern Area, ARE 7/1/6.

[35] See J. Cornford, 'The transformation of Conservatism in the late nineteenth century', *Victorian Studies*, 7 (1963), 35–66; H. Perkin, *The rise of professional society: England since 1880* (1989), 40–6; M. Roberts, 'W. L. Jackson, exemplary manliness and late Victorian popular Conservatism', in M. McCormack (ed.), *Public men: masculinity and politics in modern Britain* (Basingstoke, 2007), 123–42.

[36] Branch committee, 24 Jun. 1925, West Essex CA, Aldersbrook branch, Acc.A6853; women's branch committee, 13 Jan. 1930, West Essex CA, Woodford Bridge branch, Acc.A7347.

36   Rethinking Interwar Conservatism

popular deference to the Chamberlain name.[37] Yet Conservatives at the time were disturbed by the very absence of such continuity, as middle-class civic leadership receded and left the electorate exposed to the enticements of socialist proselytisers.[38] One factor that had a bearing on levels of activism was personal finance. Although by the mid-1920s the party's central organisers undertook initiatives to recruit 'working-class' speakers to combat the threat of Labour on the doorstep, it was felt that it was not always 'fair to ask a man to come forward ... at his own expense'.[39] Constituency parties therefore retained a preference for middle-class recruits who would boost local subscriptions and could afford to stand as self-funded candidates in municipal elections. Hannon found it 'difficult to understand the attitude of mind of leaders of industry, owners of property and those who have acquired some degree of wealth, whose resources would be seriously imperilled under a Socialist Government, but who make no contribution whatever in support of the Unionist Party Fund in Birmingham'.[40] Even elected councillors were eschewing their duty as propagandists in the community. 'Whether it be an Annual Flower Show, Bowling Club, or anything else', they were urged by the local party to step up their involvement. 'To play the showman in that sense would be effective propaganda.'[41] However, Hannon failed to consider that it was precisely because they had wealth and reputation to forfeit, and no longer felt in command of civic opinion, that significantly fewer public men now volunteered themselves or their money. Faced with the threat of costly public humiliation, these former agents of conspicuous partisanship retreated from the Conservative platform.[42]

Of course, the middle classes did not withdraw from civic life completely. The trouble for the Conservative party was that so many 'known Conservatives' now associated themselves publicly with non-party organisations, including interest-based bodies like the Ratepayers' Association and Middle Class Union, and civic ones like the Women's Institute and Rotary. Whether these imparted a genuinely impartial form of

---

[37] Davies & Morley, *County borough elections, vol. 1*, 222–3; R. P. Hastings, 'The Birmingham Labour movement, 1918–1945', *MH*, 5 (1979–80), 78–92.
[38] Central committee, 18 Oct. 1923, special sub-committee, 7 Jan. 1924, Birmingham CUA.
[39] Management committee, 14 May 1920, Birmingham CUA.
[40] Management committee, 14 Nov. 1924, Birmingham CUA; also AGM of Northumberland County and City of Newcastle CA, 8 Apr. 1922, Northumberland Archives, Northern Counties Area, NRO 4137/1.
[41] Management committee, 11 Jun. 1926, Birmingham CUA.
[42] For a general discussion of the potential indignities of public life, see J. Garrard, 'Urban elites, 1850–1914: the rule and decline of a new squirearchy?', *Albion*, 27 (1995), 583–621, esp. 603–15. See also J. Lawrence, *Electing our masters: the hustings in British politics from Hogarth to Blair* (Oxford, 2009), 7.

Local Politics and the Limits of Baldwinism

citizenship, as Helen McCarthy argues, or facilitated a diffuse anti-socialism among the growing mass of silent voters,[43] they were considered a threat by many urban Conservative parties. If the intervention of the Anti-Waste League in 1921 taught Conservatives anything, it was that middle-class ginger groups were able simultaneously to popularise aspects of Conservative thought and undermine the party's organisational strength. During the parliamentary by-election in Birmingham Moseley in February 1921, the local Ratepayers' Association publicly declared its opposition to Hannon despite their shared commitment to anti-waste politics.[44] Where before the war there had been considerable overlap, such splinter politics now exposed a growing chasm between local Conservatives and non-party activists and fostered a degree of mutual suspicion. In turn, this helps to explain why, paradoxically, party members were encouraged to join – to infiltrate – all manner of civic associations.[45] As the new organs of middle-class political sociability expanded towards mass membership, Conservative activists faced a new civic culture that threatened to disrupt the relationship between civic leadership and popular Conservatism.

Their counterparts in the countryside felt similarly hamstrung by a failure to reconstitute old social relationships, particularly with the break-up of many landed estates. For a long time, most rural Conservative parties had relied heavily on these landed estates' contributions to party funds as well as their patronage of employment, recreation, and community facilities on which rested local candidates' paternalistic appeal to labourers. Despite it being routinely contested by opponents and often voters,[46] the strategy had remained a settled feature of the rural Conservative mindset for as long as landowners were willing and able to maintain this relationship with the local community and the local party. Henry Pelling noted that in Devizes during the Edwardian years the Liberal threat rose in inverse relation to the fortunes of the Conservative Marquess of Ailesbury.[47] Such a spectre came to trouble a great many more Conservatives by the early 1920s. This happened especially as potentially valuable new forms of associational life – the British Legion,

---

[43] H. McCarthy, 'Parties, voluntary associations and democratic politics in interwar Britain', *HJ*, 50 (2007), 891–912, cf. McKibbin, *Classes and cultures*, 96–7.

[44] *The Times*, 21 Feb. 1921.

[45] E.g., central advisory women's council, 30 Jun. 1922, Birmingham CUA; *West Essex Gazette*, 27 Oct. 1922.

[46] See J. R. Fisher, 'The limits of deference: agricultural communities in a mid-nineteenth century election campaign', *JBS*, 21 (1981), 90–115; D. Eastwood, 'Contesting the politics of deference: the rural electorate, 1820–1860', in Lawrence & Taylor (eds.), *Party, state and society*, 27–49.

[47] H. Pelling, *Social geography of British elections, 1885–1910* (London, 1967), 115.

38 Rethinking Interwar Conservatism

Women's Institute, and Young Farmers' Clubs, for instance – which presented Conservatives with an opportunity to promote a culture of secular rural sociability and thereby wrest farm labourers from the historic embrace of Liberal and Labour nonconformity, failed to offset the likely electoral damage done by the sale of land.

The scale of estate dispersals was probably less than is commonly understood,[48] yet reports at the time were widespread and fuelled activists' perceptions of the challenges they faced in the countryside. According to the *Conservative Agents' Journal* in 1922, land sales had already 'obliterated old landmarks, and uprooted old family and possibly semi-feudal ideas from the mind of those owners who but a few years before proudly accepted their responsibilities'. Estates were being taken over by plutocrats, whose knowledge of the countryside was recreational and whose newness was expected to disaffect villagers' normal loyalties. The ethos of the new squire, running his estate on 'strict business principles', stood 'in sharp contrast to the methods of his predecessor whose primary thought was for those who by local ties and long tradition depended upon him for their daily bread'.[49] But even where old estates were not subjected to the vulgarities of 'new money' they were mostly dispersed among sitting tenants – a development that did not necessarily assist Conservatives. Ever since the free trade debates of 1906–10, farmers were exasperated by the party leadership's nervousness on the question of agricultural protection and resented what they saw as the disproportionate consideration shown to urban consumers over rural producers. Wartime gains as a result of statutory price guarantees were short lived, as the coalition repealed the relevant legislation in 1921. If this, the so-called 'great betrayal', provoked condemnation of the coalition government, that it occurred under a Conservative Minister of Agriculture, Sir Arthur Griffith-Boscawen, further undermined farmers' trust in the Conservative party and emboldened the National Farmers Union's flirtation with the idea of separate, single-interest representation in the form of an Agricultural Party.[50] Keeping farmers on side was important for the party's organisational integrity in the counties. Even then it was unclear if farmers were going to be able to mobilise wider local

---

[48] For a recent revision, see M. E. Turner & J. V. Beckett, 'End of the old order? F. M. L. Thompson, the land question, and the burden of ownership in England, c.1880–c.1925', *AHR*, 55 (2007), 265–84.

[49] *CAJ*, Sep. 1922, 1–2.

[50] *Political diaries of Robert Sanders*, 201–2 (11, 18 Mar., 15 Apr. 1923). See E. H. H. Green, '"No longer the farmers' friend?" The Conservative party and agricultural protection, 1880–1914', in J. R. Wordie (ed.), *Agriculture and politics in England, 1815–1939* (Basingstoke, 2000), 149–77; D. Rolf, 'The politics of agriculture: farmers' organisations and parliamentary representation in Herefordshire, 1909–22', *MH*, 2 (1974), 168–86.

opinion, since the 1921 act had also repealed the Agricultural Wages Board, which by protecting labourers' wages had placed rural labour relations under renewed strain. It was therefore not only agricultural interests that suffered; in rural communities where the traditional 'moral economy' of the landed estate was once integral to political culture, local activists believed that they saw it and their own political prospects retreat in tandem.

By 1924, with Labour holding office and with three general elections behind them, local Conservatives had had ample opportunity to detect political trends since the war. As they struggled to rehabilitate the organisational networks and social relationships upon which pre-war popular Conservatism had relied, and in light of the inglorious record of the coalition government and the faltering performance of the subsequent Conservative governments, many felt unable to dismiss the fear of imminent decline. It therefore became more incumbent than ever on the party leadership to use the powers of central government to project compelling Conservative appeals to the country.

Back in Government: Reform and Anti-Socialism, 1924–1926

Hoping to put the fragmented political landscape of the post-war years behind them, the Conservatives resumed office in October 1924 intent on consolidating and expanding their support through the projection of a successful record in government. The circumstances were almost uniquely promising. With a majority of more than 200 seats in the House of Commons, the new government was expected to serve its term in full. The return of leading coalitionist figures, including Austen Chamberlain and Lord Birkenhead, created a 'ministry of all the Conservative talents' and promised a degree of unity at the top that further eliminated the destabilising intrigues of the early post-war years. As such the second Baldwin administration was the first united, majority party government under the new franchise. For Baldwin, establishing a steady course in government was integral to the narrative of stability that hallmarked his anti-socialist message. Meanwhile, many Conservatives in the country as well as in parliament viewed stable government as a means of delivering the party's commitment to voters' interests.

Underpinning this resolve was the sobering realisation that Labour, although defeated in the face of relentless anti-Communist propaganda, had gained more than a million votes since 1923. As Beatrice Webb noted, 'The big joke of the general election is that the grave of anti-Communism, which the Liberal leaders dug so energetically for us,

40 Rethinking Interwar Conservatism

swallowed them up instead ... [and] all the Conservative leaders in the country are talking dolefully of the five and a half million "avowed socialists".'[51] Many Conservatives saw in their victory evidence of Labour's unstoppability.[52] Each Labour candidate in Birmingham increased his vote typically by 3–4,000 votes – enough to overturn a Conservative majority in the King's Norton division and to come within seventy-seven votes of unseating Neville Chamberlain in Ladywood. Patrick Hannon (whose majority in Moseley, already safe, was boosted by the withdrawal of the Liberal party) had long felt that the threat of Labour across the city necessitated a more constructive policy-based appeal, in contrast to the anti-socialist focus of the latest campaign, a sentiment which his colleagues reiterated with added urgency after polling day. 'We must bring the people into touch with the Unionist aspects of things, or at the next Election it would not be one seat we should lose, but several.'[53] Labour also advanced in Liverpool, by winning the traditionally Conservative West Toxteth division, proving a plausible challenge in Everton, and mounting a strong inaugural candidature in East Toxteth. In Stockton, although Macmillan's election owed much to the conversion of Liberal voters, Labour's poll was up by 1,500 votes. In Leeds West, where Conservatives staged a remarkable recovery from their 1923 poll, the Labour party nonetheless retained the seat.

In order to rehabilitate the party's working-class following, local Conservatives demanded a distinctly reformist culture of government. Among their demands were trade safeguards, subsidies to protect labour, measures to improve housing and restrict rent levels, schemes for slum clearance, and the expansion of insurance and pension provisions. Some felt it imperative that the government also show a commitment to protecting the legitimate right of trade unionists, a symbolic stance favoured mostly by those like Macmillan who held highly marginal seats in the north of England.[54] The leadership for such a reform agenda in government came principally from Neville

[51] *The diary of Beatrice Webb, vol. 4: 1924–1943*, ed. N. & J. MacKenzie (London, 1985), 44 (n.d. 1924). The Labour party lost forty seats and remained strongest in mining regions, east London, and Glasgow, but its total vote nonetheless went from 4,438,508 to 5,489,077 – reflecting the increased number of candidates (512 compared with 422 in 1923) and the party's growing poll presence in areas beyond its heartlands. The Labour threat was both spreading and growing, and few were the divisions in which the Conservatives did not experience, or observe elsewhere in the region, one or the other.
[52] See Frederic Wise, 'The General Election of 1924', *Ilford Monthly*, Jan. 1925.
[53] Management committee, 16 May 1924 and organisation sub-committee, 26 Nov. 1924, Birmingham CUA.
[54] Election address, Oct. 1924, Bodleian Library, Macmillan papers, 64/65–66; general meeting, 3 Dec. 1924, Stockton CA, D/X 322/4; women's section meeting, 30 Apr.,

Chamberlain. His own experience of the election revealed that the anti-Bolshevik propaganda encapsulated in the Campbell case and the Zinoviev letter failed to displace the material considerations of voters. Unemployment remained a widespread concern, and made him 'anxious, if we do come in, really to make the next Govt one that will leave behind a mark on social reforms'.[55] As Minister for Health, he entered government with a 'four year programme' comprising twenty-five measures, touching mostly on housing, the poor law, pensions, health insurance, local government, and the 'medical services'. As Mayor of Birmingham during the war and an active member of parliamentary committees on post-war reconstruction, Chamberlain had specialist experience of grappling with questions of welfare and infrastructural development. Many of his ideas on 'constructive policy' were further developed in opposition in 1924 and ranged beyond his own departmental responsibilities to include schemes for the safeguarding of particular industries, a new policy for agricultural trade, and the development of electricity supply.[56]

Chamberlain was not the only active reformer in the government. In the cabinet, Churchill as Chancellor of the Exchequer and Arthur Steel-Maitland as Minister of Labour both had strong credentials, the former as a leading light of the pre-war new Liberalism and the latter as the driving force behind the Unionist Social Reform Committee (1911–14), established to formulate Conservative social policy in response to the new Liberalism.[57] Many of their cabinet colleagues had also served on the Unionist Social Reform Committee: Baldwin himself; Edward Wood, Minister of Agriculture until he became Viceroy of India in 1925; his successor in the cabinet, Walter Guinness; Lord Birkenhead, Secretary of State for India; Leo Amery, Secretary of State for the Colonies; Sir Philip Cunliffe-Lister, President of the Board of Trade; Sir Samuel Hoare, Secretary of State for Air; and even Sir William Joynson-Hicks, the

---

28 May 1925, 5 May 1927, Stockton CA, D/X 322/9; labour advisory committee, 7 Oct. 1925, Stockton CA, D/X 322/6; women's advisory council, 13 May 1925, 7 Jan. 1926, Northumberland Collections Service, Northern Counties Area, NRO 4137/7; executive committee, 27 Feb. 1925, West Yorkshire Archive Service, City of Leeds CA, WYL 529/2.

[55] *The Neville Chamberlain diary letters, vol. 2: the reform years, 1921–1927*, ed. R. Self (Aldershot, 2000), 255 (to Ida, 26 Oct. 1924), also 249 (to Hilda, 5 Oct. 1924).

[56] Ibid., 260 (to Hilda, 15 Nov. 1924), 241–2 (to Hilda, 17 Aug. 1924). For Chamberlain's early post-war involvement in committee work, see *Neville Chamberlain diary letters, vol. 1*, 81–7.

[57] P. Addison, *Churchill on the home front, 1900–1955* (London, 1992), ch.2; E. H. H. Green, 'An intellectual in Conservative politics: the case of Arthur Steel-Maitland', in *Ideologies of Conservatism*, 72–113.

42 Rethinking Interwar Conservatism

puritanical Home Secretary.[58] Chamberlain's deputy at Health, Sir Kingsley Wood, was an established authority on insurance and came to prominence as a leading social reformer on the LCC, from where he proved instrumental in agitating for the establishment of the Ministry of Health in 1918 – along with the USRC through the publication of its influential report, *The Health of the People*.[59] However, it was Chamberlain himself, as the chief descendant of the reforming traditions of nineteenth-century municipal improvement and Chamberlainite programmatic politics, and untainted by the Lloyd George coalition, who most embodied the modern working-class Conservatism of the interwar years. As the great hope for so many Conservatives in the country, he found himself in constant high demand as a platform speaker – far more so than any leading Conservative except the prime minister.[60]

Baldwin retained a strong temperamental and strategic commitment to constructive Conservatism throughout his career. Addressing a Conservative conference in February 1924, weeks into the first Labour government, he rallied the party behind the prospect of a new age of Conservative social reform. Invoking Disraeli, he hailed a 'live, united progressive party'. 'The sordid and miserable experiences of [the] war years have left people peculiarly open to the presentation of ideals', he reasoned; it was therefore the Conservatives' duty to embrace the agenda of reform if they were ever to 'stop the drift to Labour of the young men in the towns'.[61] However, his speeches rarely focused on policy. By the time of his second government, Baldwin's statecraft had come to hinge on a distinctly didactic form of anti-socialism. He had long been disdainful of 'stunts' and extravagant 'vote-catching' promises, cultivating instead his own restrained, transparent, and moderate style of public speaking in deliberate contrast to that of opponents, especially Lloyd George. The 1923 election, and the perceived failure of voters to differentiate between

---

[58] Among USRC veterans who held junior ministerial office were William Ormsby-Gore (Colonies), Lord Wolmer (Assistant Postmaster-General), and Geoffrey Locker-Lampson (Home Office). See J. Ridley, 'The Unionist Social Reform Committee, 1911–1914: wets before the deluge', *HJ*, 30 (1987), 391–413.

[59] G. C. Peden, 'Wood, Sir (Howard) Kingsley (1881–1943)', *Oxford Dictionary of National Biography* (Oxford University Press, 2004; online edn, Jan 2011), www.oxforddnb.com /view/article/37002. See also P. R. Wilding, 'The genesis of the Ministry of Health', *Public Administration*, 45 (1967), 149–68.

[60] *Neville Chamberlain diary letters, vol. 2*, 243 (to Ida, 24 Aug. 1924), 429 (to Ida, 19 Nov. 1927); *Neville Chamberlain diary letters, vol. 3*, 126 (Mar. 1929); Macmillan, *Winds of change*, 172–8; *Parliament and politics in the age of Baldwin and MacDonald: the Headlam diaries, 1923–1935*, ed. S. Ball (London, 1992), 74 (15 Dec. 1925), 115 (2 Apr. 1927), 157 (19 Nov. 1928); education & literature committee, 17 Sep. 1924, Stockton CA, D/X 322/4.

[61] *The Times*, 12 Feb. 1924.

the Conservative policy of protection and a general tariff, had further impressed on him the pitfalls that awaited large-scale programmatic appeals in the new democracy. Correspondingly, the drift of Liberal votes to the Conservatives in October 1924 confirmed to him the effectiveness of appealing to fellow anti-socialists along ostensibly non-political lines, not so much with policy as with 'sanity and trust'. Thus began in earnest Baldwin's grand strategy to position Conservatism as the repository of anti-socialism through appeals to the universal values of public service and constitutionalism, nation and empire, Christianity and community – as Williamson has put it, 'to tap the politics of the unpolitical'.[62]

There was nothing inherently incompatible in the relationship between Baldwinite anti-socialism and activists' desire for legislative action, as the first years of the government proved. Churchill's first budget, with which he returned Britain to the gold standard and reduced income tax by 6d, and his Economy Act of 1926, marked a deflationary and orthodox economic course that pleased the 'anti-waste' sensibilities of Conservative voters in the traditional strongholds. Churchill also reimposed the revenue-raising McKenna Duties and undertook reform of income tax, cutting the burden on 'active' middle-class families at the expense of 'idle' inherited wealth. This helped to fund Chamberlain's reforms and coupled sound finance and social justice in ways that benefited both middle-class and working-class households.[63] In doing so the government's political economy arguably conformed more to the agenda of new Liberalism than the socially antagonistic version that underpins McKibbin's account of the Conservatives' 'conventional wisdom' in these years.[64] Meanwhile Chamberlain introduced a contributory pensions act, which reduced the pension age from 70 to 65 and provided maintenance to widows and orphans; an act to reform the system of local rates, intended to prepare the way for the abolition of the Poor Law, which followed in the form of the Local Government Act of 1929; a housing act, which consolidated the policy of subsidising the construction of council houses famously enshrined in Labour's Wheatley Act; and a rural workers' housing act, which offered grants to enable local authorities to make loans to those undertaking improvements to rural housing, in return for greater control over the level of future rent.[65]

Baldwin himself proved an integral part of the government's early success. As Williamson argues, he 'acquired the stature to keep these

---

[62] Williamson, *Stanley Baldwin*, 154, 222–7.
[63] Women's section meeting, 30 Apr. 1925, Stockton CA, D/X 322/9.
[64] See M. Daunton, *Just taxes: the politics of taxation in Britain, 1914–1979* (Cambridge, 2002), 98–9, 122–41; McKibbin, 'Class and conventional wisdom'.
[65] See R. Self, *Neville Chamberlain: a biography* (Aldershot, 2006), ch.6.

44   Rethinking Interwar Conservatism

different strands [of Conservatism] together, with the effect that a plurality of Conservative appeals worked to maximum effect'.[66] While Churchill and Chamberlain set the policy, Baldwin set the rhetorical tone. Often it was felt that his rhetoric on a given topic concealed his ignorance of the subject matter; in Devon, for instance, Sanders noted that Baldwin spoke 'very feebly' about agriculture but nonetheless had left a pleasing impression 'on the whole'.[67] The task of political rhetoric, according to Maurice Cowling, was 'to provide new landmarks for the electorate'.[68] Baldwin's response to the new crisis of industrial relations, which began with the coal dispute in 1925 and culminated with the General Strike in May 1926, became one such landmark. Speaking first at a party rally in Birmingham and then in parliament, he won plaudits for his reasoned and inspired rejection of a backbench bill, brought by Frederick Macquisten (MP for Argyll), which sought to disrupt the automatic flow of trade-union subscriptions to the Labour party.[69] The bill fell, an outcome which undoubtedly lodged in the gullet of some Conservatives who feared that a golden opportunity was lost. But even Cuthbert Headlam, the cantankerous County Durham MP, could appreciate the symbolic importance of desisting from challenging symbols of working-class solidarity. He 'strongly' advised a Conservative agent in his region not to join the Organisation for the Maintenance of Supplies, established in September 1925 to facilitate the movement of essential resources during a general strike, warning him that 'there is no use our Party being identified in any way as a party with what must be a strike-breaking organisation'. Given the need for sensitivity, Headlam came to appreciate Baldwin's emollient rhetoric – which, although 'exceedingly dull', seemed somehow to hold listeners in 'rapt interest' and impressed them with its 'sincerity'. 'Baldwin has a real opportunity because the great mass of the people believe in him and they will follow his lead'.[70] Baldwinite Conservatism was an enigma, and as such its strength was also its weakness.

[66] Williamson, *Stanley Baldwin*, 353. In this respect, despite his own references to Disraeli, Baldwin's methods as leader were perhaps more similar to those of Lord Salisbury. See P. Marsh, *The discipline of popular government: Lord Salisbury's domestic statecraft, 1881–1902* (Aldershot, 1978), 326.

[67] *Political diaries of Robert Sanders*, 220–1 (13 Jul. 1925).

[68] Cowling, *The impact of Labour*, 5.

[69] S. Baldwin, *On England* (London, 1926; 1937 edn), 33–59; *The Leo Amery diaries, vol. 1: 1896–1929*, ed. J. Barnes & D. Nicholson (London, 1980), 400 (6 Mar. 1925).

[70] *Headlam diaries, 1923–1935*, 55 (3 Mar. 1925), 77–8 (27–8 Jan., 3–4 Feb. 1926), 82 (6 Apr. 1926). Also P. Cambray, *The game of politics: a study of the principles of British electoral strategy* (London, 1932), 108–9; *Memoirs of a Conservative: J. C. C. Davidson's memoirs and papers, 1910–1937*, ed. R. R. James (London, 1969), 170–1 (to R. A. Butler, 20 Apr. 1955).

Policy and Platitude in Government, 1926–1929

Cracks soon began to appear. By the spring of 1926 the Conservatives had successfully defended nine seats at twelve by-elections, including Dunbartonshire in January 1926. Yet the party worried not only about its reduced majorities but also about the loss of three industrial constituencies to Labour. The first of these was Stockport, which had some tradition of working-class Conservatism, and another was East Ham North. The third and most significant was Darlington, traditionally a model of working-class Conservatism and represented since 1895 (except between January and December 1910) by a succession of paternalistic patriarchs from the Pease family.[71] Besides these incursions into its working-class industrial base, two other major developments intimidated the Conservatives and compromised the creation of a popular legacy of government: an increasingly broad-based Labour appeal in the country, the threat of which intensified significantly in the aftermath of the General Strike, and Lloyd George's succession to the Liberal leadership upon Asquith's resignation in October 1926.

From 4 May to 12 May 1926, 1.7 million workers went out on strike in support of the miners. Many contemporaries interpreted this short-lived general strike as evidence of the essential peaceableness of the British public. The revolutionary threat, they argued, masterminded by a minority of extreme agitators, came to nothing when confronted with the public-spiritedness of volunteers, who took over essential services, and the non-violence of ordinary strikers whose interests the TUC was manipulating.[72] Baldwin impressed many of his cabinet colleagues with his leadership during the crisis. His use of the radio to shape and reflect the will of the public certainly brought his skill as a communicator to the fore.[73] But it does not follow that it exemplified the Conservative leadership's strategy of bringing together working- and middle-class voters in a common-sense defence of the constitution, much less a hegemonic electoral block marching to the tune of Baldwin's didactic anti-socialism. The 'public' solidarity celebrated by Baldwin and others during and after the strike reflected little of the experience of many Conservatives on the ground, as the protracted aftermath of the strike generated a period of public debate in which Labour, despite its own constitutionalist rejection of the strike itself, successfully constructed and

---

[71] *The Times*, 19 Sep. 1925 (Stockport), 10 Feb. 1926 (Darlington), 27 Apr. 1926 (East Ham); Pelling, *Social geography of British elections*, 328.

[72] P. Mandler, *The English national character: the history of an idea from Edmund Burke to Tony Blair* (New Haven, 2006), 150–1; R. Saltzman, *A lark for the sake of their country: the 1926 general strike volunteers in folklore and memory* (Manchester, 2012).

[73] Williamson, *Stanley Baldwin*, 200–202.

46   Rethinking Interwar Conservatism

championed its own inclusive 'nation' – a workers' nation, and one of the sources of Conservative defeat in 1929.[74]

The strike and its aftermath had the effect of hardening working-class politics. Austen Chamberlain later noted that since 1926 'the working classes have been nourishing a silent resentment more like continental class hatred than anything we have experienced in our life time'.[75] He reached this conclusion as a bruised man after almost losing his seat in 1929. For most Conservatives, however, the renewed working-class politics of the late 1920s signified something perhaps less antagonistic but still damaging to their prospects, namely Labour's growing claim to represent the 'community' in the interests of all workers.

Sharing as it did social space, economic interests, and cultural and religious heritage, the urban 'community' displayed a solidarity that transcended occupational divides among workers and subsumed other hierarchies based, for example, on respectability. In her study of County Durham, Hester Barron has revealed that for miners, who mostly remained locked out until November or December, ideas of community underpinned the cross-class networks of charity and philanthropy on which their families survived.[76] 'Community', as a more or less coherent but not homogenous unit, is similarly discernible in many historical, sociological, and autobiographical accounts of the early twentieth century.[77] In this context, the popular defence of community interests, already prominent in Labour's history of campaigning, reached a new apogee in the late 1920s. The Labour party in Birmingham had provided free meals and free drinks throughout the strike and, led by Oswald Mosley, embarked on an intensive publicity campaign to forge a public view of the strike as a 'vistory [sic] for the workers' and a new dawn in the city's politics. Although dismissed as 'class propaganda', Labour's message made the Conservatives, by their own admission, 'fidgety'.[78] Once again they decided to revive the *Straightforward* as a source of counter-

---

[74] J. Lawrence, 'Labour and the politics of class, 1900–1940', in D. Feldman & J. Lawrence (eds.), *Structures and transformations in modern British history* (Cambridge, 2011), 237–60; D. Tanner, 'Class voting and radical politics: the Liberal and Labour parties, 1910–31', in Lawrence & Taylor (eds.), *Party, state and society*, 106–30.

[75] *The Austen Chamberlain diary letters*, ed. R. Self, 337 (to Ida, 6 Jun. 1929).

[76] See H. Barron, *The 1926 miners' lockout: meanings of community in the Durham coalfield* (Oxford, 2010).

[77] E.g., T. Young, *Becontree and Dagenham* (London, 1934); M. Stacey, *Tradition and change: a study of Banbury* (Oxford, 1960); R. Roberts, *The classic slum: Salford life in the first quarter of the century* (London, 1971); M. Savage & A. Miles, *The remaking of the British working class, 1840–1940* (London, 1994), esp. ch.4; T. Griffiths, *The Lancashire working classes: c.1880–1930* (Oxford, 2001); M. Brodie, *The politics of the poor: the East End of London, 1885–1914* (Oxford, 2004).

[78] Management committee, 18 May 1926, Birmingham CUA.

Local Politics and the Limits of Baldwinism 47

propaganda to combat Labour's *Town Crier*. But whether this would do enough to resist Labour's growing claims to represent Birmingham opinion was not at all clear. 'There must be put into operation a systematic and effective open-air propaganda in all parts of the City', argued one Conservative activist. 'Our Annual [event] at the Botanical Gardens ought to take a more Militant form. We ought to be able to have a procession which led up to that Demonstration, and so again give open publicity to the whole city, the same as Socialists do.'[79] In Leeds, Conservatives noted with similar alarm that Labour councillors were generating 'good propaganda' for themselves by holding public meetings after every council meeting.[80]

Labour's propaganda in municipal affairs was reinforced by a growing network of consumer and relief organisations, membership of which increased significantly between 1926 and 1929. Chief among these was the cooperative movement, whose local activities became the subject of frenzied counter-activity by the Conservatives. Mrs Parker, an activist in Stockton, reflected widespread fears within her party when she accused Labour of hijacking the ostensibly non-political cooperative society. With almost five million members nationwide, the movement 'may become as much a part of the Socialist machine as is the Trade Union Congress'. Conservative activists were therefore encouraged to join their local branch in order to oppose the election of socialist officials.[81] By the late 1920s, Labour appeared to be following the spirit of MacDonald's earlier pledge: 'The municipality should supply the communal needs – like trams, electricity and so on – which concern good government, public health and other matters of communal efficiency; the Co-operative organization should deal with the more individual needs of consumers.'[82] Moreover, by expanding their municipal agenda to include maternity and child clinics, local Labour parties addressed themselves not just to male-centred industrial concerns but also to family-oriented welfare politics.[83] This contributed to Labour's

---

[79] Management committee, 18 May, 11 Jun. 1926, Birmingham CUA.
[80] Organisation sub-committee, 20 Dec. 1926, City of Leeds CA, WYL 529/2.
[81] Women's section meeting, 10 Mar. 1927, Stockton CA, D/X 322/9; women's executive committee, 18 Mar. 1927, Devizes CA, 2305/12; management committee, 8 Jul., 14 Oct. 1927, Birmingham CUA; executive committee, 19 Dec. 1927, City of Leeds CA, WYL 529/2; women's advisory council, 3 Feb. 1928, Northern Counties Area, NRO 4137/8; general council, 28 Mar. 1928, Norfolk Record Office, Norfolk North CA, Acc.2006/152.
[82] See R. MacDonald, *Parliament and democracy* (London, 1920), 3–5, 68–75; also N. Robertson, *The co-operative movement and communities in Britain, 1914–1960* (Farnham, 2010), 36–9.
[83] D. Tanner, 'Gender, civic culture and politics in south Wales: explaining Labour municipal policy, 1918–1939', in M. Worley (ed.), *Labour's grassroots: essays on the activities of local Labour parties and members, 1918–1945* (Aldershot, 2005), 170–93.

48   Rethinking Interwar Conservatism

command of a more inclusive working-class following and helped to neutralise the effect of the controversial Trade Disputes Act of 1927, which threatened to curtail Labour's organisational strength by discontinuing the automatic transfer of union subscriptions to the party.

The spoils for Labour of this approach were first witnessed in local government. The anti-socialist London Municipal Society, commenting on the municipal election results of November 1926, feebly claimed that Labour's gains 'have not been of serious import ... except in Birmingham, Sheffield, Leeds, Stoke-on-Trent, Manchester, Nuneaton, Bolton, Liverpool, Leicester, Leyton, Mansfield, Nottingham, Dudley, Norwich, and Swansea'.[84] These were in addition to existing Labour-controlled councils in Durham, Glamorganshire, and Monmouthshire. Labour gained overall control of Birkenhead and Sheffield in 1926, Barnsley and Swansea in 1927, and Barrow-in-Furness and Leeds in 1928. In several other centres it commanded a majority of the popular vote (but not council seats) at one or more of the municipal elections between 1926 and 1929, including Bradford, Bristol, Burnley, Cardiff, Gateshead, and Grimsby.[85] In private, Neville Chamberlain, whose ministerial duties involved regular tours of the provincial cities, confessed his admiration for Labour's municipal policies. Commenting on the new Labour administration in Sheffield, he noted 'it did not appear to me that their programme contained anything that might not equally have figured in that of a progressive Conservative party'.[86] Increasingly, the urban electorate was presented with rival displays of government at local and national levels.

In response, local Conservatives urged a more active projection of the national government's achievements. In Stockton and Leeds, as elsewhere, a propaganda campaign showcasing housing and pensions reform, trade improvements, and the reduced cost of living was deemed crucial to deflecting trade-union opposition and competing with Labour municipalism.[87] Chamberlain shared this sense of urgency and anticipated the widespread reputational damage wrought by the government's failure to address unemployment, especially in the mining districts. He proceeded to launch a new slum clearance scheme and established the

---

[84] *The Times*, 4 Nov. 1926.

[85] Davies & Morley, *County borough elections in England and Wales, 1919–1938: a comparative analysis, Volume 2: Bradford – Carlisle* (Aldershot, 2000), 40–41, 222–3, 334, 540 and vol.4: Exeter – Hull (Aldershot, 2013), 110–11, 301.

[86] *Neville Chamberlain diary letters, vol. 2*, 425 (to Hilda, 30 Oct. 1927).

[87] AGM, 28 Mar. 1927, Stockton CA, D/X 322/4; women's section meeting, 24 Mar., 5 May, 20 Oct., 1 Dec. 1927, Stockton CA, D/X 322/9; advisory committee, 4 Feb. 1927, West Yorkshire Archive Service, Yorkshire Provincial Area, WYL 529/3; AGM, 16 Jun. 1928, Northern Counties Area, NRO 4137/1. Also *Neville Chamberlain diary letters, vol. 2*, 403 (to Hilda, 19 Mar. 1927).

Industrial Transference Board, 'a sort of crusade' to move '100,000–150,000 men out of these stagnant pools of labour in South Wales and Durham' to other centres of employment at home and in the Dominions.[88] Yet the government's policies were making little impression on voters. This was in part because they proved ineffective in practice, as in the case of the Transference Board,[89] but also because the message of policy achievement was being lost amid Baldwin's appeals to duty and constitutionalism. Clearly, the leadership's commitment to a didactic anti-socialism remained undimmed by developments since 1924, with Central Office orchestrating 'educational propaganda' to accompany the passage of the Trade Disputes Bill.[90] For activists on the ground, however, this approach was in danger of becoming both anachronistic, given the more immediate need to compete rather than educate, and counter-productive. As one exasperated agent argued: 'it is futile to preach platitudes about the duties of citizenship to a busy man whose efforts to earn his daily bread leave him little leisure'.[91] Stressing the appeal of the party's 'big constructive programme' of social reform in 1924, another agent posed a rhetorical question: would the party have won the last general election 'as easily and as decisively if we had offered nothing beyond the assurance of sane constitutional government?'[92]

If the General Strike helped to revivify working-class politics, it also provided conclusive evidence of Labour's commitment to parliamentary methods of reform. Not only had MacDonald opposed the strike, but the Labour party – and, crucially, the TUC – soon afterwards renounced the policy of direct action and set itself on a new course that devolved industrial disputes to collective bargaining mechanisms and saw the party appealing to voters with a wide-ranging new programme that prioritised 'social progress' for all.[93] *Labour and the Nation* (1928), as R. H. Tawney famously remarked, promised 'presents for everyone'. Containing schemes for industrial reorganisation and social reform in education, housing, pensions, and unemployment relief, the document encapsulated the combined constitutional respectability and legislative radicalism of

---

[88] *Neville Chamberlain diary letters, vol. 2*, 431–7 (to Ida, 4, 17 Dec. 1927; to Hilda, 11 Dec. 1927).

[89] W. R. Garside, *British unemployment, 1919–1939: a study in public policy* (Cambridge, 1990), 185–6, 243–6.

[90] *Davidson's memoirs and papers*, 297 (n.d.).

[91] *CAJ*, Dec. 1927, 338; also AGM, 16 Jun. 1928, Northern Counties Area, NRO 4137/1.

[92] *CAJ*, Jul. 1927, 187.

[93] See G. W. McDonald & H. F. Gospel, 'The Mond-Turner talks, 1927–1933: a study in industrial co-operation', *HJ*, 16 (1973), 807–29, and Lawrence, 'Labour and the politics of class, 1900–1940'.

50   Rethinking Interwar Conservatism

the Labour party.[94] This set the tone for the party's general election manifesto in 1929 but had already shaped how local Labour parties tailored their appeals to communities – and challenged Conservatives – well beyond their party's traditional heartlands.

This could be seen in the Ilford by-election of February 1928. The Conservative candidate, Sir George Hamilton, launched his campaign with a traditional appeal to the presumed middle-class priority of retrenchment. Echoing his predecessor, Sir Frederic Wise, he praised in particular the 'rigid economy in Government expenditure and lower taxation'.[95] In truth, the rapid growth of the Becontree estate – by 8,000 voters since 1924 – had generated a new set of pressing local interests that quickly put in jeopardy the relevance of this traditional appeal.[96] Within days of the campaign launch, up-to-date local grievances, relating in particular to transport services for commuters, dominated the agenda. All three parties campaigned in favour of extending the tube to Ilford, yet while Hamilton pledged to lobby the existing railway company the Labour candidate pressed for a state-funded project under a nationalised scheme. In addition, Labour backed a residents' campaign to prevent the introduction of greyhound racing in the borough. Together with its long-standing support for 'local option', which householders supported not only on grounds of temperance but in order to protect property values, Labour was aligning itself unashamedly with middle-class respectability. Indeed, since the general election the party's local membership had grown from 100 to 1,700.[97] Hamilton won the election, but the Conservative majority fell by 10,000 votes. The anti-waste middle-class politics of the post-war years now seemed outdated in the expanding suburbs. Conservatives were confronted with a Labour party able to cultivate its own respectability and responding relevantly to the changing interests of suburbia.

This highlighted the reasons why many Conservatives came to distrust the politics of anti-socialism when it relied on avowals of non-partisanship. In their opinion, it compounded the damaging shift already taking place in middle-class political culture away from public displays of party allegiance. This not only undermined Conservative hopes of party-

---

[94] M. Worley, *Labour inside the gate: a history of the British Labour party between the wars* (London, 2005), 117–20; Labour party, *Labour and the nation* (1928).

[95] Election address to the electors of Ilford from Frederic Wise, 14 Oct. 1924, WISE/C12; *Ilford Recorder*, 3 Feb. 1928.

[96] See Young, *Becontree and Dagenham*, ch.4.

[97] *The Times*, 13, 18, 20, 21 Feb. 1928; *Ilford Recorder*, 2 Oct., 27 Nov. 1925. Plans for the greyhound racing track went ahead and it became the second most popular source of recreation for Becontree residents after the cinema. Young, *Becontree and Dagenham*, 222.

Local Politics and the Limits of Baldwinism   51

political sociability but enabled Labour to claim a foothold on civic life, 'uncontested and unquestioned'.[98] Democracy, it was argued, relied on open disagreements. Consensus politics was flawed because it stifled rather than reconciled inevitable disagreements in society, with Conservatives doing a disservice to the electorate by closeting themselves as 'anti-socialists' rather than outing themselves as proud Conservatives.[99] In a concerted effort to demonstrate this, Ilford Conservatives branded independent politics a 'sham' and in a series of editorials in the in-house paper, the *Ilford Monthly*, depicted non-party politics as murky and clandestine. The vogue for 'independent anti-socialist' candidatures, it warned, was a dangerous departure that threatened the traditional accountability of representative government; anyone who stood as an independent was no better than 'the Vicar of Bray' – 'chameleons of the first order'.[100] Looking on at events in the neighbouring suburb of Walthamstow, the *Ilford Monthly* argued that the reason why defeat of the General Strike there had been such a close run affair was not just because of the Labour-run council's sympathy with the strikers. Rather, it was because of the feebleness of the 'alleged champions of anti-socialism', those 'hopeless old sillies' who were elected on non-party and therefore meaningless labels.[101] If, as McKibbin claims, it was through 'an "apolitical" reluctance to discuss politics' that the middle classes drifted towards the Conservative party in the 1920s, then it was also what Conservatives at the time felt permitted Labour to pursue its own apolitical strategy unchecked.[102]

Labour was not alone in developing policy platforms that challenged the Conservatives in urban and suburban districts. The biggest gain in the Ilford by-election was made by the Liberals, whose candidate, Arthur Comyns Carr, applied proposals from the so-called yellow book, *Britain's Industrial Future* (1928), to address local demands for 'traffic reform'. These included a scheme of tax-funded investment in the tube network, whereby the increase in land values as a result of infrastructural development would be appropriated (and labelled 'betterment taxes') to cover the cost of construction.[103] In fact, Liberal policy became so dirigiste that in some areas Labour was able to pose as a moderate contrast. During the by-election campaign in Liverpool East Toxteth in March 1929, a correspondent from *The Times* noted: 'It is the Labour rather than the Liberal opposition which is on the up grade ... Mr. Cleary [the Labour candidate] has been shrewd enough to seize the opportunity of

---

[98] *Ilford Monthly*, Feb. 1926.   [99] Ibid., Sep. 1925.   [100] Ibid., Feb., Mar. 1926.
[101] Ibid., Jul. 1926.   [102] McKibbin, *Classes and cultures*, 96.
[103] *The Times*, 20 Feb. 1928; Report of the Liberal Industrial Inquiry, *Britain's industrial future* (1928), 294–6.

52   Rethinking Interwar Conservatism

representing the Socialists and not the Liberals as the party offering a practical alternative Government.'[104]

The Liberals' policy projection was bound to make a wider impact on popular politics in the late 1920s as, under Lloyd George's official leadership, the party contested all by-elections and tailored its appeal to almost every region of the country. The seats gained by the Liberals were mostly rural or semi-rural constituencies. The yellow book offered a coherent set of agricultural policies to address the problems 'now aggravated by the disintegration of the old system of landlordship'. This included improved security of tenure for the growing number of small tenant farmers who in a previous generation would have been labourers, plus a system of credit supply to enable new and existing farmers to equip their holdings and embark on long-term investment.[105] The Liberals also succeeded in cutting Conservative majorities in suburban and county seats. As a rule, they did so either by intervening where they had not stood in 1924, thereby splitting the anti-socialist vote, or by crafting their own electoral recovery, as in Ilford. Only in Scotland did the Liberals struggle to make an impression at by-elections, even losing their deposits in Dunbartonshire in 1926, Aberdeen North in 1928, and North Lanarkshire in 1929. Across England and Wales, the lapsed Liberal vote, so valuable to Conservatives in 1924, returned to Lloyd George.[106] This begs the question whether erstwhile Liberals who voted Conservative at the general election did so mainly in the absence of a Liberal candidate or in sympathy with Baldwinite anti-socialism. What is clear is that by 1929 Baldwin, while shrewdly recognising the electoral value of modelling his own 'honesty' and 'character' in contrast to Lloyd George, failed to compete with the Liberal leader on popular policy.

So, with both Labour and the Liberal party responding imaginatively to the aftermath of the General Strike, Conservatism faced a hostile climate by the time of the general election in May 1929. While the consequences were not easy to predict, they were clearly serious and proved to be so. The real threat to popular Conservatism came from a resurgent progressivism. Labour was not yet a mass party, but it was no longer a sectional party; the Liberal party was no longer a party of government, but nor was it yet a marginal force. Between them they offered a home to the growing

---

[104] *The Times*, 16 Mar. 1929.
[105] *Britain's industrial future*, 318–38. The Conservatives lost to the Liberals in Bosworth in 1927, Lancaster and St Ives in 1928, and Eddisbury and Holland with Boston in 1929.
[106] G. H. Bennett, '"Part of the puzzle": Northampton and other midlands by-election defeats for the Conservatives, 1927–1929', *MH*, 20 (1995), 151–73.

Local Politics and the Limits of Baldwinism 53

millions of voters who sought a politics that combined radicalism with respectability.

By contrast, Baldwin offered the country little more than an audit of the government's work since 1924. For him, the foundations of the next Conservative majority were to be built on public trust – a recognition by voters of promises kept and, by implication, faith in new promises soon to be honoured. His message to those who backed his party at the previous election, including 'progressive men who before the War had belonged to other parties', was simple: 'I maintain . . . that we have done nothing in the last 4½ year to shake their confidence in us.'[107] This was echoed in party literature.[108] Central Office posters reminded voters of 800,000 houses built since 1924 ('PREMISES are better than PROMISES'),[109] new pension entitlements to reduce poverty ('MILLIONS SAVED FROM WANT – CONSERVATIVES GAVE YOU THESE PENSIONS!'),[110] and tax reductions to ease the cost of living ('TEA TAX abolished!').[111] Baldwin's objective was to renew his mandate for anti-socialist government. 'Moderation' and 'responsibility' therefore became the keynote of the Conservatives' 'Safety First' campaign – qualities that were to be demonstrated not only through legislative competence but also desistance from the extravagant schemes of their opponents. 'I . . . hope that you will not attempt to outbid L.G. or the Socialists in a vote-catching programme', William Bridgeman advised Baldwin. 'I see the Press continually urging you to produce an attractive bait – but it is folly to attempt a competition with irresponsible people . . . Our only safe course is to depend on our record, and make as few promises either as to what we shall do, or what we shall not do, as possible.'[112] Conservative policy, as set out by Central Office to activists, amounted to little more than a series of platitudes about 'defence of the constitution' and vague pledges to extend existing schemes of social reform and industrial safeguarding.[113]

Local Conservatives, meanwhile, were eager to highlight the government's record but reluctant to present it as the summation of Conservative appeal. After all, some policies seemed incompletely implemented. In manufacturing and agricultural areas, where mounting

---

[107] *The Times*, 15 May 1929 (speech in Exeter).
[108] E.g., *How the Conservative government has kept its pledges: a record of promises fulfilled, 1924–1929* (1929) and *Performances not promises: Mr Stanley Baldwin's great election speech at Drury Lane Theatre, April 18th 1929* (1929).
[109] CPA, poster 1929–03. [110] CPA, poster 1929–05.
[111] CPA, poster 1929–15, also 1929–17 and 1929–18.
[112] *The modernisation of Conservative politics: the diaries and letters of William Bridgeman, 1904–1935*, ed. P. Williamson (London, 1988), 218–19 (to Baldwin, 27 Mar. 1929).
[113] *CAJ*, Jan. 1929, 7.

54 Rethinking Interwar Conservatism

unemployment and slowing trade brought home to voters and activists the timidity of the government's safeguarding scheme, the slogan of 'performance not promises' struck a hollow note. Many were hopeful of pre-election budget treats, including cuts to petrol tax, betting tax, and sugar duties. Even so, the Conservative MP for Wakefield, Geoffrey Ellis, doubted if budget sweeteners would dislodge the electorate's 'general view ... that the govt <u>could</u> have done more'. The itinerant Conservative speaker, James Gardner, himself a trade unionist, reported that voters in the north of England demanded a pledge to extend safeguarding and that this should be accompanied by 'a bold lead from Mr. Baldwin', neither of which was much in evidence.[114] Moreover, the kind of publicity for which many activists had called since 1924 – that is, at the time of implementation and explicitly as an advertisement of achievements rather than a substitute for future policy[115] – now fell short in a general election campaign in which other parties' ambitious policy programmes spoke to voters' material well-being. As one agent from Newbury explained, 'Human nature being what it is we have to conclude that however excellent may be the character of the Conservative administration, the ordinary voter lives largely on anticipation of favours to come, of further social reforms, of beneficial legislation which will affect his or her interests'.[116] Such pleas were soon vindicated. In the circumstances of 1929, a visionless campaign was the inevitable prelude to defeat.[117]

In 1929 the Labour and Liberal parties each polled more votes than ever before, Labour attracting four million additional votes and the Liberals around 2.5 million. There were, of course, local factors at play. In Birmingham, where six Conservative seats were lost to Labour, party organisers blamed the impact of young women voters newly enfranchised by the 1928 act, floating voters who simply fancied 'change', and the ingratitude of a large number of voters newly resident in the city's housing estates. Their counterparts in West Yorkshire bemoaned the inadequacy of the publicity surrounding the party's safeguarding policy and also the failure of their local propaganda to penetrate through to workers in the factories. Norfolk Conservatives, who had long felt that the party's national publicity was unsuited to the interests of rural voters, blamed

---

[114] Ellis to Macmillan, 10 Apr. 1929 and Gardner to Macmillan, 3 Apr. 1929, Macmillan papers, 64/128, 142–3.

[115] E.g., *CAJ*, Jul. 1927, 187–8, Dec. 1927, 338.　　[116] *CAJ*, Mar. 1929, 40.

[117] Cambray, *The game of politics*, 66–7; *Leo Amery diaries*, 596–7 (3 Jun. 1929); Hadingham (agent) to P. Buchan-Hepburn (defeated Conservative candidate, Wolverhampton East), 17 Jul. 1929, Churchill Archive Centre, Hailes Papers, HAIS 1/1.

Local Politics and the Limits of Baldwinism 55

'the agricultural dissatisfaction generally'.[118] But it is possible also that anti-socialism itself, as an ideological world view that mobilised, and above all unified, otherwise competing constitutionalists, was approaching an existential crisis. Despite the party's grand electoral strategy to squeeze out the Liberals and position Conservatism as the dominant vehicle of anti-Labour sentiment, anti-socialism remained something imperfectly practised by many Conservatives on the ground. While the results of the 1924 election doubtlessly created a lasting appreciation of the value of the Liberal vote, 1929 highlighted how little progress was made towards entrenching it.

One reason for the failure of Conservative anti-socialism in 1929 was that it took aim at an outdated image of the Labour party. While Conservatives inevitably drew comparisons between the 1924 and 1929 elections, noting especially their attacking role in the former and their defensive task in the latter, there is less evidence that they fully comprehended the implications of recent efforts by Labour to broaden its appeal.[119] As a result, Baldwin's 'Safety First' slogan proved not only uninspiring but also suggestive of a brand of anti-socialism insufficiently responsive to changing social and political realities. Only in retrospect did this become clear to some party strategists. As the Central Office official Philip Cambray later reflected, Labour 'was no longer a Party which sought to attain economic revolution by the exercise of its industrial power, but was ... a constitutional Party sincerely aiming to solve current problems within the existing social and industrial structure'.[120] The Liberals, however, recognised this in time to make it count in their favour in 1929. Referring back to the red scares of 1924, now proved 'utterly false', the Liberal-backing *Yorkshire Evening News* noted that 'the nation is wiser after the events of 1924'. 'The Red Bogey will no longer frighten the electorate.'[121]

Conservatives dismissed the Liberal decision to put up so many candidates as counterproductive to the anti-socialist cause. The Liberal manifesto, *We can conquer unemployment*, was condemned for its unscrupulous promises. In Norfolk North an agreement was struck with the editor of the *Norfolk Chronicle*, a leading local Conservative, that the Liberal campaign 'should be ignored'.[122] But it was all too easy to dismiss Lloyd George and his party as opportunistic. Such an attitude ran the risk of

---

[118] Management committee, 14 Jun. 1929, Birmingham CUA; advisory committee, 6 Nov. 1929, West Yorkshire Archive Service, Yorkshire Area, WYL 529/3; executive committee, 26 Nov. 1928 and advisory sub-committee, 14 Sep. 1929, Norfolk North, Acc.2006/152.

[119] E.g., management committee, 14 Jun. 1929, Birmingham CUA.

[120] Cambray, *The game of politics*, 65.   [121] *Yorkshire Evening News*, 7 May 1929.

[122] Labour advisory committee, 14 Mar. 1928, 10 Apr. 1929, Stockton CA, D/X 322/6.

56   Rethinking Interwar Conservatism

underestimating the sincerity with which many voters returned to the Liberal fold in 1929; and of overestimating both Liberals' own identification with anti-socialism and their willingness to subscribe to a Conservative-led variety. Neville Chamberlain noted, albeit with hindsight, that defeated Conservative candidates 'assume[d] that in the absence of a Liberal candidate, Liberal votes would have been given to them, which seems to me very doubtful'.[123] After all, Liberal morale had been riding high since Lloyd George resumed the leadership in 1926. His policy of land reform helped to restore the party's radical credentials among workers and tenants in its rural heartlands.[124] The party also held its own in many urban areas, including the West Midlands, thanks to its policy programme as well as the latent loyalty of many nonconformists.[125] This was not a party yet ready to cede the anti-socialist mantle to the Conservatives.

Except in areas where it was most deeply rooted (Glasgow and Bristol, for example), anti-socialism as cooperation between Conservatives and Liberals went into decline in part because the Liberals withdrew. This occurred most spectacularly in the LCC in 1928, when the Liberals' Progressive Party parted company with the anti-socialist Municipal Reform Party.[126] This mirrored a similar aversion to operational cooperation on the part of many Conservatives. Renewed talk of the need to capture or coordinate the Liberal vote, which inevitably followed defeat in 1929, reminded Leo Amery of the centrist designs that destabilised his party in 1921–2, so he pledged himself to 'begin the battle over again to save us from an anti-Socialist coalitionism'.[127] In local government, which for many Conservative associations was traditionally the legitimate site of 'independent' public service, Conservatives responded to Labour's practice of fielding 'Labour' candidates by becoming more overtly partisan themselves. In Norfolk, where activists noted that 'Labour nominees were allowed to go unopposed', the party put up their parliamentary candidate, Thomas Cook, to fight a local ward. Action of this kind jeopardised relations with Liberal activists.[128] Moreover, in the context

---

[123] *Neville Chamberlain diary letters, vol. 3*, 145 (to Hilda, 9 Jun. 1929).
[124] M. Dawson, 'The Liberal land policy, 1924–1929: electoral strategy and internal division', *TCBH*, 2 (1991), 272–90; also G. Thomas, 'The Conservative party and Welsh politics in the inter-war years', *EHR*, 128 (2013), 877–913, esp. 895–9.
[125] K. J. Dean, *Town & Westminster: a political history of Walsall, 1906–1945* (Walsall, 1972), 106–10; memorandum on the election campaign in Wolverhampton East by Mr. Macdonald, 2 Jun. 1929, Hailes Papers, HAIS 1/1.
[126] *The Times*, 26 Jan. 1928 (editorial discussing LCC).
[127] *Leo Amery diaries*, 597 (3 Jun. 1929).
[128] E.g., AGM, 6 Jun. 1927, 14 May 1928, Norfolk North CA, Acc.2006/152; executive committee, 12 Nov. 1927, 11 Jul. 1929, Devizes CA, 2305/3.

of party government, and faced with a resurgent Liberal party under Lloyd George, it was perhaps inevitable that Conservatives became as much anti-radical as anti-socialist.

Yet in fact the Conservative vote expanded in 1929. Although Labour won twenty-eight more seats than the Conservative party, the Conservatives won more votes in the country – over half a million more than in 1924. Though far from obvious at the time, it seems likely that this was the consequence of a moderate gender gap, whereby a higher proportion of the women newly enfranchised in 1928 voted Conservative.[129] But in 'safe' seats like Epping, Ilford, Liverpool East Toxteth, and Devizes, where the Conservatives won with an increased poll in all cases except the last, they still stood in a minority to the progressive vote. Such results were by no means unprecedented in the three-party system of the 1920s; most Conservative MPs outside of the ultra-safe seats in Surrey, Sussex, and Kent lacked an overall majority over their opponents in 1922 and 1923. But the fact that so many Conservatives owed their victory in 1929 to a split in the progressive vote – and equally that many Conservatives elsewhere owed their defeat to a split in the anti-socialist vote – highlighted at best the fragility of the anti-socialist project and at worst its failure to yield a lasting realignment in favour of the Conservatives. Just as Labour's progress in marginal seats occurred at the mercy of Conservative-Liberal differences that precluded a stable anti-socialist bloc, so Conservative survival in not-so-marginal areas now relied on Liberal-Labour differences that precluded a progressive bloc.

Debating the Next Conservative Government, 1929–1931

MacDonald's Labour party returned to government in June 1929, again without an overall majority, and for two years relied on the erratic backing of Lloyd George's Liberals. These were years of considerable disquiet and discontent within Conservative ranks, as electoral defeat triggered a period of fraught internal debate further stoked by the launch of Lord Beaverbrook's and Lord Rothermere's populist 'Empire Crusade'. Many activists shared the sentiment expressed by Oliver Stanley, one of the leading figures of Conservatism in the industrial north of England, when he wrote to commiserate with Macmillan following his defeat in Stockton. 'If only they [the party leadership] had listened to all of us, and had at least some incling [sic] of a policy!'[130] Inevitably, some figures in the party

---

[129] See Ball, *Portrait of a party*, 118.
[130] Stanley to Macmillan, n.d. Jun. 1929, Macmillan papers, 65/28. Stanley was successfully returned as the MP for Westmorland, albeit with a much-reduced majority as a result of the intervention of a Liberal candidate.

58   Rethinking Interwar Conservatism

looked back to the Baldwin government and saw, with the clarity of hindsight, 'lost opportunities'. 'The whole handling of our industrial policy during the 4½ years', felt Patrick Hannon, 'is the most discreditable episode in the history of our Party, and I very much fear we shall pay dearly for it for years to come'.[131] In addition to pressing the leadership with demands for a constructive policy programme, activists also faced further evidence of organisational decay on the ground. The apathy of 'known Conservatives' had become a chronic problem in communities as diverse as Epping and Stockton; the absence of working-class activists caused embarrassment for the party in Yorkshire; the drop in subscriptions and donations was 'more serious than ever before' in Birmingham; and all the while the call for local activism was growing, rather than declining, as Labour continued to establish its influence in local government and through 'social service' initiatives, both urban and rural.[132]

But we should not overstate the depth of the crisis that engulfed the Conservatives in opposition. The party organisation, especially at the centre, underwent significant cultural change in these years and thereby delivered, to a degree, some of the relief sought by the party rank and file. By the spring of 1930 the newly established Conservative Research Department (CRD), charged with developing policy schemes, had been set up under Neville Chamberlain's ambitious chairmanship. 'We shall be at once an Information Bureau providing data and briefs for leaders, and a long range Research body' reporting to the Committee of Business, itself recently instigated as the core of the shadow cabinet, and to the wider party through the machinery of Central Office. An effort was made to ensure that the CRD's policy committees 'shall be composed mostly of young men including back benchers'.[133]

The early development of the CRD proved to be of a piece with the other great organisational change witnessed in 1930, namely Davidson's resignation as party chairman and the appointment of Chamberlain as his successor. The former Minister of Health and de facto national leader of working-class Conservatism thus came to command effective control of both policy and organisation within the party. This was significant within

[131] Hannon to R. H. Edwards (Chief Agent, Birmingham UA), 30 Jan. 1930, Parliamentary Archives, Hannon papers, HNN/73/3.

[132] Finance committee, 30 Jan. 1930, Stockton CA, D/X 322/4; women's committee, 13 Jan., 4 Jun. 1930, Redbridge Local History Centre, Woodford Bridge Ward (Epping CA), Acc. A7347; labour advisory committee, 28 Feb. 1931, West Yorkshire Archive Service, Yorkshire Area, WYL 1856/11/1; Hannon to Beaverbrook, 7 Jul. 1931, Hannon papers, HNN/17/1; executive committee, 11 Jul. 1929, Devizes CA, 2305/3; Council AGM, 12 Oct. 1929, Bodleian Library, Wessex Area, ARE 10/1/1; executive committee, 30 Sep. 1929, Norfolk Record Office, Norfolk North CA, Acc. 2006/152.

[133] *Neville Chamberlain diary letters, vol. 3*, 169–70 (to Ida, 22 Mar. 1930).

Local Politics and the Limits of Baldwinism 59

the party if not in the country. It signalled the end of a period in which successive party chairmen had conceived of the position as mainly managerial and detached from the business of policy development. Davidson himself conceded that his career 'had always been in big politics'. 'I had never fought in the arena. Both by training and inclination I was accustomed to use the broad brush, and I did not pretend to be a master of detail.'[134] It was for this reason that some had found Davidson's closeness to Baldwin an obstacle to progress; soon after the 1929 defeat, which highlighted the need to develop 'machinery for co-ordinated thought', one observer had predicted 'the opposition of Davidson, acting as Baldwin'.[135] Under Chamberlain, the CRD and the party chairmanship promised to galvanise Baldwin into a more active opposition leader and also to lead to future preferment for reformist figures like Walter Elliot, Billy Ormsby-Gore, Kingsley Wood, Lord Wolmer, and Geoffrey Ellis.[136] Even in opposition, such developments anticipated a more active culture of government than had been projected since 1926. How activists experienced this period in opposition is important to understanding the attitude with which they confronted the National government in August 1931.

The part played by the Empire Crusade in Conservative politics between 1929 and 1931 signified more than the interventionist whims of a single-interest ginger group. Comparisons with Rothermere's Anti-Waste League of 1921–2 were hard to resist: both campaigns tried to shake the Conservative leadership of the perceived complacency of consensual policy agendas, drew their support mostly from disgruntled Conservative activists in southern England and eastern agricultural regions, and eventually, after a spate of by-election contests, fizzled out.[137] Following closely on the heels of a full-term government and timed to capture party activists amid the post-match analysis, the Empire Crusade stoked the tension between Baldwin's model of government and that demanded by a widening cross-section of opinion within the party. The most public displays of support for the agitation once again emanated from the party's heartlands in the South and the Midlands.[138]

---

[134] Untitled memorandum, 'summer 1930', Parliamentary Archives, Davidson papers, DAV/190.

[135] Col. H. Williams to Macmillan, 17 Jul. 1929, Macmillan papers, 65/575.

[136] Chamberlain had originally tried to manoeuvre Ellis into the party chairmanship and appointed Wolmer to chair a CRD committee on agricultural policy. *Neville Chamberlain diary letters, vol. 3*, 178 (to Ida, 6 Apr. 1929), 208 (to Hilda?, 21 Sep. 1930).

[137] The comparison was a very real one for one Conservative association. In South Paddington, the party defeated an Anti-Waste League candidate at a by-election in 1922 but lost to an Empire Crusade candidate in October 1930.

[138] S. Ball, *Baldwin and the Conservative party: the crisis of 1929–1931* (New Haven, 1988), 21–5.

60   Rethinking Interwar Conservatism

Yet by no means was support for an imperial system of preferential tariffs ('empire free trade') confined to these areas. Delegates from northern English constituencies backed such a scheme on the basis that it represented a much needed extension of industrial safeguarding.[139] Given this widespread support for the crusade's policy objective, together with disquiet among many activists at the Conservative party's presence at the Round Table Conference on Indian home rule, this period in opposition undoubtedly saw Baldwin at his most vulnerable.

However, for the most part local Conservatives articulated their support for empire free trade while assiduously declaring their loyalty to Baldwin. Throughout the period in opposition there was little appetite for the dissident lead eventually provided by Churchill, who in February 1931 resigned from the shadow cabinet over the India question. Members of Churchill's own party in Epping, already competing with apathy among 'known supporters', noted caustically that 'even their Member was doing his best to get at logger-heads with the Association'.[140] It was common for constituency associations to extol Beaverbrook's scheme – variously and imprecisely referred to as 'empire development' and 'industrial safeguarding' – and in the same breath to express solidarity with Baldwin, while publicly snubbing or criticising the actions of the press lords.[141] Baldwin secured pledges of loyalty from one of the unlikeliest sources in this study. In 1929 the party in Norfolk North felt sufficiently in despair at the direction of policy under Baldwin that it considered drafting an independent manifesto on which to fight the general election.[142] A year later it welcomed Beaverbrook to the constituency and fought a strong by-election campaign on the issue of agricultural protection. Yet throughout that campaign the Conservative candidate, Thomas Cook, lost no opportunity to declare his fulsome support for Baldwin's leadership.[143] Had he wished to denounce Baldwin's leadership, the time could not have been riper.

Grassroots opinion, though unusual, was not as contradictory or duplicitous as might seem, and understanding it sheds light on important assumptions that underpinned the activist mindset on the eve of the

---

[139] Advisory committee, 6 Nov. 1929, Yorkshire Area, WYL 529/3; joint meeting of the councils Cumberland, Durham and Northumberland provincial divisions, 22 Feb. 1930, Northern Counties Area, NRO 3303/2.

[140] *West Essex Gazette*, 31 Jan. 1931.

[141] AGM, 22 Feb. 1930, Devizes CA, 2305/3; executive committee, 3 Mar. 1930, Wessex Area, ARE 10/1/1; AGM, 11 Mar. 1930, Stockton CA, 322/4; council meeting, 19 Jul. 1930, Northern Counties Area, NRO 3303/2.

[142] Advisory sub-committee, 9 Feb. 1929 and executive committee, 22 Apr. 1929, Norfolk North CA, Acc.2006/152.

[143] General council, 17 Jun. 1930, Norfolk North, Acc.2006/152.

Local Politics and the Limits of Baldwinism 61

National government. By the summer of 1931, Baldwin's leadership seemed secure once more, the result in part, as Stuart Ball has argued, of the bullying methods of the right-wing press campaign acting not as catalyst but ultimately as solvent of grassroots dissent.[144] But also crucial to his survival was the fact that his qualities as a communicator now met with a greater degree of appreciation within the party. While these had remained fundamentally unchanged since 1924, and certainly 1929, the attitude of local Conservatives, regarding the potential role of the party leader within the local sphere of popular politics, underwent subtle yet significant adjustment in response to new conditions on the ground.

One such condition was the ubiquity of the mass-media experience within British households, especially through the practice of 'listening in' to the wireless. The number of radio licences more than doubled between 1924 and 1931.[145] Whereas the 1924 election broadcast was probably Baldwin's most pioneering, his later broadcasts had wider reach and thereby greater impact, something that became empirically observable to activists for the first time by the early 1930s and was appreciated in the context of chronic activist apathy and, at times, unreliable press support. The point was well made by an agent who quoted a suburban voter: 'Neither my wife or I ... went to any of the meetings. Why should we go out at night and suffer all the inconveniences of listening to indifferent speakers when we could stay at home, switch on the wireless, and hear the "top-notchers" unfold their programme and policy?'[146] Of course, activists themselves were not immune from the 'technological attitude' which suffused society. Responding, albeit grudgingly, to the increasingly privatised lifestyle of a growing proportion of voters, local party organisers engaged new apparatus to supplement, rather than displace, traditional communitarian methods of campaigning. From 1927, for instance, some Conservatives began turning to telephone canvassing, in the realisation that 'there are always scores of people who will not answer canvassers "on the doorstep"'.[147] It was partly as a consequence of the inescapable 'technological attitude' of the late 1920s that activists pragmatically reappraised Baldwin as a national communicator.

Moreover, as industrial communities grew disillusioned with Labour's apparent failure to stem unemployment, so local Conservatives began to adopt the language of 'trust' favoured by Baldwin. Whereas 'the other two parties tried to gull the Electorate with brilliant promises', argued one

---

[144] Ball, *Baldwin and the Conservative party*, 210–12.

[145] The number of licenses per 1,000 families stood at 15.4 in 1924, 29.6 in 1929 and 44.5 in 1931 (S. Bowden, 'The new consumerism', in P. Johnson (ed.), *20th Century Britain: economic, social and cultural change* (Harlow, 1994), 246).

[146] *CAJ*, Dec. 1931, 266.   [147] *CAJ*, Aug. 1927, 216.

62 Rethinking Interwar Conservatism

speaker in Stockton soon after Macmillan's defeat, 'we, as a party, do not promise more than we can perform'.[148] By 1931, unemployment stood at more than 2.5 million and municipal elections suggested a consequent decline in Labour popularity.[149] In the context of a 'failing Labour government', appeals to 'integrity', like the slogan of 'performance not promises', obtained new traction in political debate and helped to render Baldwin's rhetoric much more a strategy than just a personal appeal. In a sure sign that his leadership was secure, Baldwin was embraced once more by the restless Conservative party in Norfolk. At a party gathering in Norwich in February 1931, the candidate showed how it was possible to politicise Baldwin's qualities to good effect. 'I don't say for a moment that Mr. Baldwin is the man of outstanding initiative and verve we might wish for', he began. 'But he is the one politician in this country you can rely on.' He went on to praise Churchill: 'He is a man after my own heart. He may not be reliable, but he is a jolly good engine, and with that engine and Baldwin's brake your motor car is safe.'[150]

On 16 February, Baldwin gave a broadcast address in which he outlined 'a national policy designed to meet a national emergency'. First, he rejected the argument, put by Keynes in a broadcast a few weeks earlier, that public expenditure could cure unemployment. 'To spend now is to shirk all the difficulties of the situation. You must economise first and try to bring back some confidence in the country, and you must make it plain that you can afford no new expenditure until times are better.' Second, he pledged to protect industrial work and wages through a tariffs policy and to protect agriculture through price guarantees, quotas, trading licences and tariffs.[151] This met with general approval throughout the party. The Conservative-controlled *Norfolk Chronicle* told its readers that 'Mr. Baldwin has once again shown that he is a realist who refuses to be panicked by political charlatans into offering one-day cures for deep-seated evils.'[152]

However, as the economic crisis deepened in the spring of 1931, it was retrenchment that came to dominate public discourse. Given that Beaverbrook was by then scaling down his Empire Crusade campaign, the issue of 'economy' once more served to unite and energise the

[148] Women's branch meeting, 3 Oct., 7 Dec. 1929, Stockton CA, D/X 322/10.
[149] S. Davies & B. Morley, 'The reactions of municipal voters in Yorkshire to the second Labour government, 1929–1931', in Worley (ed.), *Labour's grassroots*, 124–46.
[150] *Norfolk Chronicle*, 6 Feb. 1931.
[151] *The Times*, 17 Feb. 1931. For local reporting of national broadcasts, see *Darlington & Stockton Times*, 17 Jan. 1931 (Keynes), 21 Feb. 1931 (Baldwin).
[152] *Norfolk Chronicle*, 20 Feb. 1931. Ball has argued that the 'twin policies of "economy" and protection restored unity of purpose to the Party in 1931'. Ball, *Baldwin and the Conservative party*, 216.

Conservative party.[153] Yet retrenchment carried risks. Notwithstanding the enduring popularity of 'economy', especially among discontented taxpayers, for a society so sensitised to the idea of sacrifice, and in particular unequal sacrifice as experienced during the war and its aftermath, a policy of steep deflation raised the spectre of further sacrifice, and of betrayal. But betrayal by whom? This would depend on the result of a crisis election, which seemed inevitable by the summer months and filled many Conservatives with dread. In public, Conservatives tried to pre-empt the foreseeable public backlash with assurances that a Conservative government would guard against profiteering by business interests and insist on equality of sacrifice across 'all classes and interests'.[154] In private, they realised that 'economy' had become a term fatally loaded against the Conservative party. Despite the economic orthodoxy of the Labour leadership in Westminster, it was a sign of Labour's successful penetration of the electorate and its political imaginary since the war that neither 'economy' nor deference could offer a safe haven for popular Conservatism. Nothing encapsulated this more than the dole, as the single most enduring legacy of the post-war welfare settlement and, following the publication of a report on unemployment, the subject of heavy budgetary cuts. Headlam envisaged an impossible election campaign. 'The cry of the Socialist is "if you put in the Tories, they will cut off your Dole and reduce your wages – that is all they mean by Economy".'[155] Though at times Conservatives had felt relief at being out of office since 1929, the next government looked certain to be considerably more punishing to the party's reputation. Only the unique circumstances of the cross-party National government enabled Conservatives to ensure otherwise, and, in the process, to rehabilitate the local roots of popular Conservatism.

---

[153] Ball, *Baldwin and the Conservative party*, 159.
[154] E.g., Baldwin's broadcast (*The Times*, 17 Feb. 1931) and Macmillan's speech upon his re-adoption as candidate in Stockton (*Darlington & Stockton Times*, 23 May 1931).
[155] *Headlam diaries, 1923–1935*, 204 (17 Mar. 1931), also 202–3 (9 Mar. 1931), 209 (5 Jun. 1931).

3 Conservatives and the Politics of National Recovery, 1931–1937

E. H. H. Green's essay on the fall of the post-war coalition argued that Conservatives had recognised Lloyd George's indispensability at the 1918 election, as 'the man who won the war', yet 'this did not mean either that they liked the alliance or that there was no active dissent'.[1] Something similarly contradictory can be said of the party's attitude after 1931: although many did not find MacDonald – a 'socialist' leader – an obvious ally, and despite their reputed distrust of coalition, this did not rule out active support for the National government among the Conservative rank and file. In fact, there followed widespread support in all types of constituencies as Conservatives embraced the new government, seeing in it not only the most expedient political response to the financial crisis but also the opportunity to mobilise around a grand narrative of 'national recovery', which in turn provided the scope and flexibility to construct differentiated local appeals under the umbrella of 'national' politics.

The National government brought about a fundamental reconciliation between the local and national worlds of interwar Conservatism, the tensions between which were described in the previous chapter. The successful general election campaign of October 1931 immediately highlighted what became the single most important quality of the government for activists, namely its capacity to sustain a range of different appeals and traditions in the constituencies. Crucially, this initial impact shaped the reasoning with which Conservatives decided to seek a renewed National mandate in 1935. Membership of the National government enabled the party grassroots to realise many aspects of the local politics that they had tried to rehabilitate after the war. It also created new imperatives that required constituency Conservatives to make greater use of Baldwinite rhetoric and, by 1935, of Baldwin himself as a national leader.

---

[1] E. H. H. Green, 'Conservatism, anti-socialism, and the end of the Lloyd George coalition', in *Ideologies of Conservatism: Conservative political ideas in the twentieth century* (Oxford, 2002), 114–34, at 118–19.

Part II of this book discusses in detail the National government's impact in different types of constituencies. But because of the paucity of work on popular politics in the 1930s, it is useful here to outline both the overall course and key episodes of the National politics as they affected local politics. This chapter therefore sets out an overview from the formation of the government to Baldwin's resignation as party leader and begins the task of defining the characteristics of the National government during this period. It addresses certain misconceptions about grassroots involvement in, and attitudes towards, the cross-party government and introduces the key themes that explain the contribution – and challenges – of the National government to the rejuvenation of local political discourses.

This chapter has four sections. The first explores how Conservatives exploited the crisis of 1931 to construct a new anti-socialist paradigm that, forged in the aftermath of the fall of the second Labour government, gave Labour's alleged failings a degree of incontestability around which all Conservatives could mobilise. The second and third sections outline the National government's work in securing economic recovery and responding to the plight of the unemployed. This reflected a culture of active and imaginative government, which served to reinforce long-standing local Conservative appeals and also upheld the 'rationality' of the new anti-socialism. Finally, the fourth section explores the relationship between party and 'national' political identities in the constituencies. It argues that the process of defining the National government in the interests of local Conservatism introduced the rank and file to a broader range of political discourses, which complemented but did not supplant their preoccupation with rehabilitating a traditional politics of place.

'1931' and the Anti-Socialist Turn

'By the early summer of 1931', writes Andrew Thorpe, 'the Conservatives were in a happy position'. There seemed to be no danger of issues that had damaged the party in 1929 – derating and the new flapper vote, for example – resurfacing. Meanwhile, the issues around protection and Baldwin's leadership, although more complex and entrenched, had been decisively resolved. The party could therefore look forward with some confidence to replacing Labour in government.[2] But to what extent would the next Conservative administration project a more effective culture of government of the kind demanded by the constituency parties? Central Office could improve party literature and propaganda. The new Research Department could promise innovative new policies. But the

---

[2] A. Thorpe, *The British general election of 1931* (Oxford, 1991), 46, ch.2.

66   Rethinking Interwar Conservatism

party leadership still did not question the centrality or character of established anti-socialism within Conservatism.[3] There was therefore little to suggest that a future government would depart from the familiar Baldwinite model of anti-socialism defined in terms of public versus sectional interests.

The formation of the National government, although unanticipated, transformed local Conservative attitudes towards anti-socialism. Conservatives in all types of constituencies recognised that the financial crisis and the fall of the Labour government offered an opportunity to forge a more credible account of the socialist threat than had hitherto been possible. As one election agent put it, their task was to 'relate it [the crisis] in the public mind to the late Socialist Government'. Free traders were not being overly cynical when they portrayed the election as a 'Tory ramp', for there is little doubt that behind the scenes Conservatives exploited the atmosphere of national crisis, and the free hand that was granted to the National parties to advocate their own policies, to push for a tariff programme. But Conservatives also saw it as an opportunity to reverse the public's good faith in Labour, built up over the 1920s, and reset the mould of public opinion in response to 'Labour's crisis'. Apocalyptic talk of a national crisis 'would compel men of all grades and politics to think a little independently of party ties'.[4]

Unlike the anti-socialism of the 1920s, the new anti-socialism came to mean something specific. As a discrete strategy inspired by the national crisis, it signified above all Labour's incompetence in government. It was in this form that, in many places, the party rank and file embraced a concerted anti-socialist discourse for the first time. Crucially, they became reconciled to anti-socialism because the 1931 crisis gave Labour's supposed failings a concrete form around which to mobilise. Activists found themselves able to give anti-socialism a more differentiated, local flavour by focusing on particular effects of Labour's alleged mismanagement of the economy. Thus Harold Macmillan wanted the working-class voters of Stockton to see the crisis and its consequences – unemployment, reduced wages, loss of savings, assets lost by trade unions and mutual societies – as a Labour betrayal of workers' interests.[5] Similar indictments were made in relation to the agricultural industry and farm

---

[3] According to one sample analysis of grassroots opinion on the causes of the 1929 defeat, 36.8 per cent of constituency associations mentioned, among other factors, the intervention of a Liberal candidate, and 73.6 per cent cited the absence of a 'positive' policy. See S. Ball, *Baldwin and the Conservative party: the crisis of 1929–1931* (New Haven, 1988), 220–1.

[4] *CAJ*, Oct. 1931, 240. See also P. Buchan-Hepburn to H. Rathbone, 27 Sep. 1931, Churchill Archives Centre, Hailes papers, HAIS 1/4.

[5] Election address, Oct. 1931, Bodleian Library, Macmillan papers, c.141/62–3.

Conservatives and the Politics of National Recovery 67

labourers' interests in North Norfolk and Devizes. This might have represented routine political jousting – but such charges against Labour were also newly powerful after its first prolonged spell in government.

No longer contending with Central Office's manufactured and often fantastical claims of unconstitutional and revolutionary socialism, local Conservatives hoped to anchor public criticism of Labour within a more robust political discourse. The national crisis in 1931 offered them the opportunity, long anticipated, of moving decisively away from the didacticism of post-war Conservative strategy, which sought to 'educate' voters, in favour of a more competitive politics in which Conservatives vied with Labour for a reputation of effective government. This was not just about *reflecting* voters' interests. It was about *mobilising* 'the material', defined by Frank Trentmann as the resources and technologies of everyday human existence, in order to construct a narrative of Labour failure, especially in relation to the vital issues of employment and industry.[6] Chapters 4 to 7 explore how this was done in different constituencies, together demonstrating how Conservatives created a subjective '1931' – a moment when Labour incompetence was exposed. As a result of this, and the subsequent need to be seen to be responding to the depression, 'the material' became a central concern in popular politics in the 1930s. Moreover, as anti-socialism became localised and targeted, it underscored established Conservative claims to be true champions of local interests. Paradoxically, the 'National' government ushered in the last great flowering of Conservative localism.

The new rhetoric of anti-socialism was not exclusive to the grassroots, for national leaders also hung their rhetoric on the 'Labour crisis'. They made alarmist predictions of the material cost of allowing Labour back into office, even suggesting starvation as a possible consequence.[7] In turn, the grassroots could not escape the fact that they were campaigning for the election of a cross-party government. In most cases candidates tried to portray the government as guardian of the national interest, echoing not only Baldwin's national versus sectional dichotomy but also using his subtler depiction of Labour – as a party containing good and bad, constructive and destructive, elements – to explain their simultaneous alliance with National Labour and opposition to 'socialist' Labour.[8]

---

[6] See F. Trentmann, 'Materiality in the future of history: things, practices and politics', *JBS*, 48 (2009), 283–307, esp. 299–307.

[7] E.g., Thorpe, *British general election of 1931*, 222 (Baldwin), 226 (Amery), 250 (MacDonald, Steel-Maitland, Simon).

[8] P. Williamson, *Stanley Baldwin: Conservative leadership and national values* (Cambridge, 1998), 177, 222, and esp. 235–42.

68   Rethinking Interwar Conservatism

The extent of convergence between local and national should not be overstated. The tendency among Central Office strategists, as in 1929, was to consider Baldwin crucial to the success of the Conservative campaign – more so now that it was part of a wider National campaign. Before the election, senior party strategists argued 'that the Leadership of the National Party during the contest should be vested in Mr. Baldwin'. This was presented as the wish of 'large numbers of Conservatives throughout the country'. They, apparently, would not tolerate MacDonald as their leader; resented the notion of Baldwin being subordinate to him; and, thinking tactically, feared the 'embarassment [sic]' likely to be caused by 'Socialists [who] could make use of Mr. MacDonald's past utterances'.[9] Yet, among activists, Baldwin was still not recognised as the electoral asset that he came to be by 1935. Neither his vision as party leader nor his reputation as a consensual political leader were central to how they conceptualised the potential for party gain through membership of the National government. If recollections of the Lloyd George coalition meant that activists were anxious about the new government to begin, by the time of the election campaign in 1931 they had discovered for themselves compelling reasons to embrace the National government.

While Baldwin featured very little in constituency campaigns, the leaders of the other National groups were vital to Conservative appeals. In keeping with the central role of party in Conservative conceptions of mass politics, the grassroots saw their new association with Ramsay MacDonald, John Simon, and Herbert Samuel as a direct means of mobilising Labour and Liberal voters. Election addresses were replete with the wise words of these leaders. Percy Hurd devoted a quarter of his address to a column entitled 'What LIBERAL LEADERS say', with quotations from Samuel, Simon, and Viscount Grey, the former foreign secretary. It even sported a choice passage from an old speech by Lloyd George, who in fact opposed the government at the 1931 election.[10] In Stockton and Leeds West, Macmillan and Vyvyan Adams praised the 'characteristic courage' of MacDonald, J. H. Thomas, Philip Snowden, and Lord Sankey.[11] The implication was that Liberal and Labour voters who opposed the National government were not only anti-national but disloyal to their own party. Even in the 'National' campaign, therefore,

---

[9] Memorandum by R. Topping, M. Maxse and P. Gower, n.d. 1931, Cambridge University Library, Baldwin papers, 44/iii/150–2.

[10] Election address, Oct. 1931, Hurd papers. During the campaign Lloyd George delivered an infamous broadcast in which he urged voters to vote Labour where no Free Trade Liberal was standing. See Thorpe, *British general election of 1931*, 170; also J. Campbell, *Lloyd George: the goat in the wilderness* (London, 1977), 302–3.

[11] Election address, Oct. 1931, Macmillan papers, c.141/62–3; election address, Oct. 1931, London School of Economics Library, Archive Division, Adams papers, 2/2.

Conservatives and the Politics of National Recovery 69

party remained vital. Indeed, Conservatives often eschewed non-party language in favour of depicting the National government as a multi-party government combining the best talent from its constituent parts.

While the party leaders provided a means of mobilising votes in the short term, the national crisis and the National government provided opportunities to forge new political discourses and achieve longer-term objectives. Representing as it did an emergency break with conventional party government, the National government itself stood as the most striking proof of Labour's incompetence. Thus, opposition retorts of a 'Tory ramp' or 'Tory take-over' were often left undisputed since they fitted Conservatives' own depiction of 1931 as a great rescue act on behalf of the nation. 'Like firemen summoned to a blazing fire', said Macmillan.[12] Moreover, the formation of the government lent itself to comparisons with an earlier national crisis. Thorpe has found that only 7 per cent of Conservative electoral addresses made reference to the First World War.[13] This probably reflects candidates' sensitivity towards disarmament, which Labour could exploit, and a desire in any case to focus on Labour's domestic rather than international legacy. In their speeches, however, the Conservative candidate in each of the constituencies studied here made repeated reference to the Great War, asserting that the country's current travails were no less perilous than those faced in the summer of 1914 and that a coalition government that put country before party was the only solution, in peacetime as in wartime. Typical of this was Thomas Cook's closing remarks in a speech at Cromer: 'Just as in the dark days of 1914–1918 you all rallied to the defence of your country, let us realise now that we are facing an equally grave danger.'[14]

But as so many studies have shown, a single, national memory of the war proved elusive. There was disagreement over the form and meaning of commemoration, not just between regions but also within localities; and people's recollections, together with the meanings they attached to them, changed over time. A myth of unity emerged, built on a culture of mass grief and shared opposition to any hint of the war being forgotten. Yet the unequal burden of sacrifices, during and after the war, fostered lasting social divisions.[15] These carried implications – and opportunities – for politicians further into the interwar years than is currently recognised.

---

[12] Election address, Oct. 1931, Macmillan papers, c.141/62–3.
[13] Thorpe, *British general election of 1931*, 220.   [14] *Norfolk Chronicle*, 16 Oct. 1931.
[15] The literature in this field is vast, but see in particular A. Gregory, *The last Great War: British society and the First World War* (Cambridge, 2008), esp. ch.8, and A. King, 'Remembering and forgetting in the public memorials of the Great War', in A. Forty & S. Küchler (eds.), *The art of forgetting* (Oxford, 1999), 147–70.

70   Rethinking Interwar Conservatism

Therefore, when attending to Susan Pedersen's suggestion that the events of 1931 should be read 'with the memory of an earlier national crisis in mind',[16] the social divisions, and not just the overblown rhetoric of unity, need to be centre stage.

Baldwin was particularly conscious of the changes wrought by the Great War and feared their impact on the new democracy.[17] But it was the labour movement that did most to mobilise public opinion in response to the material legacy of war. In the early post-war years, the eight-hour day and other objectives negotiated during the strikes of 1919–20 could be presented as labour's fair share of the 'fruits of victory'. Then, as the initial boom subsided and financiers' and taxpayers' interests came to trump those of industrialists and organised labour, Labour was able to contest Conservative claims that this had 'public' support by presenting the new post-war settlement as a betrayal of the war generation (not just of labourers).[18] Throughout the 1920s Labour strategy was thus to propagate a feeling that nothing much had improved since the war. Against this backdrop, it seems a little less bizarre that Labour in 1931 should publish a fifty-page pamphlet, *Two Years of Labour Rule*, championing the achievements of the second Labour government, or that its manifesto should promise every effort to rescue 'this and succeeding generations' from 'the interests of big business and finance'.[19]

For Conservatives, the National government offered the most promising prospect yet of constructing an effective response to Labour's rhetoric of betrayal. Now they could claim that it was Labour that had betrayed the people by delivering a national crisis that promised nothing but further sacrifice. This way the Conservatives wrested control of what had been one of Labour's most coherent and powerful strategies, namely identification with a public long told that it deserved better from its governing classes and institutions. But Conservatives also made more radical use of the First World War, arguing that the National government would institute a recovery that not only solved the crisis caused by Labour but also recompensed people for the failures of the 1920s. While mainly

---

[16] S. Pedersen, 'From national crisis to "national crisis": British politics, 1914–1931', *JBS*, 33 (1994), 322–35, at 335.

[17] See Williamson, *Stanley Baldwin*, 137–9, 178, 185, 296.

[18] See J. Lawrence, 'Labour and the politics of class, 1900–1940', in D. Feldman &; Lawrence (eds.), *Structures and transformations in modern British history: papers for Gareth Stedman Jones* (Cambridge, 2011); L. Beers, '"Is this man an anarchist?" Industrial action and the battle for public opinion in interwar Britain', *JMH*, 82 (2010), 30–60; H. Barron, *The 1926 miners' lockout: meanings of community in the Durham coalfield* (Oxford, 2010), 62–4.

[19] Cf. Thorpe, *British general election of 1931*, 225–6; I. Dale (ed.), *Labour party general election manifestos, 1900–1997* (London, 2000), 43.

Conservatives and the Politics of National Recovery

concerned with forging a discourse of future national recovery, they also seized the opportunity to reconstruct the place of Conservatism in the public's recollection of the post-war years – not by challenging the charge of betrayal, but by recognising it. Many Conservatives spoke in doom-laden terms of Britain's economic decline, a recurring theme in political rhetoric well before 1914 but one that Conservatives like Patrick Hannon now described as a distinctly post-war problem.[20] Macmillan claimed to 'have always myself believed that we should never successfully solve the post-war problems except by a national, rather than a partisan effort'.[21] There may have been a degree of catharsis or self-satisfaction in this for Hannon and Macmillan. The former looked back on the second Baldwin government as five wasted years, with the handling of industrial policy 'the most discreditable episode in the history of our Party'.[22] For Macmillan and other young Conservatives, there was an intellectual interest in new solutions to economic and industrial problems that pre-dated the national crisis.[23]

However, a feature common to all Conservatives in 1931, activists and MPs, was the recognition that governments of all parties in the 1920s had failed to settle Britain's social and economic troubles. The result was a popular discourse that now embraced the language of 'national govern-ment', which, as Philip Williamson has shown, had been developing in some circles in Westminster since the mid-1920s.[24] In 1931, the 'post-war problem' was established as a vital paradigm in Conservative public politics. In Devizes, Percy Hurd's wife evoked the public's longing for a world of 'peace and plenty'. Hurd himself urged voters to treat the new government as a rare second chance to resolve post-war problems and make a reality of such ideals – it was 'now or never'.[25] The same themes were evident in Ilford. In his address to the Conservative association, Sir George Hamilton compared the nation's standing in 1931 to 1918 and

---

[20] *Birmingham Post*, 13 Oct. 1931. For the theme of decline in British politics since the late nineteenth century, including the pre-war Chamberlainite tradition with which Hannon was closely associated, see D. Cannadine, 'Apocalypse when? British politicians and British "decline" in the twentieth century', in P. Clarke & C. Trebilcock (eds.), *Understanding decline: perceptions and realities of British economic performance* (Cambridge, 1997), 261–84.

[21] Election address, Oct. 1931, Macmillan papers, c.141/62–3.

[22] Hannon to R. H. Edwards (chief agent in Birmingham), 30 Jan. 1930, Parliamentary Archives, Hannon papers, HNN 73/3.

[23] See R. Boothby et al., *Industry and the state: a Conservative view* (London, 1927).

[24] P. Williamson, *National crisis and national government: British politics, the economy and empire, 1926–1932* (Cambridge, 1992).

[25] Election flyer, Mrs Hannah Hurd 'To the women electors of the Devizes parliamentary division', 20 Oct. 1931; election address, Oct. 1931, Hurd papers.

72   Rethinking Interwar Conservatism

spoke of the general election of 1923 as the moment at which decisive action (in the form of tariffs) was proposed but rejected. In public addresses, he struck a note of atonement: 'He blamed every Government since the War, of all kinds, for the present situation.'[26]

The Politics of Recovery

Shortly before polling day in 1931, Lord Bridgeman congratulated Baldwin on the anticipated victory of the National government. 'The present situation', he thought, 'is a curious vindication of Safety First'.[27] Yet after their unfortunate experience of the slogan in 1929, the grassroots might be forgiven for having been rather more ambitious. Their position was better reflected by Percy Hurd, who hoped that the government would inaugurate 'a great national movement of Hope & Regeneration'.[28] Needless to say, Hurd and fellow Conservatives had their own ideological and reforming traditions to draw upon when imagining the government's agenda, but in sentiment and rhetoric their designs often echoed those of Keynes, who took to the airwaves regularly in 1931 to press the government for 'schemes of greatness and magnificence'.[29] In reality, the combination of a renewed anti-socialism and the search for a popular narrative of economic recovery enabled the Conservatives to represent a culture of government that claimed to be both responsible and industrious.

The government focused its attention during the first year on restoring Britain's balance of trade. In February 1932, Neville Chamberlain as Chancellor of the Exchequer introduced the Import Duties Act, which imposed a 10 per cent tariff on all imports except foodstuffs and raw materials into Britain. In August, following an imperial conference in Ottawa, which Baldwin attended amid much fanfare, the government entered into a global system of imperial preference that ensured free trading within the empire while raising tariffs on produce from outside the empire. These developments marked a seminal break with free trade. That the Victorian faith in free trade withstood both the Edwardian clamour for protection and Baldwin's tariffs prescription in 1923 made its eventual demise all the more significant, especially among Conservatives. Austen Chamberlain reckoned that the import duties

[26] *Ilford Recorder*, 2 and 23 Oct. 1931.
[27] Bridgeman to Baldwin, 25 Oct. 1931, Baldwin papers, 45/v/121.
[28] Hurd to General Calley (chairman, Devizes CA), 29 Oct. 1931, Wiltshire and Swindon History Centre, Devizes CA, 2305/3.
[29] E.g., *Darlington & Stockton Times*, 17 Jan. 1931.

Conservatives and the Politics of National Recovery

were as comprehensive as any scheme that 'we should have done if the Govt. had been formed from our Party only'.[30] It was celebrated within the party as the life's work of a battle-hardened generation of campaigners. In Birmingham, Chamberlain's action was marked with civic celebrations and hagiographical talk of Joseph Chamberlain as the apostolic author of Britain's economic and imperial renewal.[31] It was little wonder that such self-reverential accounts by the Conservatives of the government's work in 1932 led free-trade Liberals like Samuel to suspect their partners of exploiting the national crisis to secure a replay of battles long lost. Yet while the spirit of the Edwardian tariff campaigns undoubtedly lived long in the Conservative mind, the advent of protectionism created opportunities to forge new populist appeals in the present and for the future.

However, there were precious few immediate signs of economic recovery as a result of the government's measures, with commensurately few opportunities for Conservatives in the country to claim concrete results for voters. Even under the new trading system, they had little choice but to peddle the old refrain that employment and living standards would recover as trade recovered – that is, in the long term and without guarantee. Some, like Macmillan, tried to bolster this appeal by explaining to voters that protection was a 'scientific' policy, 'introduced because of cold and hard facts, and theories which have led Liberals of business knowledge, such as Mr. Runciman, to the certain conclusion that the system which satisfied the 19th century is not suited for the ... 20th century'.[32] Ottawa was said to signify the role of Britain and its empire in leading the world out of crisis. But as long as unemployment remained a reality for more than two million workers and their families, no degree of embellishment was likely to popularise Conservative policy in the first year of the government's life.

Nor, in this respect, was there yet much cause for optimism in domestic economic policy. True, by 'saving' the pound and averting the threat of devastating inflation of the kind witnessed in Germany, the government could claim already to have earned its spurs for economic competence. But Chamberlain's budget in April 1932, which did not reduce taxes or increase expenditure, was considered a 'flop' by many Conservatives for

[30] *The Austen Chamberlain diary letters: the correspondence of Sir Austen Chamberlain with his sisters Hilda and Ida, 1916–1937*, ed. R. Self (Cambridge, 1995), 405 (to Ida, 30 Jan. 1932).
[31] Central council, 1 Mar. 1932, Birmingham Central Library, Birmingham CUA; *The Times*, 7 May 1932.
[32] *North-Eastern Daily Gazette*, 13 May 1932.

74   Rethinking Interwar Conservatism

its strict orthodoxy and failure to make concessions.[33] A virtue could be made of such sobriety in some constituencies, for instance in Ilford where 'sound finance' chimed with the renewed anti-waste campaigns of ratepayers, or in Devizes where the traditional Liberal threat made it doubly necessary to observe Gladstonian fiscal orthodoxy. But it proved unyielding to those Conservatives in the industrial areas.[34] As the chief agent in Leeds explained, the historic election victory had not blinded them to the fact that 'there was [sic] 7 million voters who voted Socialist'; in the absence of a reform programme, or even palliatives such as a reduction in the beer tax, which the Labour government had increased, the budget did little to equip Conservatives to dampen growing discontent with the means test.[35]

The course of events in 1932 had profound implications for Conservatives' own assessment of the government and in particular how they might continue to profit from the 'National' label when, following the resignation of the Samuelite ministers, the government seemed ever more dominated by the Conservative party.[36] Williamson argues that the free traders' departure benefited the Conservatives by resolving the government's 'internal contradiction' between protectionists and their opponents and thereby restoring the Conservatives to a position of 'preeminence'.[37] However, as head of the Liberal party organisation and protector of Liberals' free-trade faith, Samuel was widely assumed to represent Liberal opinion in the country more accurately and comprehensively than Simon.[38] His resignation therefore threatened to undermine the 'national' character of the government. Ironically, although Conservatives had found Samuel and his supporters uncooperative in 1931, it was his well-known doubts about the National government that made his participation so valuable; so long as Samuel served in the cabinet alongside Simon, it was possible for Conservatives legitimately to claim

[33] For the budget and its reception among MPs, see R. Self, *Neville Chamberlain: a biography* (Aldershot, 2006), 201–2.

[34] E.g., *Ilford Recorder*, 26 Oct. 1933; executive committee, 21 Apr. 1932, Devizes CA, 2305/3. For the persistence of a Gladstonian brand of Liberalism in the south-west, see M. Dawson, 'Liberalism in Devon and Cornwall, 1910–1931: "the old-time religion"', *HJ*, 38 (1995), 425–37.

[35] *CAJ*, Dec. 1931, 268–9; council AGM, 25 Feb. 1933, Northumberland Collections Service, Northern Counties Area, NRO 3303/2.

[36] In September 1932, Samuel and his ministers resigned from the government; in November 1933, they crossed the floor and became, officially, an opposition party.

[37] Williamson, *National crisis and national government*, 516; see also D. Dutton, '1932: a neglected date in the history of the decline of the Liberal party', *TCBH*, 14 (2003), 43–60.

[38] Samuel's National Liberals polled 1,372,595 votes (6.5 per cent share) in 1931, compared with the Liberal Nationals under Simon who polled 809,302 votes (3.7 per cent). Thorpe, *British general election of 1931*, 279.

Conservatives and the Politics of National Recovery

that they, through the government, represented Liberal interests. With Samuel's departure, all such future claims would depend on Simon, whose 'national' and Liberal credentials, so helpful in 1931, were now less reliable as they came under concerted attack from the authentic Samuelite wing of the Liberal party.[39] The more Simon's backers came to be viewed as 'Conservative-minded Liberals' by the government's detractors,[40] the more the Conservatives needed to renew its claims to being 'national'.

Conservatives in the West Yorkshire region, aware of the deep roots of popular free-trade sentiment among workers, speculated that a toxic mix of 'dear food' cries and anti-means-test sentiment had fuelled Labour's partial recovery in the municipal elections in 1932. They also felt that after Ottawa, unlike during the election when the Liberals 'pretended to co-operate with us', 'they were definitely against us now ... [as] the official Liberal organisation is definitely free-trade in complexion'.[41] Yet their response was not to question the desirability of the National government. 'The general view was that it was still essential to maintain the National character of the Government. There was a large body of opinion, not definitely Conservative, which should still rally to our support at a General Election on National lines.' In other words, by dint of being 'national' the government still offered Conservatives the best means of dissolving the ties of institutional loyalty that bound 'rank and file Liberals' to Samuel.[42] Whereas 1931 had opened activists' eyes to the number of non-Conservative and other non-aligned voters it was possible to win over, 1932 alerted them to the challenges involved in renewing the national appeal.

As the economy began to show signs of recovery from 1932, so the government's popular narrative of national recovery took shape. Economic historians continue to debate whether Britain's recovery came about as a consequence of a revival of world trade; through a 'permissive' recovery at home, in which the government did little more than set the appropriate conditions enabling society eventually to pursue a consumer-led recovery, most notably by means of a 'housing boom'; or as a result of policies coherently designed and actively pursued by the government over a sustained period. The government

---

[39] See, for example, *New answers to old fallacies: a reply to Sir John Simon's defence of tariffs* (1934) and *The people's food* (1936), both published by the Liberal Free Trade Committee.

[40] E.g., G. D. H. Cole & M. Cole, *The intelligent man's review of Europe to-day* (1933), 596.

[41] E.g., advisory committee, 3 Dec. 1932, West Yorkshire Archive Service, Yorkshire Area, WYL 529/3. In Leeds the Conservatives' municipal vote in 1932 fell by 33 per cent while Labour's increased by 7 per cent.

[42] Ibid.

76   Rethinking Interwar Conservatism

packaged its own account in line with the final explanation, doing so within a chronological framework that continually reminded voters of '1931'.[43] In a pamphlet published in 1933, improvements in trade and employment were measured against the 'abyss' into which Labour had taken the country. Such an account showcased the government's activities since taking office while also serving to further embed memories of 1931 in public consciousness.[44] The idea of juxtaposing progress under the National government with incompetence under Labour climaxed in the spring of 1934 with Chamberlain's 'restoration budget', so called because it used a healthy balance of payments to restore the cuts to unemployment benefit and public sector salaries implemented in the opening days of the administration. In addition, it reduced the standard rate of income tax and cut some duties.[45] Chamberlain's statement to the House of Commons, markedly more populist than the balance-sheet style of the previous two budgets, was followed by an 'explanatory' radio broadcast and a poster campaign in the country.[46] Chamberlain told the Commons that the country had 'now finished the story of *Bleak House* and ... we are sitting down this afternoon to enjoy the first chapter of *Great Expectations*'.[47] He went on:

When the need arose in 1931, the sacrifices which were demanded then from our people were accepted by them cheerfully, and they have since been borne with unexampled courage and patience. Their truest reward is that they saved their country. I rejoice to think that at last it has been possible to afford them some relief from their burdens, and, believing as I do that this relief will itself hasten the process of recovery, I look forward with confidence to further progress in the same direction in the new financial year.[48]

The government was helped in depicting this recovery by some of the trends taking place in the popular news media of the period. As a paper that communicated, according to one historian, 'the actuality and atmosphere of Britain, its character, temper and achievements', the *Illustrated London News* continued its interest in novelty and innovation by giving

---

[43] For accounts that lend support to the government's narrative, see M. Kitson, 'Slump and recovery: the UK experience', in T. Balderston (ed.), *The world economy and national economies in the interwar slump* (Basingstoke, 2003), 88–104; A. Booth, 'Britain in the 1930s: a managed economy?', *EcHR*, 40 (1987), 499–522.

[44] *The record of the National Government: August, 1931–October, 1933* (1933).

[45] *The Times*, 18 Apr. 1934.

[46] Executive committee, 25 Apr. 1934, Redbridge Local History Centre, Ilford CA, 90/61/1/1.

[47] *Hansard, House of Commons debates*, 288, col. 905, 17 Apr. 1934.

[48] Ibid., cols. 926–7.

Conservatives and the Politics of National Recovery 77

coverage to great feats of engineering.[49] Some of these, like the launch of the *Queen Mary* ocean liner on Clydebank in 1934, the opening of the Mersey tunnel ('the world's longest under-water tunnel'), or record-breaking fast rail services linking London to the regions, spoke to the fascination with speed and modernist design that was so much the hallmark of interwar modernity.[50] Others were routine infrastructural developments promising more tangible improvements in the lives of the general public, including new bridges built, road construction, and the electrification of whole communities.[51]

Some of the *ILN*'s stories were explicitly celebratory of the government's role in generating recovery. Chamberlain emerged as the pin-up boy of the ministry, the man of the moment, 'the Chancellor of the Exchequer in a great world crisis', his restoration budget marked with a two-page spread showing 'the great achievements of the National government' (Figure 3.1). Deploying what James Thompson, in his work on political posters, has described as the combination of the 'iconic immediacy of the visual' and 'the discursive rationality of print', the special article recorded the work of the government in protecting trade, reviving industries, reducing unemployment (at an 'approximate average' rate of one man per minute), and improving services.[52] There was also special coverage of the government's announcement of a slum clearance scheme in 1933, which highlighted a story of cooperation between central government and the great municipal authorities; the emergence of cutting-edge industries, such as the refinery works brought about by the Hydrocarbon Oil Production Act of 1934 in which domestic coal was used to produce motor fuel; and a road construction scheme reported to be 'a means of reducing unemployment'.[53]

What enabled the National government to benefit more than previous governments from such coverage was the spread of newsreel at a time when cinema audiences were expanding, especially among working-class families. Newsreels came into their own after the introduction of sound in 1931 and some 80 per cent of the working class is estimated to have viewed them on a weekly basis during the 1930s. Like the *ILN*, newsreels were ostensibly non-partisan and 'consensual'; editorial decisions were informed by the topicality and visual impact of the footage, not by political allegiance. Yet,

[49] Unnamed author, 'Ingram, Sir Bruce Stirling (1877–1963)', *Oxford Dictionary of National Biography*, published 23 Sep. 2004.
[50] E.g., *ILN*, 21 Jul., 29 Sep. 1934, 16 Mar. 1935.
[51] Ibid., e.g., 23 Jul. 1932, 11 Feb., 6 May, 9 Sep. 1933, 28 Apr. 1934, 23 Nov. 1935, 4 Jan., 26 Sep. 1936.
[52] J. Thompson, '"Pictorial lies"? Posters and politics in Britain, c.1880–1914', *P&P*, 197 (2007), 177–210, at 194.
[53] *ILN*, 15 Jul. 1933, 30 Mar. 1935, 23 Nov. 1935.

Figure 3.1 *Illustrated London News*, 28 April 1934.

Conservatives and the Politics of National Recovery 79

according to Nicholas Pronay, among the leaders of the five newsreel companies that operated in Britain were several who sympathised with the Conservative party and, in the case of Movietone, secretly cooperated with Conservative Central Office.[54] So also, in a way, might the government have benefited from depression-era films in which the message of optimism and perseverance dominated. In *Sing As We Go*, Gracie Fields played the role of an unemployed Lancashire millworker who chirpily went searching for seasonal work in Blackpool. Notable for its semi-documentary footage of working-class life, but otherwise gently derided by contemporary reviewers as a 'frolicsome yarn', the film closes in rousing fashion with the re-opening of the mill works and the women's happy return to work – a peculiarly on-message outcome when the film was released in 1934.[55]

Helping to set the message on behalf of the government was a new organisation, the National Publicity Bureau, established in January 1935 as a privately funded and ostensibly non-political body for the purpose of reporting the recovery on a non-partisan basis. According to one contemporary, the NPB's strategy was to ignore political opponents and engage voters using human-interest stories and interlacing political coverage with material about the world of sport and entertainment. 'Its whole campaign was built upon the appeal of good times.'[56] Nowhere was this clearer than in its broadsheet, the *Popular Illustrated*. Decidedly eclectic in style, like the *ILN*, with a preponderance of 'real life' photographs and peppered with coverage of popular events (for instance, the All Blacks' rugby tour of that year), the paper showcased a domesticated Britain, happy 'at work and play' under the National government. By reproducing images used in well-known Conservative posters from the 1931 election campaign, the paper also mirrored Conservative efforts to entrench in political discourse a simple 'then and now' measure of the government's success. One such example was the image of the unemployed worker who, having pleaded with voters to back the National government in October 1931 – 'A call that was answered', declared the *Popular Illustrated* – was now restored to dignity and health.[57] An almost identical illustration was taken up by the Conservative party in one of its famous election posters later that year (Figure 3.2).

---

[54] N. Pronay, 'The newsreels: the illusion of actuality', in P. Smith (ed.), *The historian and film* (Cambridge, 1976), 95–119, at 112, n24.

[55] *ILN*, 22 Sep. 1934. For the film's production and reception, see J. Richards, *The age of the dream palace: cinema and society in 1930s Britain*, 3rd edn (London, 2010), 181–3.

[56] R. Casey, 'The National Publicity Bureau and British party propaganda', *Public Opinion Quarterly*, 3 (1939), 623–34, at 631. See also M. Pinto-Duschinsky, *British political finance, 1830–1980* (Washington DC, 1981), 119–23.

[57] *Popular Illustrated*, 1:1 (1935), 5.

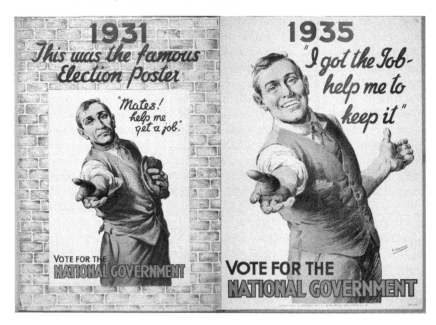

Figure 3.2 National government election poster, 1935.[58] Photo by The Conservative Party Archive / Hulton Archive / Getty Images.

Furthermore, the recovery campaign coincided with far-reaching initiatives taking place in Whitehall, within departments as well as associated non-ministerial bodies, to publicise the work of the British state. According to one pioneer of this public relations drive, the objective was to 'interest the public in work done in their name' and to 'encourage the public to take the most economic advantage of the facilities' provided for them. Given the 'general transfer of interest from the problems of production to those of distribution', he explained, and also the reduced coverage of parliamentary proceedings in the newspaper press, it was incumbent on modern government to 'project' itself.[59] Thus, as providers of public services, government agencies were increasingly impelled to sell their wares. Leading the way was the General Post Office, which established a film unit of its own, delivered a staff training programme in customer relations, and in 1933 launched an elaborate campaign to advertise the domestic and commercial benefits of the telephone

[58] CPA, poster 1935–26a.
[59] S. Tallents, 'Salesmanship in the public service: scope and technique', *Public Administration*, 11 (1933), 259–66, at 259–60, 262.

service.[60] Such practices were emulated with differing degrees of coordination across government, including by the ministries of Health and Transport, as well as bodies like the London Passenger Transport Board, established in 1933, and public utility companies. They were also used to highlight the benefits of statutory obligations brought by the government, including the contributory element of unemployment insurance and the requirement that industries comply with new standards and practices designed to improve profitability.[61]

Such developments in communication bestowed on the state a newfound culture of modernity. Indeed, the 1930s provide pre-echoes of the famous publicity that accompanied national reconstruction after the war. As in the late 1940s, which saw the government's achievements showcased in popular documentaries and publicity magazines like *Something Done* (1947), the National government's story of economic recovery similarly emphasised, first, the advantages of scientific and expert design of public policy, and secondly, an unprecedented supply of information to the public about how to access the opportunities created through government initiative.[62] As Part II of this book shows, in many cases this modernity proved crucial in cementing Conservative grassroots support for the government. It brought to the realm of popular politics a distinctive political discourse; on the one hand 'expert' in tone and thereby more compellingly impartial than politicians' own declarations of serving the 'national' interest, but not incompatible with the more plebeian demands of party politics. The growing initiative of professional public relations experts did not preclude ministerial involvement. Much of the advertising work undertaken by the Ministry of Agriculture, for example, featured the Conservative minister, Walter Elliot, a scientist by training who regularly gave radio talks and appeared in promotional newsreels. The same was true of Kingsley Wood, a reforming Postmaster General and Minister of Health from 1935, who came to public prominence through his leading role in launching the Post Office's many ventures into commercial services, from the telephone exchange's early advertising campaigns to the launch of a television service.[63]

---

[60] M. Grant, *Propaganda and the role of the state in inter-war Britain* (Oxford, 1994), ch.4.

[61] For various schemes, see H. Whitehead, 'Salesmanship in the public service: scope and technique', *Public Administration*, 11 (1933), 267–76; T. S. Simey, 'A public relations policy for local authorities', *Ibid.*, 13 (1935), 242–50; R. S. R. Fitter, 'An experiment in public relations', *Ibid.*, 14 (1936), 464–7.

[62] Central Office of Information, *Something Done: British achievement, 1945–1947* (London, 1947).

[63] For Elliot, see *The Times*, 15 Aug. 1933 (radio broadcast), *ILN*, 6 Oct. 1934; 'Wonder of the Fens', Oct. 1934, British Pathé film 797.25, 'Mr Elliot at School', 1937, British Pathé

82   Rethinking Interwar Conservatism

Crucially, this display of modern government served the interests of local Conservatives. The credibility of the government's claims to be pursuing recovery through expert and scientific methods lay in large part in the focus it placed upon assisting or reforming sectoral economies. By promoting policy that supported particular industries, whether shipbuilding, fishing, agriculture, or coal mining, ministers ensured that narratives of the recovery were mapped onto public understandings of regional economies, in ways that both highlighted the complementarity of national and local economic recovery and reinvigorated Conservative claims to champion local interests. The regional was integral to how the government articulated the recovery. 'Britain Under the National Government', a series of films produced by the Conservative and Unionist Film Association to advertise the benefits of protection, featured a special film on Lancashire; in seeking to assuage the workers of the mill towns, whose faith traditionally lay in free trade, the film addressed Lancashire's historical and contemporary interests – and, vicariously, those of other traditionally free trade regions.[64] Likewise, the NPB published targeted editions of the *Popular Illustrated*, including the *New London Pictorial* and the *Scottish Illustrated*. The former addressed London commuters, many of them shopworkers, echoing posters distributed on the underground showcasing the effects of booming consumer confidence.[65] As the *ILN* observed, the National government defended its majority at the 1935 general election with two types of poster – the national posters and those 'classified in special appeals to various sections of the electorate, such as industrial areas, shipping centres, and agricultural districts'.[66] Popular interest and pride in the regional economy went well with the grand design of national recovery. It also helped to rejuvenate popular politics in ways that further reconciled the Conservative grassroots to the opportunities presented by membership of the National government.

The Politics of Relief

In many constituencies, the image of recovery that dominated government propaganda appeared far removed from the reality of everyday life. 'In some districts the [government's] Poster Campaign had given great offence', warned one agent, 'for instance, posters in distressed areas

---

film 1615.08. For Wood and the Post Office, see *ILN*, 6 Feb. 1932, 13 May 1933, 6 Jan. 1934, 9 Feb., 17 Apr. 1935.

[64] *The price of free trade* (1932), *Empire trade* (1934), *Two Lancashire cotton workers discuss safeguarding* (1935). The first and last are available for viewing on the BFI's 'screenonline' database.

[65] Casey, 'The National Publicity Bureau', 633–4.   [66] *ILN*, 9 Nov. 1935.

Conservatives and the Politics of National Recovery

showing the improvement in employment'.[67] Moreover, Conservatives were acutely aware of what they perceived to be Labour's tightening stranglehold on welfare provision through control of local government, especially in depressed areas like South Wales and the north-east. Meanwhile in all parts of the country, a common fear among Conservatives – perhaps the most common fear by 1934 – was the proliferation of cooperative societies.[68] And so if proof were needed that Labour had not been struck dead in 1931, local Conservatives found themselves once more having to contest Labour's claims to represent voters' material, and especially welfare, interests. Conservatives in the northern counties noted that health and welfare conferences, organised by professionals and lobby groups such as the Maternal Mortality Committee, were being attended by representatives from the Women's Cooperative Guild and other Labour organisations. It was of 'extreme importance' that Conservatives did the same, not least, they argued, because their Labour opponents were blaming the second Baldwin government 'for curtailing Social Services'.[69] Even if the rationality of the new anti-socialism remained relevant – with Conservatives re-servicing the arguments of 1931 with tales of Labour's 'misdeeds' in local government[70] – it did not remain adequate for long. The politics of recovery would have to spawn a politics of relief.

Government ministers, not least Chamberlain, were well aware of these political difficulties even before the propaganda campaigns of 1934 and 1935. In addition to the narrative of recovery, the government set out to construct one of social service. The 1930s witnessed a surge both in public interest in unemployment and in voluntary efforts to address its social consequences. Both developments were harnessed by the government. As Chancellor, Chamberlain was committed to protecting the exchequer from additional obligations towards the *financial* relief of the unemployed but sought to position the government as the focus and force for a new moral economy emphasising *social* relief. In this way, although 'recovery' remained the government's leitmotif for most Conservatives, and welfare services were administered largely by delegated organisations, the politics of relief provided a vital additional subject around which local Conservatives could mobilise.

---

[67] *CAJ*, Jun. 1935, 156.

[68] Inaugural meeting of Conservative co-operators, 12 Feb. 1934, Stockton CA, D/X 322/5; labour advisory committee, 15 Jul. 1933, finance & general purposes committee, 20 Mar. 1934, council committee, 11 Jul. 1934, CPA, Home Counties North Area, ARE 8/1/1.

[69] Women's advisory council, 13 Jun. 1933, Northern Counties Area, NRO 4137/8.

[70] For an example, see Cuthbert Headlam's speech at a meeting of the Durham Lodge of the NCL. *Stockton & Darlington Times*, 26 Jan. 1935.

84   Rethinking Interwar Conservatism

Public awareness of the unemployment problem owed much to an emergent discourse that echoed the 'condition of England' question of a century earlier. The social criticism works of George Orwell, the uncomfortable truths disclosed in the travel writings of J. B. Priestley and H. V. Morton, the thinly veiled autobiographical content of Walter Greenwood's and Walter Brierley's hardship novels, and the burgeoning field of 'authentic' working-class authorship – all these introduced the reading public to the harsh realities of working-class unemployment.[71] Similar exposés were produced for the viewing public in the form of documentary films and for the listening public in the form of broadcast documentaries, both of which delved into the psychological as well as the material consequences of worklessness, often through first-hand testimonies.[72] As such it is commonplace to view this discourse as a critical commentary on the government. Certainly, the figure of the means test inspector came to personify the unyielding officialdom of the scant relief system upon which unemployed households survived. Some documentaries, like *Bread*, produced in 1934 by the Soviet-inspired Kino Production Group, represented a radically anti-establishment assault on the government, and several of the decade's most powerful commentaries were sponsored by the left-wing publisher Victor Gollancz, whose authors, notably Priestley, subsequently helped to shape popular narratives of radical renewal in the 1940s. But in general, the documentary depictions of unemployed life that proliferated in the 1930s were just as concerned with showcasing solutions as highlighting social ills. *Housing Problems* (1935), for instance, first takes viewers into the damp and infested slums of Stepney in order ultimately to dwell on the transformed living conditions enjoyed by those families who moved into modern accommodation under the auspices of a public housing scheme. Clearly the British Commercial Gas Association, which together with the Labour-run local authority had co-commissioned the film, saw in the documentary genre a form of 'agitprop', 'shocking our sympathies as the narrative urges us to support new political and economic policies'.[73]

---

[71] G. Orwell, *The road to Wigan pier* (1937); J. B. Priestley, *English journey* (1934); H. V. Morton, *What I saw in the slums* (1933); W. Greenwood, *Love on the dole: a tale of two cities* (1933); W. Brierley, *Means test man* (1935). See also V. Cunningham, *British writers of the 1930s* (Oxford, 1988) and C. Hilliard, *To exercise our talents: the democratization of writing in Britain* (Cambridge, MA, 2006), ch.4.

[72] Documentary films included *Bread* (1934); *Workers and jobs* (dir. A. Elton, 1935); *Coal face* (dir. A. Cavalcanti, 1935); *Housing problems* (dir. A. Elton & E. Anstey, 1935); *Enough to eat?* (dir. E. Anstey, 1936); *Today we live* (dir. R. Grierson & R. Bond, 1937); *Eastern valley* (dir. D. Alexander, 1937). For radio, see the compilation of transcripts in F. Greene (ed.), *Time to spare: what unemployment means, by eleven unemployed* (1935).

[73] J. Allred, *American modernism and depression documentary* (Oxford, 2010), 87.

Conservatives and the Politics of National Recovery 85

But agitprop was not the sole preserve of social-democratic critics of the government. Some within the National government appreciated its publicity value. One of these was the Minister of Health, Hilton Young, who was quoted in the *ILN:*

> Seeing is believing, and it is because many have not had the opportunity of seeing with their own eyes that I particularly welcome the help of *The Illustrated London News*, which can bring slum conditions more vividly than any speech or Blue Book before the minds of its wide circle of readers.[74]

Others directly orchestrated such publicity, including Chamberlain, who ahead of his 'restoration' budget in 1934 commissioned a series of investigative newspaper articles on the conditions of the unemployed in the north-east of England. The anonymous 'special correspondent' was one Henry Brooke, one of the Chancellor's protégés in the Conservative Research Department, who also undertook social research for the Pilgrim Trust before becoming the MP for Lewisham West from 1938 and ultimately Home Secretary in the early 1960s. 'Tyneside is not sharing much in the recovery', noted Chamberlain following a speaking engagement in Newcastle, 'and it was rather difficult to find the right note of sympathy & hope without undue optimism'.[75] Brooke's articles, published by *The Times* as 'Places without a future', gave a detailed and unvarnished account of poverty in the Durham coalfields: the helpless desperation wrought by long-term unemployment, the 'nineteenth-century' housing conditions, and the lack of 'disinterested service' on behalf of the community as many of the young and those outside the working class moved south. In the 'utterly workless' town of Jarrow he recorded 'the rare sight of even a pawnshop closed'. While critical of Labour's mismanagement of local government in County Durham, the articles were scarcely more complementary of the National government as Brooke himself conveyed his subjects' resentment of a comfortable southern electorate governing in ignorance of the North. Compared with London and the South, where 'for every 86 men working there are 14 men out of work', in Jarrow 'for every 25 working there are 75 out'. He recommended three 'special measures' that government might take to help industrial areas like the north-east: a labour transference scheme to assist migrants from the depressed areas, a regional policy that coordinated government and non-government efforts to attract investment in new industry, and provisions to alleviate the suffering of those who

---

[74] *ILN*, 15 Jul. 1933. See also J. Grierson, 'Films in the public service', *Public Administration*, 14 (1936), 366–72, at 369.

[75] *The Neville Chamberlain diary letters, vol. 4: the Downing Street years, 1934–1940*, ed. R. Self (Aldershot, 2005), 64 (to Hilda, 24 Mar. 1934).

86   Rethinking Interwar Conservatism

remained unemployed.[76] It is no coincidence that these anticipated the policy stance adopted by the government towards the distressed areas from 1934. The paradoxical combination of criticism and publicity seemed to work. Such was the level of interest that Brooke's findings were immediately reissued as a pamphlet.[77] Chamberlain, having thus helped to define public narratives of the problem, could now proceed to construct public narratives of the solution.

In December 1934 the government launched its flagship policy, the Special Areas (Development and Improvement) Act, under which four regions – South East Wales, Durham and Tyneside, West Cumberland, and Central Scotland – were to receive the dedicated attention of two special commissioners, one for Scotland and one for England and Wales. After initially focusing its modest £2 million budget on public health programmes, this experiment in regional policy soon turned to the development of government-financed industrial estates.[78] This matched what Macmillan had sought for voters in Stockton, who now stood to benefit under the scheme, namely that upon restoring the national finances the government would show its commitment to the distressed areas by giving 'first consideration' to the unemployed.[79] Indeed, Macmillan and others in the 'northern group' of MPs had advocated a regional industrial policy since the late 1920s, and there was even some legislative precedence in the form of the Industrial Transference Act of 1928.[80] Conservatives in the South were more equivocal. An activist in Epping expected such a policy to consolidate the party's standing 'as the strongest political force whose policy has been largely responsible for the recovery of the finance and trade of the country since the crisis of 1931', yet many of his peers were still unreconciled to the principle of 'Government interference with the conduct of business'.[81]

For many Conservatives elsewhere in the country it was a source of regret that their own area was excluded. Dundee and Leeds lost out, as did Lancashire. So, necessarily, did less distressed areas such as Pembrokeshire, where Conservatives felt that 'distressed area' designation would have helped them to regain the seat after their failure to do so in 1931.[82] For these

---

[76] 'Places without a future', *The Times*, 20–22 Mar. 1934.

[77] *The Times*, 24 Mar. 1934.

[78] P. Scott, *Triumph of the south: a regional economic history of early twentieth-century Britain* (Aldershot, 2007), 257–65.

[79] E.g., Macmillan's speech at the AGM, 12 Mar. 1934, Stockton CA, D/X 322/5.

[80] See Boothby et. al., *Industry and the state*; H. Macmillan, *Reconstruction: a plea for a national policy* (London, 1933); J. Tomlinson, *Public policy and the economy since 1900* (Oxford, 1990), 120.

[81] E.g., area council, 11 Jul. 1934, CPA, Home Counties North Area, ARE 8/1/1.

[82] Executive committee, 1 Dec. 1934, Pembrokeshire Record Office, Pembrokeshire CA, HDSO/51/1.

Conservatives, almost regardless of ideological reservations, the vision of an active and imaginative government represented a necessary alternative to the discourse of 'socialist planning' being developed by Labour in the mid-1930s. In the event no new special areas were created, though the Conservatives' 1935 manifesto committed the party to developing large industrial estates in the existing areas. By 1938 four estates had been built, one in each area, and the Ministry of Labour, which oversaw policy for the distressed areas, had grown in stature.[83]

By endorsing the work of the National Council of Social Service, the government also associated itself closely with the nationwide surge of voluntary responses to unemployment. Formed in 1919 to organise voluntary and charitable work after the war, from 1932 the NCSS was given a brief by government to 'stimulate voluntary work to keep unemployed men and women in physical and mental health', which it did by championing the spread of occupational and recreational clubs.[84] Activities ranged from allotment keeping to handicraft work to literature classes, depending on local needs. As the journalist and broadcaster Peter Mais explained, the clubs aimed to facilitate self-help through vocational training and greater self-subsistence. 'The unemployed do not want *charity*.'[85] Yet in practice the club movement relied on the contributions and goodwill, financial or otherwise, of the employed. In this regard the publicity attracted by the NCSS's popular patron, the Prince of Wales, proved incomparable; frequent and extensive coverage of his visits to distressed areas ensured that, alongside Chamberlain, he emerged as one of the most prominent faces of the national relief effort.[86]

If by the 1940s memories of the Prince of Wales, and his famous dictum 'something must be done', were appropriated by Labour critics of the National government,[87] at the time his involvement functioned as its own agitprop on behalf of the government. For contrary to the oppositional subtext commonly ascribed to the self-help culture of the depression years, the National government sought to make the voluntary response – by and for the unemployed – appear orchestrated by government action and not necessitated by

---

[83] R. Lowe, *Adjusting to democracy: the role of the Ministry of Labour in British politics, 1916–1939* (Oxford, 1986), 225–3.

[84] W. G. S. Adams (Chairman, NCSS) to the editor, *The Times*, 28 Nov. 1932.

[85] S. P. B. Mais, 'Time to spare', in Greene (ed.), *Time to spare*, 13–25, at 17 (original emphasis).

[86] *ILN*, 26 Nov., 3 Dec. 1932, 1, 8, 15, 22 Apr. 1933. For further discussion of the role of the royal family 'as a focus and force for social cohesion', see P. Williamson, 'The monarchy and public values, 1910–1953', in A. Olechnowicz (ed.), *The monarchy and the British nation, 1780 to the present* (Cambridge, 2007), 223–57, esp. 239–41.

[87] Central Office of Information, *Something Done.*

88   Rethinking Interwar Conservatism

government inaction. Many initiatives were private-public partnership schemes part funded by the exchequer. Adverts of government grants to help occupational centres for the unemployed were broadcast on the radio, something depicted in the documentary film *Today we live*, sponsored by the NCSS in 1937, which explained to viewers how to submit applications for financial aid. Indeed, over time the NCSS became the leading disseminator of information about government relief work, before in 1939 transforming itself into the Citizens' Advice Bureau. During this time the government also reformed the financial provisions of direct unemployment relief. In 1934, with the establishment of the Unemployment Assistance Boards under the Ministry of Labour, it switched responsibility for administering assistance (both to uninsured workers and to those whose insurance contributions had been exhausted) from the local rates to the national exchequer. By 1937 it had also extended the scope of contributory pensions and unemployment insurance schemes to previously excluded workers. 'The total picture is impressive', thought one expert, who compared Britain's 'public provision' favourably with the 'sketchy improvisations' of the United States.[88]

The politics of relief signified not just Conservative complicity in the statist trajectory of government policy in the mid-1930s but also the renewal of 'social politics' in the constituencies, as local party associations took up the ideals of civil society in the name of voluntarism. This occurred in myriad ways across the country, as will be explored in Part II, and reveals much about how local Conservatives detected opportunities to exploit the potential popularity of the National government's work. Nor should this be interpreted as an anachronistic restoration of parochial politics. An agent in Northampton, who branded traditional aspects of local political culture such as leaflets and public meetings 'ineffective', urged his party to respond to local unemployment by setting up Conservative building societies, Conservative friendly societies, Conservative coal clubs and the like. 'Social activity' of this topical kind would first engage voters, he reasoned, 'then gently but firmly lead them into the political faith desired'.[89] The appeal of voluntarism could also prove effective in the affluent south. Sir John Jarvis, a southern industrialist with business interests in Tyneside, launched the 'Surrey Fund' to support families in Jarrow and himself purchased two ships to be scrapped

---

[88] R. C. Davison, 'The state services for the unemployed', in Greene (ed.), *Time to spare*, 153–75, at 174.

[89] *CAJ*, Apr. 1935, 65.

Conservatives and the Politics of National Recovery 89

in Jarrow shipyards (all of which raised his profile as Conservative candidate in Guildford at the 1935 general election).[90] The politics of relief, like the politics of recovery, offered local Conservatives a rich seam of popular appeals, traditional and local, yet topical and aligned with the prevailing culture of national government.

Party Identity and 'National' Politics

How then were the needs of the Conservative party and a cross-party government reconciled during these years of national recovery? The challenge facing Conservatives at all levels after 1931 was how to keep the National government 'National' and the Conservative party both 'national' and Conservative. The biggest threat to the government was the potential for inter-party rivalry. Controversy over the distribution of ministerial appointments, divergent interpretations of the mandate, and disagreement over policy all bred tension, especially between Conservatives and Samuelite Liberals, until their resignation, with Snowden, in September 1932.[91] Within Conservative ranks, too, there was potential for disappointments over ministerial jobs and in certain policy areas – India, in particular – party managers foresaw trouble from the right wing. How the Conservatives responded to these and other challenges reveals much about how they saw their party identity in relation to the National government.

Unsurprisingly, party managers saw the task of maintaining unity as a question of discipline. As a result, organisational matters tended to occupy party managers more than they did local activists. Writing in the late summer of 1932, as the question of imperial preference was coming to a head with the Ottawa conference, Lord Stonehaven, Conservative party chairman, felt 'convinced of the necessity to face the fact that the dissolution of the political combination which gave the National Government its majority is only a question of time'. Failure to consolidate the cross-party cooperation would inevitably lead to conflict. With each by-election came ample scope for the parties to fall out over the national candidature and destabilise the government from within.[92] The Conservative leadership recognised that the government contained an

---

[90] *The Times*, 16 Nov. 1935.
[91] On ministerial appointments see *The Baldwin papers: a Conservative statesman, 1908-1947*, ed. P. Williamson & E. Baldwin (Cambridge, 2004), 277–8 (Wigram memorandum, 4 Nov. 1931), 355–6 (Baldwin to Londonderry, 21 Nov. 1935 and Baldwin to Winterton, 22 Nov. 1935); Bridgeman to Baldwin, 2 Nov. 1931, L. Amery to Baldwin, 6 Nov. 1931, Baldwin papers, 45/vi/194–5, 201. See also Williamson, *National crisis and national government*, 356–8 (on ministerial appointments) and 512–15 (on the resignations at the time of Ottawa).
[92] Memorandum by Stonehaven, n.d. 1932, Baldwin papers, 46/47–58.

90   Rethinking Interwar Conservatism

inherent tension that defied any solution. On the one hand, it was difficult 'claiming support for a National Coalition of Parties in which the Conservative Party predominates so overwhelmingly'; on the other hand was the impossible task of maintaining a relationship with two parties – National Labour and Liberal National – lacking their own effective organisations. Stonehaven reached the uneasy conclusion that a new National Party was the only answer, but Conservative disagreement over such a development ensured that it remained no more than a theoretical solution. Working within these confines, Stonehaven therefore did what he could to consolidate inter-party cooperation at the centre. A National Co-ordinating Committee, initially consisting of himself and the Liberal National and National Labour organisers, Leslie Hore-Belisha and the Earl De La Warr, was established in November 1932. Stonehaven built on this a year later by inviting the party's twelve area chairmen in England and Wales to London to meet the regional representatives of the Liberal National and National Labour parties.[93]

Local Conservatives' thoughts on formal cooperation between the parties were generally less advanced. Even in areas where local Conservative-Liberal cooperation in the early 1920s had outlived the Lloyd George coalition, such as in Stockton and across South Wales, attempts to restore the alliance after 1931 were seldom coordinated or sustained. There were exceptions that help to prove this rule, for instance the National Association formed between Conservatives and Liberals in Southampton in May 1932[94] – although as one of few remaining two-member seats in the country the initiative here was trouble-free in a way not applicable elsewhere. In the longer term, such alliances as were forged in the 1930s were inevitably limited to those constituencies with a Liberal National organisation.[95] But for the most part cooperation after 1931 was either absent, as Stonehaven feared, or ad hoc. If local officials sometimes responded to by-election setbacks with a renewed interest in cooperation, the results were normally inconsequential. Officials in the Wessex Area organisation, for instance, encouraged local parties to learn from the National alliance in Southampton, yet at the regional level they instituted

---

[93] 'Meeting of Area Chairmen' memorandum, by Stonehaven, 12 Dec. 1933, Baldwin papers, 46/96–100. For a detailed account of the relations between national party organisers, including the work of the National Coordinating Committee, see Stannage, *Baldwin thwarts the opposition*, 44–9.

[94] *The Times*, 12 May 1932.

[95] For Conservative-Liberal National relations, see D. Dutton, *Liberals in schism: a history of the National Liberal party* (London, 2008), chs.2–3. The Liberal Nationals renamed themselves the National Liberal party in 1948.

Conservatives and the Politics of National Recovery 91

nothing more than a genteel Lunch Club to bring together supporters of the National government.[96]

While Conservatives in the country were reluctant to venture into anything like a new National Party, they remained fully committed to maintaining the National government's distinct identity. In fact, active support for the government was the overwhelming feature of the grass-roots' mindset for most of the 1930s. Yet this remarkable fact is too often lost amid historians' more commonplace interest in the controversies and splits of the decade.

The Conservative party of the 1930s, more than that of the 1920s, has often been portrayed as a juxtaposition of two Conservative types: one young and progressive, its ranks swollen by new MPs who owed their election to the National cause, the other older and 'diehard', less reconciled to the government. They disagreed on some key policy issues, most famously Indian constitutional reform.[97] They also differed in their responses to the challenges of mass democracy. The young progressives, apparently disaffected by the old party lines and fearing that Conservatism now equated to unimaginative government, readily contemplated the formation of a National Party. Stonehaven reported to Baldwin in 1933 that 'there are undeniably members of our Party who would like to change its name to National'. These men, he noted, 'realise what is the undoubted fact that the name Conservative is taken to be synonymous with old-fashioned, unprogressive, unimaginative, etc., by large numbers of non-Party voters who think that the only real dividing line ... should be drawn between Socialists and anti-Socialists'.[98] A hundred Conservative MPs signed a letter to *The Times* in June 1934 publicly calling for a party that would make the National government 'for all practical purposes, a permanent ideal in British politics'.[99]

Insofar as the controversies of the 1930s are often exaggerated, so too is the notion that one group of Conservatives supported the government enthusiastically while the other only reluctantly 'came into line' in 1935 upon facing a general election.[100] Stannage exaggerates both the

---

[96] Finance and general purposes committee, 20 Feb., 3 Apr. 1935, Wessex Area, ARE 10/1/1.

[97] See A. Muldoon, *Empire, politics and the creation of the 1935 India Act: last act of the Raj* (Farnham, 2009), ch.6 and Stannage, Baldwin thwarts the opposition, ch.1, esp. 40–8.

[98] 'Meeting of Area Chairmen' memorandum, by Stonehaven, 12 Dec. 1933, Baldwin papers, 46/96–100, at 99.

[99] *The Times*, 14 Jun. 1934.

[100] See J. Ramsden, *The age of Balfour and Baldwin, 1902–1940* (London, 1978), 344. Stannage, *Baldwin thwarts the opposition*, talks of constituency organisations feeling '*resigned* to the fact that the general election was going to be fought on national lines' (53, emphasis added).

92   Rethinking Interwar Conservatism

coherence and extent of Conservative support for a National Party in 1934. For one thing, his claim, relating to the *Times* letter, that 'all but about ten of the signatories had been returned to the House of Commons for the first time in 1931', is incorrect. In fact the figure is thirty-one, including three elected before 1914.[101] Added to this, not all MPs who signed the letter reflected the opinion of their association. Among the signatories were four Birmingham MPs, despite the misgivings that Birmingham activists had aired some months earlier. Taking as their example the gradual courtship that brought the Liberal Unionists and Conservatives together by 1912, Birmingham Conservatives 'agreed that the necessity for a continuance of the National government still exists ... [but] many have doubts about the wisdom of premature fusion'.[102]

Any move towards a new party would only further dissatisfy and embolden 'those who are out of sympathy with the Government *on the question of India*'.[103] Activists were clearly well aware that the National Party and India questions together could destabilise Conservative unity. But they knew this not to be inevitable, because implicit in most grass-roots discussion of these issues was an understanding that many Conservatives would continue to support the National government *despite* its India policy, so long as the Conservative party retained its own separate identity, as proved to be the case. For most constituency parties it was not a significant concern. Lord Bayford, at the time chairman of the ACC and therefore in a position to test grassroots opinion, thought that opposition to Indian reform came mostly from retired colonial and military officers in the rural seats,[104] men like Colonel Purdy and Admiral Colomb in Norfolk North. Initially, many party members shared their anxiety.[105] By the summer of 1934, however, they were increasingly in a minority, as constituency parties voted to postpone further discussion until the parliamentary Joint Committee published its report on the government's White Paper.[106] This appeared later in the year and was endorsed by the

---

[101] Stannage, *Baldwin thwarts the opposition*, 47.

[102] Management committee, 9 Nov. 1933, Birmingham CUA. Similar opinions, rejecting a National Party while supporting the National government, are recorded in: Council AGM, 26 May 1933, Wessex Area, ARE 10/1/1; executive committee, 15 Feb. 1934, Eastern Area, ARE 7/1/7; council AGM, 6 Feb. 1935, Home Counties North Area, ARE 8/1/1.

[103] Management committee, 9 Nov. 1933, Birmingham CUA (emphasis added).

[104] *Real old Tory politics: the political diaries of Robert Sanders, Lord Bayford, 1910–1935*, ed. J. Ramsden (London, 1984), 249 (31 Jul. 1933).

[105] General council, 20 Jun. 1933, Norfolk Record Office, Norfolk North CA, Acc. 2006/152, at which 21 members supported Purdy's resolution registering their 'profound disquiet', which 9 opposed, with 22 abstaining; council AGM, 26 May 1933, Wessex Area, ARE 10/1/1; area council, 9 Feb. 1934, Home Counties North Area, ARE 8/1/1.

[106] General council, 7 May 1934, Norfolk North CA.

grassroots.[107] Even in Epping, where activists backed Churchill in forthrightly criticising 'Indian Home Rule', there was no questioning the government's general direction or the party's membership of it. Churchill himself urged local voters to place his views on India into proper perspective, reminding them that his stance preceded the formation of the government and that he had consistently praised the government for restoring national prestige after 1931. 'He was a supporter of the National Government, and voted with it on almost all its subjects with the exception of India', was how one journalist reported his speech at Theydon Bois at the height of the controversy in parliament.[108] A year later he was asking voters to give the new Indian constitution 'a fair chance'.[109]

By 1934, then, there were Conservative MPs publicly advocating a National Party, and many who felt that Conservative principles were being betrayed by the government on India. But beneath this lay a fundamental commitment to the government shared by the bulk of the rank and file, together with 'diehards' and 'progressives' alike. The nature of the political task that faced local Conservatives in these years differed between constituencies, as will become clear in Part II. But insofar as their ability to respond effectively was understood to be bound up with membership of the National government, there were certain shared assumptions upon which local activists sought to prolong the government.

One of these held that the government was uniquely able to engage the political consciousness of Liberals, when their own party was in disarray, and especially erstwhile Liberals, who for Conservatives represented the non-party voter whose support had been so important in 1931. Developments since then impressed the importance of continuing to cultivate this vote. By-election defeats, the fall out over India, the troubling evidence of greater fascist activity in cities including Birmingham and Liverpool, all gave the impression of a dysfunctional government that had lost its broad 'national' mandate.[110] Above all, Labour embarked on

---

[107] By 'a large majority' in the end. General council, 10 Dec. 1934, Norfolk North CA.

[108] *West Essex Gazette*, 10 Nov. 1934.

[109] Central council, 28 Jun. 1934, Redbridge Local Studies and Archives, Epping CA, Acc. A6853; election address, 28 Oct. 1935, Chartwell papers, CHAR 7/24/2.

[110] In Liverpool, a Conservative councillor defected to the fascists and in Birmingham the decline in membership of the Junior Imperial League was partly blamed on the British Union of Fascists 'endeavouring to attract young people to their ranks'. (Central council, 11 Apr. 1934, Liverpool Record Office, Liverpool CA, 329 Con/1/1/3; management committee, 9 Mar. 1934, Birmingham CUA.) See also M. Pugh, 'Lancashire, cotton, and Indian reform: Conservative controversies in the 1930s', *TCBH*, 15 (2004), 143–51, esp. 148–9; J. W. B. Bates, 'The Conservative party in the constituencies, 1918–1939' (DPhil thesis, University of Oxford, 1994), 251.

94   Rethinking Interwar Conservatism

a major propaganda campaign, with some success. Across the country, Conservatives were alarmed by Labour's victory in the London County Council elections in 1934 and soon started to identify (or imagine) similar signs of electoral and organisational recovery by Labour in their own area.[111] They rightly sensed that Labour would use its position in local government to rehabilitate its reputation for responsibility and competence in the national arena, and that both the Labour party and the burgeoning Labour press would redouble their efforts to portray the National government as just a facade for 'Tory' policies.[112]

Conservatives sought to restore the 'national' identity of the government by bidding to represent Liberalism. Some by now considered their task to be more than merely appealing to Liberals and began to entertain a more strategic desire to affect a lasting realignment of Liberal and non-party opinion in favour of the Conservatives. This, they thought, would turn on the National *government*, not any National party. J. F. Eales, MP for Birmingham Erdington, made this explicit. 'The great cleavage in the country in the future would be as to the method of government', not 'political controversies as the electors knew them years ago'. 'The Liberal Party was dead ... It could never hope to form a Government again. But the spirit which inspired Liberals in the past and the great traditions of reforming zeal associated with the Liberal Party for many years remained.' This 'great body of opinion' had to go somewhere, reasoned Eales, and insofar as it was opposed to socialism it was there for the Conservative party to harness.[113]

It is in this context that we should seek to understand Conservative MPs' public support for a National Party. Like some of the Birmingham MPs, Thomas Cook, MP for Norfolk North, signed *The Times* letter not because his association backed a shift away from traditional party lines (it made its opposition to this very clear) but because it underscored the concerted efforts already being made by his local party officials to seek 'the best means of coordinating the Liberal section of the National vote with Conservative organisation'. The absence of a Liberal National organisation (as in most constituencies), and, in any case, local Conservative hostility to any form of 'fusion', meant that 'national' politics was constructed locally on an ad-hoc basis. So, Liberal National figures like Simon, Hore-Belisha, and Ernest

---

[111] Central council, 23 Mar. 1934, Birmingham CUA; central council, 11 Apr. 1934, Liverpool CA; general council, 7 May 1934, Norfolk North CA; secretary's report to central committee, 23 Jun. 1934, Devizes CA, 2305/3; area council, 11 Jul. 1934, Home Counties North Area, ARE 8/1/1.

[112] See L. Beers, *Your Britain: media and the making of the Labour party* (Harvard, 2010), 156–7. The *News Chronicle* referred to the National government always in inverted commas (149). See also the pamphlet, *What Labour has done for London* (1936).

[113] Central council, 29 Sep. 1934, Birmingham CUA.

Brown were invited to speak at public fetes organised by the Conservatives; well-known Liberals in the locality found themselves being pursued, wined, and dined by the local Conservative chairman; and the local MP backed a National Party as a demonstration of his commitment to the National government and the high esteem with which he held his Liberal partners.[114]

Above all, the culture of national government forged after 1931, though not anticipated, enabled the Conservatives finally to reconcile the kind of national appeal rendered necessary in the age of mass-media democracy with particularist appeals that promised to underpin a traditional Tory politics of place. For most activists, anti-socialism remained the defining agenda right up to Munich. But, now allied to the task of securing national economic recovery, Conservative anti-socialism no longer precluded government intervention in the economy. In turn, government action bolstered two powerful claims that further served the interests of Conservatives in the constituencies. One was that the National government was atoning for the failure of previous governments to carry out reconstruction following the war; the other, that it was a responsive government, responding actively to public and expert interest in the social conditions of the unemployed, much like the New Liberals almost a generation earlier. The fact that Liberal opponents, like Dingle Foot in Dundee, now criticised the Conservatives for wielding excessive executive power, indeed for pursuing 'socialist' policies that endangered civil liberties, betrays the extent to which Conservatives had adapted, willingly, to the task of making the National government work.[115]

The fact that Baldwin adapted in similar fashion brought the party leadership and the grassroots into alignment. At first, the context of national crisis and 'sacrifice' gave Baldwin's traditional rhetoric a new immediacy. Addressing a rally in Ilford in 1932, he cited Thomas More's *Utopia* and referred idealistically to the 'common weal', urging his audience to be guided by More's 'spirit' over the coming years.[116] But as Williamson argues, by the time Baldwin had replaced MacDonald as prime minister in June 1935 his 'anti-statist language was replaced by pragmatic yet positive justification of state activity'. He explained this, the Chamberlainite agenda, as 'neither Socialist, nor Liberal, nor Unionist', but rather as the necessary agenda to which any determined government would have to turn.[117] This was wholly compatible with the apolitical tone of Baldwin's public persona, the same persona that Conservatives

---

[114] General council, 7 May 1934, executive committee, 13 Sep. 1934, Norfolk North CA.
[115] See P. Sloman, *The Liberal party and the economy, 1929–1964* (Oxford, 2015), 97–9.
[116] *Ilford Recorder*, 17 Mar. 1932.　　[117] Williamson, *Stanley Baldwin*, 185.

96   Rethinking Interwar Conservatism

locally now embraced enthusiastically as the embodiment of the government's 'national' credentials. Whereas in 1931 MacDonald, Simon, and Samuel were key to legitimating the 'national' identity of a primarily Conservative government, by 1935 there was an understanding that Baldwin, too, as the leader who had forfeited the top job in cabinet for four years, could play a decisive role in convincing voters once again that theirs was a National and not a partisan government. According to the party in Liverpool, 'Baldwin has strengthened his hold on our Party and enjoys the confidence of the nation'.[118] The 1935 election would bear this out.

The General Election of 1935

Most accounts of the 1935 general election have viewed the campaign as one peculiarly bound up with foreign policy. With the possible exception of the khaki election of 1918, it was the first contest since 1900 in which questions of defence preoccupied politicians on all sides. The results of the famous Peace Ballot, declared in June, revealed overwhelming public approval for the concept of collective security under the aegis of the League of Nations, with a majority of voters endorsing two seemingly contradictory policies: the reduction of armaments by international agreement and the use of League-authorised military force in defence of a country under attack. Although something of a maverick exercise, organised by the League of Nations Union and lacking statutory authority, as a national plebiscite it commanded sufficient publicity to compel politicians to frame their foreign policy deliberations, as well as their platform rhetoric, within the bounds set by their reading of public opinion in the summer of 1935. For most, the ballot signalled enthusiastic support for disarmament alongside cautious support for defensive military action where necessary. It therefore followed that when Mussolini invaded Abyssinia in October 1935, prompting questions about the League's effectiveness, the Abyssinian question came to be regarded by voters and opposition parties as a test of the government's conduct of foreign policy. For the government especially, it was a test of how to manage foreign policy controversies in an age of mass democracy; in other words, how to reconcile the inexpert but now inescapable exhortations of a mass electorate with the unpalatable military undertakings to which Britain could find itself committed under the Covenant of the League.

The Abyssinian crisis assumed a central place in the election campaign not just in response to world events but also by design, as politicians saw

---

[118] Central council, 11 Apr. 1934, Liverpool CA.

Conservatives and the Politics of National Recovery

in it opportunities to serve their party interests. It was as a consequence of the crisis and its aftermaths, Maurice Cowling famously argued, that foreign policy displaced class conflict as the organising dynamic of British popular politics by the late 1930s.[119] For many Liberals, the ideal of disarmament and the rejection of unilateralism held out the prospect of re-energising the forces of political nonconformity. Such a platform looked set to benefit Lloyd George, whose Council of Action for Peace and Reconstruction, launched earlier in the summer with the support of Free Church leaders and public figures from all parties and none, appeared poised to spearhead a 'moral' campaign similar to that which Gladstone had led in response to the Bulgarian atrocities.[120] For Labour, too, it represented an opportunity to regain respectability on questions of national and international significance and so to expand on the electoral recovery begun in London the previous year, though in the event such efforts were blunted by party division over the League's economic sanctions. Opposition parties attacked the prime minister's decision to call an election at a time of international crisis. In the first of his broadcast speeches the Labour leader, Clement Attlee, accused the Conservative leader of seeking a 'blank cheque for armaments', ostensibly in the service of the League but in reality in the interests of private industry and in pursuit of a khaki-style election, while in a subsequent broadcast J. R. Clynes mocked the government for 'looking for peace with a gun'.[121] True, Baldwin made Britain's contribution to international peace and stability through the League, including defence contributions that necessitated a degree of investment in arms, the central theme of his campaign. 'I will not be responsible for the conduct of any Government in this country at this present time', he declared in his first election broadcast, 'if I am not given power to remedy the deficiencies which have accrued in our defensive services since the War'. But allegations of warmongering appeared far-fetched to an electorate by then familiar with Baldwin's trademark caution and conciliation. 'I think you know me well enough now to know that I am no militarist', he told them.[122] Days later, in an address to the Peace Society, he gave a famous undertaking that captured his aversion to militarism and his contract of trust with voters: 'I give you my word there will be no great armaments.'[123]

---

[119] M. Cowling, *The impact of Hitler: British politics and British policy, 1933–1940* (Cambridge, 1975).

[120] S. Koss, 'Lloyd George and nonconformity: the last rally', *EHR*, 89 (1974), 77–108.

[121] *The Times*, 29 Oct., 1 Nov. 1935. See also *The Times*, 7 Nov. 1935 (Herbert Samuel), and 8 Nov. 1935 (Herbert Morrison).

[122] *The Times*, 26 Oct. 1935.   [123] Ibid., 1 Nov. 1935.

98   Rethinking Interwar Conservatism

The elevation of foreign policy by the party leaders inevitably shaped the electorate's experience of the campaign. Much has been extrapolated from the fact that audiences tuned in to Baldwin's broadcasts in unprecedented numbers, with some voters feeling sufficiently moved to write to the prime minister to express admiration for the reassuring tone and content of his message.[124] Certainly in some areas the presence of the LNU, and Conservative fears of its exploitation by Liberal and Labour infiltrators operating under the guise of non-partisanship, led many in the party to develop a new appreciation of Baldwin's qualities as a communicator capable of engaging the consciences of non-Conservatives.[125] 'I am bound to recognise', wrote Neville Chamberlain to his sister during the campaign, 'that if I supply the policy and the drive S.B. does also supply something that is perhaps even more valuable in retaining the floating vote'.[126] Polling day produced a net loss of 70 seats for the Conservatives, owing primarily to a national swing of 9.4 per cent to the Labour party, which made a net gain of 94 seats. The Conservative losses, all but eleven of them in two-way contests with Labour, occurred mainly in London and Outer London (eighteen seats, including Romford), West Yorkshire and Sheffield (thirteen), and Scotland (thirteen). In these areas it appears Liberal and Labour voters turned (back) to Labour, as if in anticipation of the patriotic radicalism that coalesced around Labour in the late 1930s, and which Chapter 8 discusses. But without Baldwin's skill in fronting the government's national campaign, the Liberal and Labour campaigns would likely have resulted in steeper swings against the Conservatives. Paradoxically, it was for this campaign, subsequently denounced by a generation of politicians and commentators for its dissembling message on rearmament, that Baldwin earned the sincerest plaudits of party activists.

But Baldwin's contribution alone does not explain why, in the final analysis, the election must be regarded a rare triumph for the party more widely. The government won 429 seats, of which 387 were Conservative, and succeeded in defending its majority to the extent that fewer seats changed hands than in any other election between the wars. Such a degree of electoral survival owed much to the scale of the swing in the Conservatives' favour at the previous general election. Despite the large swings against them in Dunbartonshire (13.3), Leeds West (8.9), Liverpool East Toxteth (15.4), and Stockton (12.7) – as well as in neighbouring seats such as Bradford East (25.8), Liverpool West Derby

---

[124] Williamson, *Stanley Baldwin*, 85, 355–6; J. Lawrence, *Electing our masters: the hustings in British politics from Hogarth to Blair* (Oxford, 2009), 97–8.

[125] See Chapter 5.

[126] *Neville Chamberlain diary letters, vol. 4*, ed. R. Self, 159 (to Hilda, 9–10 Nov. 1935).

(19.6), and Liverpool Wavertree (19.4) – the party secured a majority of votes in each. But even so, the party was not some passive beneficiary of the legacy of 1931 and must be credited with having constructed a compelling platform, of sufficient appeal nationally and locally, to retain a preponderance of those voters who rallied round the government in its first months. As the primary architects of the government's narratives of recovery and relief, the Conservatives skilfully exploited the opportunities of membership and did so to greater effect than their Liberal National and National Labour partners. MacDonald was defeated in Seaham while Simon was returned by just 642 votes; compared to the Conservatives, both parties sustained steeper swings to Labour.[127]

As the chapters in Part II make clear, the topicality of foreign affairs did not fundamentally alter the salience of domestic issues for Conservative activists, or their perception of voters' interests. 'In spite of the shadow of Hitler', wrote one agent, 'the war is still against Socialism', and the armoury remained that of domestic policy.[128] If the Peace Ballot and the Abyssinian crisis demanded a moralistic appeal to stave off a radical resurgence, it was to the more plebeian narrative of national economic recovery that local Conservatives turned for a positive appeal on behalf of the National government. Baldwin himself assured voters that he would not allow defence policy to 'divert [the government] from its programme of continuing to improve the conditions of life for our people'. He asked voters to reflect on the government's record. 'Cast your minds back to 1931', he told them, to when the achievements of recovery – a balanced budget, the creation of more than a million jobs, the restoration of cuts – would have appeared hopelessly fanciful had they been promised.[129] But the party's standard bearer in this effort was Neville Chamberlain. In election rallies nationwide and on the radio, he emphasised the government's record of industrial expansion leading to employment, citing 40,000 additional jobs since September. In a rejoinder to charges of government obstinacy on the economy, he argued that ministers and 'expert staff' in Whitehall had already succeeded in turning policy ideals, including Lloyd George's notion of 'public works', into practicable and 'definite plans' yielding measurable results. The million houses built under their stewardship of the economy, and the £30,000,000 directly invested in London Transport, generated 'employment far beyond the boundaries of London'. Economic recovery and the consequent

---

[127] In straight contests between Labour and Liberal Nationals, there was a nationwide swing to Labour of 11 per cent; in straight contests between Labour and National Labour, the swing to Labour was 16.8 per cent. See T. Stannage, *Baldwin thwarts the opposition: the British general election of 1935* (1980), 231.
[128] *CAJ*, Jul. 1935, 166.   [129] *The Times*, 26 Oct. 1935.

improvement in employment levels and living standards rested on a 'continuous policy', among the next instalment of which was to be a five-year plan to build and improve roads at a cost of £100,000,000 to the government.[130]

Such pronouncements were intended to exemplify stability, accomplishment, and dynamic policymaking as the quintessence of modern Conservative government. As such, the national campaign served the needs of constituency activists very effectively, reinforcing their support for the National government. This support rested not just on the kind of electoral calculations commonplace in coalition situations – the kind that saw cross-party cooperation as a means of manipulating party allegiances, of ensuring that Labour and Liberal voters segued in MacDonald's or Simon's footsteps towards the Conservatives. Crucially, it rested on the fact that the rehabilitation of popular Conservatism in the constituencies relied principally upon the politics of recovery, which enabled the party to project a more coherent ideal of Conservative governance than had proven possible since the advent of adult suffrage, coupling progressive competence in national administration with popular material appeals locally. Depictions of the people and their regions in the 1930s, though often borne of radicalism and soon to be commanded by the wartime left, for the time being belonged just as much to the National government and the popular and collective experience of recovery.

[130] *The Times*, 4 Nov. 1935.

Part II

Popular Conservatism and the National Government

4 Anti-Socialism and Working-Class Conservatism in the Industrial North

The great advance of Labour is in the industrial districts. This is merely a continuation of a process which has been going on for years. We have seen it for instance in Birmingham where the Socialist vote has increased at every election since 1918. This advance has been assisted materially by the fact that other parties have been in office all the time except for the brief interlude in 1924. The politicians & agitators, working on the most ignorant & credulous section of the people, have had an easy task in attributing the troubles & difficulties of the post war period to the Govt which they have always represented as a class Govt with a bias against working people ... I see no way of stopping this Labour advance except such a dose of Labour Government as will in turn disappoint and antagonise its supporters.

> (Neville Chamberlain, following the 1929 general election).[1]

Stockton-on-Tees was my next stop ... grass-grown shipyards and workshops with grimy broken windows, and middle-aged men who look like old men, sucking their empty pipes and staring at nothing, and grey-faced women remembering new clothes and good meals and holidays and fun as if they had once lived in another and better world ... [Shipbuilding] was all a highly specialised industry. You cannot build motor-cars in a shipyard, or make safety-razor blades in a marine engineering shop. For such a place as Stockton the game was up.

> (J.B. Priestley on his visit to Stockton during the autumn of 1933).[2]

Historians and 'Working-Class' Politics between the Wars

As Harold Macmillan stood for re-election in Teesside in 1935, he noted nervously that 'the electors of Stockton-on-Tees (and I shall not blame them, since nearly half of them are out of work) may relieve me by electing

---

[1] *The Neville Chamberlain diary letters, vol. 3: the heir apparent, 1928–1933*, ed. R. Self (Aldershot, 2002), 142–3 (to Ida, 2 Jun. 1929).

[2] J. B. Priestley, *English journey* (London, 1934; 1994 edn), 340, 342, 345.

104   Popular Conservatism and the National Government

my opponent'.[3] Notwithstanding the polite humility of his message, Macmillan was acutely aware of the depression that still engulfed the industrial districts of the north, and like many others in his party he reflected with some incredulity on the Conservatives' electoral buoyancy under the National government at this time. Measures of protection and imperial preference passed by the government in 1932 had been celebrated as climactic achievements by Conservatives in Birmingham and widely welcomed by business interests.[4] Yet the same tariffs were seized by opponents as evidence of the capitalist self-interest motivating Conservative membership of the government. Meanwhile, Conservatives were no longer able to counter such charges with the Tory Democratic rhetoric of social reform, since the fundamental purpose of replacing Labour in office in 1931 had been to administer cuts in public expenditure. The 1930s, then, were regarded as unpromising years for the Conservatives in working-class areas, when of necessity the reform agenda envisaged by Neville Chamberlain in the 1920s appeared destined to be displaced by the unpopular culture of the Means Test.

This chapter investigates the impact of 1931 on Conservative politics in urban, industrial, predominantly working-class constituencies. Stockton and Leeds West loom large in the telling, though as only two instances of the successful and surprising wider rehabilitation of working-class Conservatism under the National government. This was by no means a phenomenon witnessed across industrial Britain, a point amply demonstrated when Labour recovered many of its traditional strongholds at the 1935 election. Indeed, the Labour threat was everywhere present, and, together with the slow pace of industrial recovery, presented Conservative activists with formidable challenges amidst the new opportunities of the National government.

The National government continues to play an important role in how historians conceptualise ideas of working-class identity in twentieth-century Britain. In his analysis of the literary landscape of the 1930s, Valentine Cunningham concluded that, although some of the more astute contemporary authors recognised the mid-decade boom and criticised the selectiveness of George Orwell's evidence of a 'nation' unemployed, a sense of crisis and despondency formed 'the constant background and foreground' of their work.[5] The same despair was evident in the working-

---

[3] Macmillan to Mrs E. Roberts, 15 Oct. 1935, Bodleian Library, Macmillan papers, c.97/238.

[4] K. W. D. Rolf, 'Tories, tariffs and elections: the West Midlands in English politics, 1918–1935' (PhD thesis, University of Cambridge, 1975); A. Marrison, *British business and protection, 1903–1932* (Oxford, 1996).

[5] V. Cunningham, *British writers of the thirties* (Oxford, 1988), 36.

Working-Class Conservatism in the Industrial North   105

class autobiographies of the time. These, as Chris Hilliard has recently shown, proliferated through left-wing organisations such as the Left Book Club and were designed to provide 'authentic' accounts of life in the factory and on the dole.[6] Other historians have argued that the experiences they describe, of life during Britain's last period of prolonged impoverishment, became integral to notions of post-war social democracy in much the same way as they continued to inform nostalgic narratives of working-class solidarity up to the 1970s and 1980s.[7]

Yet heightened class expression did not help Labour recover the ground lost to the Conservatives in 1931. The general election of 1935 saw a modest swing back to Labour nationwide, and in 1934 the party won its first majority on the London City Council,[8] but overall there was no electoral recovery on the Left to match the proletarian character of many of the iconic images of 1930s politics in Britain, most notably the hunger marches. Marxist historians have blamed Labour's gradualist culture for this; the ravages of unemployment, they argued, had awakened the masses from the apathy of the 1920s, but the Labour leadership (even outside the National government under men like Arthur Henderson and Clement Attlee) stuck misguidedly to pre-1914 definitions of progressivism and thereby forfeited the chance to lead a revolutionary agenda.[9] Accepting the party's adherence to 'parliamentarianism', Ben Pimlott famously argued that Labour's failure lay in missing the opportunity to lead a progressive initiative with the aid of disenchanted Liberals.[10] Since the 1970s' heyday of Marxist and counter-Marxist history, however, historians less credulous of sociological explanations of political behaviour have investigated more systematically what actions the Labour organisation took in reaction to both lessons learnt in the 1920s and from the defeat of 1931. According to these accounts, Labour's turn to economic planning and mass-media communications

---

[6] C. Hilliard, *To exercise our talents: the democratization of writing in Britain* (Cambridge, MA, 2006), ch.4.

[7] J. Vernon, *Hunger: a modern history* (Cambridge, MA, 2007), ch.8; C. Waters, 'Autobiography, nostalgia, and the changing practices of working-class selfhood', in G. K. Behlmer & F. M. Leventhal (eds.), *Singular continuities: tradition, nostalgia, and society in modern Britain* (Stanford, 2000), 178–95.

[8] T. Stannage, *Baldwin thwarts the opposition: the British general election of 1935* (London, 1980), 233–4; K. Young, *Local politics and the rise of party: the London Municipal Society and the Conservative intervention in local elections, 1894–1963* (Leicester, 1975), 140–2.

[9] For the classic account see R. Miliband, *Parliamentary socialism: a study in the politics of Labour* (London, 1961). Also D. Coates, *The Labour party and the struggle for socialism* (Cambridge, 1975); S. Macintyre, 'British Labour, Marxism and working class apathy in the nineteen twenties', *HJ*, 20 (1977), 479–96.

[10] B. Pimlott, *Labour and the left in the 1930s* (Cambridge, 1977).

106   Popular Conservatism and the National Government

makes the 1930s seem less a period of failure for the party and more one of deferred success, the fruits of which were only fully realised in 1945.[11]

What renders accounts of Labour's travails in the 1930s still incomplete is the lack of attention paid to how far Conservatives, by their own appeal to the working classes, frustrated Labour's recovery in the industrial areas. When attention is paid to the active role of figures like Macmillan and Hugh Molson in the development of Keynesian economics and industrial planning, then as 'progressives' they are portrayed as too idiosyncratic and dissenting to offer broader insights into Conservative party opinion.[12] Similarly, new civic initiatives to educate the unemployed in the 'proper' use of 'enforced leisure', despite sharing the same ideals of responsible citizenship as Central Office, apparently failed to engage local associations. By the 1930s, argues Jonathan Bates, local party activists were reluctant to brave the populous new estates that formed the focus of such educational initiatives, partly because of the occasional spot of violence but also because affordable means of mass entertainment had served to erode the effectiveness of public politicking among the working classes.[13]

This chapter shows how Conservatives in depressed industrial regions did in fact succeed in constructing a distinctive working-class appeal in the 1930s. This was unexpected given how unfeasible it was for Conservatives to pursue a collectivist welfare discourse in the context of 1931. Yet it demonstrates very starkly how local parties consciously exploited the opportunities created by membership of the National government. They did so first at the 1931 election, by asserting a reworked version of anti-socialism among working-class voters; then, in relation to relief campaigns among the unemployed, by seeking to rehabilitate a conspicuous Conservative presence in working-class communities; and ultimately, in 1935, by embracing the government's cross-party example to advocate a programme of economic reconstruction that was both in

---

[11] R. Toye, *The Labour party and the planned economy, 1931–51* (Woodbridge, 2003); M. Pugh, 'The *Daily Mirror* and the revival of Labour, 1935–45', *TCBH*, 9 (1998), 420–38; L. Beers, *Your Britain: media and the making of the Labour party* (Cambridge, MA, 2009), ch.8.

[12] E.g., D. Ritschel, *The politics of planning: the debate on economic planning in Britain in the 1930s* (Oxford, 1997), 244–8, 264, 342–3; E. H. H. Green, 'The Conservative party and Keynes', in Green and D. Tanner (eds.), *The strange survival of Liberal England: political leaders, moral values and the reception of economic debate* (Cambridge, 2007), 186–211.

[13] A. Olechnowicz, 'Unemployed workers, "enforced leisure" and education for "the right use of leisure" in Britain in the 1930s', *LHR*, 70 (2005), 27–52; J. W. B. Bates, 'The Conservative party in the constituencies, 1918–1939' (DPhil thesis, University of Oxford, 1994), ch.8.

Working-Class Conservatism in the Industrial North 107

keeping with reformist Conservatism and capable of retaining erstwhile Liberal and Labour voters.

The 1931 General Election and the Industrial Worker: Redefining the Socialist Threat

For a generation of Labour activists, their party's electoral downfall in 1931 provided a signal lesson in the consequences of class betrayal. This was despite the fact that signs of popular disillusionment among voters were evident before MacDonald's act of 'betrayal', as shown by municipal and parliamentary by-election results since 1929.[14] For the Conservatives, '1931' proved a critical moment, less for any electoral realignment it proffered than for the opportunities it presented to redefine the threat of socialism and thereby rehabilitate a culture of popular working-class Conservatism among the industrial electorate. At first, it may have seemed impolitic to support a National government whose aim was to administer stringent economies. But Conservatives soon recognised that the financial crisis, together with the onerous task of restoring the national finances, might be put to good use on the public platform. Their task, according to one agent, was 'to relate it in the public mind to the late Socialist Government'.[15] In doing so, the 1931 campaign offered a concerted and newly minted anti-socialist discourse around which to mobilise working-class votes. Programmatic promises and reformist policies were obviously implausible alongside the financial imperatives of the National government; instead, a powerful narrative of '1931' was constructed, drawing attention to the lived consequences of Labour's financial crisis as well as the alleged political cowardice of the ministers who had fled the scene.

The Conservatives' new anti-socialist argument was highly contingent upon the political 'crisis' of 1931. Voters in Stockton were assured that there had been no conspiracy against the Labour government. 'It was not beaten in the House of Commons', Macmillan explained, 'but suddenly collapsed like a house of cards'.[16] Nor was the so-called 'Tory take-over' a charge that Conservatives always disputed, since it served a narrative

---

[14] J. Lawrence, 'Labour – the myths it has lived by', in D. Tanner, P. Thane & N. Tiratsoo (eds.), *Labour's first century* (Cambridge, 2000), 341–66. Cf. S. Davies & B. Morley, 'The reactions of municipal voters in Yorkshire to the second Labour government, 1929–32', in M. Worley (ed.), *Labour's grass roots: essays on the activities and experiences of local Labour parties and members, 1918–1945* (Aldershot, 2005), 124–46; T. Griffiths, *The Lancashire working classes, c.1880–1930* (Oxford, 2001), 308–13; M. Worley, *Labour inside the gate: a history of the British Labour party between the wars* (London, 2005), 141–2; A. Thorpe, *The British general election of 1931* (Oxford, 1991), ch.1.

[15] *CAJ*, Oct. 1931, 240. [16] *Darlington & Stockton Times*, 24 Oct. 1931.

108   Popular Conservatism and the National Government

that conveyed the events of August 1931 as a great rescue act on behalf of the nation. 'Like firemen summoned to a blazing fire' – that was how Macmillan explained the situation in his election address.[17] Labour's self-destruction remained a key theme throughout the election campaign and beyond because, although contingent on events in Westminster and Whitehall, it proved malleable for candidates on the stump. One constituency agent encouraged his colleagues to embellish accounts of the 'crisis' with stories of what would have happened without the intervention of the Conservatives, and to portray the new government as a deliverance that came 'just in time, and only just in time'.[18] In this way, the campaign marked a subtle but important shift away from the sensationalist anti-socialism of the 1920s, according to which Labour posed an existential threat not just to property but even the verities of political freedom, Christian faith, and the family. Now there emerged a more mundane but ultimately more potent critique of Labour's competence to govern.

While Conservatives nationwide highlighted Labour's abdication of power as proof of the party's failure to govern, those in industrial areas emphasised the material consequences of this for working-class voters. Vyvyan Adams implored the people of Leeds West to remember that 'In 1929 the Labour party won its way to office after giving "an unqualified pledge to deal immediately and practically with unemployment"'. Yet 'the Unemployed to-day', he continued, 'total one million and three-quarters more than when the Labour Party took office'. He pledged himself to a policy of scientific tariffs, for four main reasons: to halt the 'flood of Free Imports', expand employment in protected home markets, generate revenue for the exchequer, and enhance British industry's bargaining power worldwide.[19] The same arguments were inevitably made in Birmingham, the spiritual home of protectionism, where the party commissioned a 'Dumping Van' to tour the divisions with displays of 'dumped' foreign goods.[20] But they also formed the core of Florence Horsbrugh's campaign in Dundee. She declared that all other matters – including the long-standing issue of local preference – were mere 'detail' when compared with the tariffs needed to protect jobs. 'During the first six months of this year 14 million square yards of jute piece goods had been imported from Belgium and Czecho-Slovakia', Horsbrugh told one election rally. 'If that work had been done in Dundee we should have had two, if not three, local mills working full-time.'[21]

---

[17] Election address, Oct. 1931, Macmillan papers, c.141/64.
[18] *CAJ*, Sep. 1931, 223–5.
[19] Election address, Oct. 1931, London School of Economics Library, Archives Division, Adams papers, 2/2.
[20] *Birmingham Post*, 5 Oct. 1931.   [21] *Dundee Courier*, 16, 21 Oct. 1931.

Working-Class Conservatism in the Industrial North   109

Not only were more families without work than in 1929; according to Conservatives, the ability of those with jobs to survive was also diminished as a result of Labour's mismanagement of the economy. Macmillan argued that high inflation under Labour provided the root cause of the recent 'reduction' in workers' wages, the 'robbing' of pensions, and the 'wiping out' of household savings. It also had the effect of 'destroying' the assets of 'every Trade Union, Building Society, and Friendly Society'. For this reason he claimed that 'I don't want to reduce the dole'. A cut to the dole was not the intended objective of the National government, he insisted, but rather a policy that it reluctantly implemented to stave off imminent national bankruptcy.[22] Conservatives were quick to point out, as Adams did, that the Labour cabinet had 'agreed to nine-tenths of the economies', before 'escaping from responsibility and posing as the champions of the Unemployed'. It was therefore the National government's responsibility to 'improve and maintain the standard of living of the Workers', through the revival of trade and the judicious administration of public policy. To this end Horsbrugh stated that selective protection would guarantee the supply of cheap food. Macmillan pointed out that Labour's cabinet had envisaged a deeper cut in public-sector wages than that enforced by the National government's emergency budget.[23]

This re-branded anti-socialism, though rooted in the seemingly incontrovertible fact of Labour's fall from government, carried risks. In County Durham, according to a regional editorial, 'the Socialists have gone some way towards fostering the belief that their position is impregnable'.[24] It was testament to how strongly Labour had entrenched itself within many mining and industrial communities that even in the unique circumstances of 1931 the Conservatives sensed how an anti-socialist onslaught might alienate as much as rally the working class. For this reason, upon the formation of the National government, the prospective candidate in Darlington, Charles Peat, told voters that 'he did not think that the failure of the last Government was indicative of the failure of the working men and women to govern'. 'The people I would strike, and strike hard', he said, 'are those who pretend to lead the working classes but lead them only from one morass in to another'.[25] In addition to the charge of incompetence, Labour was now accused of having insulted the loyalty and intelligence of its working-class voters. Publicly and privately, Conservatives claimed that the ignominious decline of the socialist government would encourage the masses to reappraise their opinion of

---

[22] Election address, Oct. 1931, Macmillan papers, c.141/62–3.
[23] Election address, Oct. 1931, Adams papers, 2/2; *Dundee Courier*, 16 Oct. 1931; election address, Oct. 1931, Macmillan papers, c.141/68.
[24] *Darlington & Stockton Times*, 24 Oct. 1931.   [25] Ibid., 29 Aug. 1931.

110   Popular Conservatism and the National Government

Labour. Mrs. Fyfe, a women's organiser for the Northern Area, confidently proclaimed to one of her audiences that 'the Socialists who are against this [National] Government will not get the support they expect from the working man or his wife who sits down to think things out'.[26]

Indeed, the Conservatives sought to align themselves with the figure of the independent-minded working man, whose political and personal integrity they claimed was restored by the collapse of Labour. The populist Conservative paper, the *Yorkshire Evening Post*, described Labour attitudes to the workers as 'pawns on the political chess-board'. 'They are shedding crocodile tears now over the slight reduction in [unemployment] benefit ... They hope, evidently, that that will engender one of those "mass movements".' The paper valorised 'those honest folk' who prioritised the search for work in contrast to the 'small minority' for whom the 'dole' was a misplaced article of faith instilled in them by a Labour party intent on exploiting the plight of the unemployed.[27] Horsbrugh argued that if she were married to an unemployed man, she would vote for work under the National government instead of 'living on the dole' under Labour. The majority of workers, she said, 'are men with a sense of responsibility', who as citizens could be trusted to face up to the 'unpleasant truths' about the need for economies and as breadwinners could be relied upon to earn the wellbeing of their families.[28]

In this way the campaign saw the Conservatives forging a particular depiction of the 'good' worker. This differed subtly from McKibbin's famous argument, in which the working-class Conservative voter stood outside the trade union movement and shared his commitment to constitutional government with the Conservative-voting middle-class property holder.[29] Workers were now told that they belonged to either one of two conflicting forces at work within the Labour party – 'the builders' or 'the wreckers'. The 'builders' were led by Ramsay MacDonald, Philip Snowden and J.H. Thomas, a trio who had the courage to recognise, as Macmillan put it, when 'something more important than the interests of a party was at stake'.[30] Conservatives talked up MacDonald's credentials as the founding father of British Labourism. They also saluted his 'common sense' and business-like approach to the crisis. Coming from the Conservatives, this line of appeal was not certain to work, bearing in mind

---

[26] *Darlington & Stockton Times*, 29 Aug. 1931; also *CAJ*, Oct. 1931, 240.

[27] *Yorkshire Evening Post* editorial, 7 Oct. 1931.

[28] *Dundee Evening Telegraph*, 23 Oct. 1931; *Yorkshire Evening Post* editorials, 15, 19 Oct. 1931.

[29] R. McKibbin, 'Class and conventional wisdom: the Conservative party and the "public" in interwar Britain', in *The ideologies of class: social relations in Britain, 1880–1950* (Oxford, 1990), 259–93.

[30] Election address, 1931, Macmillan papers, c.141/61–5.

that all three Labour figures were well-known for ingratiating themselves to both high society and the political establishment.[31] However, Snowden's national broadcast on 17 October proved a turning point in the Conservatives' use of the figure of the Labour 'builder'. Reported in full in the national press, and commented upon in the local and regional press, the speech by Labour's only Chancellor of the Exchequer confirmed Conservative claims that the late government had indeed recognised the need for economies.[32] This rationalised the otherwise contradictory attempts by Conservatives to pursue an anti-socialist rhetoric while valorising the actions of the MacDonaldite wing of Labour, shifting the balance of authority to 'patriotic' Labour and revealing the duplicity of the 'wreckers'. In light of Snowden's account, the *Darlington & Stockton Times* asked voters to consider the simple question: 'What reliance can be placed on men who profess indignation at the adoption of means which they themselves suggested?'[33]

The purpose of aligning the common worker with the actions of MacDonald and the Labour 'builders', then, was to strip anti-socialist discourse of the trumped-up claims that defined it during the 1920s. This enabled Conservatives to escape the prevailing middle-class definitions of anti-socialism and to claim it as a mark of straightforward plebeian wisdom. Anticipating the sacrifices that would have to be borne by the workers, Horsbrugh invoked the spirit of war. 'We have got to have something of the spirit of 1914 – not staying to count what the sacrifice might be, but making every effort to join in that sacrifice.' Conservative voices elsewhere adopted similar imagery. The *Yorkshire Evening Post* described the economic crisis as a 'parallel emergency' to the war.[34] Remarkably, MacDonald, vilified as the most prominent advocate of a negotiated peace in the First World War, emerged as the most decorated combatant of this war – 'a kind of national hero', according to Headlam[35] – in contrast to Arthur Henderson and other Labour ministers who 'ratted'. One of the most popular posters used by the Conservatives during the campaign was a portrait picture of MacDonald with the slogan: 'The captain who stuck to the ship.' In Birmingham this poster was trailed in banner form behind an aeroplane hired by the Conservative organisation to shower the constituencies with leaflets.[36] The same slogan

---

[31] See N. Owen, 'MacDonald's parties: the Labour party and the "aristocratic embrace", 1922–31', *TCBH*, 18 (2007), 1–53.
[32] *The Times*, 19 Oct. 1931; *Birmingham Post*, 19 Oct. 1931.
[33] *Darlington & Stockton Times*, 24 Oct. 1931.
[34] *Dundee Courier*, 22 Sep. 1931; *Yorkshire Evening Post*, 16 Oct. 1931.
[35] *Parliament and politics in the age of Baldwin and MacDonald: the Headlam diaries, 1923–1935*, ed. S. Ball (London, 1992), 227 (22 Dec. 1931).
[36] *Yorkshire Evening Post*, 6, 8, 15 Oct. 1931; *Birmingham Post*, 15 Oct. 1931.

112 Popular Conservatism and the National Government

became commonplace in platform speeches. Addressing a mass rally in Stockton, Lady Londonderry argued that 'it was just as grave a crisis now ... as in the days of the war', which is why she urged voters to have 'more faith in the common sense of the citizens of this country than in the advice of the men who deserted the ship'. 'It will be a bad day for England if you return a deserter as the Prime Minister.'[37] The precise effect of this patriotic appeal is impossible to tell. But undoubtedly the election campaign lent itself readily to the demotic populism believed by activists to have become muted during the 1920s. Following the election, however, few of these Conservatives expected to find lasting popularity in the politics of sacrifice. Instead, they sought their own share in the government's much-vaunted economic recovery.

In Search of the Recovery

Soon after the general election, the chief agent in Leeds urged his colleagues nationwide to heed what he described as one of the 'eternal truths' of politics, namely that a government 'begins to shed its strength the day it is born'. This, he argued, applied to the National government just as to a party government.[38] Having concentrated their election rhetoric to such an extent on valorising patriotic Labour, it was now unclear to what degree Conservatives in the industrial districts could proclaim their victory a Conservative one. While many workers had voted Conservative for the first time, public displays of party triumph were rare. Across the boundary from Leeds West, in Batley and Morley, where the party won its first parliamentary election, the party president pledged to look after the interests of those local Liberals and 'Socialists' who rallied to the national cause.[39] In County Durham, when the newly elected Conservative MPs came together in January 1932 to hold an anti-socialist mass rally – 'to keep the enthusiasm of the electorate fully aroused' – they did so under the 'non-party' auspices of the Durham Municipal and County Federation.[40] To have claimed that all 'national' voters were converts to Conservatism risked offending the workers' own sense of their political independence at a crucial moment when a working-class commitment to anti-socialism seemed within reach. Yet sensitivity alone was not enough in the industrial districts and the party faced several

---

[37] *Darlington & Stockton Times*, 24 Oct. 1931.   [38] *CAJ*, Dec. 1931, 269.
[39] *Yorkshire Post*, 11 Jul. 1932.
[40] R. C. Cherry (Sec. Durham Municipal & County Fed.) to Macmillan, 30 Dec. 1931, Macmillan papers, c.68/55–6. More than 500 people attended the rally: *Sunderland Echo & Shipping Gazette*, 1 Feb. 1932.

challenges as it sought to consolidate its electoral gains among erstwhile Labour and Liberal voters.

It was tariffs, the main fruit of the National government's election victory, that most jeopardised the party's relationship with local Labour and Liberal supporters. While Birmingham celebrated the Import Duties Act of 1932, together with the Ottawa imperial agreements, popular free-trade sensibilities called for circumspection elsewhere. Anticipating this, the Conservative party in Stockton arranged a meeting with Liberal organisers 'with a view to amalgamating and forming a National Party', but expected several of those invited to 'jib' at the idea.[41] Similarly in West Yorkshire, 'the general view was that it was still essential to maintain the National character of the Government ... [as] there was a large body of opinion, not definitely Conservative, which should still rally to our support'; however, the area organisers noted that local Liberals, despite their recent cooperation, 'were definitely against us' in the aftermath of Ottawa, and consequently 'there [was] not much possibility of joint action in the future between Conservative and Liberals'.[42] With this in mind the Conservatives once more sought to present protection not as an end in itself but as a 'scientific' policy that enabled the government to serve the particular needs of regional economies by delivering industrial recovery through trade. Within a protected economy, Conservative MPs presented themselves as lobbyists on behalf of voters' interests. Adams led the efforts to increase textile duties on behalf of the mill workers of the West Riding, and Horsbrugh, in a more populist move, disclosed to her Dundee constituents that her parliamentary office was adorned with a jute rug 'as a constant reminder of the needs of the constituency she represents'.[43] In turn party activists, in pursuit of propaganda material, sought 'definite instances ... of local benefit from tariffs'.[44] Such a narrative of recovery through scientific tariffs formed the Conservatives' central plank at the by-election held in Dunbartonshire in March 1932. The Conservative candidate, Commander Archibald Cochrane, stood on the slogans 'You Did in October, Do it Again in March' and 'Fair Play for the Workers'. He was duly elected, but with twelve thousand fewer votes than his predecessor, which contemporary

---

[41] Macmillan to Cowap, 15 Dec. 1931, Cowap to Macmillan, 21 Dec. 1931, Macmillan papers, c.67/112–13, 111.
[42] Advisory committee, 3 Dec. 1932, West Yorkshire Archive Service, Yorkshire Area, WYL529/3.
[43] *Yorkshire Evening Post*, 30 Apr., 1 Jun. 1932; *Dundee Courier*, 4 Apr. 1932.
[44] Advisory committee, 3 Dec. 1932, Yorkshire Area 3, WYL529/3.

114 Popular Conservatism and the National Government

observers in the press attributed to the instructions issued to voters by the local Liberal party to support the free-trade Labour candidate.[45]

Conservatives also came to see that Labour's capacity for popular agitation among the working classes had received something of a boost following the election. It soon became apparent in Stockton, for instance, that many defeated MPs, 'let loose' from parliamentary duties, would set out to 'belittle the work of the National Government'.[46] Once more the cooperative societies became the focus of Conservative fears that non-party organisations were being infiltrated by Labour organisers for 'covert canvassing'; so too were movements like the League of Nations Union and the Townswomen's Guild.[47] The chief subject of Labour-led opposition was the means test.[48] Controversy over the means test stemmed variously from the sense of intrusion experienced by families whose income was subjected to the officious attention of inspectors; the assault on ideas of working-class respectability that stemmed from inherited assumptions about the 'undeserving poor'; and the pressure it placed on families as the existence of one earner (e.g., the son) effectively disqualified the applicant (e.g., the father). Given that the dispensers of relief, the PACs, were composed mainly of Labour representatives, it was impossible for Conservatives to escape opprobrium in industrial districts. Although some felt that it was not the unemployed but the Labour party who objected to the means test,[49] it was damaging all the same. It brought to the fore a source of tension between local and national government, and according to Conservative fears created a framework in which Labour, by calling for the test's abolition, could legitimately use bribery in municipal elections.[50] In Stockton, where in early 1932 the number of unemployed (approximately twelve thousand) exceeded Macmillan's majority, the electoral consequences were potentially devastating.[51]

---

[45] *The Scotsman*, 18, 19 Mar. 1932.
[46] Labour advisory committee, 10 Dec. 1931, 29 Jan. 1932, STCO, Durham Record Office, D/X 322/6.
[47] Council AGM, 25 Feb. 1933, council meeting, 14 Sep. 1935, Northern Counties Area, NRO 3303/2; women's advisory council, 8 Jun. 1932, Northern Counties Area, Northumberland Collections Service, NRO 4137/8; report of group advisory council meetings, Dec. 1933, Yorkshire Area 3, WYL529/3.
[48] Introduced in November 1931, this test of household income applied to unemployed applicants who, having exhausted their unemployment insurance benefit, sought transitional payments on the same basis as un-insured workers seeking public assistance. These payments were administered locally and on a discretionary basis by Public Assistance Committees, successors to the Boards of Guardians that distributed relief under the poor law, in accordance with relief scales set by central government.
[49] Women's advisory council, 13 Jun. 1933, Northern Counties Area, NRO 4137/8.
[50] *Neville Chamberlain diary letters, vol. 3*, 408 (to Ida, 28 Oct. 1933).
[51] Labour advisory committee, 14 Jan. 1932, STCO, D/X 322/6.

It became clear within the first year of the National government that Conservatives would struggle to establish a narrative of recovery in the industrial regions. Even where such a narrative could be backed with empirical evidence of trade recovery, as in Wakefield, where by the time a by-election was held in April 1932 employment had grown in response to rising exports, the Conservatives were vulnerable.[52] This was the first contest since the general election 'in which the industrial North has had a voice', declared the *Yorkshire Post*. Despite the Liberal party's non-intervention, the Conservative majority of over four thousand was over-turned by Labour's candidate, Arthur Greenwood, the former Minister of Health. Discontent with the means test played its part, even though Greenwood's opponents tried to implicate him in a similar means test said to have been considered by the previous Labour government.[53] Added to this, in its first budget since the election, held two days before the by-election, the government undermined Conservative efforts in the industrial regions by its failure to reduce the duty on beer. In a speech to Conservative women organisers at the Royal Albert Hall, Baldwin was forced to admit that 'beer lost the Wakefield election'. The measure proved very unpopular among the party grassroots, who viewed it as a 'penal duty' stemming from Liberal faddism within the cabinet.[54] Whatever the reason, it gave Labour the opportunity to further position itself as the guardian of working-class life, this time in populist defence of a staple of working men's leisure, while simultaneously pressing home to local Conservatives how far the message of patriotic austerity that played so well in the general election campaign had receded in the public imagination.

Labour continued to make gains in municipal politics up to the 1935 general election. County Durham remained in Labour control through-out the period, with twenty eight of its forty districts controlled by Labour by 1936. In 1933 Labour won control of twenty-five towns and cities, including seven boroughs for the first time, and made a net gain of 206 council seats in England and Wales. The Conservatives lost 112. Labour also regained Leeds, along with several other Yorkshire boroughs includ-ing Sheffield, Barnsley, Hull, and Rotherham. It also made considerable electoral advances in most boroughs in Merseyside and Lancashire.[55] In that same year Glasgow fell out of anti-socialist control, signalling a major breach of one of the most successful and concerted 'Moderate' (anti-socialist) coalitions to have emerged in municipal politics since the war.

---

[52] *Yorkshire Post*, 7, 18 Apr. 1932.   [53] Ibid., 21, 12 Apr. 1932.
[54] *The Times*, 30 Apr. 1932; council AGM, 25 Feb. 1933, Northern Counties Area, NRO 3303/2.
[55] *The Times*, 2, 3 Nov. 1933.

116   Popular Conservatism and the National Government

A study of one such coalition attributes its downfall, among other local factors, to popular protest among both the middle classes, in response to high rates, and the working classes, in pursuit of more generous municipal provision of the dole and of housing. Middle-class ratepayers soon returned to the anti-socialist fold, but the working classes' switch to Labour proved more permanent.[56] *The Times* tried to make sense of Labour's gains. 'There can be no doubt', it concluded, that 'whereas in 1931 the results of local extravagance were visible to all alike, in 1933 the results of the termination of extravagance were more apparent than the dangers of its resumption.'[57]

Conservatives in the industrial regions faced at least three consequences. The first was renewed reluctance on the part of 'known' supporters to present themselves in public as opponents of Labour. This was manifested in part through a self-fulfilling apathy among anti-socialists in local elections. These were the precise voters, *The Times* reckoned, whose 'indifference' had given Labour control of many boroughs and a foothold in others. In one Labour mainstay, County Durham, Cuthbert Headlam recorded with impatience the 'smaller ratepayers [who] are too frightened to vote against the miners' and also his party's failure to field a candidate in twenty-four council seats.[58] It was also the result of intimidation. In areas where Labour had refused to help with administering the means test, the task fell to councillors of other parties, including Conservatives, who in turn – like Macmillan himself – became the target of demonstrations organised by the National Unemployed Workers Movement. 'It was extremely difficult to get Councillors to undertake this work', noted party organisers in Leeds. 'It involved … considerable unpopularity and in some cases fear of violence.'[59]

The second was the emergence of a north-south divide that came to inform the political imaginary of party activists. As if intending to preempt this problematic divergence, several of Macmillan's speeches to constituents in 1932 focused on his efforts in parliament to attract investment to the north of England. 'An appalling waste of capital was now going on in the creation of new towns rather than the direction of new industries to old towns', he argued.[60] But this was an abstract policy

[56] J. Smyth, 'Resisting Labour: Unionists, Liberals, and Moderates in Glasgow between the wars', *HJ*, 46 (2003), 375–401.
[57] *The Times*, 3 Nov. 1933.
[58] Ibid.; *Headlam diaries, 1923–1935*, 290–1 (20 Jan., 4 Feb. 1934); council AGM, 23 Feb. 1935, Northern Counties Area, NRO 3303/2.
[59] Advisory committee, 3 Dec. 1932, and report of group advisory council meetings, Dec. 1933, Yorkshire Area 3, WYL529/3. For a reported attack on a Leeds councillor, see *Yorkshire Evening Post*, 29 Apr. 1932.
[60] *Darlington & Stockton Times*, 12, 19 Nov. 1932.

proposal; furthermore, it remained unimplemented until the Special Areas reforms over two years later. No matter how much party organisers in Stockton shared in Macmillan's commitment to industrial reorganisation (and they did),[61] they were unlikely to remain immune to the more demotic political references vested in the north-south divide by the mid-1930s, especially as depictions of an urban north bedevilled by unemployment and poverty became commonplace in public discourse. Observing this phenomenon, the Conservative party in Liverpool – traditionally a bastion of working-class Conservatism – extrapolated 'that the date is not far distant when they [Labour] will secure control of the City Council'.[62] Labour's sparse and inconsistent advances in the south only reinforced the fact of its progress in the north.

The third consequence was that Labour found itself in a position to enact municipal reforms that threatened to further entrench its credentials as the party of working-class interests, sometimes obscuring the efforts of the National government. Given the contentiousness of tariffs and the failure of trade-driven recovery to yield immediate electoral credit, Conservatives welcomed the government's decision to regain the initiative with the launch of a slum clearance scheme in the spring of 1933. Macmillan referred to it as an example of the benefits that stemmed from increased tariff revenues.[63] However, because the scheme operated at the level of local government, whose statutory duty it now became to draw housing plans for the next five years, many of the clearance and rehousing schemes were carried out by Labour councils. The rate of council-house building in County Durham increased from around 3,000 in 1933 to 7,000 by 1938, outstripping private building and accounting for over half of all new houses built in Stockton between the wars; in most of these schemes the council used 'direct labour' instead of outside contractors in order to relieve local unemployment.[64] Meanwhile, Leeds's newly elected Labour council embarked on the biggest clearance outside London, one that promised to rehome almost a quarter of the city's population.[65] In Dundee, the anti-socialist 'Moderate' party on the council campaigned on lower rates and lower rents, while the Labour party in opposition became the champions of Dundee's 'Five Year Housing

---

[61] Executive committee, 9 Jun. 1932, STCO, D/X 322/5.

[62] Central council, 11 Apr. 1934, Liverpool Record Office, Liverpool CA, 329 Con/1/1/3.

[63] AGM women's branch, 16 Mar. 1933, STCO, D/X 322/10.

[64] R. Ryder, 'Council house building in County Durham, 1900–39: the local implementation of national policy', in M. Daunton (ed.), *Councillors and tenants: local authority housing in English cities, 1919–1939* (Leicester, 1984), 40–100, esp. 49, 65–8.

[65] R. Finnigan, 'Council housing in Leeds, 1919–1939: social policy and urban change', in Daunton (ed.), *Councillors and tenants*, 102–53, esp. 111–13.

118   Popular Conservatism and the National Government

Plan'. Three years later, Labour took control of the city council.[66] Clearance and rehousing schemes were well-publicised as city corporations increasingly invested in civic advertising and public information campaigns. These practices were by no means confined to Labour councils, as similar campaigns were undertaken in Liverpool, Manchester, and elsewhere, in what one historian has described as the 'apotheosis of the municipal civic publicity movement' that especially flourished in the industrial cities of the north.[67] But there is little doubt that the National government's initiative, championed by the Minister of Health, Sir Hilton Young, lent Labour's municipal campaigns a degree of momentum.

For Conservatives seeking a counter-narrative to Labour's politics in the distressed areas, the National government's reformist credentials initially proved frustratingly elusive. The 'recovery' budget of 1934, which restored the unemployment benefit cuts in full, did little to help. In theory, it was a notable milestone: it restored the cuts on the basis of having balanced the budget. In practice, however, it was a poor rallying cry for a party so comprehensively tarnished by the means test. This was especially true in areas desperate to restore the benefits of employment rather than unemployment benefits, which in many instances were the same areas in which the Gladstonian commitment to retrenchment had held popular sway until very recently, including West Yorkshire and Dundee. The experience of structural unemployment, it seems, did much to destabilise this feature of working-class political thought in the 1930s.

For his part, Chamberlain was aware that his fiscal orthodoxy made others view his approach as 'humdrum, commonplace and unenterprising'. While defending his policy as key to inspiring global confidence in the British economy, he insisted that the government had in fact championed several important reform agendas: in slum clearance and housing, in regional development through the Special Areas programme, and in reforming the administration of unemployment assistance.[68] He called for more extensive publicity on behalf of the government, in part to counteract the fact that the Beaverbrook and Rothermere presses now took a largely hostile view of the government on account of its India policy, though also because he felt that 'whilst people may be aware of

---

[66] *Dundee Courier*, 12, 19, 24, 30 Oct. 1933; also K. Baxter & W. Kenefick, 'Labour politics and the Dundee working class, c.1895–1936', in J. Tomlinson & C. Whatley (eds.), *Jute no more: transforming Dundee* (Dundee, 2011), 191–219.

[67] T. Hulme, '"A nation of town criers": civic publicity and historical pageantry in inter-war Britain', *UH*, 44 (2017), 270–92, 290; C. Wildman, 'Urban transformation in Liverpool and Manchester, 1918–1939', *HJ*, 55 (2012), 119–43.

[68] *The Neville Chamberlain diary letters, vol. 4: the Downing Street years, 1934–40*, ed. R. Self (Aldershot, 2005), 67 (to Hilda, 21 Apr. 1934).

local [reform] schemes, they did not know of what was being done in the country as a whole'.[69] But given the patchy nature of recovery since 1931, national propaganda was not guaranteed to work. As one agent commented after the establishment of the National Publicity Bureau, 'In some districts the poster campaign had given great offence as, for instance, posters in distressed areas showing the improvement in employment.'[70]

No wonder then that Headlam came to the view that, barring another 'crisis' like 1931, working-class voters would desert the National government at the next general election. 'We certainly shan't gain their support for what we have done for them so far', he thought.[71] At the 1935 general election, Labour did indeed regain many mining and industrial constituencies in County Durham, West Yorkshire, and Staffordshire, as well as several seats in the East End of London. But this was by no means a comprehensive recovery. In Liverpool and Leeds, as well as large parts of Lancashire, Tyneside, and central Scotland, the majority of voters backed the National government. So how then did the Conservatives succeed in these areas despite the absence of anything like the conspicuous recovery witnessed in the south?

Relief Amid Depression

The Labour vote increased significantly in many of the constituencies retained by the Conservatives in 1935. This accounts for the reduced majorities in places like Stockton, Leeds, Dunbartonshire and Dundee. These majorities might have been smaller still, or overturned, if not for the intervention of Liberal candidates. Where such an intervention occurred, as it did in Stockton, the effect in 1935 was as likely to be a split in the anti-Conservative as the anti-socialist vote. This was in contrast to the dynamic at work in 1931, when tariffs and other factors were yet to mobilise the Samuelite Liberal party into opposition. Conservative success was therefore fragile, resting in large part on the party's ability to mitigate Labour's hold on working-class communities. Compared to the relentless and effective focus on Labour's failed stewardship of the economy during the initial crisis, the years leading up to the second election now saw Conservatives compete with Labour for presence in working-class communities.

In a series of speeches to party activists in 1933, Chamberlain gloomily forecast no significant reduction in structural unemployment for up to

[69] Management committee, 9 Mar. 1934, Birmingham CUA. [70] *CAJ*, Jun. 1935, 156.
[71] *Headlam diaries, 1923–1935*, ed. S. Ball, 302 (30 Apr. 1934).

120   Popular Conservatism and the National Government

a decade.[72] His focus, therefore, became a concerted campaign to address 'the welfare of the unemployed':

> If we are really going to have unemployment with us in considerable numbers for a long time to come ... then I would like to see measures framed to get as many of these men as possible fit in mind and body to take advantage of any work that may come along. It is not a task that can be performed only by a Government; it is one in which all of us can help ... It seems to me that these unemployed men have a moral claim upon us not only that we should do all we can to stimulate employment, but do everything to preserve their self-respect and find interest in life and occupation in other ways.[73]

It was to this end that the government enrolled the help of the National Council of Social Service and gave it control of financial grants to help invigorate voluntary networks in the country. The result was a proliferation of new club movements organised on the basis of local needs. These 'service clubs' all provided some combination of training in occupational and housekeeping skills; facilities and material for craft work, horticulture, and other activities designed to foster self-sufficiency; recreational and educational programmes; and a modest source of nourishment.[74] As such, they embodied many of the values of active citizenship espoused by Baldwin, who, in a speech to the Institute of Public Administration in 1933, praised the voluntary bodies for what he saw as their ability to assist the unemployed while safeguarding each man's 'nonconformity', 'uniqueness', and 'freedom' in ways that no government could hope to achieve.[75]

The clubs also reflected Conservatives' desire to depoliticise the experience of unemployment. They had long called for the administration of unemployment assistance to be removed from local authorities in order to protect ratepayers and for fear of its manipulation by Labour.[76] This was achieved in 1934 when the Unemployment Act delegated the task to a national statutory body, the Unemployment Assistance Board. But scarcely, in practice, did this tame unemployment relief as a topic of grievance in the depressed areas. To the contrary, in the first months of 1935 the government faced a political crisis precipitated by the board's

---

[72] *The Times*, 22 Feb. 1933 (Edinburgh), 2 Mar. 1933 (Derby); *Neville Chamberlain diary letters, vol. 3*, 380 (to Hilda, 4 Mar. 1933). See also R. Self, *Neville Chamberlain: a biography* (Aldershot, 2006), 202–3; W. Garside, *British unemployment, 1919–1939: a study in public policy* (Cambridge, 1990), 251–2.

[73] *The Times*, 22 Feb. 1933.

[74] See Pilgrim Trust, *Men without work: a report made to the Pilgrim Trust* (Cambridge, 1938), Part V, ch.2; and the 'human interest' accounts of service clubs published in the *ILN*, 26 Nov. 1932 (Liverpool), 1 Apr. 1933 (Glasgow), 15 Apr. 1933 (Dundee).

[75] S. Baldwin, *This torch of freedom: speeches and addresses* (London, 1935), 52–74.

[76] Council meeting, 1 Oct. 1932, Northern Counties Area, NRO 3303/2.

Working-Class Conservatism in the Industrial North   121

revised relief schedules, which if implemented would reduce the benefits going to half of all claimants. Despite the government intervening to urge greater leniency, the reputational price likely to be paid – in an election year, and especially when the 'independent' board was chaired by none other than the former Conservative minister who introduced the necessary legislation only months earlier – appeared great enough to force a climb-down. As a result, the scheme was reworked and its implementation postponed to 1937.[77] Throughout, however, the Ministry of Labour continued to expand its network of occupational centres. These included Juvenile Instruction Centres for those under eighteen years of age, Homecraft Training Centres for women, and a range of Training Centres for men.[78] Although attendance was compulsory for recipients of assistance, the centres were also intended to act as 'clubs' providing similar recreational and social benefits to those pioneered by the NCSS.[79]

Many instances can be cited of Conservative-organised philanthropy in working-class areas in the early 1930s. Some were ad hoc, like the decision to engage unemployed men for odd jobs or to hold recreational events that doubled as thinly veiled opportunities to treat voters. These included a sports club in Leeds, cinema parties in Darlington, and 'smoker parties' and 'pie suppers' in Stockton.[80] Other initiatives called for more sustained organisation. Several schemes were established in collaboration with Conservative volunteers in southern counties, with contributions from the latter used to set up clothing funds as well as dinner clubs for unemployed men and their families in the north. These were not exclusively Conservative, for there is evidence that the National Liberal MP for Bishop Auckland cooperated with an association of social service volunteers in Hertfordshire. But under the patronage of Lady Londonderry and Mrs Headlam, social work of this kind became integral to the work of Conservative female activists. 'It was impossible to separate politics entirely from social work', insisted Mrs Headlam. 'Conservatives must show themselves as interested in the people as their political opponents and must do their best to encourage their members to help in social service'.[81]

---

[77] Garside, *British unemployment*, 74–81.
[78] The latter were dubbed 'state apprenticeships' by party organisers in Stockton (labour advisory committee, 7 Dec. 1933, STCO, D/X 322/6).
[79] R. Lowe, *Adjusting to democracy: the role of the Ministry of Labour in British politics, 1916–1939* (Oxford, 1986), 223–4; R. H. C. Hayburn, 'The Voluntary Occupational Centre movement, 1932–39', *JCH*, 6 (1971), 156–71.
[80] Council meeting, 11 Oct. 1932, Leeds Federation of Junior Conservative Associations, West Yorkshire Archive Service, WYL 529/11; Mrs Winpenny to Macmillan, 4 Jan. 1932, Macmillan papers, c.68/451; men's branch, 15 May 1936, STCO, D/X 322/8; *Darlington & Stockton Times*, 5 Jan. 1935 (Darlington).
[81] *Darlington & Stockton Times*, 5 Jan. 1935; AGM women's advisory council, 5 Feb. 1932, Northumberland Collections Service, Northern Counties Area, NRO 4137/8.

122   Popular Conservatism and the National Government

The Pilgrim Trust report of 1938 found that the 'best remedy' for the isolation experienced by unemployed men was 'the support of already existing institutions'.[82] Notwithstanding the withdrawing effect that unemployment had on many men regardless of the associational life available to them, it was notable that the working-men's clubs, many of them political in affiliation, eschewed the distinction of employed and unemployed. After a period of decline since 1918, the Conservative working-men's clubs experienced something of a renaissance in the mid-1930s.[83] In all, over 1,500 Conservative clubs were fully functioning by 1933, serving half a million members and often cooperating with the non-political Working Men's Club and Institute Union which itself had 2,700 branches by 1935.[84] Liverpool alone had forty-six clubs. In Leeds West there were enough clubs associated with the constituency organisation to occupy the agent on fortnightly visits almost each night of the week. In Stockton, the National Conservative League, already well-established in County Durham, opened several new lodges over the course of 1933–1935. Some of these, like the Macmillan Lodge opened in Thornaby, had clubrooms of their own, while others set up shop in local pubs, including four in the neighbourhood of Tilery alone.[85] Clubs were places in which beer was cheaper than in pubs and each was typically equipped with a billiard table, a darts board, and copies of the popular and sporting press.

They were also deemed crucial for the party 'to keep the flag of Tory democracy flying'.[86] On becoming chairman of the Association of Conservative Clubs in 1933, Lord Bayford launched a nationwide campaign to urge club members to recover the sense of social and political purpose that had defined the movement in its Victorian and Edwardian heyday. He championed the government's Clubs Bill, which promised to restore pre-war privileges including longer opening hours and the right to grant themselves occasional extensions without applying to the magistrates. He urged members 'to make the club the hub' of political life in the constituencies ahead of a future general election at which their task would be to secure a second popular mandate for the National government. The sociability of club life, he suggested, offered a means through which relations between Conservatives and Liberals could be healed after the

[82] Pilgrim Trust, *Men without work*, 289–90.
[83] Cf. S. Ball, *Portrait of a party: the Conservative party in Britain, 1918–1945* (Oxford, 2013), 159–61.
[84] *The Times*, 4 Sep. 1933, 30 Oct. 1935.
[85] D. Caradog Jones, *The social survey of Merseyside, vol. 3* (Liverpool, 1934), 308; executive committee, 3 May 1933, Leeds West CA, WYL529/5; finance committee, 28 Mar. 1934, Stockton CA, D/X 322/5; *Darlington & Stockton Times*, 26 Jan. 1935.
[86] Central council, 11 Apr. 1934, Liverpool CA, 329 Con/1/1/3.

Working-Class Conservatism in the Industrial North

divisions of 1932, and would mirror similar efforts taking place between the party leaders.[87] A year later the ACC announced an initiative to establish an Information Bureau in every Conservative Club. In a direct challenge to the role played by trade unions and cooperative societies, the object of the bureau was to provide information on welfare provision, insurance schemes, employment opportunities, and the like. 'In industrial constituencies this new enterprise is being cordially welcomed and is meeting the needs of wage-earners of all political parties', commented the *Yorkshire Post*.[88]

The ACC's efforts were reflected in developments on the ground. To accompany the proliferation of clubs, the party in Stockton established a dedicated men's branch of the constituency association. This helped to bring club activities and the political work of the local party into alignment. The clubs had 'awakened to some purpose', wrote the party agent to Macmillan. Not only did they widen the Conservatives' organisational base in the constituency, they also generated their own programme of propaganda, starting in 1934 with a summer campaign of open-air meetings: Tuesdays at the Cross in Stockton, Wednesdays at the Five Lamps in Thornaby, and Thursdays in Norton Green. 'These meetings are attracting considerable attention as we have not had open air Propaganda for some considerable time. There were over 600 persons at last Tuesday's meeting on the Cross.'[89] Similar success was witnessed the following year by the Portrack Conservative Club, whose Friday night dances were supported by the local Shamrock Football Club and whose socials were compared by one activist to 'a huge family gathering'.[90]

The renewed vitality of the club movement went some way to restoring a key feature of pre-war working-class Conservatism, namely its appeal to masculinity. The fact that this was welcomed by activists should not necessarily be attributed to the lingering anti-suffragism historians have detected in some quarters of the inter war party.[91] The party in Stockton ensured that female wage-earners served alongside male wage-earners on the labour advisory committee; and campaigns to reform the administration of unemployment assistance, including replacing the household means test with an individual means test, served to champion the interests of women and girls within a welfare system still dominated by the ideal of

[87] See, for example, his speech to the annual conference of Conservative and Unionist clubs held in Exeter: *Devon and Exeter Gazette*, 12 May 1933.
[88] *Yorkshire Post*, 5 Apr. 1934.
[89] T. Keenan to Macmillan, 13 Jul. 1934, Macmillan papers, c.85/194–6.
[90] R. J. W. Ledingham (Agent, Northern Counties Area) to Macmillan, 15 May 1935, Macmillan papers, c.92/46.
[91] E.g., D. Jarvis, 'Mrs. Maggs and Betty: the Conservative appeal to women voters in the 1920s', *TCBH*, 5 (1994), 129–52, at 137.

124   Popular Conservatism and the National Government

the male breadwinner.[92] Instead, activists' attitudes stemmed from their desire to challenge public perceptions that working-class Conservatism, commonly if not always accurately understood to depend on male sociability, had become hopelessly reliant on the organisational initiative of women since the war. As one agent wrote in 1931, 'when it comes to influencing the electors ... the sooner this state of affairs can be rectified the better for the Party's prospect – especially in the industrial constituencies'.[93] The club revival of the mid-1930s, perhaps more than most developments, offered activists a comforting reminder of the pre-war and largely pre-Labour world of working-class Conservatism.

Yet the club movement held more than nostalgic appeal. It represented a renewed sense of legitimacy for Conservatives as they presented themselves as the true guardians of the working-classes' own community interests – even when these were at odds with official government policy. The fact that the party in Leeds chose to campaign against the slum clearance scheme undertaken by the city corporation serves to demonstrate this. The Conservative organisation in Leeds, while careful not to disavow the general principles behind the government's slum clearance drive, saw in it an opportunity to marshal working-class opinion against the newly-elected Labour council, while also protecting the interests of those middle-class rentiers whose security in old age relied on income from rent. The Conservative argument rested in part on the traditional defence of property rights. Vyvyan Adams, who led the campaign, drew attention to the fate that would befall respectable homeowners regardless of class. 'Doubtless large parts of our great cities must be rebuilt ... but this end must not be achieved by means of social injustice', he argued. 'What is a slum? The danger of huge clearance schemes is that property structurally sound, by no means "worn out", and conscientiously repaired by its owner, may slip into that category. This is unjust and inexcusable: it is what I mean by confiscatory socialism.'[94] Through their information bureau, the Conservative clubs offered advice to these property owners on how to claim compensation.[95] The Conservative campaign also rested on the protection of existing working-class communities in the city from the threat of break-up and removal to suburban estates. Most of these were new council estates, making more and more

---

[92] Labour advisory committee, 25 May 1933, STCO, D/X 322/6; resolutions passed at AGM, 14 Mar. 1936, Northern Area, NRO 3303/2.

[93] *CAJ*, Aug. 1931, 191.

[94] Speech to the AGM of the Leeds West CA, 11 Jan. 1935, Adams papers, 4/1.

[95] *Yorkshire Post*, 5 Apr. 1934. Grassroots objection to the confiscatory element of slum clearance was most widespread in Scotland and the industrial north of England, see Ball, *Portrait of a party*, 233–4.

voters tenants of the Labour-council landlord. 'It was not right that 2 thirds of the houses in Leeds should belong to the Corporation', argued councillor Blackburn, who went on to warn that 'such a position opened out the danger of bribery amongst the electorate'.[96] An alliance was duly forged with other local organisations against 'Socialist housing dictation', including both the Anglican and Catholic churches, who by conducting a plebiscite in the parish of St Jude's, Hunslet found that a thousand of the 1,200 households on the 'red areas' list 'wished to continue to live in the district, and preferably in their present homes'.[97]

The significance of this for historians goes wider than the slum. It signified tangible breakthroughs into working-class communities, some of which had been no-go areas for Conservatives since the war. According to Adams, speaking in 1935, 'even New Wortley' – normally a hostile slum ward where the Conservative club was reformed – 'was not safe for Socialism'.[98] Later that year the Labour council was defeated at the municipal elections. The *Yorkshire Evening Post* described what had occurred in the following broad terms: 'The Conservative victory in Leeds is a measure of Socialist mistakes in principle, failure in practice, and misjudgement of the temper and desire of the community'.[99] So Conservative achievement might well have rested on claims of Labour failings; but, crucially, Conservatives had regained the ability to be effective and trusted judges of the temper and desire of the people.

Another example of local Conservatives' newfound confidence in their ability to speak on behalf of the workers was the controversy surrounding betting reform. Gambling had been a key feature of workers' lives since before the Great War. It provided recreation and, crucially, a sporadic boost to household incomes. Despite its perceived threat to the values of self-discipline, thrift, and gainful toil, as so often expressed through middle-class 'public' anxieties, the freedom of the worker to indulge in a flutter had long been a common trope among urban Conservatives as they campaigned against the restrictive reforms proposed first by Liberal and then Labour moralists.[100] When the National government intro-duced the Betting and Lotteries Bill in 1934, some of the most concerted objections came from Conservative clubmen on behalf of working-class

---

[96] AGM, 11 Jan. 1935, Leeds CA, WYL 529/5.
[97] *Yorkshire Evening Post*, 24 Oct. 1935.
[98] Speech to the AGM of the Leeds West CA, 11 Jan. 1935, Adams papers, 4/1.
[99] *Yorkshire Evening Post*, 2 Nov. 1935.
[100] See G. McClymont, 'Socialism, puritanism, hedonism: the parliamentary Labour party's attitude to gambling, 1923–31', *TCBH*, 19 (2008), 288–313; also R. McKibbin, 'Working-class gambling in Britain, 1880–1939', *P&P*, 82 (1979), 147–78.

126   Popular Conservatism and the National Government

communities.[101] Based on the recommendations of a recent royal commission, the act illegalised two practices: tote clubs, which facilitated all-day cash gambling in pubs and clubs, and the sale of tickets for the Irish sweepstake, a state-run lottery established by Eamon de Valera's government to fund hospitals in the Irish Free State.[102] Given especially the popularity of the Irish sweep, and evidence from contemporary social studies that suggests unemployment had rendered betting ever more important for household budgets in the early 1930s, the act undoubtedly damaged the government's reputation.[103]

Paradoxically, opposition to the legislation doubled as propaganda for the club movement. It was a high-profile platform from which Conservatives reiterated their traditional defence of working-class male liberties. It was also an opportunity to seize the initiative by campaigning for the establishment of a British national lottery, the proceeds of which, as the secretary of the ACC explained, would be devoted 'to the betterment of the lot of the people'.

Had one been in existence during the past four years ... a sum would have been realised by the State sufficient to pay for slum clearance schemes throughout the country and provide decent homes for the poor instead of bleeding to death taxpayers and ratepayers ... Let then the slogan be 'a national sweep to sweep away the slums'.[104]

Conservative clubmen campaigned to this effect throughout 1934 and into 1935. Those in Liverpool and north-west England did so in favour of hospital maintenance, while their counterparts in the south-west favoured the Prince of Wales's charitable Jubilee Fund.[105] It is likely that such a campaign helped to mitigate the otherwise damaging effects of the lotteries act on the clubs just as they looked set to become once more a valuable auxiliary branch of the Conservative party in the industrial areas. At the very least it can be said that the measurable growth in club numbers and activity, described earlier, coincided with the bill's controversial passage. The timing could not have been more fortuitous. As one agent commented in December 1935, the clubs were in a position to give

[101] E.g., R. H. Smith (Chairman, Liverpool Workingmen's Conservative Association) to Buchan-Hepburn, 1 Dec. 1934, Churchill Archives Centre, Hailes Papers, HAIS 1/9; *Headlam diaries, 1923–1935*, 313 (30 Oct., 5 Nov. 1934).
[102] M. Huggins, 'Betting, sport and the British, 1918–1939', *JSH*, 41 (2007), 283–306; M. Coleman, '"A terrible danger to the morals of the country": the Irish hospitals' sweepstake in Great Britain, 1930–1987', *Proceedings of the Royal Irish Academy*, 105 (2005), 197–220.
[103] E. W. Bakke, *The unemployed man: a social study* (London, 1933), 197–200; Pilgrim Trust, *Men without work*, 98–100.
[104] *Yorkshire Evening Post*, 27 Oct. 1934.
[105] *Western Daily Press*, 23 Apr. 1934, 22 May 1935.

'great service during the recent (general election) contest – more so, by far, in many divisions, than at any previous General Election'.[106]

The General Election of 1935

Conservatives in the industrial regions committed themselves to fighting the 1935 general election as part of the National government. While the politics of recovery would feature prominently in their public campaigns, in private few of them expected working-class voters to reward the government for a job well done.[107] Instead, their decision betrayed one of the great lasting legacies of 1931, namely the calculation among Conservatives that, despite the slump, a mass of working-class voters could still be relied upon to act 'patriotically'. 'There are a large number of men and women who voted Socialist till 1931, but since that date are favourably disposed towards the conception of National Government', wrote Adams to the government chief whip. He was saying so on the basis of canvassing work conducted in 'the poorest area' of Leeds West in the summer of 1935. Of 1,338 houses canvassed, 330 identified themselves as Conservatives, 269 as National Liberal, 428 as National Labour, and 60 as Socialist.[108] The expressed objective, then, of contesting the general election in defence of the cross-party government was to reconstruct '1931'.

Conservatives did all they could to resurrect public memories of Labour in government, as exemplified by the campaign in Leeds. Speaking to voters in an area of Leeds affected by the Labour council's slum clearance scheme, Adams's message to his constituents was: 'If you object to the socialists in Municipal politics you should be just as wary to have [them in] National politics. *May I ask you not to forget 1931.*'[109] His election address claimed that Labour's clearance plans had caused 'much hardship' among working families forced to pay higher rents in the new estates.[110] He also compared the position of the local economy in 1935, under tariffs, with that of 1931: whereas at the time of the financial crisis the Armley employment exchange recorded 6,015 unemployed, up from

---

[106] *CAJ*, Dec. 1935, 261.

[107] Macmillan to Mrs E. Roberts, 15 Oct. 1935, Macmillan papers, c.97/238.

[108] Adams to D. Margesson, 9 Jul. 1935, Adams papers 1/4/2; also labour advisory committee, 10 Mar. 1934, Yorkshire Area 3, WYL 1856/11/1.

[109] Draft speech in support of Mr Spencer for council election, n.d. Nov. 1935, Adams papers 1/2/3 (emphasis added).

[110] This claim echoed the findings of Stockton's Medical Officer of Health, George M'Gonigle, who did more than any other contemporary to highlight the phenomenon of rent poverty and its harmful impact on nutritional health and thus mortality rates. See G. M'Gonigle, 'Poverty, nutrition and the public health', *Proceedings of the Royal Society*

128   Popular Conservatism and the National Government

2,257 when the Conservatives left office in 1929, by 1935 the figure stood at 2,595. The message was clear: 'Socialist administration destroys industry: keep the National Government in office and yet better times will come to us.'[111] In a further attack on Labour's fitness to govern, he sought to expose Labour's unscrupulous propaganda. He challenged in particular Labour's slur that Leeds was a 'distressed area' and that the government profligately sent subsidies to its friends in already 'profitable industries'. By standing on such a 'slender, inaccurate, unconvincing' platform, the Labour party in Leeds was 'completely lacking in local relevance and appeal'.[112] Labour had nothing to offer except another 'crisis'. 'Therefore', he suggested in his election address, 'precisely the same reasons which impelled the country to reject the Labour Party in 1931 should to-day persuade them to support the National Government'.[113]

In reality, the likelihood of repeating '1931' was jeopardised in a number of ways. One was that fewer Labour men, nationally and locally, were willing to appear as 'National Labour' figures to support Conservative candidates. MacDonald had been replaced by Baldwin as prime minister, while Snowden now allied himself with Lloyd George in direct hostility to the National government. Another was the threat of Liberal non-compliance. Lloyd George had failed to take an active part in the 1931 election due to ill health; now, in light of his decision to launch the Council of Action, Conservatives could be forgiven for anticipating a repeat of the 1929 election, at which the Liberals fought a majority of seats and did so on a radical policy programme. Speculation therefore abounded about Liberal candidatures, or, in the absence of such direct intervention, how many unreconstructed free-trade Liberal voters would exact revenge on the Conservatives by reallocating their support to Labour, and how many local Liberal dignitaries would retreat from the National platform.[114]

In addition, the context was very different by 1935 – not so much for what had been achieved by way of recovery in the industrial areas but rather the changed circumstances that altered the effectiveness of the anti-socialist appeal. The absence of a failing Labour government, or a conspicuous sense of 'crisis', proved disarming for many Conservatives whose only experience of successful anti-socialism was indelibly bound up

---

of Medicine, 26 (Feb. 1933), 677–87 and G. M'Gonigle & J. Kirby, *Poverty and public health* (London, 1936).

[111] Draft election address, n.d. Nov. 1935, Adams papers 1/2/3.
[112] Draft speech, n.d. Nov. 1935, Adams papers 1/2/2.
[113] Election address, Nov. 1935, Adams papers, 1/2/3.
[114] E.g., L. Short to Adams, 25 Jun. 1934, Adams papers 1/2/1; *Headlam diaries, 1923–1935*, 330 (17 Apr. 1935), 339 (15 Aug. 1935), 341 (10, 15 Oct. 1935).

Working-Class Conservatism in the Industrial North   129

with the events of August 1931. Headlam felt that electorates in the 'South and Midlands' had retained their fear of 'Socialist Government', whereas 'in this part of the world [County Durham] ... Labour is too strong nowadays for fear to make all the difference'.[115] Conservatives therefore felt that simply to attack Labour was not a match for impressing upon voters a positive record and programme of Conservative reform. Macmillan reminded his local party of the lessons of 1929: 'he had foreseen the defeat of 1929 and had disagreed with the Party's then policy of Safety First'.[116] Many of his followers had already expressed their concern at the anomaly in distributing anti-socialist propaganda when more than three years had elapsed since the last Labour government.[117]

The electoral success that many Conservatives secured in the industrial areas, despite the odds and so often to their own surprise, offers the most striking example of how the Conservatives exploited the National government to craft cross-party appeals locally. In Leeds West and Stockton, this was manifested most clearly in the public image of the MP. A keynote of Adams's campaign was his 'personal service' on behalf of the people of Leeds West at home and in Westminster. There is little doubt that since 1931 he had won many local plaudits through his involvement with the club movement, which played an active role in his election campaign, and also his anti-clearance work, which turned the previously forbidding slum streets into friendlier territory for him and his wife.[118] His sponsors on public platforms noted that 'in addition to his Parliamentary duties he had spoken in Leeds on an average three times a fortnight during the past four years' while Adams himself cited local trade and employment figures that 'could bring the Government's work home to West Leeds'.[119]

The precise target of his election campaign was the Liberal vote. In private he gave an undertaking to the Bramley branch of the Liberals that he supported their pursuit of electoral reform.[120] In public he highlighted above all else his record of active support for the League of Nations and the policy of peace through collective security. He contrasted this with what he described as Labour's opportunistic critique of the government's diplomatic response to the recent Abyssinian crisis. But besides constructing the spectre of another Labour 'crisis', this time international

[115] *Headlam diaries, 1923–1935*, 341 (11 Oct. 1935).
[116] Special meeting of the executive committee, 26 Sep. 1935, Stockton CA, D/X 322/5.
[117] Executive committee, 25 Feb. 1935, Stockton CA, D/X 322/5.
[118] Adams encouraged his wife to canvass in 'some of the most difficult parts of the Division' and reassured her that behind the slum doors were an anti-socialist majority. Adams to Mrs Adams, 4 Nov. 1935, Adams papers 1/2/3; *Yorkshire Evening Post*, 12 Nov. 1935.
[119] See an account of his tour of Conservative clubs, with which he launched his campaign, in *Yorkshire Post*, 6 Nov. 1935.
[120] Adams to Mrs Milestone, 13 Nov. 1935, Adams papers 1/2/3.

130   Popular Conservatism and the National Government

as well as financial, his campaign eschewed party labels in favour of his personal record as an MP. He informed voters that on collective security and peace he had given thirty speeches in parliament and addressed more than 100 public meetings. He solicited public letters of support, for printing in the Yorkshire press, from figures including Lord Cecil of Chelwood, the well-known president of the nationwide League of Nations Union; Sir Montague Burton, the Yorkshire industrialist and philanthropist who founded LNU branches in his textile factories; and Harold Lightman, a former Liberal municipal candidate in Leeds.[121] He also positioned himself as an independent supporter of the Council of Action. While the seasoned Conservative voter's distrust of Lloyd George was now a given within the party, so too was the assumption that the former prime minister's credentials as a radical reformer could help to engage the progressive vote in marginal seats like Leeds West. Adams addressed this conundrum in one election meeting by denying that he put his signature to the Council's manifesto while simultaneously expressing support for its contents and gratitude to the Council for 'think[ing] that my work in Parliament has made me worth supporting'. A request to straighten the public record – explaining that he had not signed the manifesto and did not 'adhere to Mr. Lloyd George' – was sent to the Conservative *Yorkshire Post* but seemingly *not* to the more plebeian *Yorkshire Evening Post* nor the Liberal *Yorkshire Evening News*.[122] In this way he was content for his position to appear ambivalent, on the one hand sympathetic to a programme of reform prepared by critics of the government and on the other loyal to Baldwin's National government.

Adams committed himself unequivocally to the Council of Action only after his re-election.[123] His ambivalence during the campaign was in fact a creative construct designed to portray himself as the independent representative of community interests, capable of criticising as well as supporting the National government, and further reflects the extent to which the 1935 election was fought along distinctly local lines. In the absence of the brute momentum that propelled the National vote in 1931, the task of reconvening that same multitude of Liberal and Labour voters in support of National Conservatism called for deft rhetorical persuasion. The

---

[121] Cecil to Adams, 22 Oct. 1935, Adams papers, 1/2/2; Adams to editors of *Leeds Mercury, Yorkshire Evening News, Yorkshire Evening Post*, and *Yorkshire Post*, 31 Oct. 1935, Adams to H. Morris (on behalf of Burton), 6 Nov. 1935, Adams to Lightman, 1 Nov. 1935, Adams papers 1/2/3.

[122] Draft speech, n.d. Nov. 1935, Adams papers, 1/2/2; Adams to editor, *Yorkshire Post*, 2 Nov. 1935, Adams 1/2/3.

[123] He was among sixty-seven MPs of all parties who became members of the Council of Action Parliamentary Group, chaired by Lloyd George. *Yorkshire Evening Post*, 27 Nov. 1935.

election victory is widely cited as testimony to Baldwin's personal articulation of a 'national' cross-party appeal that reached almost half the listening public.[124] But the National government required and enabled candidates to make similar appeals to the local electorate. It was an integral part of Adams's display of independent service on behalf of his constituency. Over the course of 1934–5 he addressed several non-party forums, including local branches of the Free Church council, the Royal Society of St George's, and the LNU. Like Baldwin's speeches, those by Adams were topical in their subject matter, addressing such issues as peace and industrial society, but most important was the timeless quality of the message they carried, which hinged on the broad themes of democracy, Christianity, patriotism, and regional (Yorkshire) identity. Also, like Baldwin, he lifted himself above politics. 'Let us all try to forget that there is a General Election in progress', Adams told an LNU meeting in Bramley. 'You and I are weary of the complaints and the arguments of the partisans.'[125] This context helped to salve the conscience of local Liberal figures who declared in favour of Adams, like Mr Clay from Bramley, who in his first appearance on a Conservative platform explained that he 'did not stand there to support all members of the party, but he did support Mr Adams, and urged everyone in the hall to do the same'.[126]

In Stockton, Macmillan stood as a signatory to *The Next Five Years* manifesto, a policy document drafted by a range of public figures drawn mainly from academia, the churches, and all three political parties. It advocated public works in electrification, housing, and road building, the reorganisation of industry, land settlement for rural labourers, and the expansion of 'social services' including unemployment benefit and old age pensions.[127] Members of the group were often critical of the National government, disillusioned with what they perceived to be its failure to forge a new progressivism of the centre ground, and its manifesto has been described as 'anathema to the Conservatives' grass-roots membership'.[128] However, for Macmillan and other Conservative signatories it represented not opposition to the National government but rather their standing as independent-minded representatives. This was an

---

[124] S. Nicholas, 'The construction of a national identity: Stanley Baldwin, "Englishness" and the mass media in inter-war Britain', in M. Francis & I. Zweiniger-Bargielowska (eds.), *The Conservative party and British society, 1880–1990* (Cardiff, 1996), 127–46, 136.

[125] Speech to LNU, Bramley, n.d. Nov. 1935, and other draft speeches in the Adams papers 4/2a-d.

[126] *Yorkshire Post*, 7 Nov. 1935.

[127] For a summary of Part I of the manifesto and the names of its signatories, see H. Macmillan, *Winds of change, 1914–1939* (London, 1966), 625–36.

[128] Ritschel, *Politics of planning*, 244–8; Green, 'Conservative party and Keynes', 197.

132   Popular Conservatism and the National Government

integral part of Macmillan's self-presentation to activists and voters. Headlam noted in 1934 that in a meeting of women organisers, Macmillan explained 'how free and independent he was – voting as he liked, etc., and spurring on the Government to plan and provide work – it all went down like hot cakes'.[129] Nor was there anything particularly novel about Conservative engagement with the group's policies. Many of these echoed what Macmillan and colleagues had promoted since the late 1920s, including through the 'Northern Group' of Conservative MPs set up to lobby ministers following the 1931 election.[130] To be sure, not all northern Conservatives supported a programme of industrial 'planning'. Headlam found aspects of it too 'socialistic' and its champions too abstract. Of Macmillan he thought: 'he should learn how to put his stuff over to the common people – it really is ridiculous to talk of "cheap money" to a lot of old women without explaining what it means.'[131]

Indeed, support for the Next Five Years Group or the Council of Action was initially deemed incompatible with loyalty to the Conservative party.[132] Yet in the context of the 1935 election campaign these cross-party initiatives presented real opportunities. Macmillan won over his local party by demonstrating what his adherence to the Next Five Years programme promised them politically and electorally. He consulted local Liberals, clergymen, and some Labour figures, sending them copies of the manifesto and convening dinners to discuss its contents, until many of them – including some fifty Liberals – offered the Conservative party assurances of their public support.[133] The promise of Liberal support comparable to that in 1931 was a crucial factor in the unanimous decision by the Conservative party in Stockton to endorse *The Next Five Years*.[134] It also helps to explain why the Liberal candidate,

[129] *Headlam diaries, 1923–1935*, 294 (1 Mar. 1934).
[130] See H. Macmillan, *Reconstruction: a plea for a national policy* (London, 1933).
[131] Ibid., 324 (8 Mar. 1935).
[132] Through its regular 'Notes for a Speech', the *CAJ* (Aug. 1935, 196) gave suggestions to activists on how to combat Lloyd George's Council of Action programme; and one of Macmillan's co-signatories to *The Next Five Years*, Major Hills MP (Ripon), reported being 'fiercely assaulted' by local party members. Hills to Macmillan, 21 Oct. 1935, Macmillan papers, c.97/137.
[133] Many of the arrangements were in the hands of the divisional agent and another member of the party organisation. A. C. Batty to Macmillan, 15 Aug. 1935, Macmillan papers, c.142/404; Keenan to Macmillan, 28 Aug., 4 Sep. 1935, Macmillan to Keenan, 30 Aug. 1935, Macmillan papers, c.97/157–8, 154, 155–6; list of known supporters of Macmillan as National candidate, n.d. 1935, Macmillan papers, c.142/178–80.
[134] Special meeting of the executive committee, 26 Sep. 1935, Stockton CA, D/X 322/5; *Darlington & Stockton Times*, 9 Nov. 1935. Similarly, following an initially hostile response to the group manifesto by the Conservative party in Ripon, Major Hills described his re-adoption meeting 'an outstanding triumph'. Hills to Macmillan, 30 Oct. 1935, Macmillan papers, c.97/135.

whose predecessors polled roughly a quarter of the vote for most of the 1920s, received only 10 per cent of the vote this time round and lost his deposit.

The economic recovery of the early 1930s did more than almost any other process of the twentieth century to bring Britain's regional inequalities to the fore. Observers like Priestley sensed as much at the time, as did Conservative activists in working-class areas tasked with defending the government's record. Claims of improved living conditions and a trade revival were unlikely to move the unemployed worker, while attempts to relate booming consumption in the South to increased jobs and production in the North rang equally hollow. This almost certainly contributed to the loss of many working-class seats to Labour in 1935. But, equally, it cannot explain how the Conservatives, despite the odds, retained so many similar constituencies. The answer lies in the depression itself, which brought together the party grassroots and public concerns for community relief in a way not seen since before the war. Organisations like the club movement that served a social purpose, be it relief or recreation, were also made to serve a political purpose. While there could be no serious prospect of dislodging Labour in its strongholds – as the Appendix shows, most of the industrial seats that returned to Labour in 1935 had been Labour throughout the 1920s or earlier – in areas outside the mining districts, the Conservatives made considerable progress. It was in these areas, where a tradition of working-class Conservatism had once existed, or popular Liberalism had retained a toehold, and where Labour made gains in 1929, that Conservatives successfully entrenched themselves after 1931. It was here also that the culture of the National government itself proved instrumental. It licenced Conservatives, especially individual MPs, to cultivate cross-party appeals and to fashion a more ecumenical Conservatism, acceptable to activists and unaligned voters alike. By the mid-century, regional inequalities would engender political narratives of their own. Labour authored a powerful public history of the 1930s in which the northern experience was centre stage, and the southern Conservative heartlands, by implication, the complacent beneficiaries of the recovery. In reality, however, there was little complacency about the politics of recovery in the Conservative heartlands, for, as the next chapter shows, Conservatives in the suburbs also confronted challenges as they set about shaping the National government to their advantage.

5   The Politics of Anti-Socialism in the Suburbs

This is the England of arterial and by-pass roads, of filling stations and factories that look like exhibition buildings, of giant cinemas and dance-halls and cafés, bungalows with tiny garages, cocktail bars, Woolworths, motor-coaches, wireless, hiking, factory girls looking like actresses, grey-hound racing and dirt tracks, swimming pools ... Years and years ago the democratic and enterprising Blackpool, by declaring that you were all as good as one another so long as you had the necessary sixpence, began all this. Modern England is rapidly Blackpooling itself.

(J. B. Priestley on the expanding towns and suburbs of England in the autumn of 1933)[1]

'... no ramping Tory must keep down the voice of the people!' [I]t was the duty of the Liberal Party to be on board to see fair play, to maintain an even keel, and to justify the word 'National' by their inclusion ... [And] out of the ashes of this General Election would arise a new Liberalism.

(Dr Russell Thomas, Liberal candidate, to the electors of Ilford in 1931)[2]

Historians and 'Middle-Class' Politics between the Wars

For two centuries the middle classes have been the main ascendant force in Western democratic society. In Britain, they constituted the entrepreneur-ial and professional sections of an industrial and liberal democratic state, later expanding to form the affluent population of a social democratic polity.[3] At each stage in their development, they had a formative impact on wider public opinion. The centrality thus attached to the middle classes in the political life of the nation has remained the central feature of the literature on Conservative 'hegemony' between the wars. In what remains one of the most influential essays on interwar British politics, Ross McKibbin famously argues that the 'huge' electoral coalition constructed

---

[1] J. B. Priestley, *English journey* (London, 1934; 1994 edn), 401–2.
[2] *Ilford Recorder*, 23 Oct. 1931.
[3] For a synoptic survey of the British middle classes, see L. James, *The middle class: a history* (London, 2006).

The Politics of Anti-Socialism in the Suburbs 135

by Conservatives was modelled on the prejudicial social mindset and self-serving defence of constitutional government of the 'professional and commercial suburban middle classes'.[4]

Yet despite a historiographical preoccupation with a middle-class political and cultural paradigm between the wars, what is known about the party's actual experiences in these so-called strongholds of anti-socialism is remarkably conjectural. There is, in fact, no existing study of interwar Conservatism within any largely, or typically, middle-class area. The assumption is that interwar Conservatives, like their immediate ancestors, found their electoral bedrock in the expanding suburbs of England; that the cult of domesticity, together with the quiet associationalism that marked their civic life, gave rise to residents' conservative apoliticism; and that the safe (if uninspiring) middle-brow forms of entertainment consumed by these voters, and prescribed for them by a cynical intelligentsia, defined the overall conservative spirit of the age.[5] The main objective of this chapter is to move beyond the current abstract treatment of middle-class anti-socialist politics to a sustained and detailed engagement with the experience of Conservative activists in the suburbs.

The concept of late nineteenth-century 'Villa Toryism' has already undergone a transformation in this regard. In 1963 James Cornford argued that the Conservative party under Lord Salisbury owed its strength not to the ephemeral issues which many believed determined the outcome of individual elections, but to the long-term shift in the party's 'social bases' of support. The party in the 1840s represented the landed interest and in the 1850s faced great uncertainty and predictions of decline, which circumstances were only partially solved by Disraeli's erratic pursuit of the newly enfranchised working classes after 1867. The subsequent period of Conservative 'hegemony' under Salisbury was therefore owed to the settled allegiance of the suburbs around distinctly middle-class interests that the party organisation was happy to represent.[6] Since then historians have significantly refined their thoughts on class both as a historical lens through which to analyse political trends and as an expression of social identity. As

---

[4] R. McKibbin, 'Class and conventional wisdom: the Conservative party and the "Public" in inter-war Britain', in *The ideologies of class: social relations in Britain, 1880–1950* (Oxford, 1991), 259–93, 267.

[5] See A. Light, *Forever England: femininity, literature and conservatism between the wars* (London, 1991) and D. LeMahieu, *A culture for democracy: mass communication and the cultivated mind in Britain between the wars* (Oxford, 1988). For 'patriotic' and 'conservative' film culture, see B. Melman, *The culture of history: English uses of the past, 1800–1953* (Oxford, 2006), ch.7.

[6] J. Cornford, 'The transformation of Conservatism in the late nineteenth century', *Victorian Studies*, 12 (1963), 35–66.

136   Popular Conservatism and the National Government

a result, the concept of a monolithic suburbia is no longer viable. More recent scholarship has found that the success of late-Victorian Conservatism was derived less from the allegiance of a generic middle-class electorate and more from the party's cultivation of specific local interests.[7] Moreover, Conservatism was never uncontested, especially as Liberals developed a progressivism that resonated strongly with both the social and educational aspirations of the suburban middle classes and the radical political culture of the growing working-class metropolitan suburbs.[8] This too could break down, amid further evidence of the mutability of suburban politics, leading in some instances to Liberal defections to the ranks of Liberal Unionism.[9]

If suburban politics were so hotly contested before 1914, it follows that the diversity of their political culture might have resulted in equally fierce contests after 1918. The natural counter to this is that there is little mileage in studying the party's connection with the middle classes except in a notional sense, since the party's dominance rested on the use of the middle-class 'public' as an artefact of political discourse, representing an axiomatic apolitical stance – with which all classes, especially the unorganised working classes, were encouraged to identify. In his *Classes and Cultures*, McKibbin describes how a new middle class emerged by the

---

[7] For a critique of the methodological usefulness of class, see J. Lawrence & M. Taylor, 'Introduction: electoral sociology and the historians', in Lawrence & Taylor (eds.), *Party, state and society: electoral behaviour in Britain since 1820* (Aldershot, 1997), 1–26. On identity, see D. Wahrman, *Imagining the middle class: the political representation of class in Britain, c.1780–1840* (Cambridge, 1995), which argues that the idea of a middle-class identity emerged not as the inevitable by-product of early nineteenth-century industrialisation but as a powerful construct in public political debate. For suburban Conservatism, see F. Coetzee, 'Villa Toryism reconsidered: Conservatism and suburban sensibilities in late-Victorian Croydon', in E. H. H. Green (ed.), *An age of transition: British politics, 1880–1914* (Edinburgh, 1997), 29–47; M. Roberts, '"Villa Toryism" and popular Conservatism in Leeds, 1885–1902', *HJ*, 49 (2006), 217–46; A. Windscheffel, *Popular Conservatism in imperial London, 1868–1906* (Woodbridge, 2007).

[8] J. Moore, 'Liberalism and the politics of suburbia: electoral dynamics in late nineteenth-century South Manchester', *UH*, 30 (2003), 225–50; B. Doyle, 'Urban Liberalism and the "lost generation": politics and middle class culture in Norwich, 1900–1935', *HJ*, 38 (1995), 617–34; G. Searle, 'The Edwardian Liberal party and business', *EHR*, 98 (1983), 28–60. For a case-study treatment of the working-class suburb, see T. Cooper, 'Politics and place in suburban Walthamstow, 1870–1914' (PhD thesis, University of Cambridge, 2005).

[9] J. Moore, *The transformation of urban Liberalism: party politics and urban government in late nineteenth-century England* (Aldershot, 2006); E. Biagini & A. Reid (eds.), *Currents of radicalism: popular radicalism, organized labour and party politics in Britain, 1850–1914* (Cambridge, 1991). General disaffection with both Conservative and Liberal governments by the eve of the First World War is the subject of P. Waller, 'Altercation over civil society: the bitter cry of the Edwardian middle classes', in J. Harris (ed.), *Civil society in British history: ideas, identities, institutions* (Oxford, 2005), 115–34.

The Politics of Anti-Socialism in the Suburbs

1930s that differed substantially in social background from the older suburban population, which throughout the 1920s had retained a distinctly Edwardian image. It was possible still to identify this latter group by its nonconformity and its occupational basis in business and the professions, while the newcomers, mostly resident in the new housing estates, included a high proportion of salaried white-collar workers.[10] Several historians have noted how this new middle class proved increasingly responsive to Labour's appeals after the 1935 general election. In his study of Lewisham, Tom Jeffery argues that Labour reconstituted a 'suburban radicalism' that embraced middle-class Liberals and rehearsed a rhetoric of educative and restorative politics in opposition to the National government's foreign policy. Nationally, the party improved its media strategy and enjoyed the backing of previously anti-socialist parts of the press.[11] Despite these vulnerabilities, however, for McKibbin the Conservatives' great achievement lay in their ability to accommodate the expanded and variegated middle classes within a political culture that was axiomatically *a*political in its common-sense hostility to organised labour.[12]

But as Chapter 2 showed, in the 1920s Conservatives in the suburbs rejected Baldwin's apolitical language and instead urged robust party rhetoric. Failure to stir a partisan sociability at the municipal level – even among 'known Conservatives' – led many activists to doubt their ability to respond to Labour's threat. The present chapter picks up the story of suburban Conservatism from the doldrums of the 1920s, with an account of its renewed vibrancy under the National government. As Ilford, Epping, Birmingham Moseley, and Liverpool East Toxteth demonstrate,

[10] R. McKibbin, *Classes and cultures: England, 1918–1951* (Oxford, 1998), 44–9, 73–8, 90–3.

[11] T. Jeffery, 'The suburban nation: politics and class in Lewisham', in D. Feldman & G. Stedman Jones (eds.), *Metropolis London: histories and representations of London since 1800* (London, 1989), 189–216; L. Beers, *Your Britain: media and the making of the Labour party* (Cambridge, MA, 2010), ch.8; M. Pugh, 'The *Daily Mirror* and the revival of Labour, 1935–1945', *TCBH*, 9 (1998), 420–38.

[12] McKibbin, *Classes and cultures*, 96–8. This unwittingly reinforces a long-standing view that a homogeneous middle-class conception of the nation had emerged by the inter-war years. See R. H. Trainor, 'The "decline" of British urban governance since 1850: a reassessment', in R. J. Morris &; Trainor (eds.), *Urban governance: Britain and beyond since 1750* (Aldershot, 2000), 28–46, and his 'Neither metropolitan nor provincial: the interwar middle class', in A. Kidd & D. Nicholls (eds.), *The making of the British middle class? Studies of regional and cultural diversity since the eighteenth century* (Stroud, 1998), 203–13; D. Cardiff & P. Scannell, 'Broadcasting and national unity', in J. Curran, A. Smith & P. Wingate (eds.), *Impacts and influences: essays in media power in the twentieth century* (London, 1987), 157–73; D. LeMahieu, 'John Reith, 1889–1971: entrepreneur of collectivism', in S. Pedersen & P. Mandler (eds.), *After the Victorians: private conscience and public duty in modern Britain* (London, 1994), 189–206; S. Gunn, 'Class, identity and the urban: the middle class in England, c.1790–1950', *UH*, 31 (2004), 29–47.

138   Popular Conservatism and the National Government

Conservative organisations no longer eschewed non-party affiliations and happily adopted a more 'non-party' approach after 1931. While the mantle of anti-socialism – rebooted by the spectacular fall of the Labour government – came to be the object of competition rather than cooperation between Conservatives and Liberals, the experience of the election campaign proved crucial in initiating Conservative activists to the advantages of operating under an ecumenical culture of government. Matched by greater efforts to cultivate non-party sociability in the constituencies, this accommodating culture of anti-socialism became a defining feature of suburban Conservatism throughout the decade. A measure of this was the fact that it emerged strengthened from the controversy surrounding Indian reform, which bears testament to the suburban activists' considered assessment of the benefits that stemmed from membership of the National government. Non-party sociability helped local Conservatives to elide the often conflicting social interests wrought by economic recovery in the South. The government also gave them licence to respond ecumenically to the other key feature of suburban politics in the 1930s, the Liberal threat. By 1935, the Conservatives' suburban grassroots, so often the voice of diehard Conservatism, looked enthusiastically to Baldwin as both the embodiment and key facilitator of the National government.

'1931' and the Dynamics of Anti-Socialism in the Suburbs

The general election of 1931 offered Conservatives the anti-socialist campaign *par excellence*. Nowhere was this more so than in the suburbs, where the effects of the national crisis seemed certain to rally the middle classes. It brought the 'traditional' interests of property owners, businessmen, and taxpayers to the fore. To these, the Conservatives' central message was economic security under the National government. In one election poster (Figure 5.1), John Bull, that icon of the national interest and middle-class common sense, was seen bailing himself out of the Socialist aircraft and placing his faith in the 'National' parachute. To any passing Liberal voters it suggested that, even with the National government's policy to abandon free trade in favour of protection, John Bull, historically 'the very embodiment of [their] free-trade orthodoxy',[13] would not hesitate to sacrifice orthodoxy in order to secure prosperity. The context of crisis was instrumental in enabling Conservatives to present retrenchment not just as the traditional protection of ratepayers' interests but as a self-denying act of patriotism by all suburban residents. This applied to residents of municipal estates facing the possible

---

[13] M. Taylor, 'John Bull and the iconography of public opinion in England, c. 1712–1929', *P&P*, 134 (1992), 93–128, 122–3.

curtailment of services and amenities as well as public-sector employees, notably teachers, whose salaries had already been cut. Echoes of wartime sacrifice were inevitable. Taking his cue from a Conservative poster (Figure 5.2) that featured Trafalgar Square as the unmistakable backdrop, Churchill likened the formation of the National government to a battle won, citing Pitt after victory in Trafalgar ('England has saved herself by her exertions') and steeling his voters for further worthwhile sacrifices to come.[14] Similarly in Ilford, a Conservative councillor made a plea for the 'spirit of sacrifice which gave us victory in the war and alone can give us victory now'.[15] The national crisis generated appeals that Conservatives could deploy in old and new suburbia alike.

While national crisis lent unprecedented clarity to the Conservatives' anti-socialist world view, it did little to develop grassroots cooperation between the anti-socialist parties. The fact that so many Liberal voters

Figures 5.1 and 5.2 National government posters, general election 1931.[16]
Photos by The Conservative Party Archive / Hulton Archive / Getty Images.

---

[14] Speeches reported in *Liverpool Post & Mercury*, 16 Oct. 1931 and *West Essex Gazette*, 24 Oct. 1931.
[15] *Ilford Recorder*, 9 Oct. 1931.   [16] CPA, posters 1931–05 and 1931–20.

140   Popular Conservatism and the National Government

supported National Conservative candidates is one sign of anti-socialist cooperation across party lines. But if the real dynamics of anti-socialism are to be understood, together with their impact on Conservative experiences of the National government, then a distinction must be drawn between anti-socialism as reflected in electoral outcomes and anti-socialism as imagined and practised by the rival anti-Labour parties.

A paradoxical feature of the 1931 election in many suburbs was the extent to which the contest was fought out between the Conservative and Liberal parties. Labour's reputation appeared so dissipated that local Liberal parties saw the election as an opportunity to reassert themselves as the alternative to Conservatism. As the *Liverpool Post* explained in relation to the Liberal candidature in East Toxteth: 'At the last two elections here the Conservatives won on a minority poll, and, it is believed, in view of the present temper of the Labour electors, that a Liberal candidate might just top the poll ... The temptation for the Liberals is a strong one, and it is possible that a Conservative walk-over ... will not be permitted.'[17] The leadership of anti-socialist opinion was not a role that pre-existed; it was therefore fought over. Churchill realised this as soon as the Epping Liberal association announced its plans to contest the seat. Whereas his first election address combined a crude attack on the Labour government with a confident claim of Liberal support, his second address admonished the local Liberal party for 'flouting the spirit of Conservative and Liberal cooperation'.[18] In this way the 1931 election might be said to have returned suburban politics momentarily to pre-Labour days, as Conservatives and Liberals fought over the rights to anti-socialism.

At first glance, many features of the political culture associated with the fiscal question during its Edwardian heyday remained largely unchanged. 'Between now and polling day', predicted the *Ilford Recorder* after the first week of the election campaign, 'the respective merits of Free Trade and Tariffs will be the subject of the liveliest controversy'.[19] In Birmingham the 'Dumping Van', fitted with windows on either side to display 'dumped foreign goods' and equipped with a gramophone and loudspeaker, made its rounds through the constituencies to remind voters of the ongoing tariffs crusade.[20] Liberal activists warned against the impact of increased food prices on middle-class households, while Conservatives

---

[17] *Liverpool Post & Mercury*, 14 Oct. 1931. Liberal intervention in Ilford was given the same explanation by the *Ilford Recorder*, 16 Oct. 1931. Similarly in Birmingham Moseley, where the Liberal association did not field a candidate, the *Birmingham Post* (19 Oct. 1931) argued that the self-evident failure of the Labour government served immediately to undermine the local threat of Labour and, consequently, to elevate the importance of securing the Liberal vote.

[18] Election address, 10 and 20 Oct. 1931, Churchill papers, CHAR 7/8/1 and 7/8/7.

[19] *Ilford Recorder*, 16 Oct. 1931.   [20] *Birmingham Post*, 5, 23 Oct. 1931.

The Politics of Anti-Socialism in the Suburbs

like Patrick Hannon condemned free trade as a policy that condoned imports of manufactured goods 'made by foreigners under conditions which would not be tolerated here', at a time when 'our own people' were turning in increased numbers to life on the dole.[21]

Yet the Liberals were intent on more than a rearguard defence of a cherished shibboleth. If the welfare of suburban households gave many Liberals reason to continue to deploy traditional free-trade arguments, it also saw them forging a distinctly moderate anti-socialist stance in favour of restrained economy. Since August, local Conservative parties had led a spirited and at first seemingly popular economy campaign. In Ilford an economy committee was hastily convened by the mayor and supported publicly by Sir George Hamilton (the Conservative member), followed by an announcement of a £20,000 immediate cut in borough expenditure.[22] However, there followed a backlash. The reduction to teachers' salaries, decreed nationally and implemented by local authorities, generated a good deal of public hostility to the government and sympathy for a sector whose influence spread well beyond its own boundaries.[23] Together with letters of protest, one of the unions placed a large notice in the press, stating: 'The National Union of Teachers accepts the principle of Equality of Sacrifice in a National Emergency. A cut of 15% is equivalent to permanent penalising and special taxation levied upon teachers and "IS NOT EQUALITY OF SACRIFICE".'[24] Also controversial in Ilford was the 5 per cent cut in municipal wages, which attracted a spate of letters in the local press from angry ratepayers. One of these commented: 'I, and no doubt hundreds like myself, would not appreciate the three-pence or four-pence off our rates knowing that the poorer paid workers are to lose 2s. 6d. or 3s. per week off their wages.'[25] Many of those who stood to lose from such cuts were the manual and non-manual staff of the borough council. The latter group, the so-called clerical proletariat, represented the lower-paid ratepayers, many of whom had identified with the anti-profiteering grievances represented by

---

[21] *Ilford Recorder*, 23 Oct. 1931, *Birmingham Post*, 14 Oct. 1931. See Hannon's reply to a Liberal questionnaire, ibid., 21 Oct. 1931.

[22] *Ilford Recorder*, 28 Aug., 4, 11, 25 Sep. 1931.

[23] The Conservative candidate in Liverpool East Toxteth was warned that more than 1,500 voters in the division were teachers or related to teachers (Mrs Banister to Buchan-Hepburn, n.d. Oct. 1931, Churchill Archives Centre, Hailes papers, HAIS 1/3). For letters of protest against the 'unequal sacrifices' of teachers, see *Ilford Recorder*, 18 Sep., 2 Oct. 1931 and *Birmingham Post*, 22 Sep. 1931.

[24] *Birmingham Press*, 17 Sep. 1931; for letters see ibid., 22 Sep. 1931, *Ilford Recorder*, 18 Sep., 2 Oct. 1931.

[25] *Ilford Recorder*, 9 Oct. 1931. The council decided to suspend implementation of the 5 per cent cut for three months following the threat of strike action by municipal transport workers. Ibid., 2 Oct. 1931.

142   Popular Conservatism and the National Government

Labour in the early post-war years.[26] Therefore, when Liberals like Mrs Whitten, chairman of the Ilford Women's Liberal Association, campaigned to defend free trade and curtail government economy, they positioned themselves so as to reclaim those votes that had been lost to Labour in the 1920s.[27]

Another challenge to the Conservatives was the Liberal claim to be the true 'national' party. In a letter to the *Liverpool Post* shortly before the general election, the chairman of the Liberal party in East Toxteth argued that, while the existing government was truly 'national', 'a government supported only by Tory members pledged to tariffs cannot possibly be a real National Government'.[28] Many Liberal candidates condemned the decision to call the election. It was 'nothing but a ramp', according to Granville Sharp, a former Liberal candidate addressing voters in Epping. 'The duty of the National Government had only been half-finished, and they "threw in the towel".' He laid the charge of political self-interest squarely at the feet of Conservative protectionists, who 'felt this was their opportunity, and they took it'.[29] The Liberals, by contrast, were casting aside their own ambitions. While old sectional debates were forced upon them by the protectionists, their own priority was to secure peace, and thereby prosperity, through disarmament and international order, to which ends they grandly pledged themselves to call a world conference.[30]

The Conservative provincial press responded to such Liberal interventions with scorn. The *Birmingham Post* carried editorials entitled 'Obstructive Liberals' and 'The Liberal Duty', and commented sarcastically 'how vain it is for even a National Government at a time of grave emergency to angle for the support of the Liberal Party *en bloc*'. It asserted how the Conservatives were 'in a better position to support a retrenchment policy than any Liberal can be, since they are not identified with any Yellow Book programme of extravagance'.[31] By contrast, Conservative candidates and activists responded more circumspectly. The Liberal vision of anti-socialism demanded that they did so, for it promised a 'national' culture of government that was free of class and vested interests, concerned for

---

[26] In 1920 an observer of Ilford society commented: 'It is generally thought that the vast majority of Ilford residents belong to what is regarded as the middle classes ... But the point I wish to drive home is, that there is practically no middle class in Ilford, inasmuch as all, with perhaps a few exceptions, if regarded from a certain point of view, have to labour for their daily bread. Therefore all belong to the one, viz., the working class, irrespective of each one's occupation, or where one resides.' *Ilford Recorder*, 10 Sep. 1920.
[27] *Ilford Recorder*, 9, 23 Oct. 1931.
[28] *Liverpool Post*, 17 Oct. 1931; also speech by Edgar Wallace in Birmingham, *Birmingham Post*, 17 Sep. 1931.
[29] *West Essex Gazette*, 24 Oct. 1931.
[30] Ibid., and Liberal poster printed in *West Essex Gazette*, 10 Oct. 1931.
[31] *Birmingham Post*, 5, 22 Oct. 1931.

Britain's reputation and its values, and distinguished by a revered history of reform and statesmanship. It was a reminder of the continued influence that Liberalism commanded in British society. As one party worker reflected shortly after the election, 'though the Liberals in Liverpool have never been strong numerically, they have individually been many of them outstanding figures and today just as in the past [they] wield an influence quite out of proportion to their numbers'.[32]

The Conservative party's general response to the problem of Liberal intervention, which was to 'emphasise the points which unite the two parties rather than those which divide them',[33] now bore a distinctly Baldwinian hallmark. Candidates readily expressed admiration for the Liberals' past. Patrick Hannon, not previously given to political ecumenism, referred to 'the great Liberal Party, with its individualistic character, with all its lofty conceptions of freedom, and its respect for national institutions'.[34] Great importance was placed on securing public Liberal backing, as in Ilford, where the Conservatives claimed to have the allegiance of a key Liberal worker who was 'making it his personal job to get some 50 of his old Liberal friends to work for Sir George Hamilton'.[35] In Epping, where the tone was generally less conciliatory towards local Liberals, there was much high praise for the public service of Liberal elder statesmen like Viscount Grey and Sir John Simon.[36]

In particular, Conservatives invoked British Liberalism's reputation for rational thought and intelligent reform and argued that a sentimental defence of free trade was now at odds with such a tradition of government. Tariffs were presented not as antithetical to free trade but rather as the logical successor to it, as the new guarantor of peace and plenty. Sir George Hamilton told voters in Ilford that if only the country had realised the failure of the liberal orthodoxy on trade by the time of the 1923 general election, when a protectionist solution was offered, 'he did not think they would be in the position they were today'.[37] This reflected the fact that, during the 1920s, not only had academic opinion shifted towards tariffs, but the policy's growing public profile had begun to overshadow the more plebeian wisdoms that for so long had underpinned free trade's inviolable position in political discourse. The huge press coverage accorded to Keynes's decision to abandon free trade in

---

[32] P. John to Buchan-Hepburn, 5 Nov. 1931, Hailes papers, HAIS 1/4. [33] Ibid.
[34] *Birmingham Post*, 21 Oct. 1931. [35] *Ilford Recorder*, 23 Oct. 1931.
[36] Churchill argued that the Liberal candidate's intervention showed his failure to understand the patriotic spirit and political intelligence of voters in Epping, but he went on to valorise 'statesmen like Lord Grey ... who have no ambitious axe to grind'. Election address, 20 Oct. 1931, Churchill papers, CHAR 7/8/7.
[37] *Ilford Recorder*, 23 Oct. 1931.

144   Popular Conservatism and the National Government

March 1931 was one important signal of the changing atmosphere.[38] Free trade was now a convention and therefore could be branded an anomaly within Liberalism itself. In order to maintain the dynamism and modernity that were traditionally the traits of British Liberalism, Conservatives made the case that protectionism held the only hope of 'the opening up of vast new opportunities for our people under a more liberal, a more generously conceived and a more hopeful regime than they have enjoyed before'.[39]

The scale of the Conservatives' 1931 triumph in the suburbs was unprecedented. The party's majority in already impregnable seats like Birmingham Moseley was augmented by more than 20,000 additional votes, while in safe and more marginal seats it dwarfed anything that had been achieved since the war. Whole cities – Birmingham, Manchester, Sheffield, and (almost) Liverpool – turned Conservative.[40] Perhaps this result really did reflect a definitive abandonment of free trade by the middle classes. If so, it would be in keeping with the arguments made by McKibbin and Trentmann that middle-class political outlooks had grown more defensive since the war as financial self-interest displaced the altruism of the Edwardian years, with the result that economic retrenchment took priority over free trade.[41] But it did not reflect the disappearance of suburban Liberalism. Activists attempting to fashion a Conservative-aligned anti-socialist bloc from the gains made in 1931 would continue to find the story of post-war Liberalism frustratingly equivocal, marked as much by cultural survival as electoral decline.

The Politics of Recovery in the Suburbs

In view of the overwhelming National majority that made plain the scale of anti-socialist opinion in the suburbs, represented in parliament predominantly by Conservatives, it was inevitable that the party exploited this moment to reassert its image as the true patriotic party. The fact that a number of non-party associations backed the National government also revealed to Conservatives the value of doing so. In Epping, the Royal British Legion saw in the new government a 'spirit of comradeship' that had been lacking in politics since the armistice. During the election, representatives from local branches of the Women's Institute, the Christian Brotherhood, and the League of Nations Union all expressed solidarity

---

[38] F. Trentmann, *Free trade nation: commerce, consumption, and civil society in modern Britain* (Oxford, 2008), Part II, esp. 336–47.

[39] *Birmingham Post*, 17 Oct. 1931.

[40] The only exception was the Scotland division of Liverpool, where Labour won.

[41] McKibbin, 'Conventional wisdom'; Trentmann, *Free trade nation*, 345–6.

with the National ideal.[42] This helped to thaw activists' attitudes towards non-party organisations in the 1930s. While the resulting relationship still fell short of coordinated cooperation, the overlap in personnel could now come into its own; it became more acceptable to appear on both party and non-party platforms, thereby helping to reconcile the conflicting loyalties of many others who sought membership of both types of organisations.[43] Party activists recognised this. In a bid to preserve the 'spirit' of 1931, the organisation in Epping trialled a non-political form of party membership. A letter of invitation was distributed among the local electorate promising, first, the 'essential meeting-ground' for political aficionados as well as those who sought like-minded friends in a setting that provided year-round entertainment, and secondly, membership of an educative organisation in which members could listen and contribute to informed debate on topical issues. This echoed the model of non-aligned active citizenship promoted by the voluntary associations of the interwar years, and gave recipients the option to sign up under the heading 'I am not a supporter of the Conservative Party'.[44] Nothing similar had been attempted in 1924, when Churchill stood on an anti-socialist, 'constitutional' ticket. The ability to do so now was underpinned by the cross-party culture of the government.

Not all Conservative associations were so bold as to embrace non-party membership.[45] But, after years of bemoaning the apathy of the suburban electorate, most were determined to capture the renewed enthusiasm of suburban voters with recruitment drives and social events of a more non-party flavour. The result, though not a clean break with the insistent partisanship of the 1920s, tended towards a political culture that combined the respectable sociability of the Primrose League – garden fetes, tea parties, charity appeals – and the didactic language of Baldwinite Conservatism. Crucially, this coincided with an increase in local membership, and often the creation of several new branches, that continued to

---

[42] *West Essex Gazette*, 5 Sep., 10 Oct., 21 Nov. 1931.

[43] Ibid. Several officials of the Epping CA appeared as officials of the local branch of the League of Nations Union (Mrs Gerald Buxton) and the British Legion (Captain A. Jones). Likewise, in Ilford, Mr F. Hiley was a leading organiser of the party's local executive committee (*Ilford Recorder*, 25 Sep. 1931).

[44] AGM minutes and letter of invitation (in pamphlet form), 10 Feb. 1932, Redbridge Local History Centre, Woodford Church End Branch, Epping CA, Acc. A6853. On the ethos of the voluntary associations, see H. McCarthy, 'Parties, voluntary associations, and democratic politics in inter-war Britain', *HJ*, 50 (2007), 891–912.

[45] The Liverpool organisation considered such a move but ultimately decided that non-political affiliation was unlikely to yield sufficient funds through subscription (Executive committee, 3 Apr. 1933, Liverpool Record Office, Liverpool CA, 329 CON/1/1/3).

146 Popular Conservatism and the National Government

the late 1930s. In Ilford, for instance, the party registered more than 500 new members between March 1934 and March 1935.[46]

This helps to explain some of the ways in which the party now responded to the ongoing expansion of the suburbs. In Moseley, as in the Edgbaston and Erdington divisions of Birmingham, the divisional association moved quickly to establish branch organisations in the municipal estates. Given the initial absence of familiar amenities and civic identity, which struck contemporary observers as a signal feature of life on the new estates,[47] the party sought to exploit the vacuum. In January 1932 it held 'smoking concerts' to welcome new residents to the estates.[48] The divisional agent identified a handful of volunteers in each estate to act as branch organisers. These would recruit new members (for which a target per estate was set), deliver a programme of social events, and cultivate the goodwill of other emerging institutions, notably the church. They would also be the eyes and ears of the agent, conducting a street by street canvass of the estate and reporting on social and associational activities in the vicinity. In 1936, twenty-two such branches operated within Moseley alone, nine of them women's organisations, and 265 'social' functions were held.[49] In Epping, where population growth was more modest and called for less concerted efforts, the party likewise established a handful of new branches and carefully associated itself with new sites of urban recreation. One such site was the Majestic Theatre in Woodford, an area of the constituency in which Labour was known to be most active.[50] When the theatre was transformed into a 'super cinema' in 1934, Churchill was strongly advised by the vice-chairman of the party association to accept the invitation to preside at the official opening. 'A very large number of people from Woodford and the contiguous districts will be present who do not usually attend political meetings', explained Sir James Hawkey, and the new

---

[46] E.g., executive committee, 25 Apr., 27 Jun., 16 Oct. 1934, 1 Mar. 1935, 27 Sep. 1937, Ilford CA, 90/61/1/1; management committee, 11 Dec. 1931, 15 Jan., 11 Feb. 1932, Birmingham CUA; women's committee, 7 Feb. 1933, Woodford Bridge ward (Epping CA), Acc. A7347.

[47] See R. Durant, *Watling: a survey of social life on a new housing estate* (London, 1939); R. Jevons and J. Madge, *Housing estates: a study of Bristol Corporation policy and practice between the wars* (Bristol, 1946).

[48] Management committee, 15, 21 Jan. 1932, Birmingham CUA.

[49] Moseley Division Unionist Association annual report for the year 1936, n.d., Parliamentary Archives, Hannon papers, HNN 73/3.

[50] E.g., AGM women's committee, 13 Jan. 1931, Woodford Bridge branch, Epping CA, Acc. A7347.

management had 'promised even more than I could have expected with regard to the use of the theatre for political meetings'.[51]

Suburban growth was in large part a product of government policy. Together with tariffs, the policy of 'cheap money' through low interest rates constituted what Chamberlain called the 'two main pillars' of his agenda at the Treasury. While not necessarily kind to the interests of all middle-class voters, least of all the holders of government debt, it fuelled a construction boom that served the interests of aspiring property owners and helped to propel a consumer-led recovery.[52] In this way it expanded the ranks of the property-owning 'middle classes', whose interests, as McKibbin and others have argued, formed the focus of Conservative domestic statecraft between the wars.[53] But such a migration of people to the suburbs also generated new sets of voter interests. Some of these were common to established and new residents alike, like those affecting commuters in London's eastern dormitories. In November 1932 Sir George Hamilton established the Ilford and District Railway Users' Association, 'to promote, improve and protect the interests of the travelling public of Ilford'. Together with Conservative MPs in neighbouring areas it lobbied the government for the electrification of the suburban lines and a tube extension beyond old Ilford to Chadwell Heath and Romford. Both objectives were met with a central grant worth £35million in June 1935.[54] Other interests were more divisive, reflecting sources of conflict between old and new suburbia. Within days of Churchill opening the 'super cinema' in Woodford, a mass public meeting in Epping voted by a large majority (167 to 77) to reject the proposed Sunday opening of cinemas – a reminder, if any were needed, of the enduring presence of nonconformists in public life.[55] Later in the same month, Churchill was advised that the government's Electricity Supply Bill, which gave the Central Electricity Board new powers to rationalise the supply network (in large part to feed the expanding railways), risked sacrificing the commercial interests of electricity company shareholders to the consumer interests of the new estates.[56]

---

[51] Hawkey to Churchill, 31 Oct. 1934 and souvenir programme, opening of the Majestic Theatre, Woodford, 5 Nov. 1934, Churchill papers, CHAR 7/12B (217–18) and CHAR 7/12A (43).

[52] R. Self, *Neville Chamberlain: a biography* (Aldershot, 2007), 196; N. H. Dimsdale, 'British monetary policy and the exchange rate, 1920–1938', *Oxford Economic Papers*, 33 (1981), 306–49.

[53] McKibbin, 'Class and conventional wisdom'; see also J. Ramsden, '"A party for owners or a party for earners?" How far did the British Conservative party really change after 1945?', *TRHS*, 37 (1987), 49–63, esp. 56–7.

[54] Hamilton to Churchill, 14 Apr. 1934, Churchill papers, CHAR 7/12B (279–80); *Ilford Recorder*, 6, 27 Jun. 1935.

[55] *West Essex Gazette*, 17 Nov. 1934.

[56] Hawkey to Churchill, 27 Nov. 1934, Churchill papers, CHAR 7/12B (232).

148   Popular Conservatism and the National Government

Where the interests of old and new suburbia conflicted, the Conservatives' prospects of speaking with authority on behalf of the whole community could be jeopardised by rival local organisations. This is clear in the case of Ilford, where the population increased from 131,000 in 1931 to 167,000 in 1938.[57] For the residents of North Hainault and Chigwell, the corner of the constituency to experience the most growth after Becontree, the question of civic amenities became a central concern. A new branch of the Ilford Ratepayers Association was set up to lobby on behalf of residents, initially with the encouragement of the *Ilford Recorder*, which in an editorial of 1932 lamented the lack of civic spirit among newcomers, commenting that without the 'social and other amenities which older areas enjoy ... to these new citizens Ilford is little more than a name; they are not concerned with the many interests and activities which go to make up our corporate life'.[58] The *Recorder* therefore welcomed the establishment of 'local associations' in the belief that their interest in town planning would also promote active citizenship.[59] Meanwhile, residents in old Ilford were becoming increasingly concerned with economy in local government and it was not long before the town was witness to a revival of anti-waste politics. The *Recorder* ran a provocative series of articles in the spring of 1934 which revealed that the benefit of the 6d cut in income tax announced in Chamberlain's recovery budget was to be cancelled out by an undisclosed increase of 11d in the local rates.[60] As the town's main ratepayers' association took up the issue, the focus of grievance shifted from the council to the perceived root cause of the borough's financial difficulties, namely the development of new housing of low rateable value. An unseemly public spat ensued between rival ratepayers' camps, with the North Hainault branch splintering from the main association and forming the North Ilford Ratepayers Association. The new body attacked the old for pursuing an exclusive agenda that ignored the needs of Hainault's growing population, while the old organisation, supported by the *Recorder*, created the picture of a civic infrastructure struggling to cope under the strain of a 'lesser Becontree' and suggested 'green space' or an airport as preferable alternatives.[61] As the chairman of the North Ilford

[57] W. R. Powell (ed.), *Victoria history of the county of Essex, vol. 5* (London, 1966), 63–4.
[58] *Ilford Recorder*, 17 Mar. 1932; also 14 Jan. 1932.
[59] See E. Darling, '"Enriching and enlarging the whole sphere of human activities": the work of the voluntary sector in housing reform in inter-war Britain', in C. Lawrence & A-K. Mayer (eds.), *Regenerating England: science, medicine and culture in inter-war Britain* (Amsterdam, 2000), 149–78; A. Olechnowicz, 'Civic leadership and education for democracy: the Simons and the Wythenshawe estate', *CBH*, 14 (1999), 3–26.
[60] *Ilford Recorder*, 12, 19 Apr. 1934.
[61] See the correspondence, articles and editorial in *Ilford Recorder*, 21 Feb. 1935.

The Politics of Anti-Socialism in the Suburbs 149

ratepayers diplomatically explained, 'although economy in its wisest sense is the keynote of all ratepayers' associations, the views of residents in the new and the old parts of the borough are not necessarily the same'.[62]

According to McKibbin, although relations between old and new suburbia could be tense, the Conservatives were able to remain the party of the 'middle class' because it proved itself 'open enough to incorporate both'.[63] As this chapter shows, the need to protect the gains made in 1931 had indeed produced an accommodating style of Conservatism, more muted in its partisanship. But once again Conservative efforts were not uncontested. The well-being of a large section of the new suburban population, the so-called black-coated workers employed typically as clerks and shop assistants, played an important part in the Labour party's revival in many urban centres. For many of these residents, living on stagnant salaries and contending with both job insecurity and new mortgage demands, national recovery did not always seem altogether assured. Many of them joined the cooperative movement, which the Conservatives continued to view as a Labour Trojan horse into the ranks of the respectable lower middle classes.[64] Labour opposed the anomalous position into which the government's Unemployment Bill placed black-coated workers. Contrary to the manual worker, who with a few exceptions was already in the unemployment insurance scheme and qualified for assistance upon exhausting his insurance benefit, and the agricultural labourer whose position was made the subject of statutory investigation, the non-manual worker on more than £250 a year was excluded. '[I]f they require assistance', protested the TUC, 'they will have to go to the Poor Law as at present'.[65] By engaging the interests of the new middle class in this way, Labour showed itself capable of mobilising parts of the suburban as well as the inner-city vote. This resulted in municipal gains for Labour, most notably in 1934 when the party won control of the London County Council.[66] By 1935, the architect of Labour's recovery in London, Herbert Morrison, was trying

---

[62] *Ilford Recorder*, 14 Feb. 1935.   [63] McKibbin, *Classes and cultures*, 529.

[64] AGM, 26 Feb. 1932; sub-committee meeting, 15 May 1933; labour advisory committee, 14 Apr. 1934; general council, 11 Jul. 1934, Bodleian Library, CPA, Home Counties North Area, ARE 8/1/1.

[65] *The government evades its national responsibility: TUC criticism of the Unemployment Bill, 1933* (London, 1933), 9. During the bill's parliamentary passage, Labour proposed a new clause that required the government to incorporate two occupational groups into the insurance scheme, domestic servants and clerical workers, the latter described as those 'in occupations, other than manual occupations, receiving a salary of not more than £500 per annum'; the new clause was defeated (*The Times*, 3 May 1934).

[66] *The Times*, 2, 3 Nov. 1933, 3 Nov. 1934.

150   Popular Conservatism and the National Government

to claim that the extension of the suburban railways was in fact a Labour achievement.[67]

Party Identities and Suburban Radicalism

Since the war, Conservatives had repeatedly found that few factors endangered the party's fortune in some of its own heartlands so much as the apathy of known supporters. They were reminded of this barely two years into the National government, as those 'known' (or presumed) to have voted National Conservative in 1931 appeared to threaten desertion.[68] In by-elections in Liverpool Exchange, with its large business vote, and in the safe provincial towns of Ashford, Hitchin, and Altrincham, held in 1933, Conservative majorities dropped significantly – the result not of a significant rise in the Labour vote (except in Altrincham, which was uncontested in 1931) but of a significant decline in the turnout of National Conservative voters.[69]

It struck some contemporaries that this apathy signalled discontent among traditional Conservative voters with the government's India policy.[70] From the publication of the government's White Paper in March 1933 to the Government of India Act two years later, Rothermere's *Daily Mail* ran a virulent anti-reform campaign that reached millions of Conservative-voting readers.[71] Sections of the party responded in a similar vein, with efforts to protect Conservative principles imperilled by cross-party consensus. Established in June 1933 by 'diehard' peers and MPs, including Churchill, the India Defence League was not only a pressure group – it was also intended as a reassertion of party identity. Speaking to voters in Epping, Churchill 'emphasized the necessity of the Conservative Party developing its own partisanship' and urged the parties to 'plough their separate furrows' so as not to mislead the public into imagining a consensus.[72] It was mostly in the constituencies of its leading members that the IDL operated with

---

[67] *Ilford Recorder*, 27 Jun. 1935. For Morrison's work, see Jeffery, 'The suburban nation: politics and class in Lewisham'.

[68] E.g., executive committee, 25 Apr. 1934, Redbridge Local History Centre, Ilford CA, 90/61/1/1.

[69] Compared with 1931, the Conservatives received 8,840 fewer votes in Liverpool Exchange, 4,840 in Ashford, and 11,272 in Hitchin, while in Altrincham they polled 3,120 fewer votes than in 1929.

[70] Editorial in *Yorkshire Post*, 10 Jun. 1933.

[71] For Churchill's involvement, see I. St John, '*Writing to the defence of empire*: Winston Churchill's press campaign against constitutional reform in India, 1929–1935', in C. Kaul (ed.), *Media and the British empire* (Basingstoke, 2006), 104–24.

[72] *West Essex Gazette*, 10 Nov. 1934.

The Politics of Anti-Socialism in the Suburbs 151

the blessing of local party organisers; elsewhere there is less evidence of receptiveness.

But its implications were nonetheless felt more broadly within the party, as one of its leading lights, Winston Churchill's son Randolph, emerged as the exciting young face of independent Conservatism. Following the example of his grandfather, who cultivated the party grass-roots to establish for himself a voice in the party in the 1870s and 1880s, he used the IDL to build up a following among members of the Junior Imperial League.[73] At the JIL annual conference in May 1933, the young Churchill moved a large majority of members to back his resolution opposing the government's India policy. 'The duty of patriotic organizations like the league', he told his audience, 'was to recall their leaders to their own proper path of duty'.[74] Given its deep-rooted trade connections with India, Lancashire provided a regional focus for much of Randolph's activities; he threatened to stand as an independent Conservative at the by-election in Altrincham, which shared many of Manchester's commercial interests, and eventually stood in Liverpool Wavertree in February 1935.[75] The effect of a rejuvenated JIL was similar and evident elsewhere. A leading party organiser in Ilford, David Hutchison, keen to match Labour's assertive partisanship in municipal elections, drummed up enough support on the Becontree estate to start a new branch of the Young Conservatives' Guild. This in turn helped him to fight the 1933 and 1934 municipal elections on a Conservative, rather than 'national', 'ratepayer', or 'anti-socialist' basis, to a degree considered 'unusual and remarkable' by the *Recorder*.[76]

To be sure, many Conservative associations were unwilling to reassert party identity in this way if it meant dissenting from government policy, and among those who did seek to revitalise the party, qua party, not all were exercised by India.[77] However, one overall effect of the agitation was that its electoral consequences, as they materialised, invited Conservatives to appreciate anew the advantages that membership of the National government carried. For instance, Hutchison's partisan

---

[73] Membership of the JIL was for men and women aged 14–25 and stood at 118,868 in December 1934. See S. Ball, *Portrait of a party: the Conservative party in Britain, 1918–1945* (Oxford, 2013), 154–6.

[74] *The Times*, 8 May 1933.

[75] For press coverage of his machinations in the summer of 1933, see *Yorkshire Post*, 27 May, 2 Jun. 1933.

[76] *Ilford Recorder*, 26 Oct., 23, 30 Nov. 1933.

[77] Party organisers in Liverpool spent much of 1933–5 staving off advances from Randolph, who sought adoption as a prospective parliamentary candidate in the city (central council, 30 Nov. 1934; executive committee, 29 Apr. 1935, Liverpool CA, 329 Con/1/1/3). Hutchison, the main proponent of party differentiation, supported Indian constitutional reform (*Ilford Recorder*, 15 Mar. 1935).

152   Popular Conservatism and the National Government

campaigns in Ilford rebounded badly when the party suffered significant losses to Labour in 1934 and decided thereafter to throw its weight behind Ratepayers' candidates.[78] If defence of the Raj was intended to re-engage lost Conservative votes, then a by-election held in Portsmouth North in February 1934 was a poor advertisement for such a strategy, since the Conservative association's candidate, Admiral Sir Roger Keyes – a household name in the port city, standing as a National Conservative but also an opponent of the India White paper – lost almost 9,000 votes against a Labour vote that hardly moved. In Liverpool Wavertree, Randolph Churchill succeeded only in splitting the Conservative vote and facilitating a Labour gain.

Through such experience Conservatives were reminded that success at the next general election would rely on their ability to reassemble the conditions of 1931. Besides the by-elections, the municipal elections of 1934 helped to crystallise, almost nationwide, what was at stake. Councillors served three-year terms, and therefore Labour's widespread gains represented a very public reversal of the National landslide.[79] Nor, crucially, was this realisation confined to supporters of the government's India policy. During a speaking tour of his constituency, even Churchill, notwithstanding his public insistence on separate party identities, was careful to remind voters that 'I entirely support the National Government and give them my vote – except where special reasons arise (laughter)'. He invariably towed the official line on domestic matters by propounding the great success of government policy in securing economic recovery.[80] In another speech in Theydon Bois, he reiterated his loyalty to the government and, speaking directly to local Liberals, explained that he opposed the India bill on grounds of religious freedom for the Indian people, warning that violent sectarianism would follow the withdrawal of Britain's 'impartial police force'. He concluded with a paean to the pre-war Liberal government, 'the best he had ever seen ... [with] abler men in it than any other Government he had served in'.[81] Retention of the Liberal vote, assumed to be pro-reform, was also on activists' minds in Ilford, where despite their own 'adverse' opinion of the India bill they acquiesced in the pro-reform stance of their member, Sir George Hamilton.[82]

---

[78] Municipal elections committee, 18 Mar. 1935 (cf. 14 Mar. 1934), Ilford CA, 90/61/7/1.
[79] As some had anticipated – e.g., central council, 11 Apr. 1934, Liverpool CA, Con/1/1/3.
[80] Speech in Epping, *West Essex Gazette*, 10 Nov. 1934. In preparation for the tour, Churchill's office requested from the Ministry of Agriculture 'information with regard to the beneficial effect of the various measures ... upon Essex' (Churchill's private secretary to Walter Elliot's private secretary, 27 Oct. 1934, Churchill papers, CHAR 7/11(151)).
[81] *West Essex Gazette*, 10 Nov. 1934.   [82] AGM, 13 Mar. 1935, Ilford CA, 90/61/1/1.

The Politics of Anti-Socialism in the Suburbs 153

However, by the time the Conservatives had recommitted themselves to the National government, so too had many Liberals reappraised their own position in relation to the National politics. This had implications for how – and if – '1931' could be repeated. Ever since their stand against the introduction of tariffs in 1932, the Samuelite Liberals had retained a good degree of independent agency despite officially remaining aligned with the government in parliament. The effect of this, often unpredictable, was seen in several of the by-elections. In Altrincham, a Liberal candidate stood against his Conservative counterpart on an anti-socialist platform, thus endangering the anti-Labour vote. A week earlier in Hitchin, the Liberal association decided to abstain. They advised voters that 'if you cannot conscientiously vote for a National candidate, you need not vote', and warned that if Liberal votes were found in large numbers to support the National Conservative in a repeat of 1931 they would struggle to find a 'first-class' Liberal candidate at the next general election.[83] In the famous case of East Fulham, in October 1933 the local Liberal association did not field a candidate but instructed Liberal voters to back the Labour candidate, who duly overturned the Conservative majority.[84]

The relationship of the Liberal public to the National government was undergoing change. Moreover, it was doing so according to Liberal initiative. In a speech during the National Liberal Federation conference, Samuel predicted that the Conservatives would force an early general election and use the opportunity to absorb Liberals and National Labour into the Conservative party. He particularly warned Simonite Liberals, who were 'in danger of seeing their seats handed over to the Conservative party as completely as Birmingham constituencies were handed over by the Unionist Liberals a generation ago'.[85] Shortly after East Fulham, Samuel crossed the floor of the House of Commons and with this the Liberals (except the Simonites) became, officially, an opposition party. The effect in the constituencies was twofold. First, local Liberals began to regroup. The *Liverpool Post* reported that the South Liverpool Liberal Federation had appointed a new agent, opened a new club, and launched an election fund, 'in further evidence of the increasing activity in Liberal circles in the East Toxteth and Wavertree divisions, former strongholds of the party'.[86] Whereas East Fulham showed that 'radical' Liberals

---

[83] *The Times*, 7 Jun. 1933.
[84] See M. Ceadel, 'Interpreting East Fulham', in C. Cook & J. Ramsden (eds.), *By-elections in British politics* (London, 1997), 94–111.
[85] *Yorkshire Post*, 19 May 1933.
[86] *Liverpool Post*, 25 Oct. 1934. It was perhaps no coincidence that the Liberal relaunch followed the local Conservative party's publication of *Progressive Liverpool*, intended to counteract

154   Popular Conservatism and the National Government

were capable of aligning with Labour, this degree of organisation suggested that Liberals, both radical and moderate, still had distinct ambitions of their own. Secondly, from the Conservatives' standpoint, the Liberals were able to pose as supporters or opponents of the National government at will. The Epping Liberal association opposed Churchill in 1931 and would do so again in 1935, yet spent much of 1934 campaigning alongside the government-supporting Union of Britain and India, an ostensibly non-party organisation in fact established by the India Office in collaboration with Conservative Central Office to counteract the IDL. According to the vice-chairman of Churchill's constituency association, local Liberals presided at UBI meetings and used the campaign to parade the support of a handful of Conservatives, including the former MP, General Colvin.[87]

By 1935, therefore, the cross-party politics of the National government had paradoxically made both Conservative and Liberal local parties more, not less, protective of their party identity, while also encouraging them to embrace seemingly non-party appeals in the process. This was not new; political parties had always claimed to represent the national interest and demonstrated this by cooperating with non-aligned auxiliary organisations.[88] But whereas in the 1920s associations like the Royal British Legion, the Women's Institute, and the League of Nations Union were met with suspicion among activists – precisely because their non-party ethos was thought to reflect public apathy with traditional party politics – in the 1930s they came to be viewed as representing a participatory political culture that could be harnessed to exemplify the party's non-party pretensions. It was not only the Conservatives who were inspired in this way. Whereas they sought to turn a cross-party government and the diverse (often anti-Conservative) 'National' vote of 1931 to their party advantage, the Liberals did likewise by harnessing the politics of the ultimate non-party organisation of the interwar years, the LNU – or so Conservatives thought. Founded in 1919 as a pressure group to promote the ideals of disarmament and collective security through the

---

Labour advances in the city (ibid., 23 Oct. 1934). In Ilford the Liberal Association similarly took the view that since Labour and 'Tory' party politics were foisted upon voters in local elections, it was 'vitally necessary that the Liberal point of view should be represented', duly pledging to make greater efforts to intervene in local elections and to select a parliamentary candidate (*Ilford Recorder*, 5 Oct. 1933, 18 Jan. 1934).

[87] Hawkey to Churchill, 10 Apr., 31 Oct. 1934, Churchill papers, CHAR 7/12A (133–4), 7/12B (217–18); *West Essex Gazette*, 28 Apr. 1934. For the UBI, see A. Muldoon, *Empire, politics and creation of the 1935 India Act: last act of the Raj* (Farnham, 2009), 191–5.

[88] See G. Searle, *Country before party: coalition and the idea of 'National Government' in modern Britain, 1885–1987* (London, 1995); F. Coetzee, *For party or country: nationalism and the dilemmas of popular Conservatism in Edwardian England* (Oxford, 1997); P. Ward, *Red flag and union jack: Englishness, patriotism and the British left, 1881–1924* (Woodbridge, 2004).

League of Nations, the LNU had more than 400,000 members by 1931, concentrated mostly in London, the Midlands, and the Home Counties.[89] Notwithstanding the involvement of some Conservative figures at both grassroots and national levels, by the early 1930s many Conservatives had come to view the organisation as a Liberal bandwagon. 'The kind of person who is really enthusiastic about the League', wrote Neville Chamberlain to his sister, 'is almost invariably a crank and a Liberal'.[90]

The LNU and its ideals were highly topical. The collapse of the World Disarmament Conference in October 1933 and media displays of dictatorship on the continent brought added urgency to the cause of disarmament and heightened public scrutiny of the government's defence policy. This, according to some historians, coincided with a broader shift in public commemoration of the Great War, in which international cooperation and the prevention of war began to displace the more celebratory valorisation of the sacrifice and patriotism of military service.[91] Moreover, the LNU was an especially appropriate fit for the Liberals, offering them a much-needed *raison d'être* in the post-free trade world. The pursuit of world peace enabled them to keep alive one important ideal of the free-trade faith, namely international amity through order. This resonated with the consciously moral – Conservatives would say idealistic – mindset that had remained deeply entrenched in British Liberalism since Gladstonian days, now intensely relevant to a younger generation of Britons fearful of another war.[92] Organisationally, too, the Liberals stood to benefit, as the LNU, with its close links to the Christian denominations, reinforced the political agency of nonconformist campaigners in particular.[93] What was good for the LNU was also good for the Liberals.

Like all effective non-party campaigns claiming to serve the 'national' interest, the LNU presented a challenge to Conservatives seeking to recapture the Liberal vote. Like Chamberlain, many Conservatives tended to consider the LNU either pacifist or isolationist, and politically biased to the left. Yet to say so in public would provoke damaging accusations of warmongering. For this reason, their usual strategy was to pay lip service to the LNU's enlightened campaigning while reiterating

[89] H. McCarthy, *The British people and the League of Nations: democracy, citizenship and internationalism, c.1918–1948* (Manchester, 2011), 4.
[90] *The Neville Chamberlain diary letters, vol. 4: the Downing Street years, 1934–1940*, ed. R. Self (Aldershot, 2005), 83 (to Hilda, 28 Jul. 1934).
[91] See M. Connelly, *The Great War, memory and ritual: commemoration in the city and east London, 1916–1939* (Woodbridge, 2002), ch.8.
[92] See M. Bentley, *The Liberal mind, 1914–1929* (Cambridge, 1977); Doyle, 'Urban Liberalism and the "lost generation"'.
[93] McCarthy, *The British people and the League of Nations*, ch.3.

156 Popular Conservatism and the National Government

the government's commitment to collective security. But this proved unsustainable in 1935 after the government, unlike the opposition parties, the churches, and civic organisations across the political spectrum, refused to cooperate in the so-called Peace Ballot.[94] As Martin Ceadel has argued, this decision left the Conservatives facing 'the nearest thing in the inter-war period to a true "Popular Front"'.[95]

With the general election approaching, the implications of a LNU-inspired popular front were formidable for the party in the towns and suburbs. It focused public opinion on foreign policy, which was more likely than domestic policy to reveal differences, often of a moral nature, between Conservative and Liberal voters. One Liverpool Liberal, who rejoiced in memories of Gladstone's 'idealistic' Midlothian campaign, wrote that he could not deny that Labour leaders were 'discourteous' and 'often rude', but, unlike the Conservatives, at least they shared the vision 'of a coming kingdom of heaven'.[96] This was symptomatic of a wholesome appeal that had the potential ultimately to damage irreparably the government's 'national' pretensions. Compared to the cross-class progressive alliance of the Edwardian years, the popular front's campaign for peace seemed classless. Unlike the official popular fronts of the continent, and in contrast to the Conservatives with their alleged commercial interest in the arms industry, it was rooted in the political centre ground. Moreover, it had the potential to coordinate the anti-Conservative vote, formally or otherwise, and thereby magnify the Liberal threat beyond what the Liberal party itself was capable of mustering.[97] In his post-mortem of the election, the chairman of the Conservative organisation in Liverpool noted:

It is something of a novelty in Liverpool for Liberals and Socialists to make a bargain. But such was the case. In Wavertree the Liberals did not put up a candidate, but used their influence with the electors to get them to vote for Mr Cleary (Socialist). The Socialists returned the compliment in East Toxteth where Mr Dennis (Liberal) was given Socialist help.[98]

---

[94] Officially known as 'The National Declaration on the League of Nations and Armaments', the Peace Ballot was conducted between November 1934 and June 1935 under the aegis of the LNU.

[95] M. Ceadel, 'The first British referendum: the Peace Ballot, 1934–5', *EHR*, 95 (1980), 810–39, 828.

[96] Letter to the editor, *Liverpool Daily Post*, 4 Nov. 1935.

[97] Samuel had anticipated 400 candidates (*Yorkshire Post*, 19 May 1933) but only 161 fought the 1935 election.

[98] Report to central council, 19 May 1936, Liverpool CA, 329 Con/1/1/3.

The Politics of Anti-Socialism in the Suburbs   157

Where no Lib-Lab agreement was made, as in Epping, the Liberal candidate still had the help of local LNU campaigners; where no Liberal stood, as in Ilford and across Birmingham, the LNU could help to transfer Liberal votes to Labour.

The Conservatives were determined to return the focus of public debate to domestic matters and to the recovery. Ultimately they reckoned, as Headlam observed from the North, 'that in the South and Midlands people will not be anxious to risk a Socialist Government ... when they are frightened it is all to our good'.[99] In particular, the scenario of a Labour government should concentrate Liberal minds and remind them that more united them as anti-socialists than divided them. The *Birmingham Post* regretted the Liberals' decision to abstain without expressing support for the government. 'To do so', the editorial commented, 'should not have been difficult, since Birmingham Unionists are so closely their political kindred, sprung from the same stock and heirs of the same traditions'.[100] Conservatives in and around London had the opportunity to attack the Labour administration in county hall, especially the impact of its grand housing schemes on ratepayers. But this carried some risk of alienating new residents. Anti-socialist rhetoric tended instead to emphasise the influence of those within Labour who, like Sir Stafford Cripps, leader of the Socialist League, and to a lesser extent Herbert Morrison, the leader of the LCC, were in a position to propose and enact socialist policy, over that of more circumspect moderates like Labour leader Clement Attlee. The anti-socialist message was centre stage in Churchill's campaign, as this extract from his election address illustrates:

The Socialist party have made no attempt to meet the charge that they failed the nation in 1931. Confronted with that emergency they revealed their inadequacy and moral weakness ... Have they then gained new strength and wisdom in the interval? On the contrary, all their experienced leaders are gone ... Meanwhile they continue to repeat as loudly as ever ... their predatory and moonshine doctrines about Nationalising all the means of production, distribution and exchange ... Undoubtedly their arrival as a Government would mean *at home* the collapse of credit, a landslide in values, the freezing up of enterprise and trade, and a gloomy boom in unemployment.[101]

The *Popular Illustrated* broadsheet formed the staple literature for Conservatives' publicity in the suburbs. In Ilford, 10,000 copies were

---

[99] *Parliament and politics in the age of Baldwin and MacDonald: the Headlam diaries, 1923–35*, ed. S. Ball (London, 1992), 341 (11 Oct. 1935).

[100] *Birmingham Post* editorial, 1 Nov. 1935. This echoed the view expressed by party organisers (e.g., central council, 29 Sep. 1934, Birmingham CUA).

[101] Election address, 6 Nov. 1935, Churchill papers, CHAR 7/24(3), original emphasis.

158   Popular Conservatism and the National Government

distributed each month.[102] Its pages were replete with bustling scenes of urban recovery: the bricklayer at work ('Never in history has there been such a boom in building'); cargo ships carrying goods for export; a motor-factory production line; happy postmen, teachers, and policemen ('No wonder they're all smiling – their pay cuts are to be restored in full'); new electricity stations; and modern rail travel.[103] Also receiving extensive coverage were scenes that depicted the lived results of recovery. These included pictures of contented cyclists, hikers, and day-trippers reaping the rewards of stability and progress, plus journalism that tapped into the contemporary taste for celebrity stories. Thus, in the year that Alfred Hitchcock's *The 39 Steps* stormed the cinemas, readers would find, alongside an article by Baldwin on 'The road to peace', an article headlined 'How would you like to be handcuffed to Madeleine Carroll for hours on end?'[104]

Having secured the recovery, Conservatives argued, the National government was the only force in the land capable of securing progress at home and peace abroad. From among the specific domestic policies contained in the Conservative manifesto, the most prominent in the suburban campaigns was the measure to extend health and unemployment insurance 'to the self-employed community and the great mass of workers known as "black-coated"'. In Moseley, Hannon devoted himself to promoting the 'interests of the small trader', who deserved 'an equitable share in the advantages of the nation's insurance scheme'.[105] Indeed, a notable aspect of the Conservative campaign was the breadth of the proposed programme of reforms. In one of his official addresses Churchill pledged the government to 'the use of public credit for public works', 'an active policy of rehousing', 'sympathetic treatment' of the distressed areas, and 'the continuous improvement' of education, including the extension of the school leaving age.[106] Even in areas like Epping and Moseley, where Labour did not pose anything like an immediate threat, the party's promises were a very far cry from the anti-waste campaigns of the 1920s and the popular retrenchment of 1931.

It was crucial that Conservatives also appealed directly to Liberal voters. As leader of the Liberal Nationals in the government, Sir John Simon was granted regular column space in the *Popular Illustrated*. In one article he argued that 'the only way in which Liberalism can make

---

[102] Executive committee, 25 Apr. 1934, Ilford CA, 90/61/1/1; also management committee, 5 Apr. 1935, Birmingham CUA; report to the AGM, 6 Mar. 1936, Woodford Church End Branch (Epping CA); report to central council, 19 May 1936, Liverpool CA, 329 Con/1/1/3.
[103] *Popular Illustrated*, vols. 1:1–1:6 (1935).   [104] Ibid., 1:1 (1935), 6.
[105] *Birmingham Post*, 5 Nov. 1935.
[106] Election address, 28 Oct. 1935, Churchill papers, CHAR 7/24(2).

The Politics of Anti-Socialism in the Suburbs   159

a practical contribution to the conduct of public affairs is through a National Government in which Liberals share responsibility'. While less than flattering from his own rank and file's point of view ('They must remember that there is no possibility of putting a purely Liberal Government in power'), it rehearsed the choice between 'party co-operation' and 'financial crisis', and thereby sought to renew the anti-socialist lead given to Liberals in the country.[107] The narrative of recovery also enabled Conservatives like Hannon to praise the ongoing Liberal contribution to national progress. As he noted, 'in all my speeches during the election ... I laid stress on the great services rendered to human progress by the Liberal Party and urged co-operation between the two great old parties against the assault of socialistic lunacy'.[108] In a thinly veiled sop to the Liberal grassroots on the subject of the electoral system – one of existential importance to them – Hannon also pledged himself to advocate reform.[109]

If the Liberal vote was to be mobilised, the question of peace and security also had to be broached more confidently than in previous years. For many Conservatives, it was in relation to this crucial aspect of the campaign that Baldwin, as prime minister of the National government since June, entered his own as the undisputed embodiment of the public interest. Contrary to the previous election campaign, the tactic of appealing to Liberals by invoking the example of their leaders was now much diminished; both Samuel and Lloyd George were opponents of the government, and Simon's reputation was tarnished in the eyes of many within the Liberal movement, both as a deserter of free trade and owing to his barely disguised irritation at past LNU campaigns during his time as foreign secretary.[110] In his last radio broadcast before polling day, and with his trademark air of consensual ordinariness, Baldwin began his account of the government's work with the assurance that 'our object is to maintain peace and to prevent that evil shadow of war from stalking across the world again. We seek peace, a world peace through the League of Nations'.[111] The speech demonstrated, more effectively than any ministerial declaration at the time, that the government had reflected upon and understood the public message delivered by the peace ballot.

---

[107] 'A lead to Liberals', *Popular Illustrated*, 1:6 (1935), 6.
[108] Hannon to M. Coleman, 17 Nov. 1935, Hannon papers, HNN 63/1.
[109] *Birmingham Post*, 1, 7 Nov. 1935.
[110] See e.g., a speech by Sir Archibald Sinclair, published by the Liberal Free Trade Committee as *New answers to old fallacies: a reply to Sir John Simon's defence of tariffs* (1934).
[111] Transcribed in *The Times*, 9 Nov. 1935.

160 Popular Conservatism and the National Government

There is little doubt that Baldwin's case was helped by circumstances. After failing to act over Japan's invasion of Manchuria in 1931, the League of Nations' response to Italian aggression towards Abyssinia, ongoing since early 1935, was looked upon as a make-or-break test for the doctrine of collective security. Labour was divided over the issue; some denounced the League's economic sanctions against Italy as inadequate and tantamount to the betrayal of a non-aggressor, while the official party leadership supported the government out of loyalty to the League ideal. In an echo that would have reminded listeners of the political crisis of 1931, Baldwin asked them to consider: 'What would have happened if the Labour Party had been in office at this juncture when the existence of the League of Nations was at stake?'[112] There is evidence that many voters felt genuinely moved by the morality and Christian idealism of his speeches in 1935, which Baldwin himself rated as some of his finest.[113] Many Conservatives were aware of this assessment and considered the victory to be in large part a 'personal triumph' for the prime minister, 'the modern Gladstone'.[114] In characteristic form, Chamberlain wrote to his sister that: 'I do agree with the press that S.B.'s influence in the country is immense and that he holds the mugwumps and the clericals and the conscientious, earnest, theoretical Liberals as no one else in the party can.'[115] But Baldwin's intervention was also instrumental in that it exemplified the consensual tone that Conservatives needed to strike locally. For instance, it is difficult to imagine Hannon, normally so partisan, welcoming LNU organisers to his campaign, yet in 1935 he did.[116] In this respect, Baldwin's broadcast served a similar function to Snowden's speech on 17 October 1931 – both created opportunities that Conservatives could exploit in the constituencies to destabilise normal party loyalties and reassemble them in favour of the National government, in this case by posing as supporters of the LNU even if they remained deeply suspicious of it, as many did.[117] To an extent, therefore, it was those activists in the party's southern strongholds, among whom anti-Baldwin sentiment had flourished in the past, who now had most reason to thank Baldwin.

[112] Ibid.

[113] J. Lawrence, *Electing our masters: the hustings in British politics from Hogarth to Blair* (Oxford, 2009), 97; P. Williamson, *Stanley Baldwin: Conservative leadership and national values* (Cambridge, 1998), 85.

[114] P. Williamson, 'Christian Conservatives and the totalitarian challenge, 1933–40', *EHR*, 115 (2000), 607–42, 633.

[115] *Neville Chamberlain diary letters, vol. 4*, 160 (to Ida, 17 Nov. 1935); report to central council, 19 May 1936, Liverpool CA, 329 Con /1/1/3.

[116] Hannon to Mrs McMurde, 25 Nov. 1935, Hannon papers, 63/1.

[117] E.g., area council, 2 Jul. 1936, Home Counties North Area, ARE 8/1/1.

The Politics of Anti-Socialism in the Suburbs 161

It is possible to speculate further on the effectiveness of the campaign in the suburbs by analysing the electoral results. With the exception of Epping, victory came with much reduced majorities. In East Toxteth's two-way contest, the Conservatives polled around 7,500 fewer votes than in 1931, while the Liberals reached their highest poll of the interwar years by gaining over 4,500 new votes. Because the electorate was comparatively stable in volume and the Liberal candidate in 1931 had not haemorrhaged votes to the Conservative to the same extent as his counterparts elsewhere, the likely explanation is not the drift of disaffected Liberals away from the government; rather, the decision of unaligned, or possibly Labour, voters, who in 1931 either abstained or voted 'National', to switch support to the Liberal candidate. In Ilford the Conservative poll hardly dropped at all, suggesting the party retained the favour of those who rallied to it during the crisis, yet the Labour vote increased by more than 13,000. This was likely to be connected with the Becontree estate, many of whose new residents had moved there with their party loyalty intact from the East End, where Labour had largely survived the onslaught of 1931.[118] In addition, Liberal voters with the option to support a Liberal candidate in 1931 are likely to have switched to Labour in the two-party race of 1935. Alternatively, there is no discounting the possibility that new residents, especially those in private housing, became Conservative supporters, substituting the Liberals who supported the government in 1931 before subsequently entering a popular front with Labour.

In Birmingham, the reduced majorities resulted from a fall in Conservative votes since 1931 (by around 10,000 in Moseley) and a Labour vote that held roughly level. This was reflected in the turnout, which was lower than the national average, and begs the question whether Liberal voters, presumed to have voted 'National' previously, abstained in large numbers. Despite Hannon claiming to Simon to have received 'a very substantial volume of Liberal support',[119] erstwhile Liberal voters could have followed either the lead of the Birmingham Liberal organisation by abstaining, or Samuel's advice, which was to back candidates who sympathised with the Council of Action. In his broadcast of 6 November, Samuel described the government's peace policy as typical of 'idle Toryism', based as it was on years of lukewarm commitment to the League.[120] Given that the Labour vote remained level across most of the city, it is likely that many Birmingham Liberals abstained. Where,

[118] In neighbouring Romford, with 42,598 new voters since 1931 (compared with 16,372 in Ilford), Labour overturned a Conservative majority of more than 18,000.
[119] Hannon to Simon, 26 Nov. 1935, Hannon papers, HNN 63/1.
[120] *The Times*, 7 Nov. 1935.

162   Popular Conservatism and the National Government

exceptionally, Labour's vote increased, it increased in areas with large new estates, notably Moseley and King's Norton.[121]

While the exact determinants of voting behaviour among suburban voters necessarily remain to some extent conjectural, suburban Conservatives emerge simultaneously boosted and chastened by the popular politics of the National government.

On the one hand, the party struggled to command an inclusive and settled anti-socialism. The political benefits promised by the National government, wrought from the unprecedented success of 1931 as well as the economic recovery so conspicuous in the Midlands and South, were often obscured by entrenched party identities that cut across the new National politics. Labour's initial advances had posed a threat in the 1920s, but it was the Liberals' contribution to the wider revival of suburban radicalism that defined the Conservative grassroots experience of the 1930s. It is tempting to view this, ultimately, as contributing to the long-term rehabilitation of Labour beyond its industrial heartlands, culminating in 1945, except that for contemporaries it represented a less teleological but no less intimidating progressive front, especially at the constituency level, where, as Martin Pugh has argued, Lib-Lab exchange was most commonplace.[122] The politics of peace remained the main theme of this progressivism. Bodies like the Ilford Peace Council, representative of nonconformists, teachers' groups, co-operative guilds, and branches of the League of Nations Union, did much to construct a late-1930s politics of 'crisis'.[123] Populist and intellectual, their progressive campaigns posed as an enlightened challenge to the government, with hints already towards the radical democratic polemicism later epitomised in Cato's *Guilty Men*.

On the other hand, the Conservatives successfully contained the spread of suburban radicalism. For one thing, they exploited its cosmopolitan culture. As Peter Mandler has argued, the Liberals were ambivalent about whether the national interest was best expressed through 'nationality' or 'cosmopolitanism', and grew more so in the 1930s as they enthused about the League of Nations, 'which caused them to mute their assertion of nationality'.[124] As the 1935 election campaign proved, this helped to clear a discursive field that

---

[121] Since 1931, the electorate had increased by 8,986 and the Labour vote by 4,144 in Moseley, and 10,545 and 7,668 respectively in King's Norton.

[122] M. Pugh, 'The Liberal party and the Popular Front', *EHR*, 121 (2006), 1327–50.

[123] *Ilford Recorder*, 28 May 1936. See also R. Overy, *The morbid age: Britain between the wars* (London, 2009) and M. Ceadel, 'Popular fiction and the next war, 1918–39', in F. Gloversmith (ed.), *Class, culture and social change: a new view of the 1930s* (Brighton, 1980), 161–84.

[124] P. Mandler, *The English national character: the history of an idea from Edmund Burke to Tony Blair* (New Haven, 2006), 152.

The Politics of Anti-Socialism in the Suburbs 163

Baldwin's brand of Conservatism was able to occupy, for underpinning his commitment to the League was his trademark articulation of Britain's 'national' values of Christian morality, political moderation, and constitutional democracy. Similarly, many Conservatives felt that the new radicalism's preoccupation with foreign policy meant that the attention of certain groups, through their social and economic interests, was all to play for. To this end, by the late decade the party could also claim to have secured, through the National government, legislation that raised the school-leaving age to fifteen (1936) and extended the insurance scheme to include the self-employed, clerical workers, and others (1937).

Above all, the party's position in late-1930s suburbia was stronger thanks to the new politics that the rank and file had assembled under the National government. Following the second general election victory, there was another subtle change of tack in the way suburban Conservatives approached anti-socialism. They no longer treated it as an enterprise that relied on Liberal partnership but now as a non-political, 'public' discourse that could belong uniquely to the Conservatives. A 'Non-Political Group' was founded in Ilford in 1938, led by the Conservative party and comprising all anti-socialist councillors in the borough.[125] Such adaptability was itself largely derived from grassroots experience of negotiating the new culture of national government since 1931. For in many areas the Conservatives succeeded in responding to the new radical politics with a renewed effort to establish themselves as a community party. New branches were established in the new housing estates in Moseley and Ilford. As self-contained organisations, these were able to leave the 'political' work to the divisional organisation and concentrate their own efforts on cultivating good relations with the churches, chapels, and other local institutions, even the teaching profession through the founding of Conservative Teachers' Clubs.[126] This they did with considerable success in Moseley, soon boasting around 200 members in each of the three new estates.[127] A mark of their success was that they also responded to radical opponents with a rival Conservative culture of educative politics. Few constituencies represented suburban radicalism more than Ilford, the town from which the LNU drew inspiration for its 'peace ballot', but from 1936 the local Conservative party controlled a vibrant circuit of debating societies, books clubs, radio

---

[125] Municipal elections (special) sub-committee, 4 Oct. 1938, Ilford CA, 90/61/7/1.

[126] E.g., management committee, 13 Dec. 1935, Birmingham CA; AGM, 17 Mar. 1936, Epping CA, Acc. A6853.

[127] Agent's report on the new Warstock, Dolphin Lane & Tyseley Women's Branches, 19 Jun. 1938, Hannon papers, HNN 73/3.

164   Popular Conservatism and the National Government

Listening Groups, and concert meetings, all open to non-members.[128] This may not have captured the moral high-ground that the radicals had within their sights, but, by the eve of war, it brought suburban Conservatism closer to the profoundly political formula of apolitical anti-socialism that Baldwin had long propounded.

---

[128] Report of the political education committee, 15 Oct. 1936, Ilford CA, 90/61/1/1; AGM, 18 Mar. 1937, Home Counties Northern Area, ARE 8/1/1.

6 Modernity and Paternalism in Rural Politics

'The good old days' are definitely gone for ever ... In Norfolk alone you can count on both hands large estates which have been sold and the people who were previously employed in private service have had to seek another form of employment ... I challenge anybody to show me how anybody in the district where large estates have come to an end are better off.

(Thomas Cook, addressing workers on his Sennowe Park estate, January 1932)[1]

British farmers and agricultural labourers include a larger percentage of men of brain and initiative than you find ... in the industrial areas; but have you given him a chance by allowing the flood of imports to come in and make almost every one of his operations a dead loss? Have you given him the same chance that is being given to the iron and steel industry? No, and it is about time you did.

(Percy Hurd responding to James Maxton in the debate on the Address, 23 November 1932)[2]

Rural Society and Politics between the Wars

Rural society appeared safe for Conservatives between the wars, at least compared with the brutal 'working-class' politics of the industrial areas and the dislocated communities of new suburbia. In the county seats and market towns, especially those of southern England, lay the party's 'natural' heartlands. While Liberals and Labour, nonconformists and trade unionists, continued the radical fight against landed Toryism, such challenges could normally be contained within familiar community structures. These were laid down by the country estate, acting as employer and landlord; the petty officialdom of various village institutions; and more imperceptibly the long-established customs of deference. It was

---

[1] *Norfolk Chronicle*, 8 Jan. 1932.
[2] *Hansard, House of Commons debates*, 272, col. 144, 23 Nov. 1932.

165

166   Popular Conservatism and the National Government

not all seamless, of course, and many Conservatives had long known that established hierarchies sometimes offered scant protection against the electoral advance of radical opponents, especially in heavily unionised agricultural areas like East Anglia and despite how much Labour continued to imagine feudal networks of Tory control.[3] Even so, this did not alter many Conservatives' faith in the solidity of rural society. After all, such social and political changes as had occurred in the countryside since the war, though significant, appeared perceptibly less threatening than those which confronted them in the large towns and cities. As J. B. Priestley found, whereas the expanding suburbs were becoming 'classless', the inhabitants of the countryside and small towns still lived in 'an elaborate network of relations up and down the social scale'.[4] It was the perceived stability of rural life, derived from the hierarchical and broadly accepted structure of the village community, that inspired Baldwin to draw upon it as an example of the cross-class cooperation required in the industrial regions.[5] Yet the experience of both voters and Conservative activists who lived in the countryside tells a different story – one that shows that, since the mid-nineteenth century, village life had been neither socially inert nor programmed to vote Conservative.

Studies of rural elections show that deferential voting was often contested by both tenants and labourers. It was entered into, if at all, as a means of negotiating better terms with the landlord.[6] Conservatives also had to overcome the deep-seated religious cleavage of rural politics, wrought by decades of political mobilisation through the chapels in favour of the Liberals' dissenting sympathies.[7] Nor, importantly, did the Conservative party necessarily fare much better in areas of low nonconformity, especially if a large proportion of voters worked in agriculture: as a 'general rule ... the higher the proportion of persons engaged in agriculture, the lower was the proportion of the

---

[3] N. Scotland, *Methodism and the revolt of the field: a study of the Methodist contribution to agricultural trade unionism in East Anglia, 1872–96* (Gloucester, 1981); A. Howkins, *Poor labouring men: rural radicalism in Norfolk, 1870–1923* (London, 1985).

[4] J. B. Priestley, *English journey* (London, 1934; 1994 edn), 403.

[5] P. Williamson, 'The doctrinal politics of Stanley Baldwin', in M. Bentley, *Public and private doctrine: essays in British history presented to Maurice Cowling* (Cambridge, 1993), 181–208, esp. 191–4.

[6] E.g., J. R. Fisher, 'The limits of deference: agricultural communities in a mid-nineteenth century election campaign', *JBS*, 21 (1981), 90–115; D. Eastwood, 'Contesting the politics of deference: the rural electorate, 1820–1860', in J. Lawrence & M. Taylor (eds.), *Party, state and society: electoral behaviour in Britain since 1820* (Aldershot, 1997), 27–49; E. Jaggard, 'Farmers and English county politics, 1832–80', *RH*, 16 (2005), 191–207.

[7] M. Dawson, 'Liberalism in Devon and Cornwall, 1910–1931: "the old time religion"', *HJ*, 38 (1995), 425–37; P. Lynch, *The Liberal party in rural England, 1885–1910: radicalism and community* (Oxford, 2003).

Modernity and Paternalism in Rural Politics

Conservative vote'.[8] The most heavily agricultural seats, in Norfolk for example, were less reliable than more semi-rural seats like Devizes. As we shall see, the exception came in 1931 and 1935 when the party increased its share of the vote in seven of the twelve seats in which a clear majority of the male population worked in agriculture.[9]

In addition, far-reaching economic changes in the agricultural industry ensured there was nothing inherently stable about rural society. Compared with the prosperous war years, the revival of international trade in the 1920s saw British farm profits fall to below pre-war levels as a result of foreign competition. The abolition of wartime price guarantees in 1921 and the introduction of regional wage boards in 1924 further dented farm incomes. Unlike urban poverty, the social (and political) effects of agricultural depression are too frequently overlooked in histories of interwar Britain.[10] This reflects the bias of 1930s 'social problem' literature, which focused overwhelmingly on the depressed regions and the new towns; the uninsured status of the farm labourer for most of the period, which rendered his plight less amenable to the particular investigative methods used by social scientists of the time; and, perhaps, the contemporary perception among countryfolk themselves that they possessed superior resourcefulness to ameliorate the effects of poverty.[11] Nonetheless, poverty remained a very real feature of life in many rural communities.[12] Not only did this provide grist to the Labour mill; by forcing many young people to seek opportunities in the towns and cities, it also contributed to the familiar problem of rural depopulation, a process further hastened by the widespread shift taking place from arable farming to less labour-intensive livestock and dairy farming.[13]

These difficult circumstances conditioned how rural Conservatives responded to the National government, which went on to prove itself among the most proactive peacetime administrations to address life in the

---

[8] M. Kinnear, *The British voter: an atlas and survey since 1885* (London, 1968; 1981 edn), 120, based on occupation data from the 1921 census.

[9] Cambridgeshire, Saffron Walden, Leominster, Horncastle, South Norfolk, South West Norfolk, and Central Aberdeenshire. Even then a large minority of such seats remained Liberal or Liberal National.

[10] Cf. M. Freeman, *Social investigation and rural England, 1870–1914* (Woodbridge, 2003).

[11] For a rural perspective on urban poverty, captured during wartime evacuation, see Women's Group on Public Welfare, *Our towns – a close up: a study made in 1939–42* (London, 1943).

[12] See the testimonies in R. Blythe, *Akenfield: portrait of an English village* (London, 1969) and M. Chamberlain, *Fenwomen: a portrait of women in an English village* (London, 1975); also G. Orwell, 'Hop-picking', in S. Orwell & I. Angus (eds.), *The collected essays, journalism and letters of George Orwell, volume 1: an age like this, 1920–1940* (London, 1968), 75–97.

[13] For a first-hand account of changes in interwar farming, see A. G. Street, *Farmer's glory* (London, 1951).

168   Popular Conservatism and the National Government

countryside. Tariff protection, targeted subsidies, marketing reforms, and in due course preparations for wartime food production – together, such policies transformed British agriculture in the 1930s, drawing to a close the semi-continuous depression that had engulfed much of rural Britain since the 1870s and laying the foundations of the state-aided agriculture that came after 1945.[14] This was orchestrated on behalf of the government by Walter Elliot, the ambitious and reformist agriculture minister between 1932 and 1936, who presented the policies as integral to the pursuit of self-sufficiency and improved public health which underpinned the national recovery. Despite their interventionist nature, these policies were embraced by local Conservatives as demonstrable evidence of the party's commitment to agriculture.

In challenging the government, local Labour and Liberal opponents turned to evocations of the farm labourer's historic struggle against 'Tory' landlordism. This jarred to some degree with the Labour party's official strategy in the countryside, which backed policies that recognised the changing structure of rural society (especially the new pressures on farmers, not just labourers). Nevertheless, it meant that historical critiques centred around the political and social control allegedly wielded by the Conservative landholding interest remained a common feature of county politics. As late as 1935 the Liberal candidate in Devizes exhorted voters to 'Remember [that] the ballot is absolutely secret'.[15] Under the National government, however, Conservatives were able to combine modernity and tradition. Government policies not only helped to modernise farming methods and restore profitability, but in consequence they also rehabilitated the scope for traditional paternalist politics through new methods of welfare provision. Whether by means of private largesse or public provision, the amenities and improvements championed by rural Conservatives aimed to match those already available to the urban population, to secure for the rural worker a share in the national recovery orchestrated by the government. While the focus remained on the farming community, by 1935 Conservatives were also appealing explicitly to 'black-coated' workers and other non-farming voters – a shrewd move intended to broaden their appeal, or also a defensive move arising from nervousness at Labour's growing claim on the allegiance of farmworkers apparently excluded from the agricultural recovery.

[14] J. Martin, *The development of modern agriculture: British farming since 1931* (London, 2000), esp. ch.2; A. F. Wilt, *Food for war: agriculture and rearmament in Britain before the Second World War* (Oxford, 2001).
[15] Election address, Nov. 1935, London School of Economics Library, Archives & Special Collections, Josephy Papers, 13/4. On the radical critique of landownership and its role in rural political culture, see C. Griffiths, *Labour and the countryside: the politics of rural Britain, 1918–1939* (Oxford, 2007), ch.1; A. Howkins, 'From diggers to dongas: the land in English radicalism, 1649–2000', *HWJ*, 54 (2002), 1–23.

Modernity and Paternalism in Rural Politics 169

'1931' in the Countryside: Protection and Paternalism

At first glance, the 1931 general election did not alter so much as accentuate some of the principal aspects of political culture in the countryside. In the case of many local Liberal and Labour parties, this was deliberate and done with good reason: the opportunity to contest protectionist candidates evoked the considerable success of free-trade popular politics in the late Victorian and Edwardian years. In Devizes, although the former Liberal candidate, Sir James Currie, pledged public support for Hurd and the National government, a majority in the local party ignored his example and supported the adoption of a free-trade candidate. The stated objective was to ensure that voters were given the chance to return a free-trade candidate to safeguard their interests. Privately, a more self-interested case was delivered to party activists by the veteran Liberal campaigner, Alderman James Duck, who set out a dramatic account of how a succession of lesser-known Liberals had triumphed over more established tariff reformers. The Liberals had achieved the most when they were willing to rise to the protectionist challenge, with the election victories of 1892, 1906, and 1923 proof of this. 1931, he thought, could shortly be added to this venerable record.[16] In Norfolk North, Lady Noel-Buxton, the Labour candidate, similarly sought to make tariffs 'the issue' for voters, and pleaded with Liberal notables to base their public endorsement of her candidature upon her free-trade credentials.[17] This appeared her best chance of repeating the victory won at the previous year's by-election, at which the Labour agent claimed 'a wave of Liberal support' ahead of polling day, 'the Free Trade issue being the determining factor'.[18] If in general the culture of free trade was in decline by these years,[19] little in the political culture of Norfolk reflected this.

Liberal and Labour candidates took up two discourses from the free-trade tradition. The first, food and food taxes, was the most central to their campaigns. Since the 1880s the Liberals had held large swathes of the rural electorate captive with stories of starvation and poverty on the land under the corn laws.[20] The same narrative was widespread in Liberal campaigns in

---

[16] See reports of the Liberal adoption meeting in *Marlborough Times*, 16 Oct. 1931 and *Wiltshire Advertiser*, 22 Oct. 1931.
[17] Noel-Buxton to Capt. Sears, 20 Oct. 1931, Norfolk Record Office, Noel-Buxton papers, MC 2331/1/1/2g.
[18] *Eastern Daily Press*, 3 Jul. 1930.
[19] See F. Trentmann, *Free trade nation: commerce, consumption and civil society in modern Britain* (Oxford, 2008), passim.
[20] A. Howe, 'Towards the "hungry forties": free trade in Britain, *c.* 1880–1906', in E. F. Biagini (ed.), *Citizenship and community: Liberals, radicals and collective identities in the British isles, 1865–1931* (Cambridge, 1996), 193–218, esp. 212–18. For Edwardian constructions of a collective memory of suffering, see Trentmann, *Free trade nation*, 45, and J. Vernon, *Hunger: a modern history* (Harvard, 2007), 257.

170   Popular Conservatism and the National Government

1931. In the West Country, as Lord Bayford described, the National government faced a contest that the Liberals, including J. W. Molden in Devizes, fought along precisely 'the old fashioned lines of 1906 ... [with] the Big and Little Loaf and all the old free trade stuff'.[21] Lady Noel-Buxton deployed the apparently reliable appeal of free trade to women voters. The standard of living among farm labourers would deteriorate rapidly if the '"National" Government' decided to 'impose food taxes', she argued, as this would aggravate hardship already caused by recent wage reductions. 'It is the women who suffer, when money runs short, as women are so unselfish and always go without for the sake of their children.'[22] While this was in keeping with the welfare, domestic, and consumerist issues so often associated with women's politics and the liberal free-trade tradition,[23] the women voters of Norfolk North were reminded also of the radical resolve expected of them by the example of their forebears. The women of England had fought to remove the corn laws; almost a century on, 'by voting for the Labour Party ... the women of England can prevent food taxes, and thus safeguard their homes'.[24]

The second discourse, most evident in Labour's politics in Norfolk North, offered a critique of the vested interests that lay behind both the protectionist policy and the feudalism under which labourers toiled. It represented the formation of the National government as a 'Tory trick' executed on behalf of the landowners. Lady Noel-Buxton condemned it as an already failing, elitist government: 'although giving lip-service to equality of sacrifice it has placed the burden on the weakest shoulders and caused unnecessary anxiety and suffering to the professional and working classes'. And yet, she continued, 'the "National" or Tory Government, in spite of its damaging record, expects the Electors to trust it blindly'.[25] Many reasons were given for Labour's defeat, among them, ironically,

---

[21] *Real old Tory politics: the political diaries of Robert Sanders, Lord Bayford, 1910–1935*, ed. J. Ramsden (London, 1984), 247 (12 May 1932); Molden's election address – 'Vote for Molden and No Food Taxes', Oct. 1931, Hurd papers.

[22] Election address of Lady Noel-Buxton, Oct. 1931 and notes of an address to the Cromer Labour Friendly Gathering, 17 Oct. 1931, Noel-Buxton papers, MC 2331/1/1/2g.

[23] See P. Thane, 'Women, liberalism and citizenship, 1918–1930', in Biagini (ed.), *Citizenship and community*, 66–92, esp. 76–92.

[24] Notes of an address to the Cromer Labour Friendly Gathering, 17 Oct. 1931, Noel-Buxton papers, MC 2331/1/1/2g. For women's part in the anti-corn law campaign, see S. Morgan, 'Domestic economy and political agitation: women and the Anti-Corn Law League, 1839–1846', in K. Gleadle & S. Richardson (eds.), *Women in British politics, 1760–1860: the power of the petticoat* (Basingstoke, 2000), 115–33, and for reference to how this was included in early-twentieth century accounts of the early feminist movement, see S. Stanley Holton, 'British freewomen: national identity, constitutionalism and languages of race in early suffragist histories', in E. Yeo (ed.), *Radical femininity: women's self-representation in the public sphere* (Manchester, 1998), 149–71, at 161.

[25] Election address of Lady Noel-Buxton, Oct. 1931.

Modernity and Paternalism in Rural Politics

farm labourers' 'blind faith' in MacDonald and Snowden, along with dissatisfaction with how little was done by the late Labour government in agricultural policy, the threat of dismissal by farmers and landowners, intimidation by the clergy, and even the belief that the rural poor perversely 'like to have self-denial & make sacrifices'.[26] Most common of all, however, was the belief that by assuming the 'national' label the Conservatives had inveigled the average farm labourer into thinking that patriotism demanded support for the National government.[27] The Conservatives, whose local supporters had traditionally ensured the party a strong 'non-political' presence through control of village life and institutions, were now deemed to enjoy a further hold on rural society through control of the workers' national consciousness.

The traditional course for Conservatives responding to free traders would have been to depict protectionism as an escape from a 'future dystopia', as the harbinger of a new age of modernity in which new technologies and cutting-edge industries yielded unprecedented prosperity.[28] Both Hurd and Cook were staunch protectionists. Hurd had worked as secretary to W. A. S. Hewins's Tariff Commission set up in 1904, at which time he also became a protégé of Edward Goulding, organiser of Joseph Chamberlain's Tariff Reform League. (Goulding was himself the MP for Devizes between 1895 and 1906, was followed by Basil Peto in January 1910, Hewart Bell in 1918, and orchestrated Hurd's original candidature there in 1924, thereby ensuring continuity of policy in the constituency.)[29] The 1923 general election defeat did not soften the Devizes Conservative party's protectionism, but led instead to calls for more effective propaganda and the inclusion of more agricultural sectors within the proposed tariff system.[30] Similarly, Norfolk North Conservatives held steadfast to 'Protection without any reservations' despite Lady Noel-Buxton's victory in the by-election of July 1930, in which Cook stood as an Empire Free Trade candidate with the active support of Lord Beaverbrook.[31] Hurd denied that he was a supporter of

---

[26] W. B. Taylor to Noel-Buxton, 4 Nov. 1931, J. W. N.(?) to Noel-Buxton, 29 Oct. 1931, Noel-Buxton papers, MC 2331/1/1/2e; S. J. Gee (Labour agent) to Noel-Buxton, 5 Nov. 1931; W. A. Pask to Noel-Buxton, 12 Nov. 1931, Noel-Buxton papers, MC 2331/1/1/2g.

[27] E.g., A. L. Hedge to Noel-Buxton, 12 Nov. 1931, Noel-Buxton papers, MC 2331/1/1/2e.

[28] For Edwardian depictions of protectionist modernity set against Liberal claims of free trade timelessness, see Trentmann, *Free trade nation*, 43.

[29] *The Times*, 13 Jan. 1904; sub-committee on selection of candidate, 30 Jan. 1924, Wiltshire Record Office, Devizes CA, 2305/2.

[30] *Wiltshire Gazette*, 22 Nov. 1923; executive committee, 22 Dec. 1923, Devizes CA, 2305/2.

[31] Executive committee, 28 Apr., 29 Sep. 1930, Norfolk Record Office, Norfolk North CA, Acc.2006/152.

172 Popular Conservatism and the National Government

a new party under Beaverbrook and Lord Rothermere, but publicly voiced admiration for their 'patriotic instincts' in awakening the public to 'the necessity of a policy of Home First and Empire Development'.[32]

By contrast, the protectionist campaign in Norfolk North and Devizes was conducted much less vigorously in October 1931. Cook's election address argued that 'Tariff is the quickest and the most effective weapon', but this seemed far from categorical as he also endorsed the government's request for a doctor's mandate and expressed his 'prepared[ness] to support any measure which can effect what is required'.[33] Hurd adhered to the same view: the government should 'rule out nothing'. His adoption speech highlighted the case for a balanced, scientific approach to any future tariffs policy.[34] Such reticence was not the result of a fundamental reappraisal of protectionism in the constituencies, however. Conservatives liked to claim that the case for protective tariffs had become unanswerable with the economic circumstances of 1931 and were quick to point out that many Liberals were likewise coming to realise as much. The extensive use made of the speeches of national and regional Liberal figures allowed Hurd apparently to have his policy advocated for him by a line-up of Liberal 'converts' including Lloyd George (who, given that he was now most emphatically campaigning against 'Tory protectionism', was very selectively quoted), Herbert Samuel, John Simon, Viscount Grey and the local Liberal grandee, Sir James Currie.[35]

More significantly, rural protectionists were alive to the fact that the crisis of 1931 had thrown up other political opportunities. Like Conservatives elsewhere, they realised that the fall of the Labour government enabled them to forge new political narratives, and so in Devizes, although the only official threat came from the Liberal candidate, the Conservative campaign centred upon aspects of the new anti-socialism. There was still a need to refute the Liberals' 'Dear Food' cry, but, as Hurd's election literature demonstrated, the reasoning and rhetoric used to do so became bound up with narratives of *Labour*'s 'failure' in government. In one pamphlet, Hurd argued that Labour had brought the country 'near to bankruptcy' and warned voters of the impact which Labour's return would have on standards of living. It would lead inevitably to 'Dear Food', he asserted, since a further run on the pound would render wages worthless; worse still, it could lead to 'No Food'.[36] Hurd

---

[32] *Wiltshire Gazette*, 27 Feb. 1930.
[33] Election address, Thomas Cook, Oct. 1931, Noel-Buxton papers, MC 2331/1/1/2g.
[34] *Wiltshire Telegraph*, 17 Oct. 1931.
[35] Election address, Hurd, Oct. 1931, Hurd papers. For the use of Liberal speeches by Norfolk Conservatives, see *Norfolk Chronicle*, 9, 16 Oct. 1931.
[36] *'Your Food'* (leaflet), Oct. 1931, Hurd papers.

Modernity and Paternalism in Rural Politics   173

therefore invoked the Liberal free trader's own language of starvation and poverty but pointed to Labour incompetence, and not vested interests, as the cause of this suffering.[37] The objective, clearly, was to bring about an alignment of Liberal and Conservative votes, which highlights the fact that, as a fallout of the crisis of 1931, the new anti-socialism commended itself to Conservative activists as a more effective and subtle strategy for dealing with the Liberal threat than a continuation of the combative tariff debate.

In Norfolk North, the Conservative campaign took advantage of the crisis of 1931 in order to redefine a viable paternalist appeal. Cook himself had good reason to want to rehabilitate a paternalistic and deferential relationship between landowners and their tenants and workers. He himself was only a second-generation landowner, his father having bought the 8,000-acre Sennowe Park estate near Guist, Dereham, in 1898.[38] The father's death in 1914 left the estate without a figurehead throughout the war and beyond. When Cook came of age in 1923 he therefore inherited an estate which bore little distinct identity of its own, at a particularly turbulent time for labour relations on East Anglian farms.[39] Cook finally took over the running of the estate in 1930. By then the so-called gentrification process was well underway, with Cook shedding the baggage of the family's travel-agency business and living the stately life which had formed the subject of his great-grandfather's excursions in the mid-nineteenth century, immersing himself in county affairs as master of the North Norfolk hunt, councillor for Holt, a magistrate, a governor of the Norfolk and Norwich Hospital, patron of Royal British Legion branches, and leading member of the Royal Norfolk Agricultural Society.[40] To opponents, like the Labour agent Stephen Gee, he became the 'fox hunting plutocrat' of Norfolk.[41]

Cook's paternalism, however, was not a social construct tasked only with defining his own position in society. There were compelling political reasons for it. In 1931 Cook cultivated a narrative of 'crisis' in agriculture

---

[37] For further examples, see *'Your Wages Are At Stake!'* (leaflet), Oct. 1931, Hurd papers; and a speech by Mr Gathorne-Hardy on the question: 'Is this country to be saved or is it to be starved?', reported in *Wiltshire Gazette*, 22 Oct. 1931.

[38] See F. M. L. Thompson, *Gentrification and the enterprise culture: Britain, 1780–1980* (Oxford, 2001), 184.

[39] Sennowe Park had not had a long-term resident family since it was built in 1774, but rather a series of owners. See *Eastern Daily Press*, 29 Nov. 2003. For the 'great strike' of 1923, see A. Howkins, *Poor labouring men: rural radicalism in Norfolk, 1872–1923* (London, 1985), ch.8.

[40] See Cook's obituary, *The Times*, 13 Aug. 1970. For the Thomas Cook company and tourism in the countryside, see Mandler, *Fall and rise*, 88, 93, 97, 116.

[41] During the county council elections, *Norfolk Chronicle*, 6 Mar. 1931.

174   Popular Conservatism and the National Government

in order to assert further his identity as a landlord. Conservative activists in Norfolk North shared Cook's enthusiasm for this paternalist appeal. Whether hosting garden parties and open days in their stately homes, attracting national figures to speak locally, or ensuring a flow of generous subscriptions, families like the earls of Leicester, the barons Suffield, and the Ketton-Cremers in Norfolk North, and the marquesses of Lansdowne, the earls of Pembroke, and the Gathorne-Hardys in Devizes – together with lesser gentry families – were considered crucial to the party's capacity to campaign locally. Individuals such as Lord Hastings in Norfolk North and Lord Roundway in Devizes occupied positions in the public profile of local Conservatism almost equal to the candidates. As regular attendees at the House of Lords, they enabled their local parties to boast an additional legislator representing local interests.[42]

There was also a compelling electoral reason why, in 1931, the occasion was ripe for a new paternalist appeal in Norfolk North: the local party anticipated displacing the perceived practice among farm labourers of casting a deferential vote for Lady Noel-Buxton with a deferential vote for Cook. Labour's success in Norfolk North is traditionally expressed as a product of the county's pioneering role in the development of agricultural trade unionism.[43] While recognising the contribution of this heritage to Norfolk North's exalted place within Labour rural politics, Griffiths reveals that relations between the National Union of Agricultural Workers (NUAW) and the divisional Labour party were occasionally difficult, not least when the union disagreed with the party's choice of Lady Noel-Buxton as the parliamentary candidate to succeed Noel Buxton in 1930.[44] A balanced picture of Buxton's success rightly takes account of the significant Liberal vote which followed him upon his defection to Labour in 1922;[45] but what in turn accounts for this loyalty, and what explains his appeal to workers enfranchised in 1918, is unknown. Apart from esoteric cases like 'the red Countess of Warwick', on whose estates the 'rebel peasantry' were those who voted Conservative,[46] the historiography so far fails to take seriously the role of the deferential vote in Labour electioneering.[47] Yet the

---

[42] *Wiltshire Gazette*, 10 Mar. 1932 (reporting Lord Roundway's election as chairman in Devizes); general council, 4 Nov. 1932, Norfolk CA.

[43] See Howkins, *Poor labouring men*.   [44] Griffiths, *Labour and the countryside*, 163–4.

[45] Ibid., 68.   [46] Ibid., 59.

[47] Henry Pelling believes that the culture of political neutrality which the royal estate in Sandringham set for many of the main Norfolk landowners was crucial in enabling the

Modernity and Paternalism in Rural Politics

Conservatives identified a strong deferential backing for 'the Buxton name'. The second son of Sir Thomas Buxton, third baronet, of Warlies Park in Upshire, Essex, and the grandson of the earl of Gainsborough, Noel Buxton took up residence on the family's Norfolk estate, where they had been squires for at least four generations and closely associated through marriage to the influential Norfolk Quaker family, the Gurneys of Earlham Hall.[48] This connection may explain why the Norfolk North Labour party insisted on Lady Noel-Buxton to succeed her husband in 1930. At any rate, the Conservatives on that occasion sought to 'counteract' what one activist described as 'the influence of the name of Buxton'.[49] To do this they secured the speaking services of Captain Harry Buxton, after twenty-five years' absence from the political platform. Addressing an audience in Aylsham, he declared: 'I, as one of the family, felt it my duty to come here and tell you all in this Market Place that out of one hundred of my relations who live in this county there is not more than one who supports the Socialist Party.'[50]

If this effort fell short of securing Conservative victory, the formation of the National government proved crucial in undoing the Buxton factor, as Liberals faced a choice between 'failed' Labour and a 'national' administration in which Simon and Samuel served. As in the suburbs, North Norfolk Liberals had managed to retain a public prominence that was disproportionate to the party's electoral performance. The local party lost its deposit at the only two elections it contested in the 1920s, yet it still had a sympathetic mouthpiece in the *Eastern Daily Press*, the regional paper with the largest circulation in East Anglia. Founded by the Colman family of Norwich and edited between 1897 and 1937 by Archibald Cozens-Hardy, nephew of Herbert Cozens-Hardy, Liberal MP for Norfolk North from 1885 to 1899, the paper reflected the periodic disaffection felt by some Liberals after the war, but in 1931 came out decisively in support of Simon and the Liberal Nationals.[51] Many erstwhile Liberals did likewise. Having previously supported Labour out of loyalty to the Buxtons, these voters broke

early trade union movement under Joseph Arch to develop. *Social geography of British elections, 1885–1910* (London, 1967), 97–9.

[48] See C. V. J. Griffiths, 'Buxton, Noel Edward Noel-, first Baron Noel-Buxton (1869–1948)', *Oxford Dictionary of National Biography* (Oxford University Press, 2004; online edn, Jan 2008), www.oxforddnb.com.ezproxy.york.ac.uk/view/article/35247, and O. M. Blouet, 'Buxton, Sir Thomas Fowell, first baronet (1786–1845)', *Oxford Dictionary of National Biography* (Oxford University Press, 2004; online edn, May 2010), www.oxforddnb.com.ezproxy.york.ac.uk/view/article/4247.

[49] *Eastern Daily Press*, 2 July 1930.   [50] Ibid., 4 July 1930.

[51] For the dynastic influence of the Cozens-Hardys in politics and society in Norfolk, see D. Cannadine, *Aspects of aristocracy: grandeur and decline in modern Britain* (London, 1994), ch.8, esp. 195–7.

176   Popular Conservatism and the National Government

with their traditional deference and joined the National government on point of apparent principle, citing the Gladstonian shibboleth of 'national retrenchment', now championed by the government, as the reason.[52] Lady Noel-Buxton later estimated that she lost 18,000 Liberal votes as a result.[53]

Thus 1931 offered the Conservatives a discrete opportunity to develop an alternative deferential vote, based on Cook's profile as a landowner. Under Baldwin, the Conservative leadership desisted from extending even rhetorical support to the large landowners and their estates for fear of a possible electoral backlash.[54] Cook nevertheless set out to rehabilitate a sense of the essential economic role of the country estate. In doing so he shared the same vision – if less romantically – as his uncle, the philanthropic preservationist Ernest Cook, who started his 'collection' of estates in 1931 largely in response to the threat posed to them by the crisis in the agricultural economy.[55] At this time also Lord Lothian and the National Trust were lobbying the government on the need for greater state involvement in the upkeep of stately homes.[56] While Cook undoubtedly shared many of the ideals of this movement, his objective was the economic regeneration, and less the cultural preservation, of the country estate. He expressed himself at first in the new anti-socialist language. Excessive income tax, super-tax, tithe, rates, death duties, and licenses to employ servants, all of these had made estates the 'target' of the exchequer under the Labour government. 'If by some mischance there was a return to that state of affairs', he warned, 'it would simply be the death knell of large estates'.[57] Addressing a public meeting in September 1931, he said that so far he had happily reduced his tenants' rents to reflect lost profits. But even his good nature could not sustain them indefinitely: 'unfortunately', he explained, 'reduced income met with little sympathy from the tax collector'.[58]

Placing so much faith in Cook's attributes as a local landlord did, of course, carry risks. As a modern landowner he had tractors working routinely on the Sennowe home farm, at a time when such mechanisation was still advanced practice. This undermined his claims to be a paternalistic landlord in the minds of some locals, as the Luddite reaction of Mrs Howe, the wife of one his labourers, reveals. Mrs Howe was responding to

---

[52] See *Norfolk Chronicle*, 11 Sep. 1931.
[53] Lady Noel-Buxton to Arthur Henderson, 9 Nov. 1931, Noel-Buxton papers, MC 2331/1/2/1c. She probably meant 1,800, since the Labour vote went from 14,821 in 1930 to 13,035 in 1931.
[54] Mandler, *Fall and rise*, 227–8, 241.
[55] E. J. T. Collins, *Innovation and conservation: Ernest Edward Cook and his country estates* (Reading, 1989), 21.
[56] Mandler, *Fall and rise*, 296.   [57] *Norfolk Chronicle*, 4 Sep. 1931.   [58] Ibid.

Modernity and Paternalism in Rural Politics 177

a version of the Conservatives' 'Back to the Plough' election poster (Figure 6.1) which was on display in the village of Ryburgh. The poster was clearly meant to portray agricultural recovery, and with it the security of rural employment. Mrs Howe read it differently:

As I walked down our village street today I noticed two or three Nat-Gov posters [,] one a picture of a team of horses ploughing the land [and] underneath were the words 'back to the land' and beneath that 'vote for Cook'. No doubt

Figure 6.1 National government general election poster, 1931.[59] Photo by The Conservative Party Archive/ Hulton Archive / Getty Images.

---

[59] CPA, poster 1931–17.

178   Popular Conservatism and the National Government

Mr. T. A. Cook thinks a poster of that description will entice the farm labourers' vote. If he is as patriotic as he professes to be why does he cause more unemployment by sacking the men and using machinery on his farm?[60]

It is impossible to know how widely this view was held among Cook's employees, or, for certain, if Mrs Howe had any existing allegiance to her correspondent, Lady Noel-Buxton.[61] But insofar as it reveals the potential tension between agricultural modernisation and maintaining tenant loyalty, it is noteworthy that Cook's opponent did not criticise the notion of landlordism itself, as was the wont of much Labour propaganda in the counties, but the failure of Cook to live up to the ideal landlord – which further suggests that local Labour attitudes to the paternalistic relationship were more ambivalent than is often appreciated.

Aware of such pitfalls, Cook ensured that his campaign developed a common-interest theme around the importance of the estate to rural communities. Voters were encouraged to view the large estate as the countryside's equivalent of the town factory, providing 'mass employment' in the village. To illustrate this point, and at the same time undermine Labour rumours of the threat of dismissals at Sennowe as a form of electoral coercion, repeated references were made to the situation at Sennowe Park, where long-standing tenants like Mr Ashworth had been forced by the collapse in agricultural prices to give up their farms, with repercussions for the whole community. Cook presented Mr Ashworth as a successful farmer whose plight bore testimony to the decline of rural England after two years of Labour government. He asked the audience, 'What was to become of nearly 30 men and boys employed on those 385 acres if the farmer could not make it pay?'[62] Within three months of the National government, however, Ashworth had been persuaded to stay on, with the benefits of this for local workers demonstrating 'how essential it was that something should be done for the restoration of their basic industry'.[63] Thus a common interest was created around the National government's supposed commitment to the survival of rural estates, the message to rural voters being that the National government would act decisively to foster agricultural recovery following the 'broken promises' and irresponsibility of Labour.[64] Convincing voters

---

[60] Mrs H. R. Howe to Lady Noel-Buxton, 23 Oct. 1931, Noel-Buxton papers, MC 2331/1/1/2f.

[61] Although by 1935 she was on Lady Noel-Buxton's 'List of helpers in Fulmodestone and Guist', n.d. 1935, Noel-Buxton papers, MC 2331/1/1/3e.

[62] *Norfolk Chronicle*, 16 Oct. 1931.   [63] Ibid.

[64] See, for example, the Conservative flyer in *Norfolk Chronicle*, 23 Oct. 1931.

Modernity and Paternalism in Rural Politics

of this was to occupy Conservatives in Norfolk North and Devizes throughout the early 1930s.

Private and Public Interest in the Politics of Agricultural Recovery

The 1931 election saw the first victory for the Conservatives in Norfolk North since 1918. It was also the first time that a predominantly free-trade campaign by the Liberals in Devizes was defeated. Insofar as protectionist candidates won in these areas and across the country, the election marked a watershed for rural Conservatives. It suggested the end of government indifference to agricultural decline and promised to restore the Conservatives' reputation as the party representing farming interests, something which the proliferation of agricultural pressure groups had challenged in recent decades.[65] The Agricultural Party in Norfolk withdrew its activities and its leader became active in the Conservative organisation.[66] This happened without much fanfare, however – aware of the many new votes attracted from Liberals and probably Labour under exceptional circumstances, Conservatives knew better than to gloat. Sensitivity to the 'national' Liberal vote led the party in Norfolk North to adopt the 'National' title in the hope that it might attract new subscribers from among the new voters.[67] In Devizes, Hurd referred to a scientific rather than a dogmatic application of tariffs and publicly defended Herbert Samuel's right to represent free traders' concerns at the cabinet table.[68]

The government's plan for agricultural recovery rested on the notion that protection facilitated reform of the industry. For imperial visionaries like Leo Amery, and indeed Hurd in private, the Ottawa agreement of 1932 fulfilled a grandiose notion of imperial unity. For 'pragmatic protectionists' like Neville Chamberlain, however, the Import Duties Act of 1932 'was to be sought less as an end in itself than as an instrumental step towards a far broader and more ambitious economic objective', notably industrial reorganisation leading to economic

---

[65] See E. H. H. Green, '"No longer the farmers' friend?" The Conservative party and agricultural protection, 1880–1914', in J. R. Wordie (ed.), *Agriculture and politics in England, 1815–1939* (Basingstoke, 2000), 149–77; P. Readman, 'Conservatives and the politics of land: Lord Winchilsea's National Agricultural Union, 1893–1901', *EHR*, 121 (2006), 25–69; D. Rolf, 'The politics of agriculture: farmers' organisations and parliamentary representation in Herefordshire, 1909–22', *MH*, 2 (1974), 168–86.

[66] Executive committee, 14 Dec. 1931, Norfolk North CA.

[67] AGM, 8 Feb. 1932, Norfolk North CA. Conservatives in Devizes were similarly mindful: AGM, 6 Feb. 1932, Wiltshire Record Office, Devizes CA, 2305/3.

[68] Executive committee, 3 Dec. 1931, Devizes CA.

180 Popular Conservatism and the National Government

recovery.[69] In the case of agriculture, tariffs were used to compel whole sectors to reorganise their methods of production and marketing, all in the name of meeting domestic demand and thereby restoring profitability for the farmer.

Orchestrating the government's programme from the Ministry of Agriculture was Walter Elliot. His own career as an MP lay in Clydeside, where the socialist advance informed his views on the need for a modern Conservatism that embraced greater state intervention as a route to economic regeneration and social improvement.[70] But he also enjoyed connections with farming interests, as the son of a livestock auctioneer, and, through his marriage to Katharine Tennant, herself a keen agriculturalist, his membership of the so-called cousinhood of landed Tory MPs.[71] In addition, he had a keen interest in the sciences – both physical and social – that shaped his policies on food production as well as the methods by which they were promoted to voters. During his tenure the Agriculture brief developed a higher public profile; so much so that by the mid-1930s, amid discussions on reforming the cabinet, there was talk of offering it as an influential portfolio to entice Lloyd George into the government.[72] Considered an astute political operator by contemporaries, some historians have singled out Elliot as the most successful and far-reaching of the National government ministers in reorganising and 'planning' a major industry.[73] He was popular with farmers and became something of an electoral asset for rural Conservatives. He was in high demand as a speaker and, upon his marriage to Tennant in 1934, received a gift from the National Farmers Union of a cheque – to which more than 120,000 individual farmers had subscribed – with which he purchased a tractor for his Harwood estate in the Scottish borders.[74]

The coherence of Elliot's programme rested on a raft of measures that compelled farmers to move away from ad hoc and voluntary reforms to

[69] R. Self, *Neville Chamberlain: a biography* (Aldershot, 2006), 215–16.
[70] See Elliot's own *Toryism and the twentieth century* (London, 1927).
[71] S. Haxey, *Tory M.P.* (London, 1942), 124–5; M. Linklater, 'Elliot, Katharine, Baroness Elliot of Harwood (1903–1994)', *Oxford Dictionary of National Biography* (Oxford University Press, 2004), www.oxforddnb.com.ezproxy.york.ac.uk/view/article/54942.
[72] T. Jones, *A diary with letters, 1931–1950* (Oxford, 1954), 123 (27 Feb. 1934). In the end Agriculture was considered a worthy promotion for one of Baldwin's favourite young Conservatives, William Morrison, who succeeded Elliot in the post in October 1936. *Baldwin papers: a Conservative statesman, 1908–1947*, ed. P. Williamson & E. Baldwin (Cambridge, 2004), 341 (R. A. Butler memorandum, 19–21 Jul. 1935), 447 (J. W. Robertson Scott memorandum, 28 Jan. 1938).
[73] Political diaries of Robert Sanders, 249 (31 Jul. 1933); Jones, Diary with letters, 126 (T. J. to A. F., 1 Mar. 1934); and D. Ritschel, *The politics of planning: the debate on economic planning in Britain in the 1930s* (Oxford, 1997), 189, 221.
[74] *The Times*, 24 Mar. 1934; Linklater, 'Katharine, Baroness Elliot of Harwood', *ODNB*.

Modernity and Paternalism in Rural Politics

their sector, the centrepiece of which was the Agricultural Marketing Act of 1933. Designed to rationalise the farming economy by addressing both over- and under-production, the new marketing boards were an unlikely subject of popular appeal and as such presented challenges for Conservatives in the country. Not only did they suggest an embarrassing continuity with the policy of the Labour government, which had passed its own Agricultural Marketing Act in February 1931; it was also attacked as a threat to the independence of landowners and as a bureaucratic straitjacket likely to inhibit rather than promote innovation.[75] While such criticism continued to be articulated beyond 1931, including initially by the Conservative peer Viscount Astor (who nonetheless became chairman of the Publicity Advisory Committee of the Milk Marketing Board)[76] Conservative misgivings in the country became more muted as activists now found rhetorical means of defending, even celebrating, the policy.

Whereas Labour's reforms required farmers to reorganise while exposed to foreign competition, Elliot's scheme proceeded only after protective measures were in place to maintain farm incomes and wages. Dairy and livestock farmers were protected under the Import Duties Act, while wheat producers, excluded from tariffs legislation, received subsidies under the Wheat Act, 1932.[77] Moreover, Conservatives claimed that such reforms were necessary if farms were to remain in private hands. Speaking on behalf of Cook in the Norfolk village of Aylsham, the Yorkshire MP Clifford Glossop made clear that the socialist threat demanded reform:

Woe betide if the industry failed to make the marketing boards work. If the farmers failed to reorganise themselves it would make it easier for the Socialist Party – if they came into office – to take over the whole industry on national lines and make the farmers merely servants of the State landlord. If the farmers supported the schemes they would preserve the control of their industry for themselves.[78]

Conservative propaganda charged Labour with seeking to emulate Soviet policies of nationalising all farmland and subjecting farmers to the rule of 'farm inspectors'.[79] By contrast, the National government was making amends for the way agriculture was betrayed in the 1920s, not just by the

---

[75] E.g., editorial in *Norfolk Chronicle*, 6 Feb. 1931.

[76] Viscount Astor & K. A. H. Murray, *The planning of agriculture* (London, 1933); Viscount Astor, *Farming or food control? A reply to Lord Wolmer* (London, 1934).

[77] A. Cooper, *British agricultural policy, 1912–1936: a study in Conservative politics* (Manchester, 1989), 146.

[78] *Norfolk Chronicle*, 1 Feb. 1935.

[79] See Griffiths, *Labour and the countryside*, 279–80.

182   Popular Conservatism and the National Government

coalition government, which repealed the wartime wheat act, but by the misplaced priorities of successive governments that sacrificed the interests of agriculture to those of coal mining and urban industry. In his maiden speech in November 1932, Cook claimed that 'the present Cabinet have devoted more attention to the industry of agriculture in the last 12 months than previous government have devoted during the previous 12 years'. Like Cook, Hurd also hailed a 'new attitude' towards agriculture and underlined the expertise that Elliot brought to government policy.[80]

A key theme of the government's agricultural policy was the 'modernisation' of the countryside through the application of scientific and business methods.[81] If in the attempt to convey a new golden age of agriculture the content of such material was sometimes decidedly modernist, relying on the imagery of mechanised technology and a language of 'efficiency', local Conservatives related the government's work to more familiar markers of success, in particular the return of profitability and confidence to the countryside. Cook referred to conditions on his own estate as proof. Sennowe Park's new year dinner, extensively reported in the *Norfolk Chronicle*, served as an annual opportunity to publicise the government's work as well as Cook's own commitment to rural employment. In 1934, for instance, estate foreman Mr Beck declared that 'despite that big word "depression", Mr. Cook had employed 26 extra men during the winters of 1932 and 1933', and through new projects, including privately financed afforestation and road improvement, was about to take on an additional fifteen men.[82] Speaking in 1935, Cook offered his own observations as a landowner, based on 'a comparison between 1931 and to-day'. Whereas 'in October, 1930, 50 per cent of my tenants gave me notice to quit their farms the following year ... as they could see there was no future' on the land, 'the notices were [since] withdrawn for the simple reason that confidence had been restored and they were satisfied the National Government was going to do its best to restore British agriculture'.[83]

The pace and scale of recovery was in reality more modest. Citing low farm incomes, in 1932 the NFU in Norfolk instructed its members to dismiss all but essential labourers, which in turn encouraged local Labour

[80] Cook's maiden speech appeared verbatim in the *Norfolk Chronicle*, 25 Nov. 1932; AGM, 11 Feb. 1933, Devizes CA.
[81] See the film *The country comes to town* (Empire Marketing Board Film Unit, 1933), dir. B. Wright.
[82] 'Sennowe estate dinner: where workmen find security of employment', *Norfolk Chronicle*, 12 Jan. 1934; see also ibid., 8 Jan. 1932 and 6 Jan. 1933.
[83] *Norfolk Chronicle*, 1 Feb. 1935.

Modernity and Paternalism in Rural Politics 183

officials to take up the 'wage question' as a way of rebuilding the Labour vote and boosting recruitment into the NUAW.[84] Moreover, Cooper has argued that the 'quasi-corporatism' that characterised farmers' new relationship with the state, although it gave agriculture a more permanent footing in public policy debates, rendered their interests 'functionally subordinated to those of industry'.[85] Perhaps, but it was testament to the political appeal of such corporatism that Conservatives narrated agricultural recovery not simply in terms of incomes and jobs on the land but as integral to the government's wider programme of national recovery. Thus, at the time when the Labour party cast aside much of its traditional critique of farming interests and sought to regain the initiative by appealing to farmers as 'public servants', the National government was already celebrating agriculture's substantial service to the public good.

Nowhere was this clearer than in the case of milk production, which typified the government's efforts to link agricultural recovery with the improvement of public health. As Frank Trentmann has argued, by the 1930s the pint of milk had displaced the loaf of bread as the article of popular consumer politics, as nutrition rather than cheapness came to preoccupy the concerns of consumer lobbyists.[86] In this sense, it might seem that the politics surrounding the government's agricultural marketing schemes, the flagship of which was the Milk Marketing Board established in 1933, had more to commend northern Conservatives like Macmillan and Adams than Cook and Hurd. As we have seen, Conservatives in the Northern Area were impressed by the consumer and public health issues championed by Labour through organisations like the Women's Co-operative Guild, a leading body in the campaign for a national milk policy.[87] But the government's milk scheme was developed with both urban and rural electorates in mind.

The Milk Marketing Board, according to Lord De La Warr, Elliot's National Labour deputy, was to organise dairy farmers in order to address the problem of surplus production – to get 'people to consume more liquid milk so that less of it went to cheese and butter factories' at low price for the farmer.[88] To this end, the following year Elliot announced

---

[84] Ibid., 2 Dec. 1932; J. H. Quantrill (district organiser, NUAW) to S. J. Gee (Labour agent), 2 Nov. 1932, Lady Noel-Buxton papers, MC 2331/1/2/1/d. For a history of the wage issue in the region, see Howkins, *Poor labouring men*.

[85] Cooper, *British agricultural policy*, 218.

[86] F. Trentmann, 'Bread, milk and democracy in modern Britain: consumption and citizenship in twentieth-century Britain', in M. Daunton & M. Hilton (eds.), *The politics of consumption: material culture and citizenship in Britain and America* (Oxford, 2001), 129–63.

[87] Women's advisory council, 13 Jun. 1933, Northumberland Collections Service, Northern Counties Area, NRO 4137/8.

[88] Speaking in Halstead, Essex, *The Times*, 22 Jul. 1935.

184   Popular Conservatism and the National Government

a scheme for the provision of cheap milk for schoolchildren. In doing so he extended a policy which he first introduced to Scottish schools in 1926–7, during his time as Parliamentary Under-Secretary for Health in Scotland. Above all he made agriculture more responsive to the needs of the urban population, whose poverty was brought to the forefront of public consciousness by investigative exposés like *The Times*'s series, *Places Without a Future*, and the ongoing efforts of Seebohm Rowntree, George M'Gonigle and other professionals to establish minimum nutritional standards for children as a policy objective.[89] Elliot launched the school milk scheme with a series of explanatory radio broadcasts and well-publicised school visits.[90] In the same week as Kingsley Wood announced the government's telephone campaign and Leslie Hore-Belisha unveiled the Belisha Beacon, *The Times* – which itself had recently printed a large promotional poster (Figure 6.2) – declared Elliot the frontrunner in the 'Publicity Stakes for Ministers'.[91] Such a publicity campaign placed agriculture in the vanguard of efforts to improve national fitness and self-sufficiency and thus at the heart of the moral economy of national recovery. While this ensured, at last, a level of recognition that, according to agrarian reformers, had too often been denied the industry, it also garnered support among farmers. In August 1935, the marketing scheme was placed on a permanent footing after a national poll of dairy farmers voted by 81 per cent to renew it.[92] Despite their vocal misgivings about aspects of the board's bureaucracy, farmers proved remarkably well disposed to the government's reform agenda because, although interventionist, it atoned for the perceived inactivity of government in the 1920s.

The idea that agricultural recovery was grounded in its public interestedness towards urban society was also evident on a more ad hoc local basis. Speaking in Devizes, Hurd argued that confidence among farmers was such that allotment and land settlement schemes might be expanded to enable unemployed men to become 'successful small holders'. This

---

[89] I. Gazeley, *Poverty in Britain, 1900–1965* (Basingstoke, 2003), 89–97; S. Rowntree, *The human needs of labour* (London, 1918; 1936 edn) and *Poverty and progress: a second social survey of York* (London, 1941, although conducted in 1936); J. Orr, *Food, health and income* (London, 1936).

[90] *The Times*, 27 Sep., 2 Oct. 1934; *Popular Illustrated*, 1:1 (1935). Walter Elliot would still promote the scheme after his move to the Ministry of Health in 1936 (see the Pathé film, *Mr Elliot at School*, 1937, film id. 1615.08), perhaps in response to the tendency of latter studies of poverty to invite a more critical view of the government's record on public health. See G. M'Gonigle & J. Kirby, *Poverty and public health* (London, 1936), published by the Left Book Club, and the documentary film, directed by Edgar Anstey, *Enough to eat?* (1936).

[91] *The Times*, 2 Oct. 1934.

[92] H. Sorenson & J. Cassels, 'The English milk market', *Quarterly Journal of Economics*, 50 (1936), 275–96, at 296.

Modernity and Paternalism in Rural Politics 185

Figure 6.2 *The Times*, 27 September 1934.

carried echoes of the populist 'Three Acres and a Cow' slogan promoted by Joseph Chamberlain, whose ideal of making land available to workers for a fair rent in order to encourage self-sufficiency came to influence the ideas of the leading Edwardian Conservative reformers with whom Hurd

186   Popular Conservatism and the National Government

associated.[93] By 1934 it chimed with the growing clamour for voluntary responses to the plight of the unemployed. While some land settlement schemes were managed by non-political organisations like the Land Settlement Association and the NCSS, others were attached to the Quaker Society of Friends. There is evidence that landholding chapels also offered plots at low rents, as described by Mary Chamberlain in her oral history of the East Anglian village of Gislea, and that Labour-led occupational clubs were established in rural towns like Banbury.[94] It is unclear to what extent, if any, Hurd expected farmers to make land available at low rent, but it is nonetheless clear that it became imperative for Conservatives to demonstrate a commitment to local relief initiatives – in particular the training centre for budding smallholders at Chiseldon, located on the Burderop Park estate of General Calley, the local squire and Conservative association chairman.[95] Although consistent with the ideals of rural paternalism that underpinned Cook's personalised appeals in Norfolk, for Hurd the centre served also to signal confidence in the renewal of agriculture's status as a civic-minded industry serving the interests of consumers and the nation's health.

Yet these were not selfless appeals. Rural Conservatives were acutely aware of the fact that urban victims of the depression were not confined to the distressed areas but resided in pockets of unemployment in towns and cities closer to home. In Swindon alone, which neighboured the Devizes division, more than 400 men were dismissed by the Great Western Railway in August 1934 and probably contributed to the October by-election victory of Labour's agricultural spokesman, Christopher Addison.[96] To avoid such losses, it was important that agricultural recovery contributed demonstrably to the well-being of workers in the surrounding urban districts. At the same time, paradoxically, villagers – with the possible exception of those in the very remotest regions of Scotland and Wales – were increasingly understood to desire urban standards of living. Thus, by the mid-1930s rural Conservatives, though still committed to fostering a distinctly rural culture of popular politics, had no choice

---

[93] See J. Ridley, 'The Unionist Social Reform Committee, 1911–1914: wets before the deluge', *HJ*, 30 (1987), 391–41; P. Readman, 'Jesse Collings and land reform, 1886–1914', *HR*, 81 (2008), 292–314.

[94] See P. Dearlove, 'Fen Drayton, Cambridgeshire: an estate of the Land Settlement Association', in J. Thirsk (ed.), *The English rural landscape* (Oxford, 2000), 323–35; D. Linehan & G. Pyrs, 'Unruly topographies: unemployment, citizenship and land settlement in inter-war Wales', *Transactions of the Institute of British Geographers*, 29 (2004), 46–63; Chamberlain, *Fenwomen*, 16, 22; J. R. Hodgkins, *Over the hills to glory: radicalism in Banburyshire, 1832–1945* (Southend, 1978), 190.

[95] *Marlborough Times*, 29 June 1934.   [96] *The Times*, 13 Aug. 1934.

Modernity and Paternalism in Rural Politics

but to traverse the rural-urban divide in order to remain responsive to the perceived interests of voters.

Paternalism and Modernity in Rural Welfare

The content of rural politics changed considerably with the launch of Labour's rural campaign in 1934. Questions relating to the welfare of those living off the land and in the villages became a key battleground, as Labour sought to regain the initiative and the Conservatives responded by addressing social concerns more explicitly. One important point should be stressed about the nature of the Labour threat. Whereas Labour's national strategy sought to appeal explicitly to farmers as well as labourers, in practice local appeals were often less balanced and continued to be directed at the farm labourers on a traditional class basis. Lady Noel-Buxton, who, for electoral purposes at least, had little sympathy for the inclusion of farmers as a group in the socialist state, was commended by one of her chief Labour activists for distancing herself from Stafford Cripps's 'Programme of Action'. Referring to a speech given by her to farm labourers in Yarmouth, he offered reassurance that 'a speech like this will win more votes than all the "Labour's Plan of Action" they may print', which he thought were all 'too highbrow'.[97] Lady Noel-Buxton's campaign at the general election in November would revolve around two things: foreign policy – on the grounds that Labour's 'internationalist outlook' distinguished it favourably in Liberal minds from the Conservatives[98] – and a defence of farm labourers' interests against farmers and landowners.[99]

Conservatives knew that, by highlighting the plight of the farmworker, Labour tapped into a traditional discourse of protest that enjoyed enhanced topicality in the countryside by the 1930s. Following the extensive sale of land after the war many of the new owner-occupant farmers, less cash rich than their predecessors, found themselves unable to fulfil the customary obligations of the landlord. As a result, capital investment in rural communities declined, as often did the living conditions of the workforce. As a 1936 deputation of West Country farmers explained, many of them had bought their farms in 1919, 'when we had guaranteed prices for our produce'; since then farm incomes had fallen, but there was still 'the necessity of building cottages for our labourers, who cannot be

---

[97] W. A. Pask to Noel-Buxton, 14 Feb. 1935, Noel-Buxton papers, MC 2331/1/3/2; for the speech, see *Eastern Daily Press*, 14 Feb. 1935.
[98] Notes for speech, Oct. 1935, Noel-Buxton papers, MC 2331/1/3/2.
[99] See the paper published by the Norfolk North Divisional Labour party, *Norfolk North Elector*, Nov. 1935, Noel-Buxton papers, MC 2331/1/1/3a.

188   Popular Conservatism and the National Government

expected to remain on the land and be made to live in the old and insanitary cottages that exist at present'.[100] In Norfolk, the *Chronicle* had for some time called on the government either to introduce a scheme to insure farm labourers who were dismissed through no fault of their own or offer farmers a subsidy to supplement farm wages.[101]

Nor was Labour's campaign confined to its usual haunts. In constituencies like Devizes and others in the West Country, where the threat posed by Labour was not historically as clearly defined as in the eastern counties, the perception among Conservatives was nevertheless that a Labour offensive would target the farmworkers. Four West Country seats were on Labour's campaign trail in 1934.[102] For a period, therefore, these areas experienced Labour's *official* appeal, which was comprehensive and geared towards addressing social provision, housing, village amenities – matters of concern to all in the countryside, not only those involved in agriculture.[103] The increased Labour presence was undoubtedly a disturbing development for the Conservatives in the area, but it did little to change Conservative interpretations of what the threat entailed. Labour, they thought, would always campaign on wages and improved conditions for the working poor. It is no coincidence that from 1934 Conservatives, including Hurd, started to stress the consequences of recovery for the labourer, and tried to reaffirm their party's long-standing commitment to fair and generous wages.[104]

The appeals with which local Conservatives responded to Labour once again showed their desire to couch rural progress in a culture of modernity. Those who conveyed agricultural recovery in terms of serving the nation's urban population now measured improvements in the quality of life of the rural labourer in terms of equalling the standards of town and city. In speeches and government publicity literature alike, Conservatives proclaimed not only that farm wages were 'higher than ever before' but that the government was committed to housing, road-building, and electrification in rural districts.[105] Nowhere was parity for the rural worker

---

[100] *The tithe dispute and justice for British agriculture: statement by a deputation representing the Wessex Agricultural Defence Association* (1936), 13–14.
[101] See editorial, *Norfolk Chronicle*, 16 Dec. 1932. These and other topical issues were the subject of a regular column, 'A Norfolker's Diary' (e.g., ibid., 11 Nov. 1932).
[102] These were Camborne, Frome, Penryn & Falmouth, and Thornbury; Griffiths, *Labour and the countryside*, 348–50.
[103] Ibid., 291.
[104] Council AGM, 9 Jun. 1934, Wessex Area, ARE 10/1/1; AGM, 14 Feb. 1935, Devizes CA.
[105] See Cook's speech in Norfolk, 'Work of the National Government', *Norfolk Chronicle*, 17 Nov. 1933; 'We Lead the World', National government handbill, Oct. 1935, Josephy Papers, 13/4; 'Better Times for Farming', *Popular Illustrated*, 1:6 (1935).

Modernity and Paternalism in Rural Politics 189

more clearly the aim than in the campaign to admit agricultural workers into the state's unemployment insurance schemes.

Since its inception in 1911, the system of unemployment insurance had excluded the agricultural worker. Conservatives were initially ambivalent about this, recognising the electoral appeal of inclusion but fearing that the employer contribution would become a disincentive to retaining workers. At the behest of the Unionist Social Reform Committee, and in response to Lloyd George's pre-war 'land campaign', attention shifted instead to the question of a statutory agricultural minimum wage,[106] which the wartime coalition introduced as part of the Corn Production Act of 1917. Following the 'great betrayal' of 1921, which repealed wartime statutory prices and wages, Labour staked its claim to represent farm labourers by reinstating the county wages boards through the Agricultural Wages Act, 1924 – an iconic achievement tirelessly invoked by rural Labour a decade later. In contrast, although the Conservatives in government revisited the question of unemployment insurance in 1925–6, during which they heard evidence that such a scheme would stem the flow of young men leaving the country-side for insurable urban industries, they failed to act.[107] In the context of the 1930s, and with Labour claiming both the minimum wage and the market-ing schemes as its own,[108] many rural Conservatives hoped the National government would finally steal a march on rural welfare. Asked during the 1931 election if he was in favour of unemployment insurance for agricultural workers, Hurd replied: 'Yes, I am. There are now, unfortunately, many workers out of jobs in the agricultural districts and it is not fair that they should be denied the help that would be given to them out of an insurance fund if they were town workers.'[109] A local activist deemed this pledge crucial in getting farmworkers to back Hurd.[110]

Cook was initially opposed to insuring farmworkers, despite both the long-standing support for it among East Anglia's farmworkers' unions and Labour's categorical pledge at the 1931 election. By dangling 'dole' rather than 'work' before the farmworker, he argued, Labour exposed its fundamental misunderstanding of rural folk.[111] But within a year of the

---

[106] See E. H. H. Green, 'An intellectual in Conservative politics: the case of Arthur Steel-Maitland', in *Ideologies of Conservatism: Conservative political ideas in the twentieth century* (Oxford, 2002), 72–113, at 87–92.

[107] Minutes, 3 Dec. 1925, National Farmers' Union copy of minutes of Ministry of Agriculture's Departmental Committee on Agricultural Unemployment Insurance, London School of Economics Archives, COLL MISC 1007.

[108] G. Dallas, *What Labour has done for agriculture and farm workers* (1934).

[109] *Wiltshire Gazette*, 15 Oct. 1931.

[110] R. Steward to Hurd, 30 Oct. 1931, Hurd papers.

[111] *Norfolk Chronicle*, 16 Oct. 1931. See also Christopher Addison's speech at Labour's annual conference, *The Times*, 8 Oct. 1931; election address of Lady Noel-Buxton, Oct. 1931, Noel-Buxton papers, MC 2331/1/1/2g.

190   Popular Conservatism and the National Government

election, Cook himself was campaigning openly – in parliament and in the local press – for an unemployment scheme, urging the Minister for Labour, Sir Henry Betterton, to consider the matter one of 'extreme urgency'.[112] This was testament to how quickly the language of social gain became integral to the Conservatives' narrative of economic recovery. Correspondingly, it created hostages to fortune that Labour was quick to exploit. The Unemployment Bill, published in 1933, made no provision for farm labourers and forced rural Conservatives, by way of mitigation, to argue desperately that the statutory committee set up to manage the new unemployment insurance fund, chaired by William Beveridge, would consider proposals to incorporate farm labourers in future.[113] When the Conservatives went into the 1935 general election still citing agricultural unemployment insurance as a future pledge, not an accomplishment, Lady Noel-Buxton insisted that 'in this as in most other respects, the Tories' manifesto is curiously like a list of all the things they have failed or refused to do'. By contrast, she argued, 'Had the Labour Government remained in office, our workers would have had Unemployment Insurance years ago.'[114]

It was unsurprising, then, that rural Conservatives highlighted other ways in which rural labourers shared in the benefits of national recovery. Adding to his stature as an authority on agriculture, during the 1930s Hurd forged a reputation as a campaigner for improved amenities in the countryside, giving radio talks on such themes as 'Homes for Rural Workers'.[115] As secretary of the cross-party Agricultural Committee and President of the Rural District Councils' Association, he advocated slum clearance, new houses and cottages, as well as reforms to water and electricity supply, health services, and roads and transport in the countryside. This was unglamorous work, as Hurd readily admitted. 'These many Committee meetings, held in the morning, afternoon, and evening, as occasion requires, and dealing with so many aspects of the Problems of the Countryside in Wiltshire and elsewhere, do not figure in any official records', he told his local electorate. 'Yet they are of vital importance to the men and women of a constituency like East Wilts.'[116] By championing the seemingly mundane technical and administrative politics of community amenities, Hurd was not side-lining the traditional interests of the

---

[112] *Hansard, House of Commons debates*, 272, cols. 148–50, 23 Nov. 1932 and 274, col. 1149, 16 Feb. 1933; *Norfolk Chronicle*, 11, 25 Nov. 1932.
[113] *Norfolk Chronicle*, 17 Nov. 1933.
[114] *North Norfolk Elector*, Nov. 1935, an election broadsheet published by the North Norfolk Labour party; and Lady Noel-Buxton's election address, Nov. 1935, Noel-Buxton papers, MC 2331/1/1/3a, 2f.
[115] E.g., *The Times*, 13 Mar. 1933.
[116] 'Sir Percy Hurd in Parliament' leaflet, n.d. 1935, Josephy Papers, 13/4.

farming industry so much as delineating a discourse of policy and reform that was relevant to farming and non-farming voters alike. Even his pledge to support unemployment insurance for farmworkers was now combined with a promise to extend pension schemes to cover 'small shop keepers, struggling professional men and women, and other "black-coated" workers'.[117]

The politics of amenities was embedded also in Cook's private paternalism. When he rebuilt estate dwellings in Guist in 1928, he included in the plans 'a fire station furnished with modern equipment and a Brigade of 14 members of the Estate staff – the whole scheme being maintained at his own expense'. By 1935, the service had been expanded to cover much larger swathes of north Norfolk.[118] This followed a Home Office directive requiring fire brigades in urban centres to extend their provision to surrounding rural areas through a system of 'mutual assistance', whereby rural parishes contributed to the cost of the service.[119] The Norfolk scheme, intended to operate from Norwich, collapsed owing to the parsimony of the parish councils; and in stepped Cook, with an established interest in firefighting and a desire to protect the interests of rural ratepayers. In fact, his conversion to farm labourers' unemployment insurance was partly so as to signal his commitment to the non-farming ratepayer, on whose shoulders the burden of unemployment relief would otherwise fall.[120] Given local memories of Zeppelin raids on King's Lynn and elsewhere on the eastern coast during the First World War, Cook's firefighting scheme enjoyed local resonance as a civil defence measure.[121] It also secured personal publicity for Cook as a pioneer of modern paternalism, not least in the pages of the *Norfolk Chronicle*, which he now controlled as proprietor. Throughout the summer of 1935, its pages reported extensively on every development in the fire brigade scheme, including training camps and competitions with the king's brigade on the Sandringham estate.[122]

The Rural Campaign in 1935

Both Hurd and Cook fought the 1935 election standing on their record of securing for rural voters the advantages of economic recovery. To help

---

[117] 'Last word to the electors of East Wilts' leaflet, 12 Nov. 1935, also Percy Hurd's election address, Nov. 1935, Josephy Papers, 13/4.

[118] *Norfolk Chronicle*, 7, 14 Jun. 1935.

[119] S. Ewen, 'Central government and the modernisation of the British Fire Service, 1900–1938', *TCBH*, 14 (2003), 317–38, at 330–1.

[120] *Norfolk Chronicle*, 6 Jan. 1933.

[121] *Wartime women: a Mass-Observation anthology, 1937–45* (London, 1990; 2002 edn), ed. D. Sheridan, 61–2 (diary of Muriel Green, Norfolk, 27 Dec. 1939).

[122] E.g., *Norfolk Chronicle*, 7, 14 Jun. 1935.

Figure 6.3 National government general election poster, 1931.[123] Photo by The Conservative Party Archive/ Hulton Archive / Getty Images.

them narrate this recovery, their parties had spent much of the year organising cinema-van tours and distributing copies of the *Popular Illustrated*.[124] While the idyllic depictions of village life often found in government propaganda intended, according to the *Popular Illustrated*, to be 'symbolical of the peace and security we are enjoying in this country', portrayals of agriculture itself spoke hard-headedly of profitability and economic optimism. In one issue of the broadsheet, alongside one image of a team of plough horses, ran the statement: 'Team Work: British farming is coming into its own. Farmers are getting better prices for their produce, and farm workers as a whole are getting better wages for their labour.'[125] In another, a poster from the 1931 election was reprinted (Figure 6.3) with the statement: 'The farmer's produce is now well worth the picking.'[126]

In north Norfolk, such propaganda reinforced Cook's own determined efforts to shape public ideas of the recovery. By 1935 a regular feature of the *Norfolk Chronicle* was the column entitled 'Farm Notes', written by

[123] CPA, poster 1931–18.
[124] Executive committee, 30 May 1935 and secretary's report to central committee, 6 Jul. 1935, Devizes CA, 2305/3; agent's report to executive committee, 31 May 1935 and executive committee 23 Sep. 1935, Norfolk North CA, Acc.2006/152.
[125] *Popular Illustrated*, 1:1, 1:6 (1935).   [126] Ibid., 1:3 (1935).

Modernity and Paternalism in Rural Politics

'Tenant Farmer'. This was intended to reflect the farmer's unvarnished experience of developments in his industry. For authenticity, it often referenced sources of frustration – the slow pace of recovery in such a 'naturally slow-moving business as farming', or the bureaucratic demands that accompanied the government's marketing schemes. But the central message was invariably one of government competence derived from expert knowledge of the industry, contrasted with Labour incompetence and inexperience of farming:

> Lest anyone should be tempted to allow his impatience to cause him to refrain from [voting] ... it is well to remember that the only alternative to the present government is one which would have but little understanding of, and less care for, the interests of those engaged in farming. A prosperous farming industry is of the most vital importance to everyone in the country districts, and is the only hope for the thousands of farm workers in Norfolk who have nowhere to go if the land fails to find them employment.[127]

The *Chronicle* also documented Cook's largesse as a community-spirited landowner, whose patronage benefited farmers, labourers, and non-farming villagers alike. The jubilee celebrations in May, involving a sports fete, a tea party for more than 500 children, and a fireworks display, all held at Sennowe Park, received widespread coverage at the time.[128] Six months later, voters were reminded that Cook 'had declined an invitation to St Paul's Cathedral and other ceremonies in London in order to spend the [jubilee] day with "his own people"'.[129] Cook could also rely on party activists to cooperate fully in this paternalist appeal, one local campaigner addressing a meeting in Reepham with the following simple plea:

> You have a Darts Club at Reepham, Mr. Cook is your President. You have a Pigeon Club at Reepham, Mr. Cook is interested in pigeons. You have a Bowls Club at Reepham, Mr. Cook is a Vice-President. You have a Cricket Club at Reepham, Mr. Cook is a Vice-President. You have a fire engine at Reepham. Mr. Cook, as you know, is interested in fire-fighting schemes, and does a lot for the Fire Brigade in Reepham and other places. When I go to the poll on Thursday, I am going to say 'thank you, Mr. Cook', and I want you to do the same, by putting a cross against his name, if for nothing else, for what he has done socially.[130]

The centrepiece of the Conservative campaign in Devizes was a mass meeting addressed by Sir John Simon. Given that Hurd's only opponent was a Liberal candidate, Frances Josephy, the meeting was carefully choreographed to sway Liberal voters. The meeting opened with the revelation that former Liberal candidates, including Hurd's free trade

---

[127] *Norfolk Chronicle*, 4 Jan. 1935.   [128] Ibid., 10 May 1935.   [129] Ibid., 1 Nov. 1935.
[130] Transcript, Nov. 1935, Noel-Buxton papers, MC 2331/1/1/3f.

194   Popular Conservatism and the National Government

opponent in 1931, were to join the National platform. 'We have all the Conservative and Liberal candidates since the War unanimously on one common platform', declared Lord Roundway. 'In other words, country before party'. In the course of his speech, Simon read from a letter by the Reverend Scott Lidgett, the well-known president of the United Methodist Church. Although a vice-president of the Council of Action, Lidgett, describing himself as a 'non-party man of Liberal antecedents', declared his support for Baldwin and the National government.[131] This was a major coup for the Conservatives in Devizes and owed much to their cooperation with local Liberal Nationals. In north Norfolk, too, the party enjoyed the support of leading Liberal Nationals 'so long as a National govt [sic] remained'.[132] In contrast to many urban and suburban areas, the countryside witnessed fewer instances of cooperation between Liberal and Labour opponents of the government. A. L. Rowse, who fought the Cornish seat of Penryn and Falmouth for the Labour party, attributed this to 'nuances of class differentiation' within nonconformity. The 'better off Nonconformists', he recalled, were in the 'process of moving over to becoming Tories ... and the "National" Government provided a heaven-sent opportunity for these people to cross over'.[133]

However, while the National government – its politics of recovery as well as its cross-party culture – underpinned every aspect of the Conservative campaign, it also inspired a spirited campaign on the part of its opponents. Lady Noel-Buxton's local party distributed an election broadsheet, the *North Norfolk Elector*, which challenged the very notion of recovery. Invoking the familiar divide between farmer and labourer, it argued that, despite the improvement in farm incomes and subsidies amounting to £100 million, farm wages had increased only half a penny in four years. Using slogans like 'WAGES DOWN, PROFITS UP', Noel-Buxton contested Cook's assertion that estates effectively acted as mechanisms to distribute the benefits of economic recovery and condemned the government's 'Tory' preoccupation with cosseting the interests of landowners. In this context, the *Elector* also cast aspersions on Cook himself – his 'many wealthy friends', who would supply him with cars to ferry voters to the polls; his receipt of subsidies; and his role as landowner ('Remember the Ballot is Secret').[134] By contrast, Labour was pledged to

---

[131] *Wiltshire Gazette*, 14 Nov. 1935.
[132] Executive committee, 31 May 1935, Norfolk North CA, Acc.2006/152; executive committee, 19 Sep., 24 Oct., 19 Dec. 1935, AGM, 15 Feb. 1936. Devizes CA, 2305/3.
[133] A. L. Rowse, *A man of the thirties* (London, 1979), 91.
[134] *North Norfolk Elector*, Nov. 1935, Noel-Buxton papers, MC 2331/1/1/3a.

abolishing the Trade Disputes Act and the tied cottage, thereby freeing farm labourers to pursue their legitimate demands unhindered.[135]

Similar critiques dominated the Liberal candidate's campaign in Devizes. Like Noel-Buxton, Frances Josephy strongly endorsed the Council of Action and fought the election on the twin themes of 'peace and reconstruction'. Whereas the government's landed interest was said to account for rural deprivation, its stake in the arms industry was said to account for its historic failure to lead on global disarmament. This, she argued, should leave voters in no doubt that the National government was in fact a Conservative government. Noel-Buxton was after the same effect when she suggested that the government's 'proper name' should be the "Landowners' and Arms Manufacturers' Cooperative Society".[136] So-called exposés of the government's real work ('ARMAMENTS GOING UP! TARIFFS AND SUBSIDIES GOING UP! COST OF LIVING GOING UP!') were a prominent feature of the rural campaign.[137] Together they spoke to the traditional radicalism of the land as well as the moral fervour of the nonconformist conscience, and served both Labour and Liberal attempts to rehabilitate an unmistakably Conservative target around which to agitate.

There is little doubt that the Conservatives felt the heat of the radical campaign. In the two-way contests fought in Norfolk North and Devizes, it raised the spectre of a united anti-Tory vote. In the former, the party was so exasperated by 'the many rumours which have been circulated by our opponents about our Candidate, Mr. Cook', that it distributed a last-minute 'Fact v. Rumour' leaflet to defend and celebrate Cook's conduct as landowner and landlord.[138] Following the election, the agent in Devizes attributed Hurd's reduced majority to Josephy's portrayal of the government's foreign policy.[139] Yet, in general, rural Conservatives performed exceptionally well. They lost far fewer seats than their counterparts in the industrial areas (and none in the Norfolk and Devizes areas); protected a greater proportion of the votes they gained in 1931 than their suburban counterparts; and in some cases increased their

---

[135] Lady Noel-Buxton's election address, Nov. 1935, Noel-Buxton papers, MC 2331/1/1/2f.

[136] Frances Josephy's election address, 4 Nov. 1935, Josephy papers, 13/4; *North Norfolk Elector*, Nov. 1935, Noel-Buxton papers, MC 2331/1/1/3a.

[137] 'What the National Government Posters DO NOT SAY', Liberal party leaflet, 1935, Josephy papers, 13/4. For the campaign in Pembrokeshire, see G. Thomas, 'The Conservative party and Welsh politics in the inter-war years', *EHR*, 128 (2013), 877–913, at 909–10; and on the Council of Action, see S. Koss, 'Lloyd George and nonconformity: the last rally', *EHR*, 89 (1974), 77–108.

[138] 'Mr. T. A. Cook: rumours about him & facts about him', Nov. 1935, Noel-Buxton papers, MC 2331/1/2/1c.

[139] Executive committee, 19 Dec. 1935, Devizes CA, 2305/3.

vote.[140] Although Labour and the Liberals regained some ground in the polls, neither secured any notable breakthrough in rural Britain.[141]

The success of rural Conservatives derived directly from the National government and their local uses of it. Both Cook and Hurd had made concerted efforts to appeal to the wider non-farming vote, the former by protecting the interests of ratepayers and the latter by campaigning for improved amenities. If the motive for doing so was in part defensive, triggered by fear of losing the farm labourer's vote to Labour, it soon proved to be a valuable strategy in its own right. For although it testified to the Conservatives' residual fear of a specifically rural brand of radicalism, it also testified to their faith in the government's message of competence and recovery as one capable of transcending class and occupational divides.

Above all, however, rural Conservatives – and their opponents – found that the National government neutralised the radical threat as much as it inspired it. In her analysis of the election, Lady Noel-Buxton attributed Conservative success to a number of factors. One of these was Labour's failure to develop voters' acceptance of 'any legislation which make the rich, on whom they feel dependent for their employment, poorer'. For Noel-Buxton, this peculiarity of rural life also accounted for 'widespread intimidation and bribery' by landlords and employers.[142] For Cook it signalled the success of his concerted efforts since 1931 to harness the government's narrative of recovery in order to rehabilitate a politics of paternalism locally. Another key factor, according to Noel-Buxton, was the 'National' label itself. Despite Labour's best efforts to prove its vacuity, it helped the Conservatives to shed damaging associations with Tory vested interests and proved crucial in mobilising the Liberal vote. Indeed, Lidgett's letter, reported in the national press,[143] had a considerable impact in Norfolk. It made Noel-Buxton realise, on reflection, how nonconformist voters were 'still nationally minded' – meaning that, a generation on from the campaign for disestablishment, they were still liable to vote as a bloc, in this instance with Lidgett in favour of the National government.[144]

---

[140] The Conservative vote increased in East Dorset, Holderness, Honiton, Louth, Mid-Bedfordshire, Penrith & Cockermouth, and Tavistock.

[141] The Liberals regained only two mainly agricultural seats: North Cumberland and Berwick-on-Tweed. Labour gained only four: Brigg, Carmarthen, South Ayrshire, and the Western Isles, and saw its Agricultural spokesman, Christopher Addison, defeated by the National Conservatives in Swindon.

[142] General election report, n.d. 1935, Noel-Buxton papers, MC 2331/1/1/3f.

[143] *The Times*, 9 Nov. 1935.

[144] General election report, n.d. 1935, Noel-Buxton papers, MC 2331/1/1/3f.

7   National Conservatism in Scotland and Wales

> In the politics anxiously watched by a schoolboy [in Abergavenny] in the thirties, there was the British Empire, sedulously taught but by me sullenly cursed in our Welsh grammar school, and then somewhere in the pages of the *Daily Herald*, for repulsion more than attraction but in any case for definition, an England which was an amalgam of Neville Chamberlain and Sir Samuel Hoare and Lord Halifax, of Jubilee and Coronation, of London and the Home Counties.
>
> (Raymond Williams recalling his 1930s childhood)[1]

In his public speeches, Stanley Baldwin relied heavily on the concept of 'nation' to appeal to voters. The purpose was to convey an inclusive Conservatism whose interests transcended the sectional concerns of wealth and class and, crucially, the cultural distinctions associated with regional and national differences.[2] Politicians of his generation knew all too well that regional and national identity, shaped by religious and denominational alignments, economic and civic interests, as well as linguistic traditions, had profoundly affected patterns of political allegiance in Britain since before the Second Reform Act. In the political cultures of Scotland and Wales, though different to each other, the struggle facing the Conservative party remained the tradition of dissent that drove radical anti-Tory politics, whether in the form of popular Liberalism or Labourism. The cross-party National government offered a rare opportunity to seek to neutralise such threats by putting Baldwin's values of national unity into practice. The interwar party had inherited few strongholds in the Celtic nations. In Wales these were limited to constituencies mostly near the

---

[1] R. Williams, 'Wales and England', in J. Osmond (ed.), *The National question again: Welsh political identity in the 1980s* (Llandysul, 1985), 19.

[2] P. Williamson, *Stanley Baldwin: Conservative leadership and national values* (Cambridge, 1999), 250–3; M. Cragoe, 'Conservatives, "Englishness" and "civic nationalism" between the wars', in D. Tanner, C. Williams, W. P. Griffith & A. Edwards (eds.), *Debating nationhood and government in Britain, 1885–1939: perspectives from the 'four nations'* (Manchester, 2006), 192–210.

198   Popular Conservatism and the National Government

English border. In Scotland they were, historically, highly localised – concentrated for instance around the Protestants of Glasgow, where Labour had since made notable and possibly irreversible gains – or otherwise in areas where they owed much of their support to the alliance with the Liberal Unionists.[3] However, there were marginal seats – promising ones like Dunbartonshire on the Clyde estuary and Pembrokeshire in West Wales – where the party could justifiably expect to garner advantages from membership of the National government and entrench its electoral position.

But if, as we have seen, the Conservatives' use of the 'national' label was called out by opponents in England, so too proved the case in Scotland and Wales. For the formation of the National government and the debates around national recovery brought into stark focus the national distinctions that still shaped British politics in the age of mass democracy and mass media. This chapter explores the effect of these distinctions on how Scottish Unionists and Welsh Conservatives related to the National government, how they presented its record of economic recovery to local voters, and how their opponents responded. Drawing on case studies including Dunbartonshire and Dundee in Scotland, Pembrokeshire and Gower in Wales, the chapter analyses the popular politics of National Conservatism as it traversed the so-called Anglo-Celtic frontier.[4] Starting with a discussion of the 1931 general election campaign, it demonstrates how the National government helped the Conservatives to neutralise old hostilities while also helping their opponents to renew or inspire anti-Tory sentiment. This was reflected in the election results. In Scotland, the Unionists gained twenty-eight seats, including Dundee for the first time. In Wales, it gained only five seats, all in areas that regularly voted Conservative up to 1929, and failed to regain Pembrokeshire. This in turn set the politics of recovery in Scotland and Wales on different trajectories. Through its MPs and ministers, the government enjoyed a high-profile presence in Scotland that it lacked in Wales. Even so, in both nations its claims of recovery, like the National government itself, provoked renewed anti-Tory – and often anti-Westminster – rhetoric among Liberals, Labour, and (in Scotland) nationalists. At the 1935 general election, while little changed in the relative strengths of Scottish Unionism and Welsh Conservatism, Labour emerged as the net beneficiary.

---

[3] H. Pelling, *Social geography of British elections, 1885–1910* (London, 1967), ch.16.
[4] The phrase was used to define the 'four nations' approach to British history as advocated in J. G. A. Pocock, 'British history: a please for a new subject', *JMH*, 47 (1975), 601–21, at 605.

'1931' in Scotland and Wales

Scotland

Never had Scottish Unionists enjoyed such a transformation in their electoral fortune as following the formation of the National government. Despite winning a majority of Scottish seats in 1924, albeit on a lower share of the vote than Labour, the party proved vulnerable in the face of Labour's post-war gains. This culminated in 1929 when Labour won, for the first time, a clear majority of Scottish seats.[5] Two years later, the Unionists won their own majority, also for the first time, securing 48 seats on 49.5 per cent of the vote. This outcome dwarfed the party's previous best performance in 1900, when in alliance with the Liberal Unionists it won 36 seats on 49 per cent of the vote. Nor would it be bettered by another party until 1966, when Labour secured a slightly higher share of the vote, or 1987 when Labour secured 50 seats. Dundee returned its first Unionist MP since 1832. Dunbartonshire was recaptured from Labour with a 12,000 majority. The local association attributed such gains 'in large measure [to] the support of the Liberals' as well as 'a share of the Labour vote'. Both associations also noted the 'different atmosphere' that prevailed since the crisis of the summer, one that concentrated voters' minds on Labour's record in government and was already attracting 'new blood' into the ranks of local Unionist organisations.[6]

The Unionist campaign in Dundee focused overwhelmingly on hammering home to working-class voters the failures of the Labour government. It occurred against the backdrop of considerable social tension in the city, caused by rowdy and sometimes violent demonstrations against the means test, organised by the Communist party and resulting in the imprisonment of its candidate almost up to polling day.[7] Florence Horsbrugh, the Unionist candidate, took her campaign to the gates of Dundee's jute mills and other factories, where both the employed and unemployed assembled. There she recounted the rise in joblessness and the drop in trade since 1929, the depreciation of working-class savings, and the Labour government's 'cowardly' deferral of cuts to unemployment benefit.[8] The campaign proved similarly raucous in the industrial parts of Dunbartonshire, with gangs of communist 'hooligans' descending from Glasgow to disrupt Unionist meetings and attack the candidate's

---

[5] Labour won 36 seats, Unionists 20, Liberals 13.
[6] AGM, 27 Nov. 1931, University of Dundee Archive Services, Dundee UA, MS 270/1/1/1; report for the year ended 31 Oct. 1931 and report on parliamentary election 1931, National Library of Scotland, Dunbartonshire UA, 12264/3.
[7] *The Scotsman*, 22 Oct. 1931.
[8] *Dundee Courier*, 17, 22, 27 Oct. 1931; *Dundee Evening Telegraph*, 22, 26 Oct. 1931.

200   Popular Conservatism and the National Government

car. Colonel Thom, the candidate, warned that a socialist victory 'will bring the country within measurable distance of revolution', and 'the greatest sufferers will be the wage-earners and the women and children who have suffered so much already'.[9] Like their English counterparts, Scottish Unionists saw in the crisis of 1931 ways of reversing a decade's worth of growing working-class loyalty to Labour.

The factor widely believed to hold the key to electoral success in Scotland was the Liberal vote. Despite the party's rapid electoral decline since the war, political culture in Scotland nevertheless ascribed to Liberalism a remarkable degree of public influence. The reason for this was in part dictated by electoral logic: the third party effectively held the balance of power, consequently the behaviour of the Liberals was keenly observed. So as not to alienate the Liberal vote, Unionists were careful to hedge their advocacy of tariffs. Colonel Thom went all out to disavow his doctrinal commitment to protectionism, declaring that under the circumstances he was 'not standing as a hidebound Tariff Reformer'. Instead he willingly sacrificed his own politics in order to work alongside Liberals and indeed socialists in the national interest. Faced with an unprecedented crisis, he argued that the government truly required a 'free hand', which in turn demanded sacrifices on the part of protectionists and free traders alike.[10] Horsbrugh also eschewed a doctrinal endorsement of tariffs, declaring herself opposed to food taxes and in favour of tariffs on manufactured goods that could be made in Dundee. Citing the growth in imported jute products from Belgium and Czechoslovakia in 1931, which alone represented the annual output of three mills employing 5,000 Dundonians, she spoke of 'the extravagance and cruelty of paying foreigners to do our work while our own people went idle'.[11] Tariffs, she argued, would safeguard established industries, encourage new enterprise, and bring solvency to the Unemployment Fund.[12]

In Scotland, as in Wales, there were also historical reasons underpinning the enduring influence of Liberalism. The party dominated the electoral landscape before 1914, championing the interests of the majority-nonconformist populations to the north and west of England and appealing across both class and urban-rural divides. In electoral, policy, and cultural terms, the Liberals established themselves as the party of the so-called Celtic fringe, increasingly assertive in the late nineteenth century. Containing as it did the leading advocates of 'Home Rule All

---

[9] *Kirkintilloch Gazette*, 23 Oct. 1931; election address of Lt.-Col. J. G. Thom, Oct. 1931, National Library of Scotland, Cochrane papers, 10218, 17/14.
[10] *The Scotsman*, 13 Oct. 1931; *Kirkintilloch Gazette*, 16, 23 Oct. 1931.
[11] *Dundee Courier*, 16, 17 Oct. 1931; *Dundee Evening Telegraph*, 20 Oct. 1931.
[12] *Dundee Courier*, 15, 23 Oct. 1931.

Round', a system of federal devolution designed to salvage the union in light of Gladstone's commitment to Irish home rule, as well as opponents of home rule who nonetheless favoured administrative devolution in the case of Scotland, the party could claim to represent the domestic 'national interest' of the two Celtic nations.[13] The strength of Scottish Liberalism was matched only by the strength of Scottish unionist sentiment. As has recently been argued, belief in the Union of the United Kingdom, and Scotland's place within it, was as much a pillar of Scottish life, both ideologically and culturally, as Liberalism or nationalism.[14] As such it engendered a distinctive national political culture in which Scottish Liberalism differed from Welsh Liberalism, insofar as it proved more attuned – and susceptible – to the unionist creed, and Scottish Conservatism differed from English Conservatism through its self-styled 'Unionist' identity. Nothing proved this more than that Scotland became a Liberal Unionist heartland, second only to Birmingham and parts of the West Country, following the split in the Liberal party over Irish home rule. More than a quarter of the new party's candidates in 1886 were fielded in Scotland and in 1900 the Conservative-Liberal Unionist alliance won a majority of Scottish seats. Contrasted with the many English seats where the Conservatives dominated the Unionist alliance and won elections regardless of Liberal Unionist support, in Scotland the Liberal Unionists were the dominant partner and materially boosted the Unionist vote. As the home rule issue gradually lost salience, and more especially because the separate Liberal Unionist party formally merged with the Conservatives in 1912, the Scottish unionist vote declined and Liberalism reclaimed its dominance, to be challenged only by Labour.[15]

It was no coincidence that the Unionist recovery occurred in 1931. Membership of the National government, alongside Scottish Liberals, presented Unionists with an opportunity to rehabilitate a broad alliance of Conservative and non-Conservative voters. Such an alliance had briefly looked set to emerge after the war, when a majority of Scottish Unionist MPs favoured the continuation of the Lloyd George coalition only to be outnumbered by English Conservative MPs.[16] *The Scotsman* predicted at the time that a coalition broken 'in form' could still be maintained 'in

---

[13] See K. Morgan, *Wales in British politics, 1868–1922* (Cardiff, 1963); D. Bebbington, *The nonconformist conscience: chapel and politics, 1870–1914* (London, 1982).

[14] See A. Jackson, *The two unions: Ireland, Scotland, and the survival of the United Kingdom, 1707–2007* (Oxford, 2012), ch.7.

[15] Pelling, *Social geography of British elections*, 411.

[16] Eighteen Scottish Unionist MPs voted to renew the coalition, against six who opposed it. *The Scotsman*, 20 Oct. 1922; M. Kinnear, *The fall of the Lloyd George coalition: the political crisis of 1922* (London, 1973), Appendix I.

202 Popular Conservatism and the National Government

spirit', and so it proved in some parts of Scotland, especially Glasgow, where Unionists and Liberals cooperated to ensure an anti-socialist front in municipal affairs.[17] But the cooperation was not formalised and did not always extend to parliamentary elections. What is notable about the contest in 1931 is that so few Unionists, in private or in public, invoked the idea of formal cooperation. By jointly supporting the National government, but from decidedly separate organisations, Unionist and Liberal methods of conducting the 'National' alliance were in keeping with those that underpinned the old unionist alliance. As John McCaffrey found, there were sound reasons for this 'tentative' cooperation. Retaining the support of one's own activists while also appealing to moderates of the other party was rendered easier when neither group was expected to regard themselves as 'converts'.[18]

Unionist-Liberal cooperation was secured in all but nine Scottish seats.[19] It was mostly in the east that Unionists and Liberals clashed, especially in the county seats where the unionist alliance was historically weakest and Liberalism remained anomalously stronger than Labour. In five seats in Aberdeenshire, Forfarshire, Perthshire, and Roxburghshire, the local Liberal association came out against the sitting Unionist member.[20] In Dundee, a two-seat constituency, there was no strict requirement for cooperation as the Unionist and Liberal parties encouraged voters to use their second vote reciprocally. The Unionist association recognised there were 'divergences of opinion' between the free-trade Liberal candidate, Dingle Foot, and Horsbrugh that prevented formal collaboration. But equally, it noted, 'there did not appear to be any reason whatever why the two Associations, as such, should be opposed to one another'.[21] On the need for economy, Foot preached the government's line, pleading with voters that 'cuts' were preferable to 'starvation', and that without them the 'hungry forties' of the previous century would be as nothing compared to the 'hungry thirties' of the twentieth century.[22] On the fiscal question, Horsbrugh advocated targeted tariffs rather than blanket protectionism. In this way, and based on what was already becoming an effective partnership between Horsbrugh

[17] *The Scotsman*, 19 Oct. 1922; J. Smyth, 'Resisting Labour: Unionists, Liberals, and moderates in Glasgow between the wars', *HJ*, 46 (2003), 375–401.
[18] J. McCaffrey, 'The origins of Liberal Unionism in the west of Scotland', *SHR*, 50 (1971), 47–71, at 65.
[19] The nine exceptions were Central Aberdeenshire, Dundee, Galloway, Kincardine & West Aberdeenshire, Forfarshire, Kinross & West Perth, Perth, Roxburghshire, and the Western Isles.
[20] *The Scotsman*, 17 Oct. 1931.
[21] Executive committee, 12 Nov. 1931, Dundee UA, MS 270/1/1/1.
[22] *Dundee Courier*, 24 Oct. 1931.

National Conservatism in Scotland and Wales 203

and Foot, the association 'agreed that we should endeavour as far as ever possible, to encourage a friendly spirit of one to the other'.[23] Foot won the most votes and thereby became the senior MP for the city, suggesting that he attracted a greater proportion of second votes than Horsbrugh among Labour supporters.

Likewise, in the west of Scotland, despite eliminating Unionist-Liberal clashes almost completely, the parties avoided formal cooperation. The Unionists instead enjoyed the advantage of a more valuable commodity than organisational help. This was the unspoken assumption that a majority of Liberal voters, especially those old enough to recall past alliances, would back the Unionists in the absence of a Liberal candidate. *The Scotsman* immediately interpreted news of the Liberal association's decision not to fight Dunbartonshire as a boost to Unionist prospects. The majority of Liberal voters in this part of Scotland, according to the correspondent, were 'of the old Gladstonian type who never could give a vote to a Socialist'. He cited Unionist organisers who were convinced that, under the circumstances, they could 'count on nine-tenths of the Liberal vote'.[24] Meanwhile the Labour campaign in Dunbartonshire targeted younger voters, including residents of the Knightswood council estate recently arrived from the slums of Glasgow. It did so, according to the same correspondent, in the belief that the young 'know little of the old-time party divisions'. Even those from Liberal backgrounds – 'so-called Liberals' – had not yet been conditioned to regard Unionism as an acceptable option. Together with unemployed Unionists, whose experience of the means test would disabuse them of the government's mantra of patriotic 'sacrifice', they were deemed to be among the most likely converts to Labour.[25]

Labour emerged from the election with only seven Scottish seats, having lost thirty. The Unionists gained twenty-eight. Scotland's Liberal tradition now proved to be of crucial advantage to the Unionists. It was no longer sufficiently strong in organisational and electoral terms to dominate the National partnership (as the Liberal Unionists had done before the war), but still strong enough in reputation for its collaboration to carry significant rewards. Another advantage enjoyed by the Unionists was their new association with Ramsay MacDonald. Similar to Lloyd George in Wales, MacDonald's progress

---

[23] Executive committee, 12 Nov. 1931, Dundee UA, MS 270/1/1/1. Horsbrugh herself came to embody this friendly spirit, presenting Foot with a jute carpet on the occasion of his wedding in 1932 (see photograph in *Dundee Evening Telegraph*, 19 Dec. 1932).
[24] *The Scotsman*, 12, 22, 26 Oct. 1931.
[25] Ibid., 16, 26 Oct. 1931; *Kirkintilloch Herald*, 28 Oct. 1931; election address of Willie Brooke (Labour candidate), Oct. 1931, Cochrane papers, 10218, 17/14.

from his origins as the illegitimate son of a poverty-stricken crofter in Lossiemouth to the seat of government in Westminster was the stuff of considerable folk pride in Scotland. The national crisis added further to his valorisation in some quarters, if not in the Labour movement. *The Scotsman* depicted his visit to Lossiemouth shortly after the election as the homecoming of a national hero and reported a slew of Scottish towns lining up to grant him civic honours.[26] While Baldwin is known to have possessed a deep awareness of Scottish history and culture and used this systematically to fashion his public appeals north of the border, he appeared somewhat sidelined in the Unionist campaign. There was no ignoring the importance of Sir John Simon as leader of the Liberal Nationals. But it was onto MacDonald's coat-tails that the Unionist candidates most sought to hitch their campaigns. Colonel Thom's election address referred to him as 'Leader of the National Party' and, like Horsbrugh's speeches, celebrated his 'patriotism' above that of the other leaders.[27] MacDonald's true electoral value for the Unionists is of course impossible to quantify. But the phenomenon of the 'national' political leader in Scotland and Wales can be further understood by exploring Lloyd George, whose influence on Conservative fortunes proved very different.

Wales

The outcome of the 1931 general election proved altogether less transformative in Wales. The Conservatives' failure to break through in South and West Wales cannot be fully understood without first understanding the meaning of '1931' in Wales, and in particular the way in which Welsh Liberals responded to the formation of the National government. They were supportive to begin, believing that Liberal involvement could help revive the party's fortunes in Wales. The *Cambrian News*, a regional weekly covering Mid- and West Wales and the nation's de facto Liberal paper, argued that the national crisis demanded nothing less than that Lloyd George should be invited to join the cabinet as soon as his health permitted. This way the Liberal party in Wales could secure favourable treatment in a future couponed election and make up for the 1929 election results, which according to the paper under-represented the true strength of Welsh Liberalism.[28]

---

[26] *The Scotsman*, 5 Nov. 1931.
[27] Election address of Lt.-Col. J. G. Thom, Oct. 1931, Cochrane papers, 10218, 17/14; *Dundee Courier*, 13 Oct. 1931. See G. Ward-Smith, 'Baldwin and Scotland: more than Englishness', *CBH*, 15 (2001), 61–82.
[28] *Cambrian News*, 28 Aug., 18 Sep. 1931.

National Conservatism in Scotland and Wales

By the general election in 1931, however, the Liberal party's attitude was a good deal more fractured. While continuing in general to support the government, the party divided over policy, with followers of John Simon endorsing protection as an expedient to deal with the nation's trade deficit and followers of Herbert Samuel defending free trade. Lloyd George, still outside the cabinet, rejected any move towards tariffs and attacked the decision to hold an election, arguing that the Conservatives were hijacking the national crisis to seek an emergency mandate to impose tariffs. From his sickbed in Churt he delivered a famous radio broadcast on 15 October warning voters that 'patriotism is everywhere exploited for purely partisan purposes' and urging Liberals not to allow themselves to be 'blinded by the use of the word "National" to vote for protectionist candidates'. The implication – that he endorsed Labour candidates where no Liberal free trader was standing – provoked intense commentary in the national press and placed Lloyd George firmly outside the National government.[29] Yet his influence in England was limited: the figure who mounted the Liberals' vast campaign in 1929 could no longer muster the funds to head an opposition campaign to save free trade.[30]

In Wales, however, Lloyd George still cut a patriarchal figure and was able fundamentally to shape the narrative of debate. His family constituted a small but distinct Liberal party in West Wales: his son Gwilym in Pembrokeshire, his daughter Megan in Anglesey, and his son-in-law Goronwy Owen in Caernarfonshire, were all sitting MPs. Gwilym and Goronwy had served in MacDonald's government since August but resigned in October to support their kinsman, and in doing so forfeited the clear run that local Conservatives would probably have granted them as incumbents.[31] This created a further division within Welsh Liberalism. Whereas Simonite versus Samuelite views on free trade defined Liberal differences in England and Scotland, in Wales the battle between Lloyd George on the one hand and Simon *plus* Samuel on the other engendered a more fundamental disagreement over the legitimacy of the National government itself. Backed by the *Cambrian News*, Lloyd George's stance helped to polarise public debate along pro- and anti-National government lines.[32] He was not alone in accusing the Conservatives of misappropriating the 'national' prefix. But whereas Labour candidates across Britain

---

[29] *The Times*, 16, 17 Oct. 1931.

[30] Only two Liberal candidates followed Lloyd George's lead in England: the novelist Edgar Wallace in Blackpool and Frank Owen in Hereford: A. Thorpe, *The British general election of 1931* (Oxford, 1991), 170.

[31] *Western Mail*, 17 Oct. 1931.

[32] *Cambrian News*, 16 Oct. 1931. The association with Lloyd George was forged in the years before 1914: see A. Jones, 'Sir John Gibson and the *Cambrian News*', *Ceredigion*, xii (1994), 57–83, esp. 77–9.

206   Popular Conservatism and the National Government

cast the Conservatives as the party of financiers against the interests of the unemployed, Lloyd George resurrected the vision of radical Wales, a nation whose interests could never be represented by a party rooted in English Toryism. The political and cultural prejudices wrought from the anti-Anglican and anti-landlord campaigns of the pre-war years remained deeply engrained, and relevant, in Welsh public life. Over a decade after disestablishment, anti-Anglicanism continued to function as a political frame of reference. Parts of the non-conformist press, for example, influential in Welsh-speaking Wales, were adept at switching from confessional to secular opposition to the Conservative party and its main backer in the Welsh national press, the *Western Mail*.[33] As a result, the free-trade debate lost some of its totemic status in the Welsh campaign and the national divide – the 'Anglo-Celtic frontier' – once more garnered political relevance.

Lloyd George's intervention served to reawaken traditional hostilities in Wales towards 'Tory' Westminster politics. These were to become clear during the course of the decade, but first they placed limits on the opportunities available to Welsh Conservatives in 1931. In South Wales, in the mining and industrial seats outside Cardiff and Monmouth, Simonite and Samuelite Liberals emerged as the best placed to represent the National government. Whereas the Conservatives fielded just three candidates in the region (in Caerphilly, Llanelli, and Ogmore), the Liberals fielded seven.[34] South-Wales Conservatives had yet to recover from the drubbing they received in 1929, when eleven candidates lost their deposit.[35] In Merthyr the party chose to back the New Party candidate rather than nominate its own.[36] This sense of disarray was shared by the *Western Mail*. Having been instrumental in shaping anti-socialist politics in the region in the early 1920s, and having taken ownership of the Liberal *South Wales Daily News* in 1928, the crisis of 1931 afforded the paper another opportunity to encourage a Liberal readership in a Conservative direction.[37] This led the paper to develop a benevolent editorial approach towards the National Liberals, which proved influential in placing them at the helm of the National campaign in the region.

In order to build momentum behind the National cause, and to counter Lloyd George's attempts to tar it as 'Tory Protectionist', the *Western Mail*

---

[33] E.g., see the Baptist paper, *Seren Gymru*, 23 Sep., 7 Oct. 1932.
[34] In Aberavon, Gower, Neath, Pontypool, Pontypridd, Swansea East, and Swansea West.
[35] G. Thomas, 'The Conservative party and Welsh politics in the inter-war years', *EHR*, 128 (2013), 877–913, at 893.
[36] *Western Mail*, 21 Oct. 1931.
[37] See Thomas, 'The Conservative party and Welsh politics', 889–92; A. Jones, *Press, politics and society: a history of journalism in Wales* (Cardiff, 1993), 130.

treated each move by Simon and Samuel as evidence of the Liberals' growing commitment to the National government. It praised the leadership shown by Simon and highlighted the business credentials and party loyalty of the other Liberal (and Labour) converts to fiscal reform. A series of interviews appeared with 'leading Welsh Liberals and Trade Union officials who have abandoned Free Trade'. These figures argued that a period of 'fair trade' (whereby Britain issued reciprocal trade tariffs) could help boost home industries, conjuring what they thought was the attractive image of an autarkic Britain: 'If we could produce what is required ourselves we should not only provide employment for cultivators, but also benefit the coal, steel and tin-plate industries.'[38] Indeed, one of the reasons why Conservatives in Gower so willingly supported Sir Edgar Jones as National Liberal candidate was the importance of the tin-plate industry in the Swansea district, and his expert position as chairman of the National Food Canning Council.[39] Contrasted with these figures were the Liberals who, led by Samuel, were unwilling to endorse a protectionist plea to the country. 'We are accustomed to such repudiations of national obligation on the part of the Socialists', commented the *Western Mail*, 'but better things should be expected of the Liberal party'.[40] The paper could not always disguise its frustration at the Samuelites' lukewarm backing of the government,[41] but the cabinet's decision to seek a 'free hand' nevertheless enabled the paper to assert that 'among the Liberal party there is an increasing disposition to regard the question of tariffs as no longer one to be decided on the customary controversial lines, but rather as a problem to be decided by the National government' once re-elected. By polling day, the paper was endorsing all National Liberals equally, without reference to their views on tariffs.[42]

What part this played in voters' actions – and whether it encouraged them to think that they were voting 'National' rather than 'Conservative' or 'Liberal' – is hard to tell. What is clear is that in South Wales the National Liberals performed better than the three Conservative candidates. The Liberals regained Swansea West and elsewhere managed significantly to reduce Labour majorities. It is likely that National Liberal candidates benefited considerably from Conservative votes, for with such low expectations of their own prospects in South Wales Conservative voters showed greater willingness than did Liberals to support their National partners. In areas where the Liberals had some history of popular allegiance among voters, but where no Liberal candidate stood

---

[38] *Western Mail*, 16 Sep. 1931.   [39] *South Wales Daily Post*, 13, 14 Oct. 1931.
[40] *Western Mail*, 18 Sep. 1931.   [41] Ibid., 15 Oct. 1931, editorial.
[42] Ibid., 7, 27 Oct. 1931.

208   Popular Conservatism and the National Government

in 1931, it would seem that Liberal voters were less inclined to support a Conservative standing as a National candidate. In Llanelli, Caerphilly, and Ogmore, where the Liberal party gave way to the Conservatives, Labour increased its share of the vote. Here the dissenting rhetoric of Lloyd George is likely to have legitimated the decision of many to vote Labour.

It was in Welsh-speaking West Wales that the Conservatives encountered Lloyd George's campaign most directly. In Pembrokeshire, Gwilym Lloyd George based his campaign 'on the line that there is no such thing as a National Party. It is the Tory Party & if they get in they will be a Tory government'.[43] He and his followers (many of whom had returned to active campaigning after years of apathy)[44] would exploit the National government to construct a radical appeal that blurred the barrier between the modern Liberal and Labour parties and repositioned the Liberal tradition as the expression of popular anti-Tory dissent. Gwilym stood in defence of voters' democratic right not to be governed by Conservative deceit. The 'National' government was anything but inclusive, he insisted, as it had arbitrarily decided to adopt tariffs and was behaving unconstitutionally by asking for a 'doctor's mandate'. Voters could either give the government a 'Free Hand' or defend their rights as 'Free People'.[45] The *Pembrokeshire Telegraph*, supporting his campaign, echoed this argument: 'We live under a Representative form of Government, and there is something alien to the whole spirit of our constitution in asking for a mandate for something not specified'.[46] In a further bid to make an example of the National government's hypocrisy, Gwilym's activists mocked the Conservatives' alliance with the erstwhile Labour prime minister. 'What had the "Western Mail" to say about Ramsay MacDonald during the war?', asked one speaker. 'Who was the traitor then?'[47]

In keeping with the party's exploits elsewhere, the Conservatives in Pembrokeshire used the election to reframe their opponents – in particular to obscure the distinction between Lloyd George and Labour. The candidate, Major Charles Price, presented it as a choice between National and Socialist government, between himself and Gwilym Lloyd George. Having argued prior to the election that 'a vote for Liberalism had … come to mean a vote for Socialism',[48] he now maintained that events proved his point. David Lloyd George would normally be 'one of the first

---

[43] Gwilym to D. Lloyd George, n.d. Oct. 1931, Parliamentary Archives, London, Lloyd George papers, LG/I/3/2/20.
[44] Ibid.   [45] See the poster in *Pembrokeshire Telegraph*, 22 Oct. 1931.
[46] *Pembrokeshire Telegraph*, 15 Oct. 1931.   [47] Ibid., 15 Oct. 1931.
[48] *Cardigan and Tivy-side Advertiser*, 3 Jul. 1931.

National Conservatism in Scotland and Wales 209

to say "Help the National Government"', yet his position as a leader without a party had corrupted his judgement and led him to oppose the government in a desperate 'bid' for the leadership of the Labour party. Gwilym's departure from the government was 'egotistical' and in tune with the elder Lloyd George's personal ambition: both wanted to do down MacDonald in order to coalesce with Arthur Henderson in the leadership of Labour.[49] The withdrawal of the Labour candidate in Pembrokeshire was taken as further proof of the collusion. 'The plain reason' for Labour's decision, Price asserted, 'is because they do not want two Socialists in the same constituency'.[50]

Under the National guise, Price appeared more emboldened than in previous elections to appeal to the Liberal north of the county. The pacifist sensitivities of the Liberal nonconformists were clearly in his mind when, addressing a British Legion rally in Crymych, he stressed his admiration for the organisation's work for the 'cause of peace' and dismissed as 'fallacy' rumours that it perpetuated a 'war spirit'.[51] Furthermore, he did what Conservative candidates throughout Britain did, which was to embrace the political character of a given area and claim that the cross-party National government was best placed to represent it. Thus, Price did not contest the Liberal allegiance of the people of north Pembrokeshire but never missed an opportunity to remind them that it was he, and not Gwilym Lloyd George, who promised co-operation with Simon, Samuel, Lord Reading, Lord Grey, and Lord Buckmaster.[52] This proved effective up to a point. Some senior local Liberals, including Rees Davies (the former member for Pembrokeshire), came out in support of the government.[53] Despite their loyalty to Lloyd George, many Liberals struggled with the notion of opposing a 'National' government. As Lloyd George's agent in Caernarfon explained to him, 'they do not understand why you are not NATIONAL'. They feared that, amid his critique of the Conservatives, he had 'not brought out that [he is] just as intent as the Tories to safeguard the interests of the country ... [w]hilst the Tories are using the Union Jack ... our folks are all as mild as Moses, almost apologising that they are Liberals'.[54]

Liberal concerns were understandable but ultimately exaggerated, as West Wales remained solidly Liberal. In rural areas especially, among

[49] *Pembrokeshire Telegraph*, 15, 22 Oct. 1931; *Cardigan and Tivy-side Advertiser*, 16 Oct. 1931.
[50] *Pembrokeshire Telegraph*, 22 Oct. 1931.
[51] *Cardigan and Tivy-side Advertiser*, 2 Oct. 1931.
[52] *Pembrokeshire Telegraph*, 22 Oct. 1931. See poster in *Cardigan and Tivy-side Advertiser*, 23 Oct. 1931.
[53] W. Rees Davies to Price, in *Cardigan and Tivy-side Advertiser*, 23 Oct. 1931.
[54] Agent to D. Lloyd George, 24 Oct. 1931, PA, LG/G/33/1/34.

210 Popular Conservatism and the National Government

y werin bobl ('the folk'), a renewed culture of dissent saw the labouring classes, many of whom had flirted with Labour in the 1920s, return to the Liberal fold.[55] Gwilym Lloyd George remarked that 'the North [of Pembrokeshire] seems solid for me and I think I shall more than make up for anything I may lose [in the south]'.[56] Indeed, despite his best efforts, almost all of Price's speeches in north Pembrokeshire were interrupted by voters insisting that the election had little to do with 'National' rehabilitation and everything to do with Tory ambitions. In Fishguard, he was forced to abandon an impromptu speech when voters succeeded in singing him down with a repertoire intriguingly alternating between The Red Flag and *Hen Wlad Fy Nhadau* ('Land of My Fathers'). The same evening a fracas broke out as Price admonished an individual for refusing to sing God Save the King.[57] Such overt displays of dissent were a real boost for Gwilym Lloyd George and revealed a momentum that he attributed in part to his father's controversial radio broadcast.[58]

The Politics of Recovery in Scotland and Wales

The revival of trade, and with it the reduction of unemployment, was the central feature of the government's early narrative of recovery. As we have seen, measures to protect home industries and to promote imperial free trade were intended to underpin the image of a government acting decisively in the economic interests of communities across the United Kingdom. In Dundee, where, as Jim Tomlinson has argued, the increasingly adverse forces of globalisation shaped the political agenda in the 1930s, Florence Horsbrugh presented herself as the champion of the jute industry in parliament.[59] She lobbied ministers on import duties, pressed Whitehall departments for government contracts, undertook ambassadorial trips abroad, and led by example in extolling the quality of Dundee's manufactured goods by kitting out her Westminster office with jute carpet – all of which received publicity in the local press.[60] But in addition to securing Britain's share of global trade, it was necessary for the government – and the Conservative party – to demonstrate responsiveness and competence across the so-called Anglo-Celtic frontier by

---

[55] 'Labour Men Return to the Fold', *Pembrokeshire Telegraph*, 22 Oct. 1931.
[56] Gwilym to D. Lloyd George, 18 Oct. 1931, PA, LG/I/3/2/21.
[57] *Pembrokeshire Telegraph*, 22 Oct. 1931.
[58] Gwilym to D. Lloyd George, 18 Oct. 1931, PA, LG/I/3/2/21.
[59] J. Tomlinson, *Dundee and the empire: Juteopolis, 1850–1939* (Edinburgh, 2014), chs.7–8 and 'The political economy of globalization: the genesis of Dundee's two 'united fronts' in the 1930s', *HJ*, 57 (2014), 225–45.
[60] E.g., *Dundee Courier*, 4 Apr., 16 Aug., 23 Sep., 20 Oct. 1932; *Dundee Evening Telegraph*, 19 Dec. 1932.

National Conservatism in Scotland and Wales 211

addressing peculiarly Scottish and Welsh problems. This proved the most difficult in Wales since, beyond the handful of 'safe' Conservative seats secured in 1931,[61] there were no Conservative MPs to embody the dialogic relationship between government and local interests. This had implications for government's standing in West and South Wales and created opportunities for the opposition parties to 'represent' Welsh interests. Scottish Unionism enjoyed a much higher profile thanks to its unprecedented number of MPs. Yet incumbency generated its own distinct disadvantages as, to varying degrees, opposition parties mobilised around a 'nationalist' critique of the recovery. In both countries, the Conservative message of economic recovery encountered a rejuvenated anti-Tory radicalism; far from neutralising the historic anti-Westminster scripts of Celtic politics, the National government provoked their renewal.

Recovery and the Absentee 'National' Government in Wales

Given the outcome of the general election in Wales, Conservatives in the principality predictably struggled to capitalise directly on their membership of the National government. The difficulties were partly organisational in nature. Faced with Lloyd George's triumphant Liberal party, Conservatives in West Wales did not enjoy the influx of erstwhile Liberal members that their counterparts elsewhere experienced. In Pembrokeshire, they had difficulty finding a candidate willing to take on the task of 'nursing' the constituency. Some of those put forward by Central Office replied that 'they did not intend contesting Divisions in Wales'. Local officials questioned the wisdom of fighting the next election and, having done so and lost, even contemplated closing down the association office.[62] Yet at no point did these difficulties bring into question the desirability of the party's continued membership of the government. The advantages of the National government in Liberal Wales – including, as one activist put it, the ability to field 'a "National" Candidate without the word Conservative being applied' – still held true.[63] The same was broadly true of the party's position in Labour-dominated South Wales, except that their experience of the government involved more interaction with other National parties. In Gower, where the historically weak

---

[61] All in 'English Wales': Brecon & Radnor, Cardiff East, Cardiff South, Llandaff & Barry, Newport, and Monmouth.

[62] Executive committee, 13 Oct. 1934, 5 May, 12 Oct. 1935, 14 Jul. 1937; candidate sub-committee, 24 Sep., 16 Oct., 8 Nov. 1937; finance committee, 4 Dec. 1937, Pembrokeshire CA, HDSO/51/1.

[63] Executive meeting, 12 Oct. 1935, Pembrokeshire CA, HDSO/51/1.

212   Popular Conservatism and the National Government

Conservative association backed the Liberal National candidate, local Conservatives claimed to have augmented an election campaign that, while unsuccessful in unseating the long-serving Labour MP, at least managed to divert Labour activists from the neighbouring marginal seat of Swansea West, where the Liberal National duly won.[64] While hardly a victory, they had nonetheless secured a stake in the National government's (albeit limited) representation in the region. Thereafter, there is no evidence of any orchestrated opposition to membership. The situation was unsurprisingly more fraught in Cardiff Central, following the decision of Central Office to compel the local association to support the National Labour MP. As a result, they lost the services of their much-admired candidate, the Hon. Evan Morgan, whose father – Lord Tredegar – promptly withdrew funds from the association, endangering the agent's salary.[65] Yet even in this case the associational records show no systematic opposition to the National government.

The difficulties facing Welsh Conservatives were exacerbated by the government's failure to project itself in Wales. Not a single Welsh Conservative MP served as a minister between 1931 and 1940, while the most senior Welsh representative in the government was the National Labour MP for Cardiff Central, Sir Ernest Bennett, who held the minor role of Assistant Postmaster-General. Just as the government lacked representation in Wales, so the government in turn lacked an intuitive awareness of regional sensitivities. This was reflected in the government's failure to produce a programme of propaganda systematically attuned to Welsh interests. Following the establishment of the Scottish National Development Council in 1931, South Wales received its own Industrial Development Council in 1932 and Special Area status in 1934, both designed to attract new enterprises and encourage consumer support of existing industries.[66] But such schemes rarely applied to West Wales. Pembrokeshire Conservatives noted with envy the activity of the area commissioner in South Wales and petitioned ministers for inclusion in parts of the scheme.[67] This would have generated considerable publicity for the government in the county. But in the absence of such schemes, and without a government MP to both champion and lobby the government,

---

[64] Sir G. Bowyer to G. Hutchinson, 21 Nov. 1934, West Glamorgan Archive Services, Hutchinson papers, D16/4/1.

[65] Special executive meeting, 21 Jan. 1932, special finance committee, 6 May 1932, National Library of Wales, Cardiff Central CA, 1987/26/22.

[66] The Industrial Development Council gave its support to the 'Back to Coal' movement, initiated by the Liberal National candidate in Pontypridd, Captain Bernard Acworth RN, during the election campaign and calling on the Royal Navy to revert to coal. *The Times*, 29 Oct. 1931, 22 Apr., 24 Nov. 1932.

[67] Executive committee, 1 Dec. 1934, Pembrokeshire CA, HDSO/51/1.

the task of narrating the recovery became increasingly onerous for activists in the farthest corners of West Wales, especially as they felt excluded from the party's propaganda efforts in the designated Special Areas. By 1938, the Pembrokeshire association felt compelled to protest to the area organisation, the South Wales Committee, that 'assistance was arranged for ... constituencies which there was no possible chance of winning, while Pembrokeshire, one of the few seats that could be won is neglected'.[68] Meanwhile the *Western Mail* provided constant support for the government, but in view of the party situation had to be equally attentive to all three National parties.

Moreover, many Conservatives failed to grasp the significance of Welsh-language propaganda. In Pembrokeshire the party officials reassured themselves that, contrary to the doubts expressed by one activist, its poor showing in the north of the county had nothing to do with their candidate's inability to speak Welsh.[69] Similarly, in a meeting of party representatives from Cardiganshire, Carmarthenshire, Pembrokeshire, and Breconshire, it was decided that Welsh-language literature was 'not needed as the Welsh could not be understood in South Wales' – even though, according to the 1931 census, the language was spoken by more than 80 per cent in the former two counties and by a third in the other two.[70] Given that voters' cultural, even ethnic, identity was historically entwined with *yr iaith gymraeg*, the Conservative position was naive.[71] It suggests an obliviousness to the unspoken assumption, embodied by Welsh Liberalism and grasped by Welsh Labour, that the language mattered, especially in rural West Wales. As a result, the Conservative organisation in Pembrokeshire unwittingly laid bare one of the vital factors distinguishing its 'National' politics from the 'national' politics of its rivals and many in the electorate.

Under the circumstances, the National government was vulnerable to charges of operating a form of absentee government in large swathes of Wales. The Conservative project in Wales was further undermined by the activities of the Liberal and Labour parties, each intent on articulating 'Welsh' experiences of the National government. Although mocked by

---

[68] Executive committee, 26 Mar. 1938, Pembrokeshire CA, HDSO/51/1.
[69] Executive committee, 28 Dec. 1935, Pembrokeshire CA, HDSO/51/1.
[70] South Wales committee, 16 Jul. 1937, in Pembrokeshire CA, HDSO/51/4; M. Kinnear, *The British voter: an atlas and survey since 1885* (London, 1968), 134–6.
[71] For detailed discussion of the role of 'ethnicity' in political mobilisation in Wales, see D. Howell, 'A "Less Obtrusive and Exacting" nationality: Welsh ethnic mobilisation in rural communities, 1850–1920', in D. Howell (ed.), *Roots of rural ethnic mobilisation* (Aldershot, 1993), 51–97; also K. Verdery, 'Ethnicity and local systems: the religious organisation of Welshness', in C. A. Smith (ed.), *Regional analysis, vol. ii: social systems* (New York, 1976), 191–227.

214   Popular Conservatism and the National Government

Baldwin as a 'prophet in his own family',[72] David Lloyd George's ambition to lead a Welsh Liberal bloc gathered momentum in the early 1930s. This began with the Cardiganshire by-election in September 1932, which he viewed in histrionic terms as a battle between 'the narrow and the Liberal interpretation of nationality'. If he could mobilise the protest of those disillusioned by the government's narrow conception of the 'national', and do so in a constituency whose Liberal association had not always seen eye to eye with him, he would be on course to orchestrate a Welsh group of MPs whose objective, like that of *Cymru Fydd* in the 1890s, would be to lead enlightened radical opinion against Tory Westminster. 'I cannot see a gleam of Liberalism anywhere', he remarked, only a 'Tory Government of the Eldon era'.[73] According to the local press, the 'famous Welsh statesman' was given a 'warm welcome' on every leg of his tour through the county, and put in a series of bravura performances, ridiculing the naivety of the Conservative candidate, Colonel Fitzwilliams, a county squire, for dropping the 'Tory' label in favour of 'National'. He compared the Conservative to 'Hen gi wedi bod yn lladd defaid' (a dog guilty of savaging sheep): no matter how much it was disciplined to change its ways, it was the same old dog and should be kept away from the flock – or strangled.[74] Nor was the momentum of Lloyd George's campaign limited to Cardiganshire. Around this time at least two Welsh Liberal MPs who opposed the government's policies of imperial preference joined the Lloyd George group: R. T. Evans in Carmarthenshire, elected as a Samuelite, and even Llewellyn Jones in Flintshire, elected as a Simonite.[75] By 1933, Lloyd George was convening meetings of all the Liberal MPs in Wales, in order 'to act as a group on all Welsh matters'.[76]

Through his rhetoric and interventions, Lloyd George could still pervade Welsh national politics. He never confined his crusade to Welsh-speaking Wales. One of his supporters, Victor Evans, contested the Merthyr by-election in June 1934. The local Conservative association decided not to field a candidate, yet a faction promised nonetheless to

---

[72] *Hansard*, House of Commons, 27 Nov. 1933, vol. 283, col. 649.
[73] Lloyd George to Prof. Levi, 24 Aug. 1932, PA, LG/G/33/3/58. He discussed ways of forming a 'Welsh group' as early as 1926; see K. O. Morgan, 'Twilight of Welsh Liberalism: Lloyd George and the "Wee Frees", 1918–35', *Bulletin of the Board of Celtic Studies*, 12 (1968), 389–405, at 404.
[74] *Cardigan and Tivy-side Advertiser*, 23 Sep. 1932.
[75] *Western Mail*, 12 Oct. 1935; D. Dutton, 'Liberalism in crisis: Liberals, Liberal Nationals and the politics of North-east Wales, 1931–1935', *Welsh History Review*, 26 (2003), 106–23, at 115–16.
[76] *The Times*, 15 Feb. 1933. Although there is little evidence that this remained an established group.

National Conservatism in Scotland and Wales

support Evans on anti-socialist grounds (delivering the votes of '60 or 70 per cent of the Merthyr Conservatives') and to do so 'quietly', in the knowledge that public support from the Tories would 'injure' the Liberal candidate with his own supporters.[77] Thus the anti-socialist impulse remained strong among some Conservative activists even when the Liberals were mounting anti-Tory campaigns. That same month Lloyd George intervened in the Monmouth by-election, advising Liberals to support Labour against the Conservative candidate.[78] These actions – opposing Labour in Merthyr Tydfil while supporting Labour in Monmouth – testify to something more profound than Lloyd George's legendary opportunism. They testify above all to his ability to mobilise the Welsh radical tradition and pervade Welsh politics to an extent far in excess of the organisational resources at his disposal. In this regard he was helped by developments in British and world politics – notably the breakdown of the disarmament conference in Geneva and the prospect of rearmament at home – which increased the topicality of some Welsh radical shibboleths. It was no coincidence, for example, that the twelve highest turnouts in the Peace Ballot in 1935 were in Welsh divisions;[79] nor, by the same token, that Lloyd George fought the subsequent general election at the head of the Council of Action, campaigning on the twin pillars of Peace and Reconstruction.

If Lloyd George commanded the historic rhetoric of Welsh radicalism, across South Wales it was Labour that dominated municipal government in the 1930s.[80] The scale of unemployment and poverty became – and remained in social memory – the National government's chief legacy in the region; and compounding this perception was the fact that (until 1934) the burden of funding the dole, on which the long-term unemployed relied after exhausting their insurance entitlement, fell on hard-pressed local ratepayers.[81] Against this backdrop, Special Area grants from central government were, unsurprisingly, a poor substitute for a general revival of trade. Paradoxically, however, because many of the grant-funded schemes to improve public health in the region – including

---

[77] T. Naylor to D. Lloyd George, 31 May and 2 Jun. 1934, PA, LG/G/35/1/7, 11.

[78] D. Lloyd George to Mrs I. Harries, 12 Jun. 1934, PA, LG/G/35/1/22. This advice was forwarded to *The Daily Herald* for publication: F. L. Stevenson to W. H. Stevenson (editor), 12 Jun. 1934, PA, LG/G/35/1/23.

[79] See table 6 in H. McCarthy, 'Democratizing British foreign policy: rethinking the Peace Ballot, 1934–5', *JBS*, 49 (2010), 358–87, at 381.

[80] The main exception was Cardiff, where Labour was the largest single group on the city council but stood in a minority to the Conservatives and Liberals.

[81] C. Williams, 'Labour and the challenge of local government, 1918–1939', in D. Tanner, C. Williams & D. Hopkin (eds.), *The Labour party in Wales, 1900–2000* (Cardiff, 2000), 140–65.

216   Popular Conservatism and the National Government

plans for a general hospital, a mental hospital, a midwifery service, sewage construction[82] – were delegated to municipal authorities for implementation, they went some way to reinforcing narratives of Labour's commitment to municipal provision in mining and industrial communities. Throughout the 1930s, public health served as the touchstone of Labour's municipal campaigns. As Duncan Tanner demonstrated, this reflected an important reorientation of the party in South Wales: with a shift towards a greater focus on healthcare, the party not only responded with 'practical measures' to local needs, it specifically improved provisions for women and families. This expanded the range of people with a stake in municipal provision and marked a major shift in the definition of Labour's 'community' away from the male-dominated trade unionist towards a more inclusive social constituency.[83] The government's politics of relief in the mining valleys of South Wales, far from heralding a working-class Conservatism, further entrenched Labour as the defender of community interests.

'Scotland's Best National Party'?

The first test for the National government in Scotland came in the form of a by-election in Dunbartonshire in March 1932. The National Unionist candidature went to Commander Archibald Cochrane, a decorated submariner and former MP for East Fife who withdrew from that seat at the general election in favour of a Liberal National. Although a four-cornered contest with Labour, Communist, and Scottish Nationalist candidates, the main subjects of debate differed little from the general election campaign. The Labour candidate, Tom Johnston, a member of the previous Labour cabinet, campaigned to abolish the means test and reject 'food taxes'. The test had 'already broken up and starved thousands of households', he argued, and furthermore it forced ex-servicemen to maintain their unemployed relatives out of their pensions.[84] Meanwhile Cochrane stressed the 'crisis' still facing the country, urged voters to renew the government's mandate, and hailed a return of confidence in the British economy under the new administration.[85] In the event, Labour's vote declined, but so too did the Unionist majority, from twelve to three

---

[82] *The Times*, 8 Nov. 1934, 28 Mar., 7 Dec. 1935.
[83] D. Tanner, 'Gender, civic culture and politics in South Wales: explaining Labour municipal policy, 1918–1939', in M. Worley (ed.), *Labour's grass roots: essays on the activities and experiences of local Labour parties and members, 1918–1945* (Aldershot, 2005), 170–93.
[84] Election address of T. Johnston, Mar. 1932, Cochrane papers, 10218, 17/14.
[85] Election address of A. D. Cochrane, Mar. 1932, Cochrane papers, 10218, 17/14; *Kirkintilloch Herald*, 16 Mar. 1932.

National Conservatism in Scotland and Wales 217

thousand. The Unionist association attributed this to the 'divergent instructions' issued by the Liberal party.[86] Sir Archibald Sinclair, the Liberal Secretary of State for Scotland, voiced the Liberal party's official support for Cochrane. Yet a fortnight before polling the local Liberal association, which regarded the Import Duties Act 'as a gross breach of the pledges' given at the general election, declared that it 'cannot ask Liberals to support any Candidate who approved of the Government's Protectionist Policy'.[87]

According to *The Scotsman*, the Liberals who disengaged from the National alliance formed the bulk of support for the Scottish Nationalist candidate. It was therefore the Nationalists, rather than Labour, that most eroded the Unionist majority.[88] Robert Gray, the Nationalist candidate, held Scotland's economic plight to be the direct consequence of 'English-controlled political parties' and 'London Government'. He described the means test in Scotland, where joblessness was 'more than 30% worse than in England', as a 'scheme to balance England's Budget'; and the wheat quota, introduced by the 'English National Government', as of 'no use' to Scottish farmers, whose communities were offered no help to stem the flow of rural depopulation. 'English Control means Scottish Ruin' became his campaign slogan.[89] Cochrane's election posters countered with the slogan 'National Government: Cochrane represents Scotland's best National Party'. Johnston, a former minister in the Scottish Office, countered that he had always supported Scottish Home Rule to deal with 'purely Scottish affairs', but did not consider it the definitive formula for the eradication of poverty.[90] Ultimately, the impact of the Nationalist intervention proved more far-reaching than Gray's 13 per cent share of the vote would suggest. Local Unionists noted with some alarm the 'exceedingly active' presence of the SNP since the election, and the formation of fourteen local associations in Dunbartonshire alone.[91] Moreover, it represented, potentially, a distinct challenge to the government's politics of recovery north of the border.

Political developments in the autumn of 1932, again involving the Liberals, validated the Scottish Nationalist challenge to the National government. In October, a number of Liberal ministers, including Sir Archibald Sinclair at the Scottish Office, resigned from the government in

---

[86] Report for the year ended 31 Oct. 1932, Dunbartonshire UA, 12264/3.
[87] *The Scotsman*, 16 Mar. 1932; D. Macmillan (President, Dunbartonshire Liberal Assoc.) to A. Whitelaw (President, Dunbartonshire UA), 2 Mar. 1932, Cochrane papers, 10218, 23/5.
[88] *The Scotsman*, 19 Mar. 1932.
[89] Election address of R. Gray, Mar. 1932, Cochrane papers, 10218, 17/14.
[90] *The Scotsman*, 11, 18 Mar. 1932.
[91] Report for the year ended 31 Oct. 1932, Dunbartonshire UA, 12264/3.

218   Popular Conservatism and the National Government

protest at the Ottawa tariff agreements. The Scottish Liberal Federation endorsed their decision, its chairman labelling the government's tariffs policy 'the greatest political betrayal in history'. The Liberal party, he argued, like 'millions of electors', had been 'duped and tricked' by the promise of limited and scientific tariffs, given by Unionists who now made 'fraudulent misuse of a majority given on a national non-party' basis. The federation reflected the language of 'betrayal' voiced by Liberal figures and associations across Scotland, including Foot and his supporters in Dundee.[92] Throughout 1932, the Liberal language of 'betrayal' carried echoes of the Nationalist language of 'betrayal', and some Liberals elided the two, advocating a restoration of free trade alongside the case for Home Rule.[93] Attempts at this time to launch a genuinely cross-party movement to advance the case for 'moderate' Home Rule involved some senior Unionist figures, notably the Duke of Montrose, as well as representatives of Labour.[94] But the resignation of the Samuelites turned Home Rule into what Unionists perceived to be the basis of a distinct Nationalist-Liberal alliance, which Samuel's pronouncements seemed only to confirm. He pledged to a deputation of the National Party of Scotland that the Liberal party 'will regard the establishment of a measure of Home Rule for Scotland as among its main purposes', and urged nationalists to do their bit to secure public backing. Just as he urged Liberals to stand firm in defence of free trade to avoid being subsumed into the Conservative party like the 'Unionist Liberals a generation ago', so in Scotland he used Home Rule to reassert Liberal independence.[95]

Although the Nationalist share of the vote remained modest throughout the 1930s, the growing topicality of Home Rule among Scottish Liberals posed a threat to the cohesion of the anti-socialist alliance on which the Unionist electoral success of 1931 rested. Unionists sought to ward off any resulting 'apathy' among voters by contrasting the emerging recovery to the crisis that prevailed in 1931. Addressing a public meeting in Dundee, Horsbrugh cited improvements in the export and employment figures of the jute industry and publicised her own efforts to secure further government orders, as well as a place for the Caledon shipyard on the Admiralty list of approved shipbuilders.[96] In addition, she stood to win cross-party plaudits – including from the League of Nations Union – for her role on the British delegation to the League of Nations Assembly in

---

[92] *Dundee Courier,* 1 Oct. 1932; *The Scotsman,* 29 Sep. (Galloway), 4 (Glasgow), 13 (Edinburgh), 15 (SLF) Oct. 1932.
[93] E.g., the Galloway Liberal Association, *The Scotsman,* 29 Sep. 1932.
[94] See details of the Scottish Home Rule Conference in Glasgow, *The Scotsman,* 15 Sep. 1932.
[95] *The Scotsman,* 15 Oct. 1932, 19 May 1933.   [96] *Dundee Courier,* 20 Jan. 1934.

Geneva; which, in turn, eased the way for several Unionist activists to support the Dundee branch of the LNU.[97] The ability to claim a hand in local economic recovery was integral to the public profile of a government MP. Cochrane, for instance, cultivated a reputation for assiduous constituency work through his surgeries, his annual summer tour of the division, and his campaign to re-open the Argyll works, a vast factory complex in the Vale of Leven.[98] Claims of hard-won recovery at home, amid mounting tensions in Europe, were also useful in obligating Liberal voters to reappraise their drift from the National alliance. Thus, the Unionists' speaker of choice at a mass rally in Dundee in 1934 was Sir John Simon, who testified to Horsbrugh's enterprise on behalf of Dundee as well as her role on the British delegation to Geneva.[99]

Moreover, the spectre of Home Rule presented a unique challenge to the National government's attempt to show that Scotland shared in the economic recovery. In this connection it is worth highlighting the number of Scottish MPs who sat in the cabinet or held ministerial rank. These included, among the Unionists, Walter Elliott, John Gilmour, Noel Skelton, John Colville, James Stuart, and Henry Scrymgeour-Wedderburn, and, among the Liberal Nationals, Ernest Brown and Godfrey Collins. At their disposal were well-established mechanisms to enable the Westminster government to respond to Scotland's national needs. The cabinet contained a Secretary of State for Scotland whose duties were defined geographically rather than functionally; whose remit included overseeing the 'board' system of administrative devolution, developed in the nineteenth century, which delegated agriculture, education, and health in Scotland to the Scottish Office.[100] As a result, while foreign, economic, and defence policy remained centrally controlled, it was commonplace for legislation relating to local government and social policy in Scotland to differ from that applied to England and Wales. This precedent was seized upon by the National government. For example, it was originally envisaged that responsibility for all four Special Areas, including central Scotland, would be vested in one commissioner answerable to the Ministry of Labour. The Minister insisted that the effective administration and presentation of the scheme demanded a single commissioner. Yet the cabinet sided with Sir Godfrey Collins, the Secretary of State for Scotland and Liberal National MP for Greenock, who

---

[97] *Dundee Courier*, 1 Aug. 1933; executive committee, 20 Dec. 1934, Dundee UA, MS 270/1/1/1.
[98] Reports for the year ended 31 Oct. 1933 and 31 Oct. 1934, Dunbartonshire UA, 12264/3. His surgeries were advertised in the local press, e.g., *Kirkintilloch Herald*, 22 Aug. 1934.
[99] *Dundee Courier*, 24 Feb. 1934.

220   Popular Conservatism and the National Government

recommended a separate Commissioner for Scotland answerable to the Scottish Office. 'He advocated this proposal on political as well as economic grounds', warning the cabinet that 'the Government scheme would be open to very severe criticism in Scotland if Scottish sentiment on this point did not receive adequate recognition by the appointment of a separate Commission'. Summing up the discussion, the President of the Board of Trade, Walter Runciman, stated 'there was greater administrative convenience in having a single Commissioner, but politically there was a great deal to be said for a separate Commissioner for Scotland'.[101] A month later, Commander Cochrane celebrated Dunbartonshire's inclusion in the Scottish Special Area, emphasising that it was not a costly scheme for 'relief work' but an expert-led programme to attract new jobs in the motor car and wireless industries to Scotland.[102]

The same attentiveness to Scottish sentiment was reflected in the government's publicity campaign north of the border. As the general election approached, the NPB produced the *Scottish Illustrated* as a counterpart to the *Popular Illustrated* distributed in England and Wales. The written content was similar and often identical, while the images were strikingly different. Whereas the *Popular Illustrated* showed a soldier in regular army fatigues, the *Scottish Illustrated* showed him in the uniform of the Scots Guards; and where the former presented a London power station as an example of infrastructural development and Wherwell in Hampshire as the scene of English rural life, the latter presented images of the newly reconstructed Glencoe Pass and a crofter's cottage on the shore of Loch Long in Dunbartonshire.[103] Sources relating to the internal workings of the NPB have not survived, making it impossible to discern the precise editorial process. But the very presence of the *Scottish Illustrated*, compared to the absence of a dedicated pictorial broadsheet in Wales, highlight once more the advantages to be wrought from a large Scottish representation in the government, from which the Unionist party in the constituencies profited. Distribution of the pictorial broadsheet became a staple of Unionist activity throughout 1935.[104] So too did the cinema vans which toured Scotland in the summer months, accompanied by the local Unionist MP. In Dundee the agent scheduled a programme

---

[101] Committee on the reports of the investigators into the Distressed Areas, vol. ii, 6 Nov. 1934 and minutes of the cabinet committee on the reports of the investigators into the Distressed Areas, 12 Nov. 1934, in *The Scottish Office: depression and reconstruction, 1919–1959*, ed. I. Levitt (Edinburgh, 1992), 89–91.

[102] *Kirkintilloch Herald*, 12 Dec. 1934.

[103] *Scottish Illustrated*, 1:1–1:5 (1935), cf. *Popular Illustrated*, 1:1–1:5 (1935).

[104] Report for the year ended 31 Oct. 1935, Dunbartonshire UA, 12264/3. Cochrane's association records reveal that he was 'a member' of the NPB, but no further details of his involvement can be found.

of lunchtime and early-evening shows outside major factories in the city, including the Caledon shipyard and the works of Lindsay & Low Ltd confectioners, at which Horsbrugh spoke. The 'talkies', in addition to general scenes of trade recovery and social improvements nationwide, depicted scenes of industrial revival in Dundee itself – an illustration, Horsbrugh explained, of how unemployment in the jute trade had been more than halved since 1931.[105]

Defending the National Government in Scotland and Wales: the 1935 General Election

At first sight, the National government did well to preserve its parliamentary strength in Wales at the 1935 general election. As in 1931, eleven National candidates were elected, six of them Conservatives standing in the party's strongholds near the border.[106] Yet there was very little to celebrate, since Welsh Conservatives failed once again to emulate the success of their English counterparts. Whereas the party achieved more than half of the total votes across the United Kingdom as a whole, it lost support in all parts of Wales.[107] Labour, meanwhile, emerged as the net beneficiary in Wales between 1931 and 1935 despite an overall decline in the number of Labour votes. This derived in part from the fact that Labour held ten seats entirely unopposed, compared to just four in 1931. But, in those seats that Labour fought in contested elections in both 1931 and 1935, it gained on average 2,574 extra votes, while the Conservative and Liberals both lost ground by a larger average margin. Using the party's average gain in South Wales (2,984 votes), it is possible to project that Labour would have gained an extra 167,943 votes had it been obliged to fight a contested election in the six constituencies where it was newly unopposed in 1935. This would have brought Labour's total Welsh vote in 1935 to 563,778 (56.6 per cent), suggesting a more-or-less full recovery to its peak performance in 1929. Thus, it was the distorting effect of Labour's unopposed returns that accounted for the increase in the Conservatives' share of the Welsh vote (from 22.1 per cent in 1931 to 27.5 in 1935). In the twelve seats contested by the Conservatives in 1931

---

[105] *Dundee Courier*, 2 Jul. 1935. Also *The Scotsman*, 17 May, 23 Jun. 1935; *Kirkintilloch Herald*, 28 Aug., 18 Sep. 1935; executive committee, 18 Apr., 19 Sep. 1935, Dundee UA, MS 270/1/1/1.

[106] Cardiff East, Cardiff South, Flintshire, Llandaff & Barry, Newport, and Monmouth.

[107] For a detailed breakdown of electoral trends in 'English' Wales, 'Welsh' Wales, and 'Industrial' Wales, see table 3 in Thomas, 'The Conservative party and Welsh politics', 908.

222   Popular Conservatism and the National Government

and 1935, the party experienced on average a decrease of 7.2 per cent in its share of the vote.

The National government lost fourteen seats in Scotland, all but one of them Unionist. All went to Labour, mostly in Glasgow and the central industrial belt of Lanarkshire and Stirlingshire, except Fife West, which elected the well-known Communist candidate from Clydeside, Willie Gallacher. As a result, Labour went from seven to twenty-four seats in Scotland (including four ILP MPs). This still fell short of the number of seats secured in the 1920s. However, the number of seats obscures a steeper rise in Labour's share of the Scottish vote. The Unionist party and Labour (including the ILP) each polled 42 per cent of the vote. The total number of votes cast for Labour and the ILP stood at 975,045 – more than the Unionist vote (962,595) and more than at Labour's peak in 1929.[108] Indeed, Labour came close to capturing additional seats, including Rutherglen and Glasgow Kelvingrove, where Walter Elliott's majority was slashed to 149, while the Unionist candidate in North Lanarkshire was saved only by a split vote between the ILP and Labour candidates.

Wales

Welsh Conservatives fought the 1935 election on much the same basis as their English counterparts. They reminded voters of the crisis of 1931 and juxtaposed this with the fruits of economic 'recovery' enjoyed after four years of the National government. In particular the Conservative local and regional press drew the attention of rural voters to the 'great record' and 'inspiring leadership' of Walter Elliot in transforming the fortunes of agriculture.[109] In Pembrokeshire, radical Liberalism could still prove effective in the face of a Conservative-dominated Westminster government. Though Lloyd George's dissident Liberal campaigns might appear to be mainly rhetorical in function, and outdated, even irrelevant, in substance, they continued in fact to carry powerful and current critiques of government. Thus during the campaign, Gwilym Lloyd George was quick to associate himself with the North Pembrokeshire and South Cardiganshire Tithepayers' Association, not simply out of historical affinity but because it lobbied to protect the interests of farmers, a group he long feared was susceptible to the Conservatives on financial and business grounds.[110] His

---

[108] Although the ILP disaffiliated from the Labour party in 1932, these calculations reflect the combined strength of Labour organisations and sentiment facing the Scottish Unionists.

[109] *Cardigan and Tivy-side Advertiser*, 1, 8 Nov. 1935.

[110] *Cardigan and Tivy-side Advertiser*, 8 Nov. 1935; Gwilym to D. Lloyd George, n.d. Oct. 1931. Lloyd George papers, LG/I/3/2/20.

father, meanwhile, highlighted the 'neglect' of West Wales. He attributed the closure of Pembroke Dockyard to its remoteness from the London clubs of government ministers and taunted the government that 'Unemployment is becoming an ancient British institution and you must not abolish it. It is like the House of Lords . . . It is like the feudal system . . . the longer it lasts the more will Conservatives feel that it is a cherished British institution which must not be touched.'[111] Yet, even in its heartlands, Welsh Liberalism was not inviolable. The Liberal vote declined markedly in Pembrokeshire, Cardiganshire, and Carmarthenshire, in large part because Labour intervened and garnered more votes than ever before – enough to regain Carmarthen.

In South Wales, the *Western Mail* once more backed the government. It presented the industrial voters with sensationalist eve-of-poll stories about the prospect of large-scale employment, for instance at the reopened Ebbw Vale steelworks, and the 'expert' explanation given by its owner Sir William Firth that this turnaround was 'due entirely to the National government'.[112] The Ebbw Vale steelworks was an isolated case, however, and South Wales remained an area of mass unemployment. The Conservative campaign therefore focused on the government's work to alleviate the social conditions of mass unemployment. In a speech that formed the centrepiece of the National campaign in South Wales, Neville Chamberlain announced a £30 million programme of electrification and re-construction of the railway network, with preference given to firms in the distressed areas. He praised the special commissioner for the region, who, with a block grant from the government, had put in place schemes to 'keep up the spirit, to keep up the health of the people', including a 300-bed hospital in Glamorgan, new additions to the Rhondda Infectious Diseases Hospital, seaside holidays for children, cookery and dietary classes, open-air swimming baths, drainage systems, public libraries, and a land-settlement programme for horticulture.[113]

This campaign represented a very different, more 'progressive' anti-socialism to the 'Red Scare' variety of the 1920s. But its failure to compete with Labour brings into focus how little the political landscape in postwar Wales had changed in favour of the Conservatives despite the catharsis of disestablishment and the electoral decline of the Liberal party. The party's decision to leave so many South Wales constituencies uncontested suggests, up to a point, that they recognised as much. In other ways, too, Conservative actions had the effect of conceding the mining electorate to Labour. In Gower, besides trying rather routinely to placate Liberal

---

[111] Lloyd George speaking at Pembroke Dock, *Western Mail*, 11 Nov. 1935.
[112] *Western Mail*, 13 Nov. 1935.   [113] Ibid., 5 Nov. 1935.

224   Popular Conservatism and the National Government

concerns on peace and security, the Conservative campaign appeared to take heart from the suburban expansion of Swansea. Taking the view that 'the Socialist vote is almost invariably constant and steady', the *South Wales Evening Post* calculated that residential building in areas such as Sketty, Bishopston, and Oystermouth in the Mumbles had produced a new 'suburban vote' that might bring the Conservative candidate, Geoffrey Hutchinson, within range of victory.[114] Hutchinson concentrated his efforts on these areas, and on the eve of poll the paper declared confidently: 'IF MUMBLES COMES OUT, HUTCHINSON GOES IN'.[115] It is clear that the Conservative press and candidate interpreted suburbanisation as a sociological phenomenon that favoured Conservatism. Not only did this effectively concede the non-suburban working-class vote to Labour, it also showed little consideration for the possibility that voters in the new households might bring with them entrenched allegiances formed in the chapels and workplaces of their old neighbourhoods.

By focusing his campaign on the suburban and outlying rural areas of the constituency, Hutchinson sought to combat the 'apathy' of the non-Labour voter and overcome the sense of inevitability of a Labour victory. He therefore asked voters to question Gower's reputation as an industrial seat. He stressed the importance of rural communities and trumpeted the government's record in agriculture, arguing that 'the prosperity of the agricultural areas was linked up with the prosperity of the big towns'. He denounced Labour's disregard for farming and attacked the unfairness of what he called the 'block vote', which he insisted was under the dictatorial command of the South Wales Miners' Federation.[116] Such interventions meant that the Conservative campaign – not to mention press warnings of 'another 1931' unless the National government was returned – was liable to offend more voters than it attracted. Little wonder then that, according to local Conservative party leaders, Hutchinson's defeat was attributed to him being, simply, 'a stranger and an Englishman' in a South Wales mining community.[117]

Scotland

The general election in Scotland showed that, notwithstanding the Labour gains, the government's claims of economic recovery resonated

---

[114] *South Wales Evening Post*, 12 Nov. 1935.
[115] Ibid., 13 Nov. 1935; list of election meetings, 4–14 Nov. 1935, Hutchinson papers, D16/3.
[116] *South Wales Evening Post*, 5 Nov. 1935; *Western Mail*, 9 Nov. 1935; election address of G. Hutchinson, Nov. 1935, Hutchinson papers, D16/1.
[117] Capt. Aeron-Thomas to Sir G. Bowyer, 18 Nov. 1935, Hutchinson papers, D16/4/3.

effectively enough with voters to ensure the preservation of a majority of the Unionist gains made in 1931. The Unionist campaign in Dundee, historically a hopeless seat for the party, hinged almost entirely on the local experience of recovery. It also provides one of the most striking examples of how a National MP seized on the power of incumbency to cultivate a powerful public following. In addition to reporting Horsbrugh's campaign, the *Dundee Courier* carried articles recalling her 'indefatigable' efforts over four years to 'bring trade and industry to the city, so that workers, skilled and unskilled, might earn a livelihood'. Through interviews and negotiations with British and foreign ministers, listed among her accomplishments were trade agreements with seventeen countries, accounting for the increase in exports of jute goods; the future security of the Caledon shipyard under Admiralty sponsorship; the inflow of new industry, including a canning factory that helped to revive business for local fishermen; and her ongoing campaign to build a road bridge across the Tay.[118] The paper also reported a letter from John Colville, Secretary to the Department of Overseas Trade, testifying to Horsbrugh's industriousness. 'Of all the members of parliament with whom I was brought in touch in my official position I know of no one who was more assiduous in following up all trade questions.'[119] The fact that Labour gained votes, partly as a result of the Communist party's withdrawal, accounted for Horsbrugh's reduced majority from almost 16,000 to 6,000. Even so it was a historic victory, and the Unionist vote increased at the expense of the Liberal vote, enabling Horsbrugh to displace Foot as the city's senior MP.

The recovery proved all too elusive in some other parts of Scotland. Unemployment remained high in the Scottish Special Area, such that the scheme itself threatened to become a liability for the government as Labour attacked its failure to create jobs.[120] Most of the Unionist losses to Labour occurred in seats within or adjacent to the area, prompting the conference of the Scottish Unionist Association, in a resolution to the government on the subject of the Special Areas, to stress the objectives of 'industrial rehabilitation' and 're-employment', and not just social amelioration.[121] Compared to 1931, many Scottish Unionists struggled to penetrate working-class, especially unemployed, communities

---

[118] *Dundee Courier*, 12 Nov. 1935.   [119] Ibid., 7 Nov. 1935.

[120] R. H. Campbell, 'The Scottish Office and the Special Areas in the 1930s', *HJ*, 22 (1979), 167–83; W. W. Knox & A. Mackinlay, 'The re-making of Scottish Labour in the 1930s', *TCBH*, 6 (1995), 174–93.

[121] SUA conference programme, 29 Nov. 1935, 8, Cochrane papers, 10218, 2/3; *The Scotsman*, 30 Nov. 1935. Labour gains included Camlachie, Maryhill, Springburn, and Tradeston in Glasgow; Bothwell, Coatbridge, and Motherwell in Lanarkshire; Linlithgowshire and both East and West Stirlingshire.

226   Popular Conservatism and the National Government

precisely because Labour had rehabilitated its own voice among the poor; and not only in mining areas like Lanarkshire, but in parts of Glasgow where working-class Unionism had previously flourished. The implications of this were felt in Dunbartonshire, where the Labour vote reached its interwar peak, reducing the Unionist majority by more than 13,000 votes. The Kirkintilloch Unemployed Workers' Union, for instance, responsible for charitable relief work as well as recreational activities, adopted the stance of a mass organisation by 1935 and campaigned on behalf of the Labour candidate, Thomas Cassells. Meanwhile there was ongoing speculation about the political allegiance of residents of the new housing estates, who had moved from a solidly Labour part of Glasgow.[122]

Moreover, it was no longer clear whether the cross-party National government was capable of neutralising the anti-Westminster rhetoric of the Unionists' opponents. Since 1931, the withdrawal of Scottish Liberalism from the National alliance and the parallel rise of the Scottish Nationalist Party wrought a degree of influence on the discursive course of Scottish politics that was out of proportion to those parties' electoral strength. The Unionist campaign testifies to this. In contrast to the Labour and Liberal manifestos, the government manifesto contained a special reference to Scotland. This innovation, not seen in any other manifesto of the interwar years, reinforced the message that Scotland's economic recovery was underway precisely because special attention had been paid to Scotland's needs. As to the future, 'the programme outlined will be generally applicable to the United Kingdom, but in many spheres separate treatment is necessary to meet the special circumstances of Scotland'.[123]

Faced once more with a Nationalist candidate, the Unionist campaign in Dunbartonshire highlighted Scottish, as distinct from narrowly local, successes since 1931. In his speeches, for example, Cochrane pointed to higher expenditure on social services in Scotland than England, and the increased tonnage of Scottish compared to English shipbuilding.[124] The SNP tried to claim credit for such developments, describing the reopening of the Argyll Works under Admiralty control as a concession brought about by the agitation of Nationalists to 'stem the drift of industry southwards'. The SNP candidate also urged voters not to 'waste' their vote on Labour. 'It is ridiculous', he argued, 'to expect the progressive people in Scotland to wait until Mr Cassells [the Labour candidate] and

---

[122] *Kirkintilloch Herald*, 13, 22 Nov. 1935; *Kirkintilloch Gazette*, 5 Jul. 1935; *The Scotsman*, 2 Nov. 1935.

[123] *A call to the nation: the joint manifesto of the leaders of the National government* (1935).

[124] *Kirkintilloch Herald*, 6, 13 Nov. 1935.

National Conservatism in Scotland and Wales

his friends have converted 40 million Imperialistic English to some form of Socialism before we can expect any progress in Scotland'.[125] While Labour in turn dismissed the SNP as the 'wasted vote', Cochrane condemned it in stronger terms as a threat to Scotland's economic recovery. He accused the nationalists of peddling 'propaganda which for political purposes decries Scotland as a spent and done country trailing at the heels of England'. The effects on business confidence, he argued, would be just as adverse as those generated by the Communist threat on Clydeside. 'How could they expect anyone to bring fresh industries to Scotland when that propaganda was going on?' In many of his campaign speeches, he depicted the nationalists – 'these dismal Jimmies' – as doom-laden purveyors of a misplaced victimhood and took upon himself the mantle of representing the true, enterprising Scotsman.[126]

The fall in the SNP vote in Dunbartonshire was such that the candidate lost his deposit – as did his counterparts in Glasgow Hillhead, Greenock, Kilmarnock, and both East and West Renfrewshire.[127] Reflecting on the result, Unionist organisers attributed their own success to the support of Liberal voters. The very voters who were rumoured to have drifted from the National alliance and boosted the SNP's performance in the 1932 by-election had once more 'put country before party and voted for Commander Cochrane'.[128]

Labour's recovery in the west of Scotland continued steadily in the years after 1935. In March 1936, at a by-election occasioned by Cochrane's appointment as Governor of Burma, the voters of Dunbartonshire overturned the Unionist majority of more than 4,000 votes in favour of Labour. All three parties – including the SNP – lost votes, but the Unionists disproportionately so, shedding almost 5,000 votes since the general election. The local association attributed this to voter 'apathy', noting also a decline in local membership made more significant by the fact that it was 'more apparent in the residential districts than in the industrial areas'.[129] Eight months later, and across the Clyde estuary, Labour captured Greenock for the first time, following the death of Sir Godfrey Collins. This occurred against the backdrop of a resolution by the Labour party conference, held in Edinburgh in October, to launch a commission of inquiry into the distressed areas and the administration of the Special Areas.[130] Thus while the

---

[125] *The Scotsman*, 2 Nov. 1935; R. Gray to the editor, *Kirkintilloch Herald*, 27 Nov. 1935.
[126] Election address of A. Cochrane, Nov. 1935, Cochrane papers, 10218, 21/2; *Kirkintilloch Herald*, 6 Nov. 1935.
[127] Only in Inverness and the Western Isles did SNP candidates keep their deposits.
[128] *Kirkintilloch Herald*, 20 Nov. 1935.
[129] Report for the year ended 31 Oct. 1936, Dunbartonshire UA, 12264/3.
[130] H. Dalton et al., *A programme of immediate action: interim report of the Labour party's commission of enquiry into the distressed areas* (1937); *The Scotsman*, 20 Nov. 1936.

228   Popular Conservatism and the National Government

government candidate, a National Liberal, focused on the advantages of rearmament for the local shipbuilding and armaments industries, and announced that imminent government orders could hinge on the election outcome, the Labour candidate struck a more idealistic note. Condemning the government's cynical 'war means work' approach to public policy, he demonstrated the vulnerability of the National government's programmatic culture of government to charges of bribery, especially when compared to Labour's legitimate policy of peaceful industrial planning for the long term.[131]

Yet enthusiasm for the National government remained strong among most Unionist associations in Scotland. In Dunbartonshire and Dundee, where it was assumed the next general election would be fought 'under the banner of the National Government', it was still spoken of as a means of neutralising old threats and attracting new members from across the National parties.[132] They also commended the government's legislative accomplishment. Public knowledge of the government's work in Scotland was enhanced not only by the high-profile advocacy of several Scottish politicians of cabinet rank, including Sir John Gilmour, Walter Elliott, Ernest Brown, and Malcolm MacDonald, but also by the evolution of a 'distinctly Scottish sub-system of government' in the 1930s. During Elliott's tenure as Secretary of State from October 1936 to May 1938, the Scottish Office further consolidated its image as 'Whitehall in Scotland' with the construction of St Andrew's House as a central hub for the administration of agriculture, education, health, and home affairs.[133] Together with the Scottish Development Council it also set up the Films of Scotland Committee, tasked with producing a series of films for the 1938 Glasgow Empire Exhibition, including *Wealth of a Nation*, which narrated the government's role in coordinating efforts to attract new industries.[134]

Such concerted and pioneering efforts to project the National government in Scotland stood in stark contrast to the situation in Wales. There the lack of a critical mass of National MPs to act as advocates for local

---

[131] *The Scotsman*, 21 Nov. 1936.

[132] Executive committee, 10 Sep. 1937, Dundee UA, MS 270/1/1/1; report for the year ended 31 Oct. 1937, Dunbartonshire UA, 12264/3. For a famous case of grassroots re-affirmation of the National government in Scotland, see S. Ball, 'The politics of appeasement: the fall of the Duchess of Atholl and the Kinross and West Perth by-election, December 1938', *SHR*, 69 (1990), 49–83.

[133] Mitchell, *The Scottish question*, 69, 85.

[134] The imagery of industrial planning seen in *Wealth of Nations* (dir. D. Alexander) shared much in common with that printed in the *Scottish Illustrated*, 20,000 copies of which were distributed by the Dundee UA in the spring of 1937. Executive committee, 18 Mar. 1937, Dundee UA, MS 270/1/1/1.

interests when in London and as defenders of government policy when in Wales, created a reputational vacuum. 'Welsh' interests thus continued to be monopolised by Labour and Lloyd George. Like their counterparts in Scotland, by presenting the nation as the victim of establishment neglect, they saw in the National government an opportunity to rehabilitate radical anti-Conservative and anti-Westminster sentiment. Though electorally more successful in Wales than in Scotland, in both cases the strategy spawned a discourse of betrayal – of community and of nation – that inspired the political left as well as Celtic nationalists for decades to come.

Part III

Reputations of Government

8 The Unravelling of National Anti-Socialism?

> I keep on wondering what practical value there is to the Party in these everlasting political schools. Central Office ... has gone mad about them and all the leading wire-pullers in London (who know little or nothing about rough and tumble politics) are 'educational' enthusiasts. I feel that if we were to concentrate our forces on more active propaganda we should be doing a deal more practical good ... However, there it is, education is apparently the *dernier cri* among those in authority and we must not be behind hand in it in this part of the world, or we shall be considered retrograde!
>
> (Cuthbert Headlam, diary entry, 29 Nov. 1937)[1]

Had Baldwin gone to the country some weeks later than November 1935, the public's verdict might have been very different. For on 10 December the press leaked the controversial terms of a draft agreement, reached between the British Foreign Secretary, Sir Samuel Hoare, and the French Prime Minister, Pierre Laval, that sought to resolve the Abyssinian dispute. According to these terms, two thirds of Abyssinia was to be partitioned to Italy. The news prompted a blistering backlash in parliament, including among Conservative MPs like Vyvyan Adams, and in the country among voters who felt betrayed by a government whose course of action contradicted its manifesto commitment to pursue a collective League response. The reputational damage proved instant and intense, so much so that the cabinet decided to disown both the agreement and Hoare, who resigned on request. That the government was so buffeted by public reactions so soon after its election triumph exposed something of the transient and conditional nature of the 'National' vote. As Tom Hopkinson of the *Picture Post* noted in 1943, when the Beveridge Report appeared before the public, '[only] once before, over the Hoare-Laval Pact, this country spoke its mind, and the Government had to follow'.[2]

---

[1] *Parliament and politics in the age of Churchill and Attlee: the Headlam diaries, 1935–1951*, ed. S. Ball (Cambridge, 1999), 119 (29 Nov. 1937). *Dernier cri*: the last word.

[2] Cited in D. Waley, *British public opinion and the Abyssinian War, 1935–6* (London, 1975), 49.

234   Reputations of Government

The abdication crisis of 1936 had the potential to jeopardise the government's standing still further. The political Establishment and the churches reacted with hostility to the prospect of Edward VIII marrying Mrs Simpson. But public opinion was unclear and possibly sympathetic to the king. As Prince of Wales, he had already commanded affection from the masses. His visit to the stricken industrial towns of South Wales in November 1936 proved a personal triumph. Viewed as a moderniser with a progressive interest in social welfare, his comments in South Wales – including 'Something should be done to get them at work again', which upon subsequent appropriation turned into the more familiar 'something must be done' – appeared in the *Daily Mail* as criticism of the government.[3] The *Daily Express*, the *Daily Mirror*, the *Daily Sketch*, and the *News Chronicle*, which together with the *Mail* had a circulation of near nine million, backed the king in his personal predicament.[4] At all costs the government wished to avoid a constitutional crisis that might culminate in the shocking spectacle of a popular king being forced by his ministers to renounce his crown. In the event, the manner of the abdication was orderly and voluntary. Once again, contemporaries attributed this to Baldwin's personal qualities as much as his skill as a statesman. One of very few modern prime ministers to retire at a time of his own choosing, Baldwin did so in May 1937, a fortnight after the coronation of George VI.

The National government entered a new phase in the spring of 1937. Under the new prime minister, Neville Chamberlain, the government would step up the rearmament programme, turn its attention to civil defence, and pursue appeasement on the continent. On the face of it, little changed politically. The Conservatives went on constructing their popular appeals around the government's record of economic recovery; appeasement, though controversial, preserved peace in the present; and the opinion polls suggested further electoral success in the future. Still embodying the anti-socialist settlement of 1931 and presenting itself as the engineer of national recovery and social reform, the National government looked set to achieve an unprecedented third election victory. But the war intervened and, eight months later, in May 1940, Labour returned to government as part of Churchill's new coalition. Only then, just as the Phoney War ended, did the phoney 'National' government of 1931 – as Labour would soon characterise it – collapse.[5]

[3] *Daily Mail*, 23 Nov. 1936.
[4] S. Williams, *The People's King: the true story of the abdication* (London, 2003), 105.
[5] R. McKibbin, *Parties and people: England, 1914–1951* (Oxford, 2010), 117–23; J. Lawrence, 'Labour and the politics of class, 1900–1940', in D. Feldman & Lawrence (eds.), *Structures and transformations in modern British history* (Cambridge, 2011), 237–60.

The Unravelling of National Anti-Socialism? 235

Yet such a serene reading obscures the challenges facing its Conservative supporters in the constituencies by the late 1930s. By 1937, Labour had begun to regain the initiative. This occurred despite rearmament appearing to boost employment and despite the demonstrable results of Chamberlain's social reforms, especially in the new housing estates. While such reforms reflected the ongoing project of 'national recovery' and highlighted the enduring vitality of domestic issues in the period of appeasement, they also point to the peculiarities of Labour's recovery as experienced by Conservatives in the constituencies. For Labour was now restoring its reputation through its own well-publicised programme of municipal social reform (especially in London), its growing presence in neighbourhood organisations (including among the suburban electorate), and its critique of the government's handling of the distressed areas. In doing so, Attlee's party not only contested the government's narrative of recovery; it also began the process of articulating a particular version of 1930s Britain that ultimately defined British society's political and historical imaginary for several generations to come. Among the Conservatives' responses, and standing testament to the perceived threat of Labour, was a return to the notion of 'educating' the voter. Thus, the Conservative party ended the interwar years with much the same predicament as occupied it in the 1920s: whether to educate or appeal to the electorate.

Peace and Progress on the Eve of War

Almost immediately upon taking up his new office, Chamberlain found himself presiding over a string of by-elections. Over the course of June and July 1937, contests were fought in no fewer than twelve seats across rural and urban areas of Scotland and England, including Ilford.[6] The outcome was a clean sweep for the government, the Conservatives winning in ten seats and the Liberal Nationals in two. Turnout was down, and consequently so also was the Conservative vote. According to *The Times*, however, the most remarkable feature of this 'miniature General Election' was the decline of the Labour vote.[7] In Ilford, Labour's vote declined by more than 9,000, while in the other contests it declined by an average of more than 2,000. Under Chamberlain, anti-socialism looked

---

[6] The other constituencies were Glasgow Hillhead, Buckingham, Plymouth Drake, Cheltenham, Hemel Hempstead, Holland with Boston, Bewdley, St Ives, Kingston-upon-Thames, Chertsey, and North Dorset.

[7] *The Times*, 15 Jul. 1937. The Independent Conservative who triumphed in Cheltenham, despite standing against the official National Conservative candidate, pledged himself to support the government.

236   Reputations of Government

set to remain electorally robust. But to what extent were its appeals still rooted in notions of economic recovery?

One of Chamberlain's last main acts as chancellor, in February 1937, was to raise a loan of £400 million to spend on defence.[8] While the real impact of this expenditure on the economy is debated among economic historians, it undoubtedly marked a significant watershed in public policy as the government, having set itself the task of rearming, abandoned fiscal orthodoxy in favour of deficit-financing a near-war economy. According to one estimate, rearmament created more than a million jobs and accounted for about 81 per cent of the increase in civilian employment since 1935.[9] Albeit 'due more to Mr Hitler than Mr Keynes' therefore, as Barry Eichengreen has noted, rearmament nonetheless generated new employment in ways similar to the public-work schemes advocated by Keynesian planners.[10] Yet the political implications for the government were far from straightforward. Two years on from the Peace Ballot and Baldwin's cautious election pledge to pursue rearmament as a defensive measure, it was unclear if rearmament should be actively publicised like any other job-creating measure or downplayed for fear of exacerbating public fears of war and energising sections of the political left. Meanwhile, senior figures in the Labour leadership, while endorsing rearmament, seized on Chamberlain's belated conversion to deficit finance. Referring to the government's consistent refusal to undertake loan expenditure at the height of the depression, Hugh Dalton criticised the intransigence of a government that conceded the principle of deficit finance in order to fund arms yet still refused to raise smaller loans 'for the restoration of employment in those areas where unemployment remains most intractable'.[11]

Yet in practice the government had two means of defending rearmament. The first centred on the positive economic consequences. Throughout 1937–8, reports of the recession hitting the American economy raised concerns about the impact of decreasing trade and rising prices on Britain's recovery. Against this backdrop, rearmament, although temporary, appeared a decisive project in helping industry to weather the storm, with orders, jobs, and production all holding up

---

[8] *House of Commons Debates*, 5 ser., 320, col. 1205–1217, 17 Feb. 1937.
[9] M. Thomas, 'Rearmament and economic recovery in the late 1930s', *EcHR*, 36 (1983), 552–79, at 567.
[10] B. Eichengreen, 'The British economy between the wars', in R. Floud & P. Johnson (eds.), *The Cambridge economic history of modern Britain, vol. II: economic maturity, 1860–1939* (Cambridge, 2004), 314–43, 337; also N. Craft & T. C. Mills, 'Rearmament to the rescue? New estimates of the impact of "Keynesian" policies in 1930s' Britain', *Journal of Economic History*, 73 (2013), 1077–1104.
[11] *House of Commons Debates*, 5 ser., 320, col. 1300, 17 Feb. 1937.

The Unravelling of National Anti-Socialism? 237

favourably with international comparisons. Having struggled to harness the political spoils of national recovery in the mid-decade, Conservatives in the Northern Area, where the multiplier effect of new factory jobs presented a second chance at economic regeneration, embraced rearmament and echoed ministerial commitments to prioritise the depressed regions.[12] According to Peter Scott, many rearmament activities did in fact locate in the Special Areas, since the designation of the Midlands, the South East and the East coast as unsafe zones in the event of air attack led policymakers to exploit the skills endowment and surplus workforce found in South Wales, Lancashire, and Central Scotland.[13]

The implications for wage earners were soon laid bare in the press and in political speeches. The *Dundee Courier*, referring to a War Office order for 40 million sandbags, described rearmament as 'an enormous boon' for Dundee. 'It will keep thousands of looms running throughout the winter which, without it, would certainly have been closed down.'[14] Other regions celebrated similarly large-scale orders. British steel production, announced Oliver Stanley, the President of the Board of Trade, had reached 'a record for all time', while factories in West Yorkshire and Lancashire were working to capacity.[15] Meanwhile, the pictorial press provided vivid accounts of the transformative effect on each armed service and the economy, the *ILN* reporting that the rearmament budget equalled the sum necessary to build 300 ocean liners like the *Queen Mary* and its financial journalist, Hartley Withers, explaining that factory-building and rearmament would be 'keeping the industrial pot boiling' just as the housebuilding boom slowed down. Coverage of the king and queen on their extensive tour of factories became a familiar encounter for cinemagoers.[16] Although Labour opponents sought to construe rearmament as symptomatic of Tory warmongering, in the short term the rearmament programme did more to boost than jeopardise the politics of recovery.[17]

The second defence of rearmament, paradoxically, was the increasingly fraught foreign policy context that accompanied it. As Nick Crowson has

[12] Council AGM, 27 Feb. 1937, Northern Counties Area, Northumberland Collections Service, NRO 3303/2. Sir Samuel Hoare, First Lord of the Admiralty, claimed that 80 per cent of defence expenditure was spent in the distressed areas ('Notes for a speech: the Special Areas', *CAJ*, Nov. 1936, 272–4).

[13] P. Scott, *Triumph of the south: a regional economic history of early twentieth century Britain* (Aldershot, 2007), 274–7.

[14] *Dundee Courier*, 29 Oct. 1937.

[15] E.g., *Yorkshire Post*, 30 Nov. 1938; *ILN*, 8 Jan. 1938.

[16] *ILN*, 13, 27 Feb. 1937, 8 Jan. 1938; *Britain and Prosperity: boom in industry and trade* (1937), Pathé, no. 903.17.

[17] Report for the year ended 31 Oct. 1937, National Library of Scotland, Dunbartonshire UA, 12264/3.

238   Reputations of Government

shown, while developments including the Anschluss, Kristallnacht, and the Munich talks all raised concerns about Germany's intentions, most Conservatives – in the constituencies and in parliament – supported the government's restrained foreign policy and in any case favoured a stance of public loyalty to Chamberlain's official policy.[18] Rearmament could be cast as a defensive measure, underpinning popular diplomatic efforts and ensuring preparedness in the event of their failure. For opponents of appeasement, too, rearmament provided a cause around which to demonstrate continued support for the government. In the summer of 1936, Macmillan and Adams resigned the government whip in order to back an opposition motion objecting to the abandonment of sanctions against Italy. Yet in 1937 by endorsing rearmament and framing it as indivisible from the principle of collective security enshrined in the League of Nations, they were able to placate their local activists. Soon upon Chamberlain's accession to the premiership, Macmillan applied to receive the whip once more.[19] When attitudes within the party hardened in favour of a more defiant policy, following Eden's resignation as Foreign Secretary in February 1938 and then Munich and the fall of Prague, Conservatives could still look to rearmament – as well as the domestic record – for a rationale to underpin their continued support of the government. Thus when Adams voted against the government on a censure motion in February 1938, he did so with the understanding of his association in Leeds West, while Macmillan, who abstained, sought to put his differences with the government on foreign policy into context by declaring to activists that 'no other party has ever done so much towards social reform' as the National Conservatives since 1931.[20] Of the opponents of appeasement studied here, it was Churchill who endured most difficulty with members of his local association, a minority of whom disapproved of his public criticism of the prime minister, but even so a majority praised Churchill's role in forcing 'national defence' onto the agenda.[21] Notwithstanding concerns about the pace of rearmament, pro- and anti-appeasers could find in it a source of consensus. Therefore, while Anglo-German relations deteriorated and appeasement itself wrought disunity in parliament, rearmament and war preparation in fact provided a policy

[18] N. Crowson, *Facing fascism: the Conservative party and the European dictators, 1935–1940* (London, 1997).
[19] Men's branch AGM, 25 Mar. 1937, Durham Record Office, STCO, D/X 322/8; *Yorkshire Post*, 17 Feb., 12 Mar. 1937 (Adams); *Lancashire Evening Post*, 6 Apr. 1937 (Adams); *Leeds Mercury*, 31 Jul. 1937 (Macmillan).
[20] Executive committee, 28 Feb. 1938, Leeds West CA, West Yorkshire Archive Service, WYL 529/5; men's branch AGM, 10 Mar. 1938, STCO, D/X 322/8.
[21] Special meeting of central council, 4 Nov. 1938, Redbridge Local History Centre, Epping CA, Acc.A6853.

The Unravelling of National Anti-Socialism? 239

that largely satisfied contemporary opinion – more so than subsequent Churchillian and leftist assessments chose to acknowledge.

However, the government did not allow rearmament to define its domestic agenda. By 1938, many of the policies promised at the time of the 1935 election had been enacted. These included the Education Act, 1936, which raised the school-leaving age to fifteen and provided grants to local education authorities; the Midwives Act, 1936, compelling local authorities to provide a salaried midwifery service; the Holidays with Pay Act, 1938, which gave workers the right to paid annual leave; and the extension of health insurance benefits to workers aged 16–18. These, together with other measures discussed below, coalesced around the theme of progress in public welfare, which formed the centrepiece of Chamberlain's vision for the government at home. In a filmed personal address, the prime minister stated that the 'aim of a statesman ought to be the improvement of the condition of the people'. Setting out the government's priorities,

he placed health first, and in the case of ill-health the best available medical attention; then a sufficient income to keep a man and his family in at least a minimum of comfort; then leisure and the means to enjoy art; and, lastly, moral and intellectual freedom without fear of persecution.[22]

Such an agenda marked a step change in the government's ambitions, from fighting unemployment to highlighting the social benefits of economic recovery. As such, it promised to continue to serve the interests of many local Conservatives.

The last of the government's peacetime programmes of reform came in the shape of a national health campaign launched in the autumn of 1937. Instigated by the Ministry of Health and the Board of Education in response to official fears about the inadequate physical fitness of the British population, the campaign is inevitably viewed as the activity of a government preparing for war.[23] But it was also the activity of a government battling hard to keep the narrative of social progress at the forefront of public discourse. It coincided with a new publicity drive following a string of Labour electoral successes. Labour had held on to the London County Council with an increased majority in March, won a parliamentary by-election in Islington North in October, and made

---

[22] *The Times*, 9 Oct. 1937.

[23] M. Grant, 'The National Health Campaigns of 1937–1938', in D. Fraser (ed.), *Cities, class and communication: essays in honour of Asa Briggs* (London, 1990), 216–33; I. Zweiniger-Bargielowska, *Managing the body: beauty, health and fitness, 1880–1939* (Oxford, 2010), ch.7.

240   Reputations of Government

further gains in the municipal elections held in November – taking control of 17 out of 28 London boroughs (up from 5 in 1931 and 10 in 1934) and 43 towns and cities in England and Wales, including Bristol, Coventry, and South Shields for the first time.[24] While the Conservative vote held up well in many places, including Birmingham and Liverpool, Labour's gains now obscured the by-election successes of the summer and generated doubts about the government's ability to renew its appeal. Apathy, contrasted with Labour's activity, appeared to pose a threat once more.[25] A film tour undertaken by the National Publicity Bureau therefore received the enthusiastic approval of activists. The reasons were in part practical: the latest cinema vans were adapted for use indoors, which boosted audience numbers and enabled their use all year round. In a rural seat like Devizes, the novelty of an indoor cinema attracted audiences of up to 2,000 people.[26] But above all, the content was deemed clear, relevant, and often entertaining. Typically containing a voiceover that explained government policy, a cameo appearance by the relevant minister, and the use of 'before' and 'after' footage to exemplify the immediate impact of policy implementation, the films combined expert commentary on public policy with the demotic appeals of a party political broadcast.

One of the most professional films, produced by Pathé for the Ministry of Health, was *The Great Crusade: the story of a million homes* (1937). It opens with a girl, Molly, returning home from school to the grim conditions of life in the slum. 'The children of today are the parents of the next generation', declares the narrator, 'and unless these breeding places of dirt and disease are swept away, what sort of generation will it be? Are we going to perpetuate a C3 race?' The film cuts to footage of Sir Kingsley Wood, the Minister of Health responsible for the five-year plan to abolish the slums, before embarking on a sustained assessment of clearance and rehousing schemes in a range of English cities from Bristol and Portsmouth to Manchester and Bradford. 'During the first two years of the five-year plan', the narrator claims, 'already more people have been rescued from these hovels than for the whole previous fifty-eight years'. In addition to the cleanliness, spaciousness, and comfort of the new housing,

---

[24] *The Times*, 3, 4 Nov. 1937.
[25] E.g., 'Learn from the Opposition', *CAJ*, Oct. 1937, 238–9; branch committee, 20 Feb. 1938, Woodford Church End Branch (Epping CA), Acc.A6853; executive committee, 25 May 1938, Norfolk Record Office, Norfolk North CA, Acc.2006/152.
[26] *CAJ*, Feb. 1938, 36; chairman's report to the AGM, 12 Feb. 1938, Wiltshire Record Office, Devizes CA, 2305/3. Also executive committee, 25 Feb. 1938, Ilford CA, 90/61/1/1; executive committee report, 19 Mar. 1938, Northern Counties Area, NRO 3303/2; executive committee, 25 May 1938, Norfolk Record Office, Norfolk North CA, Acc.2006/152.

The Unravelling of National Anti-Socialism? 241

there are scenes of busy building works, bustling trade in allied industries, and cheery workers on pay day, all highlighting the direct boost to employment and wages. The film concludes with Molly as a healthy schoolgirl, her childhood – and future – duly transformed by the move from the slum to new accommodation.[27] Another popular film, *Deeds, Not Words* (1938), featured a dialogue between two working men in which they discussed industrial recovery under the National government and contrasted this with what one local paper called 'the extravagant pretensions of the Socialist Party'.[28]

Another feature of the national health campaign was a scheme to promote physical fitness. As early as 1934, Chamberlain had hoped to develop a 'general scheme for the improvement of the physique of young people' that would address maternal and infant mortality, nursery services, and juvenile health insurance. 'Taken separately these would be merely a series of electoral bribes of rather petty character', wrote Chamberlain in his diary. 'But as parts of a scheme for raising the level of national health they present an ideal which is both right in itself and attractive to the public.' Significantly, by the time the scheme materialised in 1937, it encompassed adults as well as the young and recreational life as well as physical fitness.[29] In this way it echoed the growing acknowledgement among contemporary social scientists, notably Rowntree, that basic well-being depended not only on a subsistence level of material provisions but also on the discretionary consumption of recreational items and pastimes.[30]

Under the terms of the Physical Training and Recreation Act of 1937, local committees were established under the auspices of a National Advisory Council for England and Wales, with another for Scotland. Comprising representatives of local authorities and voluntary organisations, the committees were charged with reviewing existing facilities and, where appropriate, securing grants for 'gymnasiums, playing fields, swimming baths, bathing places, holiday camps and camping sites, and other buildings and premises'.[31] Within a year, the scheme was also responsible for the construction or improvement of 'community centres' nationwide. Often furnished with some combination of a dance hall, gymnasium,

[27] *The Great Crusade: the story of a million homes* (1937), prod. Pathé, film no. 3467.04.
[28] *Wells Journal*, 16 Sep. 1938. This film, whose title and message of achievements bear some similarity to the Nazi propaganda film *Wort und Tat* (1938), was probably the NPB's most widely disseminated film in 1938. References to it are commonplace in the local press: e.g., *Sunderland Daily Echo*, 9 Jul. 1938, *Western Daily Press*, 2 Sep. 1938.
[29] *The Neville Chamberlain diary letters, vol. 4: the Downing Street years, 1934–1940*, ed. R. Self (Aldershot, 2005), 216 (31 Oct. 1936).
[30] B. S. Rowntree, *The human needs of labour* (London, 1918; revised edn 1936), 126–7.
[31] *Physical Training and Recreation Act*, 1937, 1 Edw. 8 & 1 Geo. 6, ch.46.

242   Reputations of Government

reading room, cinema, and canteen, the social centre of the late 1930s helped the slum dweller to adjust to the new conditions of the housing estate.[32] As the *Yorkshire Post* noted, such a community hub promised to combat a major problem of the age, namely the 'loneliness of people removed from slums and rehoused amid strangers', offering a facility around which residents could rehabilitate the 'old sociability that made life in the slums tolerable and even jolly'. It would create, said the National Liberal Robert Bernays of the Ministry of Health, 'a centre of corporate life'.[33] For a voluntary organisation like the NCSS, the shift from containing the distress of the unemployed to the implementation of government-subsidised schemes of this kind marked a welcome return to its original agenda of social improvement. Referring to 'the tide of increased opportunities and possibilities' made possible by government legislation, especially the Physical Training and Recreation Act, a report of the NCSS's Liverpool branch noted that 'schemes vaguely thought of in the past have now become realities, and this has not only given encouragement to physical fitness, but to the many other sides of club life'.[34]

While the full implications of the national health campaign on the political life of local communities were soon to be obscured by the outbreak of war, Conservative activists were alive to the opportunities it afforded them. Sporting and handicraft facilities for recreation, together with amenities including maternity clinics and libraries, provided further evidence of government activity – and in turn also brought into focus what might be described as the trend towards the conspicuous consumption of state provision by British society on the eve of the Second World War. In 1938 the NCSS launched a grant scheme to help village halls, which boosted the movement for rural amenities and promised to decelerate the problem of rural depopulation.[35] Likewise in urban areas it made for ready propaganda on behalf of the government and, according to some studies, proved instrumental in entrenching 'community' norms in ways that helped to stabilise the hitherto transitory population of the new estates.[36] Moreover, new sites of corporate life created new spaces for the political parties to work within. In Wiltshire, for example,

---

[32] E.g., R. Jevons & J. Madge, *Housing estates: a study of Bristol corporation policy and practice between the wars* (Bristol, 1946), 81–3.

[33] *Yorkshire Post*, 2, 4 Apr. 1938.

[34] Annual report for 1938, cited in H. R. Poole, *The Liverpool Council of Social Service* (Liverpool, 1960), 64.

[35] *Dundee Evening Telegraph*, 22 Aug. 1938; *Yorkshire Post*, 23 Aug. 1938; *Wiltshire Times*, 24 Sep. 1938.

[36] R. Durant, *Watling: a survey of social life in a new housing estate* (London, 1939), 42–9, ch.4; Jevons & Madge, Housing estates, 79–83; also A. Olechnowicz, *Working-class housing in England between the wars: the Becontree estate* (Oxford, 1997), 163–79.

The Unravelling of National Anti-Socialism? 243

membership of the Women's Institute expanded in the late 1930s just as meeting facilities in the villages improved.[37] While still officially non-aligned, many of its branch members were Conservative activists – Chamberlain's sister, Hilda, served as Treasurer of the National Federation – and thereby ensured for the party in Devizes and neighbouring seats enhanced access to community activity.[38] The utility of such connections was to be found not only in the potential recruitment of new members but also in that they looked to be in a position to mediate public opinion. The WI at this time abandoned its own organisational concerns that had for so long preoccupied its activities and developed more of a pressure-group identity, working on behalf of the 'public' interest in cooperation with the government. The ministers of health, education, and agriculture were careful to strike a confiding and collaborative tone whenever they addressed its audiences, and the organisation was represented on several government commissions.[39] Members often reciprocated with proud declarations of how their views were shaping public policy. 'It was really only through the Women's Institutes', declared the dowager Countess of Radnor, president of the Wiltshire federation, 'that opinions could be got on all sorts of questions – housing, health and education ... The Government realised that the Movement was a means of getting things done'.[40] Such communal leadership anticipated the role played by the WI and Townswomen's Guild in wartime and, as James Hinton has argued, proved an asset for the Conservatives.[41]

But community itself remained, as ever, a contested space. As the party upped its political activity, so on occasion the social pitfalls of doing so became apparent. This came to light in Birmingham Moseley, where the party spent much of the late 1930s trying to establish itself in the new estates, when the chairman of a ward committee threatened to resign following complaints from fellow activists that he introduced undue 'political propaganda' into social functions attended by 'members of the

[37] The National Federation of the WI was one of the first recipients of a grant under the Physical Training and Recreation Act. *The Times*, 22 Oct. 1937.

[38] The Wiltshire Federation of the WI comprised 130 village branches with a membership of almost 6,000 (*Wiltshire Times*, 2 Apr. 1938). Party officers in Norfolk North scheduled their events so as not to clash with WI events (general council, 22 Oct. 1937, Norfolk North CA, Acc.2006/152).

[39] *The Times*, 26 Nov. 1937 (Sir Kingsley Wood addressing a conference on health services called by the WI), 17 Apr. 1938 (the Board of Education's committee on cookery teaching in schools), 1 Nov. 1938 (deputation of the WI to the Minister of Health on milk for children).

[40] *Wiltshire Times*, 2 Apr., 14 May 1938.

[41] J. Hinton, 'Conservative women and voluntary social service, 1938–1951', in S. Ball & I. Holliday (eds.), *Mass Conservatism: the Conservatives and the public since the 1880s* (London, 2002), 100–19.

244   Reputations of Government

opposition'.[42] Yet faced with the prospect of Labour expanding its own activities in the estates, there was no alternative. By 1938, the Conservative agent had set up women's branches in three of the largest estate areas, each seeking cooperation with and the use of the new churches and local schools, and holding fortnightly 'socials' attended by up to 150 residents.[43] Ultimately it is difficult to tell how such developments might have helped the party at a general election in 1940. The question of whether the Conservative party seized on the renewal of community organisation that accompanied the national health campaign of the late 1930s to any great effect against its main rival is discussed in the next section.

But first it is worth highlighting one important implication of the government's national health campaign – namely that it elevated state welfare provision to a central place in British popular politics at a time when the problem of unemployment no longer demanded it. To be sure, the fruits of most policies were realised only with the involvement of voluntary organisations like the NCSS and the WI, together with local authorities and private enterprise. Housing schemes and other municipal improvements were undertaken largely because central government compelled or enabled local government to act. In turn many such developments relied on the commercial supply industry, in particular utility companies like the Gas Light and Coke Company, whose mascot – 'Mr Therm' – became an icon of 1930s domestic modernity.[44] Therefore although the central state – and state funding – was integral, it was not yet a welfare state. When government grants under the 1937 act were advertised, as in the documentary film *Today We Live* (1937), which showed the construction of a village hall in Gloucestershire and a community centre in a South Wales mining town, it was the NCSS rather than any government department that instructed viewers how to prepare applications.[45] When the Midwives Act expanded professional midwifery services, the effect was to augment existing charitable organisations rather than create a new state service.[46] As such, the role played by the voluntary and local authorities in shaping what the public saw of welfare provision on the ground obscured the significant strides made by

[42] C. Edwards to Hannon, 14 Nov. 1938, Hannon to Edwards, 17 Nov. 1938, Parliamentary Archives, Hannon papers, HNN 72/1.

[43] Report on the new Warstock, Dolphin Lane and Tyseley Women's Branches, 19 Jun. 1938, Hannon papers, HNN 73/3.

[44] A. Clendinning, *Demons of domesticity: women and the English gas industry, 1889–1939* (Aldershot, 2004), 233–5.

[45] *Today We Live* (1937), dir. R. Grierson & R. Bond.

[46] C. Braithwaite, *The voluntary citizen: an enquiry into the place of philanthropy in the community* (London, 1938), 287–8, 312.

The Unravelling of National Anti-Socialism? 245

the National government since 1935 to distribute the rewards of economic recovery, which it did by moving away from a policy designed primarily to combat the distress of unemployment, providing relief in place of wages, to one that offered welfare alongside wages.

The continued dominance of Victorian-style philanthropic and local networks is, on the one hand, of a piece with the notion that the British state underwent limited change in the interwar years. Eichengreen points out that economic recovery took place 'without forcing the socialisation' of the economy, while Duncan Tanner, E. H. H. Green, Jon Lawrence and others have stressed the extent to which the 'liberal' – or 'Tory liberal' – impulses of nineteenth-century British political discourse inculcated the world view of Conservative reformers and Labour politicians in the twentieth century.[47] Such a reading reinforces the commonplace view that the National government, despite the reformist narrative inherent in its abandonment of free trade and its relaxation of fiscal orthodoxy, remained too hamstrung by its own adherence to laissez-faire dogma to pursue significant social reform. Chamberlain himself did not renounce the ideal of the balanced budget, nor did wider Conservative opinion alter fundamentally its preference for limited government. Indeed, many of the most striking examples of state-led reforms available to contemporaries were those set by the European dictators, and thus gave ministers good reason to disavow state incursions into everyday life as militaristic and distinctly un-British.[48] And yet politically the National government insisted that voters should recognise, and indeed embrace, the growing range of services provided by the state. In the late 1930s the General Post Office produced several films advertising the services it offered, imparting a duty on Britons to avail themselves of the telephone exchange, the post office savings scheme and other services, in order thereby to secure the future of the GPO as a large employer and crucial cog in the nation's modern infrastructure.[49] Indeed, the national health campaign involved a six-month publicity drive entitled 'Use Your Health

---

[47] Eichengreen, 'The British economy between the wars', 337. See E. H. H. Green & D. M. Tanner (eds.), *The strange survival of liberal England: political leaders, moral values and the reception of economic debate* (Cambridge, 2006); J. Lawrence, 'Paternalism, class and the British path to modernity', in S. Gunn & J. Vernon (eds.), *The peculiarities of liberal modernity in imperial Britain* (Berkeley, CA, 2011), 147–64.

[48] When launching a regional fitness campaign in Liverpool, Kingsley Wood stressed the voluntary nature of the scheme and argued that 'compulsory methods were against our best traditions'. *Yorkshire Post*, 6 Oct. 1937.

[49] E.g., *A Job in a Million* (1937), dir. E. Spice; *Big Money* (1937), dir. H. Watt; *Book Bargain* (1937), dir. N. McLaren.

246   Reputations of Government

Services'. This revealed that medical assistance was freely available to 16.5 million wage earners under the national health insurance scheme, and implicit in many of the declarations by ministers was the assumption that public utilisation of services would serve to secure the further expansion of welfare schemes. Wood himself stated that 'extensions to our health services were desirable' and that therefore all facilities should be 'fully utilised', prompting the *Lancashire Evening Post* to express 'confiden[ce] that far greater progress will be made when wider and fuller use is made of all the health services by the people who need them'.[50]

Labour's Cultures of Government

Electoral success under Chamberlain did not continue unabated nor unchallenged. For all the signs of stable public support for the government, it is worth noting that the by-election victories of the summer of 1937 were secured on reduced polls. In Ilford, for instance, only about a third of voters turned out to vote at the by-election in June, at which the Conservative majority was halved. Organisers in the south-west could take little comfort from their victory in North Dorset, since the Liberals came within just 500 votes of recapturing the seat for the first time since 1923.[51] Then, between October 1937 and the outbreak of war, the Conservatives lost six by-elections to Labour and saw their share of the vote dwindle in virtually all other parliamentary contests.[52] While such by-elections offer only impressionistic evidence of Labour's recovery, they nevertheless echoed Conservatives' own perceptions of the challenges facing their party in the late 1930s. One of these was apathy. Albeit less endemic than in the 1920s, the threat of apathy among known supporters – in the form of declining or an inactive membership, floundering finances, or the retreat of club members from the political fray – looked certain to endanger the electoral gains of 1931.[53] Canvassers reported growing discontent among farmers, while in suburban areas the

[50] *Lancashire Evening Post*, 1 Oct. 1937. For a similar sentiment expressed by the Minister of Agriculture following the passage of the Housing (Financial Provisions) Act 1938 and the Housing (Rural Workers) Amendment Act 1938, see *Wiltshire Times*, 5 Nov. 1938.
[51] Annual report for the year ending 31 Dec. 1937, CPA, Bodleian Library, Oxford, Wessex Area, ARE 10/1/2.
[52] These were Islington North, Ipswich, Fulham West, Dartford, Kennington, and Brecon and Radnor. Labour's share of the vote increased in all but two of the twenty-six seats it contested in 1935 and again in by-elections between October 1937 and September 1939.
[53] E.g., executive committee, 8 Apr. 1937, Devizes CA, 2305/3; branch committee, 20 Feb. 1938, Redbridge Local History Centre, Woodford Church End Branch (Epping CA), Acc.A6853; executive committee, 25 May 1938, Norfolk North CA, Acc.2006/152; 'Learn from the Opposition', *CAJ*, Oct. 1937, 238–9.

The Unravelling of National Anti-Socialism?

rapidly growing electorate of the new estates continued to present new organisational challenges.[54] This was underscored by the Labour party's new strategies for appealing to erstwhile Labour and Liberal supporters. Though far from assured, Labour's recovery was finally underway, and signified above all the fragility of the National vote in the face of an effective challenge.

The fact that this challenge materialised when the government's record of reducing unemployment stood at its most incontestable stands testament to how Labour successfully began to wrestle back control of the political initiative. Several historians have addressed Labour's strategy in the late 1930s, highlighting in particular the significance of *Labour's Immediate Programme*, published in March 1937. As Richard Toye notes, although the party remained formally committed to the principles contained in a previous document, *For Socialism and Peace* (1934), including wholesale nationalisation of industry and banking as well as the pursuit of world peace through the establishment of a 'Co-operative World Commonwealth', the *Immediate Programme* represented an important presentational change. It eschewed the boldly idealistic language of the party's post-1931 radicalism and outlined in more pragmatic terms what the party, under Clement Attlee, would do in its first term in office.[55] By cultivating a more contractual relationship with voters, Labour could begin to rehabilitate its credentials as a party of government. If this seemed unduly optimistic to some within the party, it appeared less so to their opponents in the light of Labour's gains at the municipal level. Under Herbert Morrison, the London Labour party campaigned successfully on its record since 1934. On housing, education, hospitals, public assistance, public spaces, and public-sector employment, 'London has had nearly three years of sane progress', claimed a Labour pamphlet, 'of sweeping but unhurried reform, of humane administration without extravagance'.[56] Conservatives privately reflected that Morrison won because he had 'not shown himself an extremist', whereas the Conservative-run Municipal Reform campaign, so Headlam thought, 'consisted of anti-Red propaganda where Reds were practically non-existent'.[57] If Labour could

---

[54] Secretary's report to executive committee of women's association, 31 Jan. 1938, Devizes CA, 2305/13; executive committee, 25 May 1938, Norfolk North CA, Acc.2006/152; report for the year ended 31 Oct. 1936, Dunbartonshire UA, 12264/3; redistribution sub-committee, 17 Nov. 1937, finance and general purposes committee, 17 Dec. 1937, CPA, Bodleian Library, Oxford, Home Counties North Area, ARE 8/1/1.

[55] R. Toye, *The Labour party and the planned economy, 1931–1951* (Woodbridge, 2003), 70–3.

[56] *What Labour has done for London* (1936), 2.

[57] *Parliament and politics in the age of Churchill and Attlee: the Headlam diaries, 1935–1951*, ed. S. Ball (Cambridge, 1999), 107 (5 Mar. 1937).

248   Reputations of Government

prove itself competent on policy and implementation, it was equipped both to challenge the government's claims to the same and to impede the Conservatives' resort to familiar anti-socialist attacks.

Conservatives perceived in Morrison's successes something more endemic and far-reaching in the Labour threat. They saw that Attlee's party had learnt how to make systematic use of local government in order to project its national policies in the constituencies and cultivate its own culture of government. One agent, writing anonymously, observed that Labour's strategy in municipal elections was 'more and more making use of national questions . . . bringing to bear the whole weight of mass bribery and specious promises to gain support', noting, as an example, that 'Socialist canvassers were employing the promises of the Parliamentary Socialists to give pensions at 60'.[58] Another agent, writing from the south London seat of Streatham, analysed Labour's growing hold on voters in the new council estates. 'The Socialists do look after their own when it comes to a question of housing accommodation', he concluded – an electorally astute strategy when allied to the 'deliberate policy of the Socialists to build these flats in politically vulnerable constituencies'. He lamented that municipal Conservatism, by contrast, had gone 'economy mad in 1931' and consequently 'failed to capture the imagination of the masses'. If the Conservative party was to retain a presence in London, it would have to reinvent itself as a municipal party committed to social reform. 'Our local administrators must have big hearts as well as calculating heads. They must know and be known by the people.'[59]

While Labour's municipal threat was most acute in the capital, it was emblematic of the evolving threat facing Conservatives nationwide. There is little doubt that Labour was in part forced by circumstances, not least the general election result, to seek its recovery in local government. Yet in doing so the party was well placed to reprise a familiar and effective strategy. As Duncan Tanner showed, some of Labour's early advances occurred in areas where a policy of 'municipal interventionism' succeeded in demonstrating a commitment to social improvement and protection of consumer interests.[60] The power of this strategy became most evident in mining areas like South Wales, where, as the previous chapter showed, Labour's 'right' to represent community interests remained entrenched even beyond 1931. By the late 1930s, Labour was claiming similar rights in more residential areas, or so it appeared to local Conservatives as they found their own everyday organisational interests

[58] 'Recent local government elections', *CAJ*, Dec. 1937, 289.
[59] 'Thoughts on London elections', *CAJ*, Dec. 1937, 292.
[60] D. Tanner, *Political change and the Labour party, 1900–1918* (Cambridge, 1990).

checked by perceptible shifts in the behaviour of residents.[61] In Birmingham, concerns grew that Labour was exploiting or indirectly benefiting from the new community centres, introduced under the 'non-political' sponsorship of the NCSS, as these became in effect incubators of new political or protest initiatives. In 1938–9 alone they spawned a network of Ratepayers Associations, hitherto largely absent in the city's politics, and the Birmingham Municipal Tenants' Association, which went on to lead a ten-week rent strike the following year.[62] Moreover, the community interests on which Labour staked its reputation in municipal affairs, once extrapolated to the national arena, held the prospect of a coherent challenge to the government's narrative of recovery and, at the same time, projected an alternative, Labour vision of government.

In 1937 Labour published its plans for the distressed areas. Instead of proselytising a predetermined socialist solution, the party undertook a detailed empirical investigation of the government's administration of the Special Areas. In a series of regional reports by the party's commission of enquiry into the distressed areas, headed by Hugh Dalton and based on a scientific gathering of evidence from local workforces as well as industrial and public health experts, it charged the government with failing to secure a nationwide recovery.[63] The long-term unemployed in the distressed areas bore testimony to 'the Government's utterly disgraceful failure to show either determination, competence or human sympathy in its handling of the question' – and now faced the 'immediate peril of a sheer breakdown of communal life and of local government', according to Dalton's report. The distressed areas had experienced nothing but crisis since 1931. Eluded by the recovery, 'the magnitude and the duration of [the resulting] social disaster' was exacerbated by the government's ineffectiveness. Labour offered 'a number of practical proposals, capable of being translated immediately into action, if the Government and Parliament were willing'.[64] These included replacing the Special

---

[61] In some wards in Ilford they had difficulty finding venues for meetings and social events, while in Dunbartonshire the decline in party membership was more apparent in the residential areas than the industrial areas. Executive committee, 7 Dec. 1937, Ilford CA, 90/61/1/1; reports for the years ended 31 Oct. 1936 and 31 Oct. 1937, Dunbartonshire UA, 12264/3.

[62] Management committee, 13 May, 9 Dec. 1938, Birmingham City Archives, Birmingham CUA. The rent strike took place May–July 1939; see *Birmingham Post*, 10 Jan., 6 Apr., 3 May, 4 Jul. 1939.

[63] *Durham and the North East Coast: report of the Labour party's commission of enquiry into the distressed areas* (April 1937); *South Wales: report of the Labour party's commission of enquiry into the distressed areas* (May 1937); *Lancashire: report of the Labour party's commission of enquiry into the distressed areas* (September 1937).

[64] H. Dalton et al., *A programme of immediate action: interim report of the Labour party's commission of enquiry into the distressed areas* (1937), 2–3.

250   Reputations of Government

Commissioners with a cabinet minister equipped with a bigger budget, the authority to approve full-cost grants, and the power to control the location of new businesses; expanding the boundaries of the Special Areas; the immediate raising of the school-leaving age to fifteen; the expansion of health services; and public work schemes to improve transport links and 'spring clean' derelict industrial sites.[65]

Labour claimed that public indignation at the condition of the distressed areas was felt 'in all parts of the country and in all sections of the community'.[66] In doing so it set about trying to recast the plight of the depressed regions into a sweeping nationwide indictment of the government. This process of historicising the decade continued into the 1940s and beyond, with far-reaching consequences for how the British public remembered – or reimagined – the 1930s.[67] In the short term there were more modest, but still significant, rewards to reap from such a process. Some of the government's most unexpected by-election defeats occurred in southern seats with low unemployment. Here Labour sought to cultivate not only sympathy with the distressed areas but also new grievances of nationwide relevance, one such being the increased cost of living, which dominated the contest in Islington North. While the unsuccessful Conservative candidate campaigned on the government's twin record of economic recovery and peace, his Labour opponent, Leslie Haden-Guest, attacked the government for the rise in food prices caused by increased taxes on consumers and subsidies for producers.[68] The *Daily Mirror* continued the campaign by ridiculing the 'physical jerkers of the Government health crusade':

Cost of living has risen 33 per cent in four years. British Medical Association's recommended *minimum* diet for health in a male adult – cost about 6s. a week. Now nearly 8s. a week. Will the jerks provide the extra cash for the health diet minimum?[69]

A number of protests took place, including a mass rally of Lancashire housewives in Manchester. The interests of the housewife consumer were also taken up by the Liberal party, which ran a well-publicised nationwide campaign culminating in the presentation of a parliamentary petition signed by more than 800,000 housewives.[70] As a result, the cost of living, together with the charge that government policy was protecting vested interests in the

[65] Ibid., 3–15.   [66] Ibid., 2.
[67] See A. Thorpe, 'Myth and counter-myth in Second World War British politics', in C. Williams & A. Edwards (eds.), *The art of the possible: politics and governance in modern British history, 1885–1997: essays in memory of Duncan Tanner* (Manchester, 2015), 121–42.
[68] *The Times*, 9, 13 Oct. 1937.
[69] *Daily Mirror*, 11 Oct. 1937, 11 Jan. 1938 (original emphasis).
[70] *Daily Mirror*, 19 Nov. 1937; *Yorkshire Post*, 3 Feb. 1938; *The Scotsman*, 3 Feb. 1938.

The Unravelling of National Anti-Socialism? 251

Conservative party, became a source of contention – enough to provoke a reply from the Conservative party in the form of a leaflet.[71]

Another grievance was the threat allegedly posed by the government's handling of the rearmament programme, including to the maintenance of public services. A fortnight after the famous Oxford by-election was won by a pro-appeasement Conservative, the government lost in Dartford, where the Conservative campaign focused on recovery and Chamberlain's diplomatic triumph in Munich: 'a vote for me', explained the candidate, 'is, in effect, a vote of thanks to Mr. Neville Chamberlain for salvation from the unspeakable horrors of war'.[72] While the Labour candidate first focused her attack on the government's foreign policy, it was her subsequent claim that the government intended to make 'cuts' in social services, in order to spend more on rearmament, which appeared materially to have swung the poll in her favour.[73] While emergency cuts in the name of national solvency proved feasible in the crisis atmosphere of 1931, discretionary cuts were fraught with political perils. Having launched a scathing attack on the government's inadequate defence preparations, which it claimed to be the real rationale behind the government's capitulation to Hitler in Munich, the Labour leadership argued that the sacrifices necessary for the funding of national defence 'must be made by those best able to bear them', not by curtailing public services. In a manifesto published ahead of the municipal elections, Labour argued categorically that 'the social services must be maintained' as an integral part of ensuring the nation's defence.[74] This commitment, argued Attlee, stood in stark contrast to 'the Gradgrind economy campaign' of the government, whose rearmament programme looked likely only to favour the industrial profiteer, now once more the subject of disapproval in the popular press.[75] Labour thus emerged from the shadows of Munich with a programme that neatly aligned the socialist ideals of national control (of arms manufacture, food production, finance, transport) with the national interest.

---

[71] Finance & general committee, 17 Feb. 1938, Stockton CA, STCO, D/X 322/5.

[72] *The Times*, 2 Nov. 1938.

[73] Ever since defence expenditure was raised in 1937, the Conservative party had been at pains to explain that spending on social services would remain protected ('Notes for a speech: the budget', *CAJ*, May 1937, 115). The spectre of Conservative 'cuts' commanded all the more public attention because Jennie Adamson, the Labour candidate, cited Walter Elliot, Minister of Health, as saying that rearmament would make 'inroads' on the social services budget – a statement he immediately refuted and claimed was 'lifted out of context' (*The Times*, 1, 2 Nov. 1938). Nonetheless, within days the argument was repeated by Labour politicians in municipal elections and parliamentary by-elections elsewhere (e.g., *Western Morning News*, 31 Oct. 1938, *The Scotsman*, 9 Nov. 1938).

[74] *The Times*, 29 Oct. 1938.

[75] *The Times*, 22 Oct. 1938; *Daily Mirror*, 19, 29 Oct., 16 Nov. 1938.

252   Reputations of Government

Critically for the government, Labour's efforts coincided with a renaissance of polemical discourse, both investigative and fictive. George Orwell's famous account of life among the unemployed and working poor of Wigan appeared in 1937. So did A. J. Cronin's bestselling realist novel about malpractice and institutional decay in the medical profession, *The Citadel*, which 'impressed' more contemporaries than any book except the Bible, according to a Gallup poll.[76] At the same time the Mass Observation project got underway, dedicated to building an 'anthropology of ourselves' through the fieldwork of observers nationwide.[77] Its publications, though infrequent in the pre-war years, served to articulate public sentiment sometimes at odds with the National government – including a corrective to the pro-Chamberlain hysteria that seized the national press at the time of Munich.[78] That same year witnessed the launch of the *Picture Post*, a staunchly anti-fascist and mostly left-leaning current affairs magazine with a circulation totalling almost a million and a half by early 1939.[79] That Labour might exploit these sources of social and political commentary was hardly a new threat. Extracts from H. V. Morton's travelogue, *What I Saw in the Slums* (1933), in which he describes the slums of Leeds, appeared in the *Daily Herald*, the newspaper part-owned by the TUC, as well as in a Labour pamphlet, *A City of Back to Backs*, within months of their publication.[80] The radio, too, could be a vehicle for 'tendencious [sic] Socialist propaganda'. Writing to the Director General of the BBC in 1934, the Conservative party chairman argued that 'the "Poverty in Plenty" talks, the title of which is itself part of the Left wing jargon, have been used very subtly by Left wing theorists to secure publicity for their view'.[81]

Labour exploitation of the work of 'independent' public experts continued later into the decade,[82] but the relationship between contemporary public discourse and leftist politics became altogether more threatening for the Conservatives following the establishment of the Left Book Club in 1936. Although ostensibly a Popular Front initiative designed to unite

[76] R. McKibbin, 'Politics and the medical hero: A. J. Cronin's *The Citadel*', *EHR*, 123 (2008), 651–78, 651.
[77] C. Madge & T. Harrisson, *Mass-Observation* (London, 1937), 10.
[78] C. Madge & T. Harrisson, *Britain by Mass-Observation* (Harmondsworth, 1939), 23–108.
[79] T. Hopkinson (ed.), *Picture Post, 1938–1950* (London, 1970), 11.
[80] J. Giles & T. Middleton (eds.), *Writing Englishness, 1900–1950: an introductory sourcebook on national identity* (London, 1995), 250–3, 268. For a letter protesting this 'socialist belittlement of Leeds', see *Yorkshire Post*, 16 Mar. 1934.
[81] Memorandum by Chief Publicity Officer to Miss Gow, 30 Nov. 1934, and Stonehaven to Reith, 3 Dec. 1934, Bodleian Library, Oxford, CPA, CCO 4/1/23.
[82] E.g., Dr M'Gonigle and Sir John Orr are cited as authorities in Dalton, *A programme of immediate action*, 15.

The Unravelling of National Anti-Socialism?

opposition to the National government, a majority of LBC members were Labour and regarded the movement as distinctly Labour – as did local Conservatives, who monitored its activities with palpable concern.[83] By 1939 it had almost 57,000 members and 1,200 local groups. In addition to holding discussions, lectures, and socials, these groups acted as 'recruiting centres' for the Labour left and encouraged closer activist cooperation with cooperative societies, trade unions, and the League of Nations Union.[84] Identified by Mass Observation as operating one of the dominant propaganda campaigns of the period,[85] the LBC reached beyond Labour's heartlands and prospered in southern suburban seats, hinting ominously at the revival of middle-class radicalism. If this radicalism was in part borne of the anti-fascist sentiment that animated many LBC books, it also reflected the added scrutiny brought to bear on the government's economic record. *The Times* published a series of themed articles in 1938 describing Scotland's return to depression.[86] With unemployment back up to nearly two million by January 1939, the *Picture Post* published a feature article on the long-term unemployed based on the experience of one Alfred Smith of Peckham and his daily search for work.[87] Whereas earlier in the decade this kind of investigative journalism could be used by the government to frame policy responses, it now appeared too unambiguously critical of the government to favour any party except Labour.

Preserving the National Vote

The best available indicators of voting intention show that public support for the National government remained, on the whole, remarkably stable up to 1940. Notwithstanding the infancy of polling techniques, it is worth noting that only twice during Chamberlain's government did the British Institute of Public Opinion find a majority intending to vote for the 'Opposition', in April 1938 (54 per cent) and January 1939 (51 per cent).[88] Yet the combination of municipal interventionism and neighbourhood

---

[83] E.g., AGM, 18 Mar. 1937, Home Counties North Area, ARE 8/1/1.
[84] P. Laity (ed.), *Left Book Club anthology* (London, 2001), ix–xxxi.
[85] M. Hinton, *The Mass Observers: a history, 1937–1949* (Oxford, 2013), 77, 77n.
[86] While the North Hillington industrial estate brought fifty or so new firms to the Special Area, Scotland as a whole was falling behind. In Dundee, despite government contracts, the jute factories continued to lose trade because of cheap Indian imports and the city was unable to compete with Hillington to attract new industries of its own. *The Times*, 20, 21 Jun. 1938, 27 Jun. 1939; *Dundee Courier*, 22 Jan., 1 Mar. 1938.
[87] 'Unemployed!', *Picture Post*, 21 Jan. 1939.
[88] 'Public Opinion', *Cavalcade*, 16 Apr. 1938, 11; J. Hinton, P. Thompson & I. Liddell, British Institute of Public Opinion (Gallup) Polls, 1938–1946 [computer file], Colchester, Essex: UK Data Archive, Apr. 1996, SN: 3331, http://dx.doi.org/10.5255/UKDA-SN-3331-1.

254   Reputations of Government

organisation displayed by Labour, at a time of industrious polemicising by the left, suggested that Labour was in a position to break out of the heartlands to which it had retreated in 1931. A burning question for the Conservative party on the eve of war was how best to preserve its electoral position. Almost a decade on from the perfect anti-socialist moment – a historical 'accident' whose opportunities were inevitably to diminish with time – how should the party keep supporters active and mobilised?

Two responses can be discerned. The first was the decision to fight the next election as a member of the National government. Not all activists were satisfied with the state of relations between the National parties: the South Tottenham Conservative Association, having stood down their candidate in favour of National Labour in 1931, resented the inter-party agreement that prevented a Conservative candidate from standing, and it is doubtful if the Dunbartonshire association would have remained so sanguine had the National candidature passed to the Liberal Nationals following the by-election defeat in 1936.[89] Yet such demurrals concerned the question of candidature, not membership of the government. Given how Labour's threat to the government's reputation might reasonably be expected to prompt a return to the comforting certainties of party, as happened in 1922, it is notable that such sentiment was conspicuous mostly by its absence. The widespread disaffection with the government reported among farmers, compounded by Labour's launch of a new agricultural policy, did not generate debates about the merits of the government among party members in North Norfolk or Devizes. Benefits, including the backing of Liberal voters, were sufficiently discernible still.[90] In light of the changing nature of the urban and especially suburban electorates, it is perhaps less surprising that Conservatives preferred the cross-party security of the National government. Nonetheless, their position serves to highlight the degree to which Conservative organisations, so highly partisan in the 1920s, had come to embrace the National government as instrumental to their survival.

The second response came in the form of 'political education'. In a manner that betrayed the impact of the left's resurgence on Conservative self-confidence, sections of the right set out to respond in

---

[89] Council meeting, 2 Mar. 1938, Home Counties North Area, ARE 8/1/1; joint meeting with Liberal National committee, 1 Apr. 1936, Dunbartonshire UA, 12264/3.

[90] A canvasser who toured ten of the larger villages within the Devizes division reported 'many Liberals who support the National Government . . . and several small farmers who told her they were really Conservatives but would not vote at all at the next Election unless the Government improved its agricultural policy'. Secretary's report to executive committee of women's association, 31 Jan. 1938, Devizes CA, 2305/13.

The Unravelling of National Anti-Socialism? 255

kind to the polemical discourse emanating from Labour. The Right Book Club was established in 1937 to counteract the influence of the LBC. Tasked with 'opposing and exposing Left propaganda . . . [and] educating an active and effective fighting body' in the constituencies, it was intended to instruct party members in political debate.[91] Interest was shown early on in Yorkshire and associated 'Discussion Classes' were organised by the Conservatives in Ilford and Epping and elsewhere, but in general these were considerably less active than LBC groups and national membership stood at just 20,000 in 1939.[92] Further educational efforts were initiated by Conservative Central Office and implemented by party staff in the Area organisations. These included discussion groups, sometimes called 'Ashridge Circles' after the party's training college for staff and followers, and were meant to equip activists for the task of debunking Labour propaganda. So too were the Listening Groups, which brought party members together to monitor, listen to, and discuss broadcast material on the radio.[93] Both were symptomatic of Conservative attempts to harness the ethos of the adult education movement, whose influence on the left in this period is well documented. The Listening Groups, in particular, imitated a form of educative recreation already established among voluntary organisations including the WI, the YMCA, and the Workers' Educational Association.[94] Meanwhile, the Conservative Teachers' Circles, also established in 1937, were intended to scotch any public assumption that 'teachers were all Socialists' and encourage Conservative teachers to proclaim their beliefs publicly. According to the party chairman, the Teachers' Circles would also guide government policy on education, at a time when fears over the susceptibility of juveniles to socialist propaganda were growing.[95]

However, fighting the war of ideas remained secondary to fighting the battle of popular appeals. Cultural hegemony was a desirable ambition

[91] 'The Right Book Club', *CAJ*, Feb. 1938, 31–3.
[92] *Yorkshire Post*, 7 Mar. 1937; *Birmingham Mail*, 10 Mar. 1939; annual report, 1936–37, Ilford CA, 90/61/1/1. Birmingham Conservatives declined the RBC's invitation to collaborate (management committee, 14 Oct. 1938, Birmingham CUA). On the RBC's publications, see E. H. H. Green, *Ideologies of Conservatism: Conservative political ideas in the twentieth century* (Oxford, 2002), ch.5.
[93] CCO expected constituency associations to establish such groups with the assistance of Area organisers. Executive committee report, 19 Mar. 1938, Northern Counties Area, NRO 3303/2; advisory committee, 17 Nov. 1937, West Yorkshire Archive Service, Yorkshire Area, WYL 529/3; education sub-committee, 3 Feb., 20 Jun. 1938, Home Counties North Area, ARE 8/1/1; also *CAJ*, Jun. 1937, 151, Apr. 1938, 110–11.
[94] The Home Counties North Area organisation invited the Educational Officer of the BBC to address them on the subject of listening groups and heard that over a thousand such groups met weekly. Council AGM, 18 Mar. 1937, Home Counties North Area, ARE 8/1/1.
[95] *The Times*, 22 Mar. 1937; *Yorkshire Post*, 2 Jan. 1939; executive committee report, 19 Mar. 1938, Northern Counties Area, NRO 3303/2.

256   Reputations of Government

sure enough, but one that few activists associated with instant electoral success or viewed as a formula for renewing the popular politics of the National government. The experience of London, where the party implemented the new methods most vigorously yet failed to dislodge Labour, did nothing to shake this assumption. With a general election expected before 1940, it served, if anything, to reaffirm local Conservative views of what drove electoral success. As one Leeds agent put it, whereas the political agenda was once dominated by tithes and church, it was now material 'problems' – 'economic, social, and political' – that demanded a political response.[96] The growing volume of constituency case work generated by successive reforms to unemployment benefit, pensions, insurance, housing, and public services crated new imperatives for local parties. Members found themselves expected to advise voters on how to access such schemes, in response to which agents began to suggest manuals in public policy as recommended reading.[97] Although technical and challenging, this aspect of economic recovery – the shifting expectations of voters as consumers of statutory and non-statutory services – presented opportunities to develop additional methods of representing local interests through advisory and advocacy roles. Soon these roles would be taken up systematically by the Citizens' Advice Bureau, established in 1939. But they provide a further glimpse of how, in the context of economic recovery, the rights of voters in relation to the emerging welfare state came to shape local Conservative practices in the constituencies.

If the popular Conservatism of the 1930s appeared endangered by the eve of war, it was not for the imminent breakdown of the National government. Local Conservatives on the one hand felt vulnerable to a revitalised Labour opposition and on the other in tension with the agenda of political education that once more preoccupied their party's central organisers. Shaping a public 'culture' of Conservatism to serve as a home for 'Right'-minded voters and an intellectual hinterland for the party in its battles with Labour, had been a key objective throughout the interwar years.[98] The organisational innovations of the late 1930s served a well-defined purpose in this sense; and the initiative of local parties in launching discussion groups, listening groups, and teachers' circles reveals a level of grassroots appreciation of the educative imperative. But the project of 'educating' the voter was liable to entail a return to the negative and contrived anti-socialism that prevailed before 1931.

---

[96] *CAJ*, Jan. 1936, 7–8.   [97] *CAJ*, Jul. 1937, 179–80, Jun. 1938, 140–1.
[98] C. Berthezène, *Training minds for the war of ideas: Ashridge College, the Conservative party and the cultural politics of Britain, 1929–1954* (Manchester, 2015); G. Love, 'The periodical press and the intellectual culture of Conservatism in interwar Britain', *HJ*, 57 (2014), 1027–56.

The Unravelling of National Anti-Socialism? 257

Headlam, as was his wont, decried the discussion groups and teachers' circles as the modish 'stunt' of 'wire-pullers' in the capital 'who knew little or nothing about rough and tumble politics'.[99] He was not alone. Agents who themselves showed commitment to political education in principle had doubts about its rate of electoral return. It was feared that it reached only those voters who were already 'unshakeable in their belief' and thus detracted from the critical task of converting voters.[100] After almost a decade in which a range of popular Conservatisms had rehabilitated in the name of economic recovery, the mantra of education once more threatened to stifle the demotic practice of appealing to voters' sense of material well-being.

[99] *The Headlam diaries, 1935–1951*, 110 (23 Apr. 1937), 119 (29 Nov. 1937).
[100] *CAJ*, Dec. 1938, 293–5.

Conclusion

This study of political campaigning, the place of central government in popular politics, and the shifting fortunes of British Conservatism between the wars, began with a simple question. Why did the Conservative party, temperamentally so hostile to coalition following its experience of the Lloyd George government in 1918–22, support membership of the National government from 1931? Support was, undoubtedly, contingent upon electoral success. With 473 seats in 1931 and 432 in 1935, out of a total of 615 and on 55 and 48 per cent of the vote respectively, the scale of the Conservatives' electoral performance was unprecedented and has remained so.[1] These results enabled the party to dominate its National Labour and Liberal National partners, thereby limiting the dissipation of party influence normally associated with power-sharing and obviating the reaction that in 1922 had led Conservatives to withdraw from the post-war coalition. Compared to Lloyd George, the Labour leader Ramsay MacDonald proved a more palatable non-Conservative prime minister, his public persona, though not unblemished given his stance during the war, standing in stark contrast to the Welsh Wizard's demagoguery. Moreover, the events of 1931 rendered him a peculiarly valuable asset for Conservative co-option, both as the embodiment of 'country before party' and, alongside Philip Snowden, the most authoritative inside witness to Labour's failure to respond decisively to the financial crisis.

While election outcomes and the contingencies of leadership and 'events' were critical to shaping how Conservatives assessed the viability of membership, they alone do not explain why and how party members reconciled themselves to the National government, nor how they made sense of their success in doing so. Previous studies have explored the formation and early years of the National government with reference to the actions, beliefs, and strategies of those political, financial, and

---

[1] Labour secured 393 of 635 seats in 1945 with 47.8 per cent share of the vote, and 419 of 659 seats in 1997 with 43.2 per cent share.

Conclusion 259

industrial figures who together formed the country's power elite.[2] But however necessary it is to understand the actions of the political leaders, an essential preliminary is to understand the opinion of the grassroots members on whose support, or at least acquiescence, they relied. This study has therefore sought to reconstruct the experiences of local Conservatives, locating them within their local and regional settings, and also in relation to the high-political strategy of the party leadership. The resulting analysis has highlighted important phenomena that shaped the character of popular politics, in particular those wrought from the fraught process of party members' acclimatisation to the extension of the franchise. In order to understand the assumptions and concerns with which the Conservatives entered the National government, we must understand at least four of these phenomena.

First, Conservative activists saw the task of cultivating the new electorate in resolutely local terms, reflecting their abiding commitment to pre-war understandings of what constituted popular Conservatism and how it operated. The active and public participation of leading local Conservatives was key to its operation. In reality, however, while overall party membership and subscriptions increased, local parties lamented the retreat of prominent figures from the arena of community politics. The waning fortunes of landowners, the impact of wartime inflation on middle-class incomes, and fear of embarrassing public humiliation at the hands of Labour, all took their toll. Traditionally, these figures had served as beacons of conspicuous partisanship, acting as local intermediaries between party and electorate and thus facilitating powerful social mechanisms for the maintenance of popular allegiance. Their retreat coincided with a trend towards non-aligned forms of associational life, frequently cited by historians and sociologists as advantageous to the Conservative party.[3] However, contemporary activists were acutely aware that voters had to be engaged within a finite public realm. For them, this space was now encroached on by the new associational movements of the 1920s, contested by municipal Labour and residual Liberalism, and rhetorically conceded by Baldwin's trademark disavowal of party politics. On the

---

[2] R. Bassett, *Nineteen thirty-one: political crisis* (London, 1958); P. Williamson, *National crisis and national government: British politics, the economy and empire, 1926–1932* (Cambridge, 1992).

[3] M. Stacey, *Tradition and change: a study of Banbury* (Oxford, 1960); M. Pugh, *The Tories and the people, 1880–1935* (Oxford, 1985); R. McKibbin, *Classes and cultures: England, 1918–1951* (Oxford, 1998), ch.3; L. Black, 'The lost world of young Conservatism', *HJ*, 51 (2008), 991–1024.

260   Reputations of Government

eve of the 1931 crisis, therefore, Conservative grassroots anxiety was shaped as much by disruption to Victorian norms of conducting local popular politics as by the principal challenges of mass democracy and socialism.

The world of popular politics was not, of course, entirely a social phenomenon. Another, second phenomenon, fundamental to how activists understood the doctrine of representative politics, concerned their perception of the local electorate's material interests. There is a methodological point here, for the scholarship on interwar Conservatism – more so than studies of local Labour politics – exemplifies the linguistic turn, which rightly cautioned historians against a sociologically deterministic reading of political behaviour and highlighted the capacity of politicians, through the agency of language and the reach of broadcast media, to construct and contest voters' world view.[4] But as Frank Trentmann has argued, such a conception of politics presents a 'lopsided view of representation' as something concerned more with the 'identity' of voters than the 'objects of concern' to them.[5] The most influential explanations of Conservative electoral success after 1918 argue that through its national publicity appeals the party succeeded in creating class and gender stereotypes whose exemplary sensibilities – of fiscal orthodoxy, faith in the constitution, hostility to organised labour – shaped voters' political consciousness.[6] Indeed, so influential have these accounts been that the material realities of voters' daily lives, as experienced and perceived by party activists locally, have remained mainly outside the gaze of most modern treatments. However, the constituencies studied here remind us of the enduring relevance of community interests to political discourse. These were economic interests, embedded in the historical industrial and occupational make-up of each constituency and its wider region, as well as the more protean social and infrastructural concerns wrought by residential and demographic change. They commonly cut across class and gender. Activists, though in the business of constructing appeals, did not presume to do so in a vacuum. Their autonomy as local architects of popular Conservatism was circumscribed by existing and inescapable agendas defined by trade, employment and

---

[4] S. Pedersen, 'What is political history now?', in D. Cannadine (ed.), *What is history now?* (Basingstoke, 2002), 36–56, esp. 44–5.

[5] F. Trentmann, 'Materiality in the future of history: things, practices, and politics', *JBS*, 48 (2009), 283–307, 301.

[6] R. McKibbin, 'Class and conventional wisdom: the Conservative party and the "public" in inter-war Britain', in his *Ideologies of class: social relations in Britain, 1880–1950* (Oxford, 1990); D. Jarvis, 'British Conservatism and class politics in the 1920s', *EHR*, 111 (1996), 59–84; D. Jarvis, 'Mrs Maggs and Betty: the Conservative appeal to women voters in the 1920s', *TCBH*, 5 (1994), 129–52.

Conclusion 261

economic prosperity, living standards, and amenities. Grassroots experience is thus intelligible only upon realising that the primary objective, as they saw it, was to represent the industrial and social interests of the constituency, less so to construct constituencies based upon formulaic identity.

Yet by no means did the community and regional focus of popular Conservatism render it parochial, for the third phenomenon is the growing significance of modern central government to the enterprise of popular politics between the wars. Electoral strategies in the constituencies rested on the assumption that living standards could be successfully managed by government initiative. These were closely tied to the health of the regional economies, the heterogeneity of which ensured that grassroots priorities for central government often appeared segmented. But for as long as the idea of a 'national' economy continued to gain traction in political discourse in the way described by Jim Tomlinson, partly shaped by interwar Conservatism's retreat from a predominantly laissez-faire conception of the economy, so these diverse priorities coalesced around a political instinct that favoured active, at times interventionist, government.[7] The idea that electoral support could be garnered from the pursuit of active government, rather than by protection against government encroachment, became more universally held after 1918. Economic and social problems, wrought from the dislocation of war and exacerbated by the failure of post-war reconstruction and the industrial depression of the 1920s, compelled activists to lobby the government – and to be seen to be doing so while also eschewing collectivist or corporatist outcomes at odds with Conservative anti-socialism. To this end, the dialogic relationship between the plebeian politics of the constituency and the political authority of central state institutions remained a crucial concern for activists. Above all, they sought displays of competence. Public perceptions of a party's competence in government, according to political scientists, can be understood in terms of its ability to gain and retain long-term 'ownership' of a set of issues – housing, unemployment insurance, industrial safeguarding, education, local amenities – as well as its performance in handling exogenous shocks like economic crises.[8]

If the party was to succeed in showcasing its competence to govern, the objectives and accomplishments of its leading figures had to be communicated effectively. The advent of radio broadcasting undoubtedly brought new possibilities that Baldwin and Central Office quickly exploited. It

[7] J. Tomlinson, *Managing the economy, managing the people: narratives of economic life in Britain from Beveridge to Brexit* (Oxford, 2017).
[8] J. Green & W. Jennings, *The politics of competence: parties, public opinion and voters* (Cambridge, 2017).

262   Reputations of Government

enabled the party leader to reach millions of voters simultaneously, including swing groups like anti-socialist Liberal voters whose favour was critical to Conservative success. But efficient communication was not always effective communication. For even in the early age of mass broadcasting, activists continued to understand an effective political appeal to be a dialectical process involving the claims of local Conservatives to champion the aspirations of voters on the one hand and the administrative responsiveness of national leaders on the other, with the former drawing its authority from the latter. This is why the fourth phenomenon is the reception of national political rhetoric among party activists. Alongside their recognition of radio's unprecedented reach, Conservative activists held grave doubts about the relevance of Baldwin's message. He crafted his apolitical, classless, and ecumenical rhetoric precisely in the belief that 'what we were at present fighting was not a programme, but an atmosphere, which no amount of promulgation of counter programmes would affect'.[9] It was for this reason, according to Philip Williamson, that Baldwin 'did not intend anything so pointless and sterile as to represent or interpret "public opinion"', prioritising instead 'the presentation of an appropriate political culture'.[10] Many local Conservatives lamented this strategy, finding that it marginalised policy and administration as the basis of popular appeals. Despite the extensive programme of social reforms enacted after the 1924 election, and (notwithstanding the General Strike) a period of political stability and party unity not experienced since the war, Baldwin failed to capitalise on the government's record. In consequence he ceded the political initiative to Labour, whose success in both municipal elections and parliamentary by-elections in the late 1920s highlighted the vulnerability of working-class as well as suburban Conservatism. Meanwhile in places as diverse as Devizes, Ilford, and Leeds, the Conservatives also feared the susceptibility of voters to a newly radicalised Liberal programme pledging traditional land reform alongside neo-Keynesian policies of public works. In the face of Labour encroachment and the prospect of a Liberal revival, Baldwin's Conservatism, for all its rhetorical coherence, came to signify inaction in government.

Yet in the 1930s Baldwinite Conservatism came into its own in response to the decade's prevailing contingencies, its political ecumenicism proving critical to the formation of the cross-party National government and its Christian message rendered pressingly relevant by the

[9] *Memoirs of a Conservative: J. C. C. Davidson's memoirs and papers, 1910–37*, ed., R. Rhodes James (London, 1967), 306 (Baldwin reported in Lord Irwin to Davidson, 25 Feb. 1930).
[10] P. Williamson, 'The doctrinal politics of Stanley Baldwin', in M. Bentley (ed.), *Public and private doctrine: essays in British history presented to Maurice Cowling* (Cambridge, 1993), 188.

Conclusion 263

spectre of fascism. But if the National government showcased Baldwin's unique brand of Conservatism, so too did it facilitate the local Conservatisms envisaged by party activists. The financial crisis, the depression in trade, and the scale of unemployment necessarily pivoted the national political agenda towards avowedly materialist concerns, marking an alignment of priorities between the party leadership and the party grassroots that dissolved many of the tensions that previously hindered the aspirations of local Conservatives. By exploiting this moment, the Conservative party was able to re-cast its anti-socialist mantra to considerable effect. A more plebeian critique of Labour rule was forged from the lived experience of a society now sliding into poverty, displacing the constitutionalist refrain previously prioritised by the party leadership. At the 1931 election the party emphasised the manifest cost to the country of a socialist government incapable of responding to the crisis and the consequential harm done to the economic viability and material well-being of local communities. Staking its reputation on the pursuit of economic recovery, the National government cultivated a narrative of skilful stewardship orchestrated by Neville Chamberlain as Chancellor of the Exchequer and implemented by leading administrators whose schemes responded to the sectoral and regional interests upon which the party grassroots campaigned. Examples of this include Walter Elliott in agriculture and subsequently in Scotland, Henry Betterton and Oliver Stanley in industrial and labour matters, Hilton Young in health, and Kingsley Wood in housing and infrastructure.

The role of policy innovation in engineering economic recovery in the 1930s has long preoccupied economic historians and continues to be debated to this day.[11] But the 'fact' of recovery was rarely disputed among Conservative contemporaries, even by self-styled progressives like Macmillan who advocated a more expansionary state solution to unemployment. By 1935 most activists regarded the narrative of recovery, as publicised by the party and the National Publicity Bureau, to be the most effective projection of the work of central government offered to them since the war. Not all the government departments most closely associated with the recovery were headed by Conservatives; Walter Runciman, a Liberal National, dominated the Board of Trade (1931–7) and his colleague, Sir Godfrey Collins, the Scottish Office (1932–6). But

---

[11] D. Winch, *Economics and policy: a historical study* (London, 1969), ch.10; S. Howson, *Domestic monetary management in Britain, 1919–1938* (Cambridge, 1975); S. Howson & D. Winch, *The Economic Advisory Council, 1930–39: a study in economic advice during the depression and recovery* (Cambridge, 1977); A. Booth, 'Britain in the 1930s: a managed economy?', EcHR, 40 (1987), 499–522; B. Eichengreen, *Hall of mirrors: the great depression, the great recession, and the uses and misuses of history* (Oxford, 2015).

264   Reputations of Government

for as long as 'recovery' constituted a usable narrative of government, and the example of senior Liberal Nationals like Sir John Simon assisted appeals to local Liberal voters, the electoral advantages of the National government remained clear – and explain why so many local Conservative parties embraced coalition government in the 1930s having rejected it so decisively in 1922.

Paradoxically, Conservative activists also used the new 'National' politics of the 1930s to revive the faltering traditions of localism in British politics. They emphasised certain national policies depending on the dominant socio-economic group in the constituency. The range of idiosyncratic appeals extended across different regional economies reflected the ideological pluralism of British Conservatism. It also points further to the dialectical construction of both Conservative appeals and Conservative ideology in the mass democratic age. While studies of political culture have focused comprehensively on the party's appeals, future studies would do well to explore the consequences of the party's electoral strategies for the British state. For Conservatives from across a range of constituencies held one assumption increasingly in common after 1918: that the administration of government should be an active enterprise, its priority to champion existing socio-economic interests and not to arbitrate between them. This assumption was not often articulated in ideological terms, shaped as it often was by practical considerations of electoral competition, but nor as anti-socialists did activists feign to be ideologically rootless. Above all, as we have seen, there could be no guarantee that governments produced the desired effect. Given how economic recovery eluded large parts of industrial Britain, ultimately aiding Labour's march to 1945, the National government itself fell short of the ideal of nationwide economic recovery. Yet through measures including slum clearance and housing, unemployment insurance, public amenities, and the Special Areas schemes – designed to relieve regional poverty through the proceeds of national economic recovery – most contemporary Conservatives continued to embrace the government as an asset whose actions complemented philanthropic efforts by the party in the constituencies.

Through its pursuit of recovery and relief, the National government represented the biggest peacetime break with government orthodoxy since the New Liberals. After 1932, it was not just in respect of the trading system that economic protectionism proved a radical measure, although this was important given popular understating of national solvency as a matter primarily of trade. It was also in respect of the scope it afforded for ministerial intervention, which demonstrated to local parties the political and electoral capital inherent in a quasi-corporatist system in which MPs – protectionists and free traders – could publicly lobby

Conclusion 265

government on behalf of regional and sectoral interest groups. The maintenance of low interest rates to boost consumer demand; quota systems to compel agricultural modernisation; tariff protection to facilitate industrial diversification; central state aid to assist economic planning and infrastructural development in the distressed areas – though modest by the standards of the subsequent Attlee settlement, these controls represented a new immediacy between the national political economy and everyday life. Notwithstanding occasional and localised protests, the Conservative grassroots proved remarkably accommodating of such statist and technocratic innovation, avoiding the internal rifts that bedevilled both their own and the Liberal party in the Edwardian years.[12] Few of them thought to articulate an ideological defence of this statism, which may explain why mainstream Conservative statism has remained marginal to histories of 1930s Britain for so long. This also explains why the likes of Macmillan and Adams emerge as maverick figures at odds with party opinion.[13] But across a range of constituencies, the project of economic recovery generated a profound political impulse in favour of the statist, nationalistic, technocratic state – the kind that David Edgerton has recently argued was distinguished from its nineteenth-century liberal heritage as much by its autarky as its welfarism.[14] It was the National government's politics of recovery, as much as Keynes's academic interventions, that laid the foundations for what became the post-war settlement. Indeed, the Conservative party was the first to recognise the political potential of the programmatic, activist government that became so prevalent in Britain after the war, mobilising patriotic sentiment behind economic nationalism and cultivating the interests of different sectional groups.

That the political dividend of this important moment of radical Conservatism was so soon dissipated is testament to how Labour in the 1940s, building on the polemical discourse begun by the Left Book Club, successfully cast public memory of the interwar past. The Labour manifesto, *Let Us Face the Future,* urged voters to 'think back over the depressions of the 20 years between the wars, when there were precious few public controls of any kind and the Big Interests had things all their own way. Never was so much injury done to so many by so few.' The party's

---

[12] Cf. E. H. H. Green, *The crisis of Conservatism: the politics, economics and ideology of the Conservative party, 1880–1914* (London, 1995). For contrasting grassroots experiences of the New Liberalism, see P. Clarke, *Lancashire and the New Liberalism* (Cambridge, 1971) and G. L. Bernstein, *Liberalism and Liberal politics in Edwardian England* (London, 1986).

[13] E. H. H. Green, 'The Conservative party and Keynes', in Green & D. Tanner (eds.), *The strange survival of Liberal England: political leaders, moral values and the reception of economic debate* (Cambridge, 2007), 186–211.

[14] D. Edgerton, *The rise and fall of the British nation: a twentieth-century history* (London, 2018).

266   Reputations of Government

posters at the 1950 election similarly evoked mass unemployment, featuring images of the Jarrow Crusade ('Remember? Don't give the Tories another chance') and, in one famous example, an elderly couple whose stoic gaze betrayed the hardships of betrayals past ('They remember – and they're voting Labour').[15] Indeed, two themes stand out in Labour's post-war rhetoric: the notion that interwar Britain was a land of preventable poverty, especially for the working classes who suffered the brunt of unemployment; and that interwar governments, because of the Conservatives' failure to honour the promises of post-war reconstruction made during and after the First World War, betrayed the interests of British society as a whole. This became a conventional wisdom that shaped attitudes in post-war Britain – 'the script of British social democracy', according to James Vernon. It entered further into folk memory through the work of leftist historians like Noreen Branson and Claude Cockburn.[16]

In this context, where so many narratives of post-war reconstruction were set up in antipathy to the interwar years, it is remarkable to see how far the Conservative party initially disavowed its time in office, and in particular the work of the National government. In 1945, the party naturally preached the urgent relevance of Conservative ideals to the pressing agenda of post-war reconstruction, yet offered little concerted defence of their application under the National government. It presented Conservative social reform as a timeless commitment stretching back to Disraeli and to Shaftesbury, and the free market – not the protectionist experiment of the 1930s – as the optimal model to boost production.[17] Not until 1949 was there a direct rebuttal formulated, in the wake of the devaluation crisis that momentarily lent credence to warnings of another 'economic collapse' under Labour. 'To divert public attention from their own shortcomings and failures', declared one pamphlet,

the Socialists are now assiduously plugging the legend of 'Tory misrule' ... no calumny, no matter how base, no allegation, no matter how sweeping, is disregarded in building up a picture in the public mind of a supposedly 'Dark Age' under the Tories before the war. Once this is done they feel they may safely

---

[15] Labour party, *Let Us Face the Future: a declaration of Labour policy for the consideration of the nation* (1945), 2; H. G. Nicholas, *The British general election of 1950* (London, 1951), 240–1.

[16] J. Vernon, *Hunger: a modern history* (Cambridge, MA, 2007), ch.8; N. Branson & M. Heinemann, *Britain in the nineteen thirties* (London, 1971); C. Cockburn, *The devil's decade* (London, 1973).

[17] E.g., *Forty years of progress* (1945) and *Who has worked for the workers?* (1945) set out to validate the Conservative record, but mainly up to 1929. For the most unapologetic defence of their record in the interwar period as a whole, see *50 things the Tories have done* (1947).

Conclusion 267

compare the infinitely worse conditions to-day with that period without fear of contradiction.

The pamphlet proceeded to set the 'factual truth' under the following headings: restoration of agriculture, extension of employment, rising standard of living, improved health standards, industrial aid and reform, and imperial development.[18] It was too late: by the 1950s, even the party leadership had internalised the past as polemicised by the left. When challenged to choose between two types of Toryism – the 'humanitarian Toryism ... of the welfare state' and the 'neglectful' 'big-majority Toryism' of the pre-war variety – Anthony Eden appeared to accept the latter characterisation, correcting it only with reference to the Conservative record in housing.[19] Like most of his party after 1945, Eden complied with the hostile, condemnatory, and polemical historicisation of interwar Conservatism.

Later in the century, Thatcherites' more admiring evocations of the National government failed to challenge the idea that interwar Conservatism practised archetypal laissez-faire government. The government's example, according to Thatcher, charted the path to salvation for the Conservative party following its post-war apostasy. According to her close ally, Sir Keith Joseph, 'It is often forgotten that the thirties was a period of growth, expanding employment, [and] rising living standards for a majority of manual workers.' He attributed the recovery – 'well before Keynes published his General Theory' – to the abandonment of gold in 1931, which represented the true Conservative's design to 'let the economy look after itself' following the hubristic interventionism that characterised the restoration of gold in the 1920s.[20] Few Conservative activists in the 1930s would have recognised, much less championed, such an ideal of minimalist government.

In reality, the popular Conservatism of the 1930s and 1950s shared much in common – above all a statist culture of government. As John Ramsden has noted, the party's winning coalition of voters in the 1950s was built on similar foundations to that of the National government, using housebuilding and property ownership, fiscal orthodoxy and tax cuts, and social reforms to rally support from skilled workers and the middle class.[21] However, the precise political economy projected by the government and harnessed by local parties differed between the periods. The Conservative party moved away from overt protectionism and began to

[18] *The truth about the inter-war years: an exposure of the Socialist myth*, by M. Maybury with a foreword by R. A. Butler (1949), 11.
[19] Conservative party election broadcast, 17 May 1955; *The Times*, 18 May 1955.
[20] K. Joseph, *Monetarism is not enough*, with foreword by M. Thatcher (London, 1976), 6–7.
[21] J. Ramsden, '"A party for owners or a party for earners?" How far did the British Conservative party really change after 1945?', *TRHS*, 37 (1987), 49–63.

268   Reputations of Government

talk the emancipatory language of the free market.[22] The purpose of doing so was to forge a coherent Conservative vision of welfare capitalism in which socialist state controls were roundly condemned but welfarism embraced. Standing on this national platform, the party commanded over 13 million votes in each of the 1951, 1955, and 1959 elections – over a million more than in 1931. But, compared to the 1930s, these votes were drawn from a narrower range of constituencies as Labour consolidated its gains in the wake of 1945. Mobilising nearly 14 million votes in 1951 and never fewer than 12 million up to February 1974, the post-war Labour party amassed support in the industrial regions, including in seats like Stockton and Dunbartonshire that had appeared marginal in the 1920s, as well as in rural seats including Norfolk North and Pembrokeshire. This was offset for the Conservatives by the Liberal swing in their favour in southern boroughs and suburbs, and in parts of Lancashire and Leeds.[23] Electorally, therefore, the long-term legacies of the National government proved to be mixed for the Conservative party.

Even so, Conservative membership of the cross-party government signified a more permanent development in British political culture after the First World War: the normalisation of activist government in popular politics. The search to rehabilitate local brands of popular Conservatism rooted in community interests, which continued to define grassroots ideas of representation, compelled local parties to forfeit the prospect of single-party government and to support the National government. The expediency of this decision rested not only with the capacity of the cross-party government to neutralise the Liberal threat; crucially, it also derived from grassroots embracement of activist government in whose project of national economic recovery the regional and sectoral interests of voters loomed centre stage. In this way the National Conservatism of the 1930s presided over the last great flowering of localist politics in post-Victorian Britain. Paradoxically, it also did more than its opponents on the left to extend the appeal of modern government, eroding the Victorian ideals of the minimal state and ushering in an age of programmatic government.

---

[22] J. Freeman, 'Reconsidering "Set the people free": neoliberalism and freedom rhetoric in Churchill's Conservative party', *TCBH*, 29 (2018), 522–46, esp. 537–42.

[23] See M. Kinnear, *The British voter: an atlas and survey since 1885* (London, 1968), 58.

Appendix   Parties' Share of the Vote in the Constituency Case-Study Areas, 1918–1945

The following tables show the Conservative, Liberal, and Labour share of the vote in each of the constituency case studies, and surrounding seats, from 1918 to 1945. For each constituency an additional notional figure has been calculated to show the 'swing' in the Conservative party's share of the vote from the pre-war period (1885–1910) to the post-war years (from 1918 to the eve of the National government). This is calculated as the difference between the party's average share of the poll over six of the eight elections between 1885 and 1910, as calculated in Henry Pelling's study, and the party's average share of the poll over the five elections from 1918.[1]

Where the 1918 boundary changes prevent perfect comparisons, I have chosen the pre-war constituency – or combination of constituencies – that offers the closest alignment with the new post-war constituency.

Where the Conservatives did not contest the seat, or were returned unopposed, a probable share of the vote has been extrapolated from the preceding general election using the actual average swing in surrounding seats. Where the preceding general election was also uncontested, the extrapolation has worked backwards from the next subsequent contested election. The probable share appears within brackets and is underlined in the case of unopposed returns. For all regions, the greater the number of probable results calculated, the wider the margin of error, which is why in some cases (e.g., Gower and Pembrokeshire) it was decided that too little data was available to calculate reliably.

Key to Symbols:

Underlined poll figures denote the winning candidate (or unopposed return).

In two-member seats (e.g., Dundee, Norwich), I record the combined share of the vote where more than one Conservative candidate stood; in these cases, twice underlined signifies that both seats were won by the party.

---

[1] H. Pelling, *Social geography of British elections, 1885–1910* (London, 1967), 4–5.

Key

U'd = unopposed return
–   = no candidate
(%) = projected/extrapolated share of the Conservative vote

	(A) 1885–1910 avg	1918	1922	1923	1924	1929	(B) 1918–1931 avg	Swing in Con vote, A to B	1931	1935	1945
Stockton											
Conservative	47.3	(35.1)	(35.5)	34.3	42.0	36.1	36.6	−10.7	61.6	48.9	37.4
Co/N Liberal		U'd	38.0	34.5	24.9	22.7			–		–
Liberal		–	–	31.2	33.1	41.2				10.8	7.5
Labour		–	34.3						38.4	40.3	55.1
Sedgefield											
Conservative	47.3	42.1	40.5	50.0	52.7	39.5	45.0	−2.3	58.8	47.7	36.2
Co/N Liberal	(S E Durham)	–	–	–	–	12.8			–	–	–
Liberal		21.1	15.9	50.0	47.3	47.7			–	–	–
Labour		36.8	43.6						41.2	52.3	63.8
Seaham											
Conservative		(24.2)	24.6	28.7	34.5	13.9	25.2	−22.1	–	–	19.9
Co/N Liberal		–	–	–	–	10.7			–	–	
Liberal		58.7	15.5	71.3	65.5	72.5			–	–	–
Labour		41.3	59.9						43.7	68.2	80.1
Nat Labour									55.0	31.8	
Middlesbrough E											
Conservative	42.8	(38.6)	39.0	25.5	34.7	28.1	33.2	−9.6	–	43.7	34.9
Co/N Liberal	(Middlesbrough)	–	–	40.6	26.8	30.6			–	–	
Liberal		69.2	27.6	33.9	38.5	41.3			60.4	12.3	65.1
Labour		30.8	33.4						39.6	44.0	
Middlesbrough W											
Conservative		(30.6)	(31.0)	(29.8)	(34.5)	22.5	29.7	−13.1	–	–	–
Co/N Liberal		–	30.7	69.4	U'd	40.6			–	–	–
Liberal		67.2	69.4	30.6	–	36.9			66.6	36.2	46.5
Labour		32.8	–						33.4	33.7	53.5
Nat Labour										30.1	
Darlington											
Conservative	50.6	61.5	49.7	42.2	53.8	40.2	49.5	−1.1	60.7	55.2	30.0
Co/N Liberal		–	–	24.2	–	15.8			–	–	

(cont.)

	(A) 1885–1910 avg	1918	1922	1923	1924	1929	(B) 1918–1931 avg	Swing in Con vote, A to B	1931	1935	1945
Liberal		38.5	16.5	33.6	46.2	44.0			–	–	21.0
Labour		–	33.8						39.3	44.8	49.0
Bishop Auckland											
Conservative	34.4	(23.9)	(24.3)	23.1	(27.8)	14.1	21.0	–13.4	–	–	–
Co/N Liberal		37.3	46.3	25.7	44.9	30.1			51.4	–	35.9
Liberal		12.1	–	51.2	55.1	55.8			–	37.7	–
Labour		50.6	53.7						48.6	62.3	64.1
Barnard Castle											
Conservative	39.0	30.1	50.7	44.9	50.8	38.1	42.9	+3.9	55.3	44.1	41.7
Liberal		17.1	–	–	–	19.9			–	6.1	–
Labour		42.8	49.3	55.1	49.2	42.0			44.7	49.8	58.3
Durham											
Conservative	45.6	50.6	44.8	43.2	35.1	20.9	38.9	–6.7	–	–	–
Co/N Liberal	(Durham + Mid	–	–	–	–	–			–	40.9	33.8
Liberal	Durham)	–	–	56.8	10.0	22.3			50.4	–	–
Labour		49.4	55.2		54.9	56.8			49.6	59.1	66.2
Spennymoor											
Conservative		(27.2)	27.6	34.3	37.0	28.2	30.9	–14.7	43.8	28.8	23.2
Liberal		53.5	22.1	–	–	–			–	–	–
Labour		46.5	50.3	65.7	63.0	71.8			56.2	71.2	69.9
Avg Con swing		+0.4	–1.2	+4.7	–12.0			–9.0			
Avg Conservative share of vote in Stockton area	43.9						35.3				

Sources: H. Pelling, *Social geography of British elections, 1885–1910* (London, 1967); F. W. S. Craig, *British parliamentary election results, 1918–1949* (London, 1969); *Report of the Boundary Commission (England & Wales), Vols. II–III*, 1917 (Cd. 8757–8).

Appendix

By-elections 1918–1939

Darlington (28 February 1923)

Conservative	56.6
Labour	43.4

Darlington (17 February 1926)

Conservative	43.3
Liberal	12.2
Labour	44.5

Middlesbrough West (7 March 1928)

Conservative	27.8
Liberal	36.2
Labour	36.0

Bishop Auckland (7 February 1929)

Conservative	13.0
Liberal	29.9
Labour	57.1

	(A) 1885–1910 avg	1918	1922	1923	1924	1929	(B) 1918–1931 avg	Swing in Con vote, A to B	1931	1935	1945
Leeds W											
Conservative	43.0	–	(32.7)	33.6	42.5	33.0	35.5	−7.5	63.2	54.3	27.6
Co/N Liberal		61.9	–	–	–	–			–	–	–
Liberal		–	51.7	25.7	15.0	19.8			–	–	13.3
Labour		29.5	48.3	40.7	42.5	47.2			36.8	45.7	59.1
Leeds C											
Conservative	50.4	–	50.0	56.2	59.6	41	51.5	+1.1	–	–	34.2
Co/N Liberal		70.6	–	–	–	–			–	–	–
Liberal		–	22.2	–	–	14.4			–	–	8.6
Labour		–	27.8	43.8	40.4	44.6			28.6	43.6	57.2
Nat Labour									71.4	56.4	
Leeds S											
Conservative	37.3	–	(28.1)	29.0	39.9	27.5	31.1	−6.2	42.1	43.0	25.6
Co/N Liberal		60.6	–	–	–	–			–	–	–
Liberal		–	46.3	26.8	13.8	20.0			17.8	–	13.4
Labour		31.5	53.7	44.2	46.3	52.5			40.1	46.0	61.0
Leeds SE											
Conservative	37.3	–	(27.8)	(28.7)	(38.3)	24.8	29.9	−7.4	47.4	34.3	15.9
Co/N Liberal	(Leeds S)	–	–	–	–	–			–	–	–
Liberal		–	41.1	36.8	41.1	–			–	–	12.2
Labour		U'd	58.9	63.2	58.6	75.2			52.6	65.7	71.9
Leeds N											
Conservative	52.0	–	51.4	54.0	70.0	48.2	55.9	+3.9	78.8	69.0	42.0
Co/N Liberal		74.7	–	–	–	–			–	–	–
Liberal		–	26.9	25.4	–	24.4			–	–	16.2
Labour		18.4	21.7	20.6	30.0	27.4			21.1	31.0	41.8

Leeds NE											
Conservative	43.3		75.5	46.1	46.7	57.8	47.0	54.6	+11.3	75.5	64.8	37.5
Liberal	(Leeds E)	–	29.5	22.0	10.6	20.5			–	–	9.4
Labour		24.5	24.4	31.3	31.6	32.5			24.5	35.2	53.1
Spen Valley											
Conservative	40.2	–	23.9	22.0	(31.6)	(18.1)	23.9	−16.3	–	–	–
Co/N Liberal		55.6	–	–	–	–			64.6	50.8	43.3
Liberal		–	39.2	40.6	56.9	51.7			–	–	–
Labour		44.4	36.9	37.4	43.1	47.7			35.4	49.2	56.7
Bradford E											
Conservative	47.8	–	(22.6)	23.5	(33.1)	(19.6)	24.7	−23.1	58.8	33.0	26.0
Liberal		21.0	21.4	28.4	50.1	45.3			–	18.7	14.3
Labour		37.9	45.4	48.1	49.9	54.7			–	21.7	44.9
Pudsey & Otley											
Conservative	43.6	–	46.5	43.7	51.0	41.0	45.6	+2.0	76.0	51.7	43.3
Co/N Liberal	(Pudsey + Otley)	75.2	–	–	–	–			–	–	–
Liberal		–	31.7	35.4	23.7	28.7			–	25.0	16.4
Labour		24.8	21.8	20.9	25.3	30.3			24.0	23.3	40.2
Batley & Morley											
Conservative	33.5	–	24.8	(25.7)	(35.3)	(21.8)	26.9	−6.6	61.2	46.4	28.4
Co/N Liberal	(Morley)	52.9	–	–	–	–			–	–	–
Liberal		–	29.1	47.4	50.6	41.7			–	–	13.5
Labour		47.1	46.1	52.8	49.4	58.3			38.8	53.6	58.1
Dewsbury											
Conservative	36.6	42.3	28.5	(21.5)	31.1	19.8	28.6	−8.0	–	–	–
Co/N Liberal		–	–	–	–	–			–	–	29.9

(cont.)

	(A) 1885–1910 avg	1918	1922	1923	1924	1929	(B) 1918–1931 avg	Swing in Con vote, A to B	1931	1935	1945
Liberal		27.6	34.1	55.6	27.8	34.0			63.7	23.3	13.9
Labour		30.1	37.4	44.4	41.1	46.2			36.3	47.2	56.2
Nat Labour									–	29.5	
Avg swing[2]			–	+0.9	+9.6	−13.5		−5.2			
Avg Conservative share of vote in Leeds W area	42.8						37.1				

Sources: H. Pelling, *Social geography of British elections, 1885–1910* (London, 1967); F. W. S. Craig, *British parliamentary election results, 1918–1949* (London, 1969); *Report of the Boundary Commission (England & Wales), Vols. II–III,* 1917 (Cd. 8757–8).

[2] Because the Conservative party contested only two of these seats in 1918, we lack sufficient raw material to calculate a reliable average swing for the 1922 election.

Appendix

By-elections 1918–1939

Spen Valley (20 December 1919)

Co Liberal	26.8
Liberal	33.8
Labour	39.4

Leeds Central (26 July 1923)

Conservative	47.6
Liberal	11.0
Labour	41.4

Leeds South East (1 August 1929)

Labour	95.8
Communist	4.2

Batley & Morley (9 March 1939)

Conservative	44.6
Labour	55.4

Birmingham Moseley

Birmingham Constituency	(A) 1885–1910 avg	1918	1922	1923	1924	1929	(B) 1918–1931 avg	Swing in Con vote, A to B	1931	1935	1945
Moseley											
Conservative	64.7	69.2	U'd (56.9)	71.3	77.2	56.8	66.3	+1.6	79.8	71.4	51.2
Liberal	(Worcs E)	14.6	–	28.7	–	15.7			–	–	–
Labour		16.2	–	–	22.8	26.4			20.2	28.6	48.8
King's Norton											
Conservative	64.7	54.5	41.6	43.4	42.8	42.0	44.9	−19.8	57.5	56.8	34.0
Liberal	(Worcs E)	30.3	25.6	25.9	13.9	17.4			13.8	–	10.8
Labour		15.1	32.8	30.7	43.3	40.6			28.7	43.2	55.2
Yardley											
Conservative	67.1	56.3	58.1	53.5	53.2	39.9	52.2	−14.9	65.2	57.7	29.5
Liberal	(Birmingham	5.4	–	–	–	11.2			–	–	10.0
Labour	Bordesley)	38.3	41.9	46.5	46.8	48.9			33.8	42.3	60.5
Deritend											
Conservative	67.7	82.7	48.9	56.1	51.5	42.5	56.3	−11.4	66.0	59.5	34.7
Liberal	(Birmingham S)	17.3	22.3	–	–	6.8			–	–	–
Labour		–	28.8	43.9	48.5	50.7			34.0	40.5	65.3
Sparkbrook											
Conservative	67.7	78.1	49.5	56.0	58.1	46.2	57.6	−10.1	73.4	68.5	34.6
Liberal	(Birmingham S)	6.4	27.1	19.4	5.8	16.4			–	–	–
Labour		15.5	23.4	24.6	36.1	37.4			26.6	31.5	57.8
Duddeston											
Conservative	59.0	(73.4)	61.1	59.6	51.2	39.0	56.9	−2.1	61.1	57.8	35.0
Liberal	(Birmingham E)	20.6	–	–	–	–			–	–	–
Co Labour		79.4	–	–	–	–			–	–	–
Labour		–	38.9	37.2	48.8	61.0			36.6	42.2	65.0

Erdington											
Conservative	73.0	66.0	U'd (53.7)	66.0	59.5	43.1	57.7	−15.3	68.1	58.3	39.2
Liberal	(Aston Manor)	6.9	–	–	–	13.4			–	–	
Labour		27.1 (Ind Lab)	–	34.0	40.5	43.5			31.9	37.4	60.8
Aston											
Conservative	73.0	62.4	60.8	56.2	54.6	47.8	56.4	−16.6	70.8	68.8	38.1
Liberal	(Aston Manor)	–	–	12.0	–	–			–	–	
Labour		27.8	39.2	31.8	45.4	52.2			19.2	31.2	61.9
Edgbaston											
Conservative	68.0	76.4	U'd (64.1)	72.2	76.6	63.7	70.6	+2.6	86.5	81.6	53.5
Liberal	(Birmingham	23.6	–	27.8	–	12.9			–	–	14.5
Labour	Edgbaston)	–	–	–	23.4	23.4			13.5	18.4	32.0
Ladywood											
Conservative	73.8	69.5	55.2	53.2	49.1	50.0	55.4	−18.4	71.8	71.7	44.1
Liberal	(Birmingham C)	11.5	–	–	2.0	–			–	–	
Labour		19.0	44.8	46.8	48.9	50.0			28.2	28.3	55.9
West											
Conservative	74.2	U'd (73.9)	61.6	58.3	67.4	50.1	62.3	−11.9	68.1	64.3	36.5
Labour	(Birmingham	–	38.4	41.7	–	49.9			–	–	
Communist	W + C)	–	–	–	32.6	–			31.9	35.7	63.5
Handsworth											
Conservative	58.3	56.4	59.6	U'd (59.5)	65.6	53.9	59.0	+0.7	78.4	73.0	37.9
Liberal	(Handsworth)	–	–	–	–	16.8			–	–	12.0
Labour		–	–	–	34.4	29.3			27.0	27.0	34.3
Avg swing			−12.3	−0.1	−0.4	−11.0		−9.6			
Avg Conservative share of vote in Birmingham	68.0						58.0				

Sources: H. Pelling, *Social geography of British elections, 1885–1910* (London, 1967); F. W. S. Craig, *British parliamentary election results, 1918–1949* (London, 1969); *Report of the Boundary Commission (England & Wales), Vols. II–III*, 1917 (Cd. 8757–8).

280   Appendix

By-elections 1918–1939

Birmingham Moseley (4 March 1921)
Conservative   Unopposed

Birmingham West (31 March 1921)
Conservative   Unopposed

Birmingham Erdington (20 October 1936)
Conservative   56.5
Labour   43.5

Birmingham West (29 April 1937)
Conservative   56.6
Labour   43.4

Birmingham Aston (17 May 1939)
Conservative   66.3
Labour   33.7

Liverpool East Toxteth

Liverpool Constituency	(A) 1885–1910 avg	1918	1922	1923	1924	1929	(B) 1918–1931 avg	Swing in Con vote, A to B	1931	1935	1945
E Toxteth											
Conservative	62.8	U'd (56.8)	60.3	U'd (45.5)	59.9	47.9	54.1	−8.7	75.6	60.2	49.3
Liberal	(E + W Toxteth)	–	39.7[3]	–	15.5	25.2			24.4	39.8	17.1
Labour		–	–	–	24.6	26.9			–	–	33.6
W Toxteth											
Conservative	60.5	65.6	59.6	50.3	49.4	44.9	54.0	−6.5	57.9	47.1	40.3
Labour	(A'cromby + W Toxteth)	34.4	40.4	49.7	50.6	55.1			42.1	52.9	59.7
Wavertree											
Conservative	60.4	59.9	61.6	34.7	47.4	40.0	48.7	−11.7	77.9	58.5	48.2
Liberal	(Walton +	13.1	–	37.3	17.6	27.8			–	–	13.4
Labour	E Toxteth)	27.0	38.4	28.0	35.0	32.2			22.1	41.5	38.4
Fairfield											
Conservative	62.3	50.6	72.3	U'd (57.5)	62.9	52.9	59.2	−3.1	75.6	62.5	42.2
Co Liberal	(W Derby +	27.5	–	–	–	–			–	–	–
Liberal	Walton)	–	–	–	–	–			–	–	12.1
Labour		21.9	27.7	–	37.1	47.1			24.4	37.5	45.7
Edge Hill											
Conservative	65.0	63.8	59.8	43.1	47.0	36.5	50.0	−15.0	62.8	50.5	35.1
Liberal	(W Derby)	–	–	–	–	8.1			–	–	–
Labour		36.2	40.2	56.9	53.0	55.4			37.2	49.5	64.9

[3] Eleanor Rathbone stood as an Independent candidate but received the support of the local Liberal party.

Liverpool Constituency	(A) 1885–1910 avg	1918	1922	1923	1924	1929	(B) 1918–1931 avg	Swing in Con vote, A to B	1931	1935	1945
Everton											
Conservative	66.0	52.4[4]	60.6	54.5	51.5	47.1	53.2	−12.8	48.9	49.6	34.6
Labour		–	39.4	45.5	48.5	52.9			31.2	50.4	65.4
Nat Labour		–	–	–	–	–			19.9	–	–
Kirkdale											
Conservative	66.0	67.4	U'd (70.9)	U'd (56.1)	60.6	48.7	60.7	−5.3	45.2	38.8	32.6
Labour	(Everton)	32.6	–	–	39.4	51.3			–	36.7	54.2
Liverpool Protestant Party		–	–	–	–				24.7	24.5	13.2
W Derby											
Conservative	62.8	67.4	70.5	45.8	52.5	42.7	55.8	−7.0	78.0	58.4	54.3
Liberal	(Walton +	–	–	54.2	17.9	21.3			–	13.5	–
Labour	Everton)	32.6	29.5	–	29.6	36.0			22.0	28.1	45.7
Walton											
Conservative	59.5	71.4	U'd (74.9)	U'd (60.1)	55.3	42.7	60.9	+1.4	73.6	61.6	37.4
Liberal	(Walton +	–	–	–	7.9	15.1			–	–	19.0
Labour	Kirkdale)	28.6	–	–	36.8	42.2			26.4	38.4	43.6
Scotland											
Conservative		–	–	–	–	–			37.5	34.3	–

[4] The Conservatives' only opponent was the nominee of the local branch of the National Federation of Discharged and Demobilised Sailors and Soldiers.

Labour									56.5	65.7	U'd
Irish Nationalist		U'd	U'd	U'd	U'd	U'd			–	–	–
Exchange											
Conservative	52.3	55.6	55.4	50.5	U'd (54.4)	50.3	53.2	+0.9	68.8	57.2	48.0
Labour		–	–	–	–	49.7			31.2	42.8	52.0
Irish Nationalist		44.4	44.6	49.5	–	–			–	–	–
Avg swing			+.35	–14.8	+3.9	–9.2		–6.8			
Avg Conservative share of vote in Liverpool (excluding Scotland div.)	60.6[5]						55.0				

Sources: H. Pelling, *Social geography of British elections, 1885–1910* (London, 1967); F. W. S. Craig, *British parliamentary election results, 1918–1949* (London, 1969); *Report of the Boundary Commission (England & Wales), Vols. II–III*, 1917 (Cd. 8757–8).

[5] Given the extent of boundary changes in Liverpool in 1918, whereby post-war seats were carved from a multiplicity of pre-war seats, this figure is the simple average of the Conservative share of the vote in eight Liverpool divisions (those in parentheses) between 1885 and 1910.

284   Appendix

By-elections 1918–1939

Liverpool West Derby (26 February 1919)

Conservative   56.5
Labour   43.5

Liverpool Exchange (13 March 1922)

Conservative   Unopposed

Liverpool Edge Hill (6 March 1923)

Conservative   47.3
Labour   52.7

Liverpool West Toxteth (22 May 1924)

Conservative   45.7
Labour   54.3

Liverpool East Toxteth (19 March 1929)

Conservative   43.2
Liberal   27.6
Labour   29.2

Liverpool East Toxteth (5 February 1931)

Conservative   75.4
Labour   24.6

Liverpool Wavertree (23 June 1931)

Conservative   65.0
Labour   35.0

Liverpool Exchange (19 January 1933)

Conservative   55.0
Labour   45.0

Appendix   285

Liverpool Wavertree (6 February 1935)

Conservative	31.2
Ind Conservative	23.9
Liberal	9.5
Labour	35.4

Liverpool West Derby (6 July 1935)

Conservative	Unopposed

Liverpool West Toxteth (16 July 1935)

Conservative	39.1
Labour	60.9

Ilford

	(A) 1885–1910 avg	1918[6]	1922	1923	1924	1929	(B) 1918–1931 avg	Swing in Con vote, A to B	1931	1935	1945[7]
Ilford											
Conservative	50.7	66.8	44.4	44.4	58.4	42.4	51.2	+0.5	67.2	63.1	
Liberal	(Romford)	13.7	24.0	37.5	19.9	36.9			14.1	–	
Labour		19.5	17.1	18.1	21.7	20.7			18.7	36.9	
Romford											
Conservative		(59.1)	(43.9)	35.8	44.6	32.6	43.2	–7.5	61.5	46.0	34.7
Co/Nat Liberal		57.5	58.5	–	–	–			–	–	–
Liberal		–	–	30.3	17.1	22.5			–	54.0	12.3
Labour		28.1	41.5	33.9	38.3	44.9			38.5		52.8
East Ham N											
Conservative		(44.9)	29.7	30.3	39.6	35.5	36.0	–14.7	65.9	50.9	29.8
Co/Nat Liberal		58.3	19.7	–	–	–			–	–	–
Liberal		–	6.2	34.0	24.6	22.4			–	–	–
Labour		–	27.8	35.7	35.8	42.1			34.1	49.1	70.2
East Ham S											
Conservative		30.3	(15.1)	13.0	(25.2)	25.4	21.8	–28.9	53.8	40.7	26.0
Liberal		–	30.0	37.8	48.1	20.3			–	–	–
Labour		26.9	48.1	49.2	51.9	54.3			46.2	59.3	74.0

[6] East Ham South and Walthamstow West were won by National Democratic candidates.
[7] The Ilford constituency was divided in 1945 to form Ilford North and Ilford South.

Epping											
Conservative	63.1	72.6	59.9	52.9	58.9	48.5	58.6	−4.5	63.8	59.1	41.3
Liberal		20.6	40.1	47.1	29.9	38.4			27.8	24.4	14.6
Labour		-	–	–	11.2	13.1			8.4	16.5	44.1
Stratford											
Conservative	49.9	63.8	40.5	26.2	44.0	28.2	40.5	−9.4	49.6	36.9	20.5
Liberal	(West Ham N)	36.2	12.7	18.7	–	13.3			–	–	–
Labour		–	46.8	55.1	56.0	58.5			50.4	63.1	74.6
Upton											
Conservative		61.2	46.0	34.7	54.0	32.3	45.6	−4.3	58.5	46.8	25.5
Liberal		16.6	21.2	26.0	–	18.7			–	–	–
Labour		22.2	32.8	39.3	46.0	49.0			41.5	53.2	74.5
Plaistow											
Conservative	44.2	–	36.7	25.4	32.9	22.5	29.2	−15.0	–	26.7	12.4
Labour	(West Ham S)	94.9	63.3	74.6	67.1	77.5			U'd	73.3	87.6
Walthamstow E											
Conservative	51.8	63.3	46.8	35.9	48.5	34.7	45.8	−6.0	58.8	54.0	29.8
Liberal	(Walthamstow)	36.7	20.6	29.5	16.1	25.7			10.0	–	19.1
Labour		–	32.6	34.5	35.4	39.6			31.2	46.0	51.1
Walthamstow W											
Conservative	51.8	(36.7)	(21.5)	13.4	(26.9)	14.1	22.5	−29.3	41.9	38.2	17.0
Liberal	(Walthamstow)	19.1	25.8	39.0	50.9	31.9			12.9	–	17.8
Labour		29.3	43.3	47.6	49.1	54.0			45.2	61.8	65.2
Leyton E											
Conservative		34.0	38.6	32.4	46.4	33.6	37.0	−14.8	62.4	46.1	34.3
Co/Nat Liberal		35.7	22.4	–	–	–			–	–	–

(cont.)

	(A) 1885–1910 avg	1918	1922	1923	1924	1929	(B) 1918–1931 avg	Swing in Con vote, A to B	1931	1935	1945
Liberal		–	8.1	28.1	13.9	23.5			–	9.2	–
Labour		30.3	30.9	39.5	39.7	42.9			–	44.7	65.7
Leyton W											
Conservative		67.4	46.8	34.5	46.7	35.8	46.2	–5.6	63.7	49.8	28.9
Liberal		32.6	29.4	34.3	18.6	22.1			–	–	12.6
Labour		–	23.8	31.2	34.7	42.1			36.3	50.2	58.5
Avg swing			–15.2	–8.1	+12.2	–12.8		–12.6			
Avg Conservative share of vote in Ilford area	51.9						39.8				

Sources: H. Pelling, *Social geography of British elections, 1885–1910* (London, 1967); F. W. S. Craig, *British parliamentary election results, 1918–1949* (London, 1969); *Report of the Boundary Commission (England & Wales), Vols. II–III*, 1917 (Cd. 8757–8).

Appendix 289

By-elections 1918–1939

Leyton West (1 March 1919)

Conservative	42.7
Liberal	57.3

Ilford (25 September 1920)

Conservative	54.4
Liberal	22.7
Labour	22.9

East Ham North (29 April 1926)

Conservative	34.5
Liberal	24.8
Labour	40.7

Ilford (23 February 1928)

Conservative	44.7
Liberal	33.4
Labour	21.9

Upton (14 May 1934)

Conservative	40.1
Labour	56.4

Ilford (29 June 1937)

Conservative	61.2
Labour	38.8

Epping

	(A) 1885–1910 avg	1918	1922	1923	1924	1929	(B) 1918–1931 avg	Swing in Con vote, A to B	1931	1935	1945
Epping											
Conservative	63.1	72.6	59.9	52.9	58.9	48.5	58.6	−4.5	63.8	59.1	41.3
Liberal		20.6	40.1	47.1	29.9	38.4			27.8	24.4	14.6
Labour		–	–	–	11.2	13.1			8.4	16.5	44.1
Saffron Walden											
Conservative	44.1	(66.1)	43.6	44.3	51.6	44.5	49.0	+4.9	77.7	67.1	46.9
Co/Nat Liberal		70.1	13.7	–	–	–			–	–	–
Liberal		–	12.6	26.4	21.8	27.2			–	–	9.4
Labour		29.9	30.1	29.3	26.6	28.3			22.3	32.9	43.7
Chelmsford											
Conservative	61.3	66.9	52.6	44.2	54.7	43.8	51.7	−9.6	80.5	70.8	43.2
Liberal		–	29.8	55.8	35.3	33.4			–	–	10.1
Labour		33.1	17.6	–	10.0	22.8			19.5	29.2	–[8]
Ilford											
Conservative	50.7	66.8	44.4	44.4	58.4	42.4	51.2	+0.5	67.2	63.1	
Liberal	(Romford)	13.7	24.0	37.5	19.9	36.9			14.1	–	
Labour		19.5	17.1	18.1	21.7	20.7			18.7	36.9	
Edmonton											
Conservative	50.7	49.4	36.0	35.6	46.9	40.7	41.7	−9.0	56.8	44.8	29.0
Liberal	(Romford)	16.1	18.9	–	–	–			–	–	–
Labour		25.7	45.1	64.4	53.1	59.3			43.2	55.2	68.2

[8] The successful candidate, Ernest Millington (Common Wealth Party), received the support of the local Labour party and joined the Labour party in 1946.

Romford												
Conservative		(57.5)	(40.0)	35.8	44.6	32.6	42.1		−8.6	61.5	46.0	
Co/Nat Liberal		57.5	58.5	–	–	–				–	–	
Liberal		–	–	30.3	17.1	22.5				–	–	
Labour		28.1	41.5	33.9	38.3	44.9				38.5	54.0	
Walthamstow E												
Conservative	51.8	63.3	46.8	35.9	48.5	34.7	45.8		−6.0	58.8	54.0	29.8
Liberal	(Walthamstow)	36.7	20.6	29.5	16.1	25.7				10.0	–	19.1
Labour		–	32.6	34.5	35.4	39.6				31.2	46.0	51.1
Walthamstow W												
Conservative	51.8	(35.1)	(17.6)	13.4	(24.3)	14.1	20.9		−30.9	41.9	38.2	17.0
Liberal	(Walthamstow)	19.1	25.8	39.0	50.9	31.9				12.9	–	17.8
Labour		29.3	43.3	47.6	49.1	54.0				45.2	61.8	65.2
Avg swing			−17.5	−4.2	+10.9	−12.1			−8.4			
Avg Conservative share of vote in Epping area	54.3						44.8					

Sources: H. Pelling, *Social geography of British elections, 1885–1910* (London, 1967); F. W. S. Craig, *British parliamentary election results, 1918–1949* (London, 1969); *Report of the Boundary Commission (England & Wales), Vols. II–III*, 1917 (Cd. 8757–8).

292   Appendix

By-elections 1918–1939

Ilford (25 September 1920)
Conservative	54.4
Liberal	22.7
Labour	22.9

Chelmsford (30 November 1926)
Conservative	47.8
Liberal	30.2
Labour	22.0

Ilford (23 February 1928)
Conservative	44.7
Liberal	33.4
Labour	21.9

Ilford (29 June 1937)
| Conservative | 61.2 |
| Labour | 38.8 |

Norfolk North

	(A) 1885–1910 avg	1918	1922	1923	1924	1929	(B) 1918–1931 avg	Swing in Con vote, A to B	1931	1935	1945
Norfolk North											
Conservative	43.4	50.6	47.8	42.4	40.6	41.4	45.4	+2.0	60.5	55.3	41.3
Liberal		49.4	–	–	10.7	11.1			–	–	–
Labour		–	52.2	57.6	48.7	47.5			39.5	44.7	58.7
King's Lynn											
Conservative	47.3	50.9	37.2	36.1	41.6	40.7	41.3	−6.0	70.2	50.0	39.9
Liberal	(Norfolk NW +	–	30.1	38.7	32.6	30.3			–	15.5	10.2
Labour	King's Lynn)	49.1	32.7	25.2	25.8	29.0			29.8	34.5	48.7
Norfolk SW											
Conservative	48.2	(65.2)	(58.4)	53.5	58.0	39.1	54.8	+6.6	66.3	57.4	49.9
Co/Nat Liberal	(Norfolk SW	U'd	54.7	–	–	–			–	–	–
Liberal	+ Mid)	–	–	–	–	19.1			–	–	–
Labour		–	45.3	46.5	42.0	41.8			33.7	42.6	50.1
Norfolk E											
Conservative	45.7	44.9	41.0	35.6	44.6	37.0	40.6	−5.1	–	–	–
Co/Nat Liberal		–	–	–	–	–			79.8	68.8	55.8
Liberal		42.8	39.7	49.6	36.0	39.6			–	–	–
Labour		–	19.3	14.8	19.4	23.4			20.2	31.2	44.2
Norfolk S											
Conservative	48.0	(62.4)	55.6	48.1	55.5	42.0	52.7	+4.7	65.5	57.9	32.5
Co/Nat Liberal		64.3	–	–	–	–			–	–	–
Liberal		–	–	–	–	23.5			–	–	–
Labour		35.7	44.4	51.9	44.5	34.5			34.5	42.1	50.3

(cont.)

Norwich (2 seats)

	(A) 1885–1910 avg	1918	1922	1923	1924	1929	(B) 1918–1931 avg	Swing in Con vote, A to B	1931	1935	1945
Conservative	48.6	(40.5)	33.7	28.5	27.4	23.8	30.8	−17.8	28.9	27.6	21.4
Co/Nat Liberal		–	33.7	–	–	–			30.4	29.1	23.0
Liberal		43.3	–	30.6	27.4	26.2			–	–	–
Labour		11.6	32.6	40.0	44.9	50.0			21.0	37.8	55.6
Co Labour		45.1									
Avg swing			−6.8	−4.9	+3.9	−7.3		−2.7			
Avg	47.1						44.1				
Conservative share of vote in Norfolk North area											

Sources: H. Pelling, *Social geography of British elections, 1885–1910* (London, 1967); F. W. S. Craig, *British parliamentary election results, 1918–1949* (London, 1969); *Report of the Boundary Commission (England & Wales)*, *Vols. II–III*, 1917 (Cd. 8757–8).

Appendix

By-elections 1918–1939

Norfolk South (27 July 1920)

Coalition Liberal	34.5
Liberal	19.8
Labour	45.7

Norfolk North (9 July 1930)

Conservative	49.7
Labour	50.3

Norfolk East (26 January 1939)

Nat Liberal	62.9
Labour	37.1

Devizes

	(A) 1885–1910 avg	1918	1922	1923	1924	1929	(B) 1918–1931 avg	Swing A to B	1931	1935	1945
Devizes											
Conservative	51.5	63.8	59.3	48.2	60.9	47.8	56.0	+4.5	66.3	59.3	47.0
Liberal		36.2	40.7	51.8	39.1	42.7			33.7	40.7	23.1
Labour		–	–	–	–	9.5			–	–	29.9
Swindon											
Conservative	45.2	48.4	56.4	45.1	55.1	38.1	48.6	+3.4	55.9	51.2	37.7
Liberal	(Cricklade)	11.7	–	22.3	–	18.3			–	–	–
Labour		39.9	43.6	32.6	44.9	43.6			44.1	48.8	62.3
Chippenham											
Conservative	49.4	53.1	46.3	48.3	54.6	46.6	49.8	+0.4	56.8	53.3	42.6
Liberal		29.2	48.6	51.7	45.4	40.6			36.0	34.5	25.6
Labour		17.7	5.1	–	–	12.8			7.2	12.2	31.8
Westbury											
Conservative	45.4	49.1	39.0	39.4	44.2	38.8	42.1	–3.3	51.2	49.0	39.0
Liberal		32.1	41.7	43.2	37.7	38.7			33.3	33.5	36.5
Labour		18.8	19.3	17.4	18.1	22.5			15.5	17.5	24.5
Frome											
Conservative	47.0	46.6	51.2	45.6	52.8	40.3	47.3	+0.3	58.3	46.3	44.9
Liberal		8.4	–	–	–	14.2			–	9.8	–
Labour		43.9	48.8	54.4	47.2	45.5			41.7	43.9	55.1
Salisbury											
Conservative	51.8	53.3	50.7	48.6	56.3	47.3	51.2	–0.6	76.9	71.5	44.0
Liberal		46.7	49.3	51.4	35.6	39.3			–	–	23.5

Labour	(Wilton + Salisbury)	–	–	–	8.1	13.4			23.1	28.5	32.5
Basingstoke											
Conservative	59.3	64.1	56.0	49.3	57.3	50.4	55.4	−3.9	69.7	57.8	46.0
Liberal	(Andover)	–	30.4	50.7	34.7	35.4			18.1	32.2	20.2
Labour		35.9[9]	13.6	–	8.0	14.2			12.2	10.0	33.8
Newbury											
Conservative	54.1	U'd (60.2)	57.4	49.9	55.9	51.0	54.9	+0.8	U'd	73.0	52.4
Liberal		–	42.6	50.1	39.5	39.0			–	–	13.0
Labour		–	–	–	4.6	10.0			–	27.0	33.7
Abingdon											
Conservative	55.0	U'd (54.1)	51.3	49.4	56.4	47.4	51.7	−3.3	U'd	U'd	44.5
Liberal		–	48.7	50.6	37.8	40.1			–	–	18.5
Labour		–	–	–	5.8	12.5			–	–	31.5
Avg swing			−2.8	−4.8	+7.5	−9.5		−0.2			
Avg Conservative share of vote in Devizes area	51.1						50.6				

Sources: H. Pelling, *Social geography of British elections, 1885–1910* (London, 1967); F. W. S. Craig, *British parliamentary election results, 1918–1949* (London, 1969); *Report of the Boundary Commission (England & Wales), Vols. II–III*, 1917 (Cd. 8757–8).

[9] The candidate, A. Close, stood as 'Independent Labour'.

298   Appendix

By-elections 1918–1939

Basingstoke (31 March 1920)
Conservative	44.2
Liberal	28.0
Labour	27.8

Abingdon (14 May 1921)
| Conservative | Unopposed |

Newbury (10 June 1922)
| Conservative | Unopposed |

Westbury (16 June 1927)
Conservative	40.1
Liberal	39.5
Labour	20.4

Salisbury (11 March 1931)
Conservative	53.9
Liberal	32.7
Labour	13.4

Basingstoke (19 April 1934)
Conservative	53.7
Liberal	30.8
Labour	15.5

Swindon (25 October 1934)
| Conservative | 46.6 |
| Labour | 53.4 |

Gower

	1885–1910 avg	1918	1922	1923	1924	1929	1918–1931 avg	1931	1935	1945
Gower										
Conservative	24.6	–	–	–	42.8	17.1	30.0	–	33.2	–
Liberal		45.2	45.8	40.9	–	28.9		–	–	–
Nat Liberal		–	–	–	–	–		46.6	–	31.5
Labour		54.8	54.2	59.1	57.2	54.0		53.4	66.8	68.5
Llanelli										
Conservative	28.8	–	–	14.2	–	7.7	11.0	34.7	–	18.9
Co/Nat Liberal	(Carmarthen E)	53.1	40.7	–	–	–		–	–	–
Liberal		–	–	30.7	47.1	36.9		–	–	–
Labour		46.9	59.3	55.1	52.9	55.4		65.3	U'd	81.1
Swansea E										
Conservative	44.4	–	–	–	–	10.2	10.2	–	–	–
Co/Nat Liberal	(Swansea Town)	63.6	49.1	–	–	–		–	–	24.2
Liberal	44.4	–	–	42.6	45.4	33.3		43.5	–	–
Labour	(Swansea Town)	36.4	50.9	57.4	54.6	56.5		56.5	U'd	75.8
Swansea W										
Conservative		34.4	32.4	30.9	30.2	20.8	29.7	–	–	–
Co/Nat Liberal		40.0	35.5	–	–	–		58.5	52.9	42.0
Liberal		–	–	34.3	36.4	38.6		–	–	–
Labour		25.6	32.1	34.8	33.4	40.6		41.5	47.1	58.0
Neath										
Conservative	20.4	–	–	–	–	10.0	10.0	–	–	–
Co/Nat Liberal	(Swansea Dist.	64.8	40.5	–	–	–		–	–	16.9
Liberal	+ Mid Glamorgan)	–	–	37.7	–	29.8		36.0	–	–
Labour		35.2	59.5	62.3	U'd	60.2		64.0	U'd	75.8

(cont.)

	1885–1910 avg	1918	1922	1923	1924	1929	1918–1931 avg	1931	1935	1945
Aberavon										
Conservative	–		36.1	44.4	–	10.9	30.5	–	–	27.5
Co/Nat Liberal		62.8	17.3	–	46.9	–		–	–	–
Liberal	–	–		55.6	53.1	33.2		41.6	–	–
Labour		35.7	46.6			55.9		58.4	U'd	72.5

Sources: H. Pelling, *Social geography of British elections, 1885–1910* (London, 1967); F. W. S. Craig, *British parliamentary election results, 1918–1949* (London, 1969); *Report of the Boundary Commission (England & Wales)*, *Vols. II–III*, 1917 (Cd. 8757–8).

Appendix

By-elections 1918–1939

Swansea East (10 July 1919)
Co Liberal   53.1
Labour   46.9

Gower (20 July 1922)
Co Liberal   42.5
Labour   57.5

Llanelli (26 March 1936)
Nat Liberal   33.2
Labour   66.8

Pembrokeshire

	(A) 1885-1910 avg	1918	1922	1923	1924	1929	(B) 1918-1931 avg	Swing in Con vote, A to B	1931	1935	1945
Pembrokeshire											
Conservative	43.9	–	–	34.0	40.4	31.3	35.2	−8.7	44.3	35.0	–
Liberal	(Pembroke Borough + County)	–	–	38.3	36.2	41.8			55.7	37.4	–
Co/Nat Liberal		69.8	69.0	–	–	–			–	–	50.2
Labour		28.0	31.0	27.7	23.4	26.9			–	27.6	49.8
Cardiganshire											
Conservative	38.4	–	–	25.4	–	39.4	32.5	−5.9	–	–	–
Liberal		–	49.0	27.7	U'd	60.6			76.0	61.1	63.8
Co/Nat Liberal		U'd	51.0	–	–	–			–	–	–
Ind Liberal		–	–	46.9	–	–			–	–	–
Labour		–	–	–	–	–			24.0	38.9	36.2
Carmarthen											
Conservative	34.5	–	29.4	30.1	–	25.2	28.2	−6.3	24.0	18.8	–
Liberal	(Carmarthen W, E + District)	–	12.8	45.1	68.5[10]	36.6			39.5	33.8	51.7
Nat Liberal		U'd	41.9	–	–	–			–	–	–

[10] Sir Alfred Mond defected to the Conservative party in 1926.

Labour	–	–	24.8	31.5	38.2	36.5	47.5	48.3
Other	–	15.9[11]	–	–	–	–	–	–
Avg swing							−7.0	
Avg Conservative share of vote in Pembrokeshire area	38.9				32.0			

Sources: H. Pelling, *Social geography of British elections, 1885–1910* (1967); F.W.S. Craig, *British parliamentary election results, 1918–1949* (1969); *Report of the Boundary Commission (England & Wales), Vols. II–III,* 1917 (Cd. 8757–8).

[11] National Farmers' Union candidate.

304   Appendix

By-elections 1918–1939

Cardiganshire (18 February 1921)
Liberal   42.7
Co Liberal   57.3

Carmarthen (14 August 1924)
Conservative   27.2
Liberal   44.0
Labour   28.8

Carmarthen (28 June 1928)
Conservative   29.1
Liberal   35.5
Labour   35.4

Cardiganshire (22 September 1932)
Conservative   32.1
Liberal   48.7
Labour   19.2

Dundee

	(A) 1885–1910 avg	1918	1922	1923	1924	1929	(B) 1918–1931 avg	Swing in Con vote, A to B	1931	1935	1945
Dundee (2 seats)											
Conservative[12]	36.2	(27.4)	(18.7)	19.7	22.7	19.7	21.6	−14.6	27.7	26.8	18.9
Co/Nat Liberal		37.5	36.1	–	–	–			–	–	–
Liberal		–	5.7	22.4	20.6	19.8			29.6	26.4	19.5
Labour		47.4	25.6	22.7	26.5	27.7			18.6	46.8	57.0
Scottish Prohibition Party		15.1	27.6	25.1	23.5	29.2			18.3	–	
Forfar											
Conservative	39.3	52.4	45.2	47.1	49.1	42.2	47.2	+7.9	61.4	60.2	51.6
Liberal		47.6	54.8	52.9	28.0	32.8			38.6	39.8	17.3
Labour		–	–	–	22.9	25.0			–	–	31.1
Perth											
Conservative	40.5	U'd (55.0)	46.3	46.8	49.4	40.4	47.6	+7.1	50.2	73.7	63.1
Co/Nat Liberal	(Perthshire E +	–	10.9	–	–	–			–	–	–
Liberal	Perth City)	–	23.9	53.2	30.4	36.1			40.1	–	–
Labour		–	18.9	–	20.2	23.5			–	26.3	32.6
Fife E											
Conservative	45.8	54.2	44.0	44.5	53.0	41.1	47.4	+1.6	–	–	–
Co/Nat Liberal	(Fife E +	–	–	–	–	–			U'd	82.3	69.4
Liberal	St. Andrews)	42.2	56.0	55.5	47.0	42.9			–	–	–
Labour		–	–	–	–	16.0			–	17.7	30.6

[12] The Conservative party fielded just one candidate in each election.

(cont.)

	(A) 1885–1910 avg	1918	1922	1923	1924	1929	(B) 1918–1931 avg	Swing in Con vote, A to B	1931	1935	1945
Avg swing			−8.7	+1.0	+4.0	−7.7		+0.5			
Avg Conservative share of vote in Dundee area	41.3						41.0				

Sources: H. Pelling, *Social geography of British elections, 1885–1910* (London, 1967); F. W. S. Craig, *British parliamentary election results, 1918–1949* (London, 1969); *Report of the Boundary Commission (Scotland)*,1917 (Cd. 8759).

Appendix 307

By-elections 1918–1939

Dundee (22 December 1924)

| Liberal | 30.8 |
| Labour | 69.2 |

Fife East (2 February 1933)

Nat Liberal	52.2
Ind Liberal	7.6
Labour	22.0
Agricultural Party	14.6
SNP	3.6

Perth (16 April 1935)

| Nat Liberal | 68.7 |
| Labour | 31.1 |

Dunbartonshire

	(A) 1885–1910 avg	1918	1922	1923	1924	1929	(B) 1918–1931 avg	Swing in Con vote, A to B	1931	1935	1945
Dunbartonshire											
Conservative	49.6	55.8	50.4	36.0	55.8	41.6	47.9	−1.7	63.6	50.3	49.3
Liberal		13.3	–	21.0	–	12.7			–	–	–
Labour		30.9	49.6	43.0	44.2	45.7			36.4	41.9	50.7
SNP		–	–	–	–	–			–	7.8	–
Lanarkshire N											
Conservative	46.2	43.1	36.4	34.3	53.9	44.1	42.4	−3.8	55.3	48.1	40.4
Liberal	(Lanarkshire NE	18.5	16.3	15.2	–	–			–	–	–
Labour	+ NW)	34.1	47.3	50.5	46.1	55.9			–	14.6	59.6
ILP		–	–	–	–	–			44.7	37.3	–
Coatbridge											
Conservative	46.2	64.5	39.6	44.5	49.9	30.0	45.7	−0.5	51.3	42.8	38.9
Liberal	(Lanarkshire NE	–	11.4	–	–	15.0			46.6	–	–
Labour	+ NW)	35.5	49.0	55.5	50.1	55.0				57.2	61.1
Bothwell											
Conservative		50.9	43.0	32.0	43.7	39.3	41.8	−4.4	50.0	39.7	34.2
Liberal		–	–	7.8	–	–			–	–	–
Labour		49.1	57.0	60.2	56.3	55.2			43.5	60.3	65.8
Glasgow Maryhill											
Conservative	51.8	60.2	39.6	39.7	52.6	41.2	46.7	−5.1	55.5	45.0	39.9
Liberal	(Partick)	11.9	13.1	12.2	–	8.2			–	–	–
Labour		27.9	47.3	48.1	47.4	50.6			44.5	55.0	60.1

Glasgow Hillhead											
Conservative		75.4	62.7	51.0	67.7	66.3	64.6	+12.8	73.8	68.2	58.5
Liberal		–	37.3	22.6	–	–			–	–	7.9
Labour		24.6	–	26.4	32.3	36.7			26.2	31.8	33.6
Glasgow Partick											
Conservative		(50.5)	(38.7)	33.1	57.8	44.1	44.8	−7.0	62.7	54.0	51.6
Co/Nat Liberal		70.1	65.2	–	–	–			–	–	–
Liberal		–	34.8	22.9	–	10.3			–	–	–
Labour		29.9	–	44.0	42.2	45.6			37.3	46.0	48.4
Argyll	46.8										
Conservative		(64.7)	(52.9)	47.3	46.2	44.1	51.0	+4.2	U'd	53.6	56.5
Co/Nat Liberal		81.4	58.8	–	–	–			–	–	–
Liberal		–	41.2	52.7	31.1	32.1			–	46.4	11.6
Labour		–	–	–	22.7	23.8			–	–	31.9
Renfrewshire E	53.9										
Conservative		(51.8)	40.0	42.3	55.7	52.2	48.4	−5.5	59.4	55.6	53.6
Co Liberal		72.2	–	–	–	–			–	–	–
Liberal		–	17.5	13.1	–	–			–	–	–
Labour		27.8	42.5	44.6	44.3	47.8			26.7	34.0	46.4
SNP		–	–	–	–	–			13.9	10.4	–
Renfrewshire W	50.6										
Conservative		(51.0)	(39.2)	33.6	54.1	39.4	43.5	−7.1	53.5	49.8	44.9
Co Liberal		61.8	46.0	–	–	–			–	–	–
Liberal		–	–	18.3	–	8.7			–	–	–
Labour		38.2	54.0	48.1	45.9	46.5			–	38.9	4.8

(cont.)

	(A) 1885–1910 avg	1918	1922	1923	1924	1929	(B) 1918–1931 avg	Swing in Con vote, A to B	1931	1935	1945
ILP		–	–	–	–	–			31.5	–	–
SNP		–	–	–	–	5.4			11.0	11.3	6.3
Stirling W											
Conservative	43.5	51.9	47.6	34.7	50.7	43.3	45.6	+2.1	53.3	44.9	45.6
Liberal	(Stirling)	19.4	–	13.4	–	–			–	–	–
Labour		28.7	52.4	51.9	49.3	56.7			46.7	55.1	54.4
Stirling & Falkirk											
Conservative	39.2	(43.6)	(31.8)	(26.2)	(40.7)	31.3	34.7	−4.5	63.6	48.8	43.9
Nat Liberal	(Stirling Dist. +	–	46.7	–	–	–			–	–	–
Liberal	Falkirk Dist.)	64.3	–	50.4	46.1	–			–	–	–
Labour		35.7	53.3	49.6	53.9	47.4			36.4	51.2	56.1
Avg swing			−11.8	−5.6	+14.5	−9.4		−1.7			
Avg Conservative share of vote in Dunbartonshire area	46.7						46.4				

Sources: H. Pelling, *Social geography of British elections, 1885–1910* (London, 1967); F. W. S. Craig, *British parliamentary election results, 1918–1949* (London, 1969); *Report of the Boundary Commission (Scotland)*, 1917 (Cd. 8759).

Appendix 311

By-elections 1918–1939

Argyll (10 March 1920)
Co Liberal	64.9
Labour	35.1

Dunbartonshire (29 January 1926)
Conservative	48.0
Liberal	8.1
Labour	43.9

Renfrewshire East (29 January 1926)
Conservative	52.0
Labour	48.0

Bothwell (26 March 1926)
Conservative	35.2
Liberal	5.1
Labour	59.7

Lanarkshire North (21 March 1929)
Conservative	33.4
Liberal	9.1
Labour	57.5

Renfrewshire East (28 November 1930)
Conservative	53.6
ILP	33.3
SNP	13.1

Dunbartonshire (17 March 1932)
Conservative	43.5
Labour	35.6
SNP	13.4
Communist	7.5

Dunbartonshire (18 March 1936)
Conservative	45.7
Labour	48.1
SNP	6.2

Glasgow Hillhead (10 June 1937)
Conservative	60.2
Labour	29.7
SNP	9.0

Bibliography

Primary Sources

Conservative Party Records

Birmingham Central Library
Birmingham Conservative and Unionist Association

Birmingham University Library, Special Collections Department
Midland Union of Conservative Associations

Bodleian Library, Oxford
Conservative Party Archive
Eastern Area
Home Counties North Area
Wessex Area

Durham County Record Office, Durham
Stockton & Thornaby Constitutional Organisation

Liverpool Record Office
Liverpool Constitutional Association

National Library of Scotland
Dunbartonshire Conservative Association

National Library of Wales
Cardiff Central Conservative Association

Norfolk Record Office, Norwich
Gresham Polling District Conservative Association
Norfolk North Conservative Association

Bibliography 313

Northumberland Collections Service, Woodhorn, Ashington
Northern Counties Area

Redbridge Local History Centre, Ilford
Ilford Conservative Association
Epping (West Essex) Conservative Association

Pembrokeshire Record Office, Haverfordwest
Pembrokeshire Conservative Association
South Wales Area

University of Dundee, Archive Services
Dundee Conservative Association

West Yorkshire Archive Service, Leeds
City of Leeds Conservative Association
West Leeds Conservative Association
Yorkshire Area

Wiltshire and Swindon History Centre, Chippenham
Devizes Conservative Association

Other Organisations
Club and Institute Union, London
Annual reports of the Working Men's Club and Institute Union

Private Papers
Bodleian Library, Oxford
Macmillan papers

British Library (Asia, Pacific, and Africa Collections)
Halifax papers

Cambridge University Library
Baldwin papers

Churchill Archives Centre, Cambridge
Chartwell papers
Hailes papers
Horsbrugh papers
Margesson papers

314 Bibliography

London School of Economics Library, Archive Division
Adams papers
Josephy papers
Wise papers

National Library of Scotland
Cochrane papers
Johnston papers

Norfolk Record Office, Norwich
Noel-Buxton papers

Parliamentary Archives, London
Beaverbrook papers
Davidson papers
Hannon papers
Lloyd George papers

West Glamorgan Archive Service, Swansea
Hutchinson papers

Privately Held
Hurd papers, in the possession of Lord Hurd of Westwell

Newspapers and Journals
Armley & Wortley News
Birmingham Post
Cambrian News
Cardigan & Tivy-Side Advertiser
Conservative Agents' Journal
Daily Telegraph
Darlington & Stockton Times
Diss Express
Dundee Courier
Dundee Evening Telegraph
Eastern Daily Press
Evening Standard
Kirkintilloch Gazette
Ilford Guardian
Ilford Monthly
Ilford Recorder
Illustrated London News
Lancashire Evening Post
Leeds Mercury
Liverpool Mercury

Bibliography 315

Liverpool Post & Mercury
Marlborough Times
New London Pictorial
Norfolk Chronicle
North-Eastern Daily Gazette
North Norfolk Elector
North Wiltshire Herald
Pembrokeshire Telegraph
Picture Post
Popular Illustrated
The Scotsman
Scottish Illustrated
Seren Gymru
South Wales Daily Post
Straightforward (Birmingham)
Sunderland Daily Echo
Sunderland Echo & Shipping Gazette
The Times
Western Daily Press
Western Mail
West Essex Citizen
West Essex Gazette
Wiltshire Advertiser
Wiltshire Gazette
Yorkshire Evening News
Yorkshire Evening Post
Yorkshire Post

Party Literature & Film

Conservative Party (and the National Government)
How the Conservative government has kept its pledges: a record of promises fulfilled, 1924–1929 (1929).
Performances not promises: Mr Stanley Baldwin's great election speech at Drury Lane Theatre, April 18th 1929 (1929).
The price of free trade (film, 1932).
The record of the National Government: August, 1931–October, 1933 (1933).
Empire trade (film, 1934).
Progressive Liverpool: a record of the past, a peep at the present, and a vision of the future (1934).
Two Lancashire cotton workers discussing safeguarding (film, 1935).
A call to the nation: the joint manifesto of the leaders of the National government (1935).
Forty years of progress (1945).
Who has worked for the workers? (1945).
50 things the Tories have done (1947).

316   Bibliography

The truth about the inter-war years: an exposure of the Socialist myth, by M. Maybury with a foreword by R. A. Butler (1949).

Labour Party

Labour and the nation (1928).
Vote Labour (1931).
The government evades its national responsibility: TUC criticism of the Unemployment Bill, 1933 (1933).
Dallas, G., *What Labour has done for agriculture and farm workers* (1934).
What Labour has done for London (1936).
H. Dalton et al., *A programme of immediate action: interim report of the Labour party's commission of enquiry into the distressed areas* (1937).
Let Us Face the Future: a declaration of Labour policy for the consideration of the nation (1945).

National Labour Committee

On the home front: a succinct account of the domestic record of the National government, August 1931–March 1934 (1934).
The case for the National government, by Earl de la Warr (1934).

Liberal Party

Britain's industrial future: the report of the Liberal Industrial Inquiry (1928).
We can conquer unemployment: Mr. Lloyd George's pledge (1929).

Liberal Free Trade Committee

New answers to old fallacies: a reply to Sir John Simon's defence of tariffs (1934).
The people's food (1936).

Other

Mr. Lloyd George's New Deal, by Lord Snowden (1935).

Diaries and Memoirs

Ball, S., (ed.), *Parliament and politics in the age of Baldwin and MacDonald: the Headlam diaries, 1923–1935* (London, 1992).
Barnes, J. & Nicholson, D. (eds.), *The Leo Amery diaries, vol.1: 1896–1929* (London, 1980).
James, R. R. (ed.), *Memoirs of a Conservative: J. C. C. Davidson's memoirs and papers, 1910–1937* (London, 1969).
Jones, T., *A diary with letters, 1931–1950* (Oxford, 1954).
Mackenzie, N. & J. (eds.), *The diary of Beatrice Webb, vol.4: 1924–1943* (London, 1985).
Macmillan, H., *Winds of change, 1914–1939* (London, 1966).
Norwich, J. J. (ed.), *The Duff Cooper diaries, 1915–1951* (London, 2005).

Bibliography 317

Ramsden, J. (ed.), *Real old Tory politics: the political diaries of Robert Sanders, Lord Bayford, 1910–1935* (London, 1984).

Roberts, R., *The classic slum: Salford life in the first quarter of the century* (London, 1971).

Rowse, A. L., *A man of the thirties* (London, 1979).

Salvidge, S. (ed.), *Salvidge of Liverpool: behind the political scene, 1890–1928* (London, 1934).

Self, R. (ed.), *The Austen Chamberlain diary letters: the correspondence of Sir Austen Chamberlain with his sisters Hilda and Ida, 1916–1937* (Cambridge, 1995).

 The Neville Chamberlain diary letters, vol. 1: the making of a politician, 1915–1920 (Aldershot, 2000).

 The Neville Chamberlain diary letters, vol.2: the reform years, 1921–1927 (Cambridge, 2000).

 The Neville Chamberlain diary letters, vol. 3: the heir apparent, 1928–1933 (Aldershot, 2002).

 The Neville Chamberlain diary letters, vol. 4: the Downing Street years, 1934–40, (Aldershot, 2005).

Shakespeare, G., *Let candles be brought in* (London, 1949).

Stuart, C. (ed.), *The Reith diaries* (London, 1975).

Williamson, P. (ed.), *The modernisation of Conservative politics: the diaries and letters of William Bridgeman, 1904–1935* (London, 1988).

Williamson, P. & Baldwin, E. (eds.), *Baldwin papers: a Conservative statesman, 1908–1947* (Cambridge, 2004).

Contemporary Works & Records

Astor, Viscount & Murray, K. A. H., *The planning of agriculture* (London, 1933).

 Farming or food control? A reply to Lord Wolmer (London, 1934).

Bakke, E. W., *The unemployed man: a social study* (London, 1933).

Baldwin, S., *On England* (London, 1926; 1937 edn).

 This torch of freedom: speeches and addresses (London, 1935).

Barker, B. (ed.), *Ramsay MacDonald's political writings* (London, 1972).

Boothy, R., et. al., *Industry and the state: a Conservative view* (London, 1927).

Braithwaite, C., *The voluntary citizen: an enquiry into the place of philanthropy in the community* (London, 1938).

Brierley, W., *Means test man* (London, 1935).

Cambray, P., *The game of politics: a study of the principles of British political strategy* (London, 1932).

Casey, R., 'The National Publicity Bureau and British party propaganda', *Public Opinion Quarterly*, 3 (1939), 623–34.

'Cato' [M. Foot, P. Howard & F. Owen], *Guilty men* (London, 1940).

Central Office of Information, *Something Done: British achievement, 1945–1947* (London, 1947).

Cole, G. D. H. & Cole. M., *The intelligent man's review of Europe to-day* (London, 1933)

Durant, R., *Watling: a survey of social life in a new housing estate* (London, 1939)

Elliot, W., *Toryism and the twentieth century* (London, 1927).

318   Bibliography

Fitter, R. S. R., 'An experiment in public relations', *Public Administration*, 14 (1936), 464–7.

Greene, F. (ed.), *Time to spare: what unemployment means, by eleven unemployed* (London, 1935).

Greenwood, W., *Love on the dole: a tale of two cities* (London, 1933).

Grierson, J., 'Films in the public service', *Public Administration*, 14 (1936), 366–72.

Hansard, House of Commons debates (Fifth Series).

Haxey, S., *Tory M.P.* (London, 1942).

Hinton, J., Thompson, P. & Liddell, I., *British Institute of Public Opinion (Gallup) Polls, 1938–46* (Colchester, 1996).

Hopkinson, T. (ed.), *Picture Post, 1938–1950* (London, 1970).

Houston, H. J. & Valdar, L., *Modern electioneering practice: a manual for candidates, election agents, M.P.s, etc.* (London, 1922).

Jevons, R., & Madge, J., *Housing estates: a study of Bristol corporation policy and practice between the wars* (Bristol, 1946).

Jones, D. C., *The social survey of Merseyside, vol. 3* (Liverpool, 1934).

Joseph, K., *Monetarism is not enough*, with foreword by M. Thatcher (London, 1976).

Levitt, I. (ed.), *The Scottish Office: depression and reconstruction, 1919–1959* (Edinburgh, 1992).

Macadam, E., *The new philanthropy: a study of the relations between the statutory and voluntary social services* (London, 1934).

MacDonald, R., *Parliament and democracy* (London, 1920).

Macmillan, H. M., *Reconstruction: a plea for a national policy* (London, 1933).

Madge, C., & Harrisson, T., *Mass-Observation* (London, 1937).

Britain by Mass-Observation (Harmondsworth, 1939).

Maxton, J. P. (ed.), *Regional types of British agriculture* (London, 1936).

M'Gonigle, G., 'Poverty, nutrition, and the public health', *Proceedings of the Royal Society of Medicine*, 26 (1933), 677–87.

M'Gonigle, G. & Kirby, J., *Poverty and public health* (London, 1936).

Morton, H. V., *In search of Wales* (London, 1932).

What I saw in the slums (London, 1933).

Next Five Years group, *The Next five years: an essay in political agreement* (London, 1935).

Orr, J., *Food, health and income* (London, 1936).

Orwell, G., *The road to Wigan pier* (London, 1937).

Orwell, S. & Angus, I. (eds.), *The collected essays, journalism and letters of George Orwell, volume 1: an age like this, 1920–1940* (London, 1968).

Physical Training and Recreation Act, 1937, 1 Edw. 8 & 1 Geo. 6.

Pilgrim Trust, *Men without work: a report made to the Pilgrim Trust* (Cambridge, 1938).

Priestley, J. B., *English journey* (London, 1934).

Rowntree, B. S., *The human needs of labour* (London, 1936 edn).

Poverty and progress: a second social survey of York (London, 1941).

Sheridan, D. (ed.), *Wartime women: a Mass-Observation anthology, 1937–45* (London, 1990; 2002 edn).

Simey, T. S., 'A public relations policy for local authorities', *Public Administration*, 13 (1935), 242–50.

Sorensen, H. & Cassels, J., 'The English milk market', *Quarterly Journal of Economics*, 50 (1936), 275–96.

Stacey, M., *Tradition and change: a study of Banbury* (Oxford, 1960).

Street., A. G., *Farmer's glory* (London, 1951).

Tallents, S., 'Salesmanship in the public service: scope and technique', *Public Administration*, 11 (1933), 259–66.

The tithe dispute and justice for British agriculture: statement by a deputation representing the Wessex Agricultural Defence Association (1936).

Whitehead, H., 'Salesmanship in the public service: scope and technique', *Public Administration*, 11 (1933), 267–76.

Women's Group on Public Welfare, *Our towns – a close up: a study made in 1939–42* (London, 1943).

Young, T. *Becontree and Dagenham* (London, 1934).

Documentary Film & Newsreel

A job in a million (dir. E. Spice, 1937).

Big money (dir. H. Watt, 1937).

Book bargain (dir. N. McLaren, 1937).

Bread (1934).

Britain and prosperity: boom in industry and trade (Pathé, 1937).

Coal face (dir. A. Cavalcanti, 1935).

The country comes to town (dir. B. Wright, 1933).

Deeds, not words (1938).

Eastern valley (dir. D. Alexander, 1937).

Enough to eat? (dir. E. Anstey, 1936).

The Great Crusade: the story of a million homes (Pathé, 1937).

Housing problems (dir. A. Elton & E. Anstey, 1935).

Mr Elliot at school (newsreel, 1937).

Today we live (dir. R. Grierson & R. Bond, 1937).

Wealth of a nation (dir. D. Alexander, 1938).

Wonder of the Fens (newsreel, 1934).

Workers and jobs (dir. A. Elton, 1935).

Secondary Sources

Reference Works

Craig, F. W. S., *British parliamentary election results, 1918–49* (London, 1969).

Dale, I. (ed.), *Conservative party general election manifestos, 1900–1997* (London, 2000).

Dale, I. (ed.), *Labour party general election manifestos, 1900–1997* (London, 2000).

Erskine May's parliamentary practice: treatise on the law, privileges, proceedings and usage of parliament (1st edn, 1884).

Oxford Dictionary of National Biography (online edition).

320   Bibliography

Powell, W. R. (ed.), *The Victoria history of the county of Essex, vol. 5* (London, 1966).

Books

Adams, R. J. Q., *Bonar Law* (London, 1999).

Addison, P., *Churchill on the home front, 1900–1955* (London, 1992).

Allred, J., *American modernism and depression documentary* (Oxford, 2010).

Ball, S., *Baldwin and the Conservative party: the crisis of 1929–1931* (London, 1988).

  Portrait of a party: the Conservative party in Britain, 1918–1945 (Oxford, 2013).

Barron, H., *The 1926 miners' lockout: meanings of community in the Durham coalfield* (Oxford, 2010).

Bassett, R., *Nineteen thirty-one: political crisis* (London, 1958).

Beers, L., *Your Britain: media and the making of the Labour party* (Cambridge, MA, 2009).

Bentley, M., *The Liberal mind, 1914–1929* (Cambridge, 1977).

Bergonzi, B., *Reading the thirties* (Pittsburgh, 1978).

Bernstein, G. L., *Liberalism and Liberal politics in Edwardian England* (London, 1986).

Berthezène, C., *Training minds for the war of ideas: Ashridge College, the Conservative party and the cultural politics of Britain, 1929–1954* (Manchester, 2015).

Biagini, E., *Liberty, retrenchment and reform: popular Liberalism in the age of Gladstone, 1860–1880* (Cambridge, 1992).

Biagini, E. & Reid, A. (eds.), *Currents of radicalism: popular radicalism, organized labour and party politics in Britain, 1850–1914* (Cambridge, 1991).

Blaazer, D., *The popular front and the progressive tradition: socialists, liberals and the quest for unity, 1884–1939* (Cambridge, 1992).

Black, L., *Redefining British politics: culture, consumerism and participation, 1954–1970* (Basingstoke, 2010).

Blake, R., *The Conservative party from Peel to Churchill* (London, 1970).

Blythe, R., *Akenfield: portrait of an English village* (London, 1969).

Booth, A. H., *British hustings, 1924–1950* (London, 1956).

Bracco, R. M., *Merchants of hope: British middlebrow writers and the First World War, 1919–1939* (Oxford, 1993).

Branson, N. & Heinemann, M., *Britain in the nineteen thirties* (London, 1971).

Brasnett, M., *Voluntary social action: a history of the National Council of Social Service, 1919–1969* (London, 1969).

Brassley, P., Burchardt, J. & Thompson, L. (eds.), *The English countryside between the wars: regeneration or decline?* (Woodbridge, 2006).

Bridge, C., *Holding India to the empire: the British Conservative party and the 1935 constitution* (New Delhi, 1986).

Briggs, A., *History of Birmingham, vol. 2: borough and city, 1865–1938* (London, 1952).

Briggs, A. & Burke, P., *A social history of the media: from Gutenberg to the internet* (Cambridge, 2002).

Bibliography   321

Brodie, M., *The politics of the poor: the East End of London, 1885–1914* (Oxford, 2004).

Bulmer, M., Bales, K. & Sklar, K. K., *The social survey in historical perspective, 1880–1940* (Cambridge, 1991).

Burchardt, J., *Paradise lost: rural idyll and social change since 1800* (London, 2002).

Burnett, J., *A social history of housing, 1815–1985* (2nd edn, London, 1986).

Campbell, J., *Lloyd George: the goat in the wilderness* (London, 1977).

Cannadine, D., *Aspects of aristocracy: grandeur and decline in modern Britain* (London, 1994).

Carey, J., *The intellectuals and the masses: pride and prejudice among the literary intelligentsia, 1880–1939* (London, 1992).

Carr, R., *Veteran MPs and Conservative politics in the aftermath of the Great War: the memory of all that* (Farnham, 2013).

Chamberlain, M., *Fenwomen: a portrait of women in an English village* (London, 1975).

Chatterji, B., *Trade, tariffs and empire: Lancashire and British policy in India, 1919–1939* (Delhi, 1992).

Clarke, P., *Lancashire and the New Liberalism* (Cambridge, 1971).

A question of leadership: Gladstone to Thatcher (London, 1991).

Hope and glory: Britain, 1900–2000 (3rd edn, London, 2004).

Clendinning, A., *Demons of domesticity: women and the English gas industry, 1889–1939* (Aldershot, 2004).

Coates, D., *The Labour party and the struggle for socialism* (Cambridge, 1975).

Cockburn, C., *The devil's decade* (London, 1973).

Coetzee, F., *For party or country: nationalism and the dilemmas of popular Conservatism in Edwardian England* (Oxford, 1997).

Collins, E. J. T. (ed.), *Innovation and conservation: Ernest Edward Cook and his country estates* (Reading, 1989).

Connelly, M., *The Great War, memory and ritual: commemoration in the city and east London, 1916–1939* (Woodbridge, 2002).

Cook, C., *The age of alignment: electoral politics in Britain, 1922–1929* (London, 1975).

Cooper, A. F., *British agricultural policy, 1912–1936: a study in Conservative politics* (Manchester, 1989).

Cowling, M., *The impact of Labour, 1920–1924: the beginning of modern British politics* (Cambridge, 1971).

The impact of Hitler: British politics and British policy, 1933–1940 (Cambridge, 1975).

Cragoe, M., *An Anglican aristocracy: the moral economy of the landed estate in Carmarthenshire, 1832–1895* (Oxford, 1996).

Culture, politics and national identity in Wales, 1832–1886 (Oxford, 2004).

Croft, A., *Red letter days: British fiction in the 1930s* (London, 1990).

Crowson, N. J., *Facing fascism: the Conservative party and the European dictators, 1935–40* (London, 1997).

Cunningham, V., *British writers of the thirties* (Oxford, 1988).

Daunton, M., *Just taxes: the politics of taxation in Britain, 1914–1979* (Cambridge, 2002).

Bibliography

Daunton, M. & Rieger, B. (eds.), *Meanings of modernity: Britain from the late-Victorian era to World War II* (Oxford, 2001).

Davies, S., *Liverpool Labour: social and political influences on the development of the Labour party in Liverpool, 1900–1939* (Keele, 1996).

Davies, S. & Morley, B., *County borough elections in England and Wales, 1919–1938: a comparative analysis. Volume 1: Barnsley – Bournemouth* (Aldershot, 1999).

County borough elections in England and Wales, 1919–1938: a comparative analysis. Volume 2: Bradford – Carlisle (Aldershot, 2000).

County borough elections in England and Wales, 1919–1938: a comparative analysis. Volume 3: Chester – East Ham (Aldershot, 2006).

County borough elections in England and Wales, 1919–1938: a comparative analysis. Volume 4: Exeter – Hull (Aldershot, 2013).

Day, G., *Community and everyday life* (Abingdon, 2006).

Dean, K. J., *Town & Westminster: a political history of Walsall, 1906–1945* (Walsall, 1972).

Dutton, D., *Austen Chamberlain: gentleman in politics* (London, 1985).

Liberals in schism: a history of the National Liberal party (London, 2008).

Edgerton, D., *Warfare state: Britain, 1920–1970* (Cambridge, 2005).

The rise and fall of the British nation: a twentieth-century history (London, 2018).

Eichengreen, B., *Hall of mirrors: the great depression, the great recession, and the uses – and misuses – of history* (Oxford, 2015).

Fielding, S., Thompson, P. & Tiratsoo, N., *'England arise!' The Labour party and popular politics in the 1940s* (Manchester, 1995).

Freeman, M., *Social investigation and rural England, 1870–1914* (Woodbridge, 2003).

Fry, G., *The politics of crisis: an interpretation of British politics, 1931–1945* (Basingstoke, 2001).

Gaffney, D., *Aftermath: remembering the Great War in Wales* (Cardiff, 1998).

Gardiner, J., *The thirties: an intimate history* (London, 2010).

Garside, W., *British unemployment, 1919–1939: a study in public policy* (Cambridge, 1990).

Gazeley, I., *Poverty in Britain, 1900–1965* (Basingstoke, 2003).

Gilbert, D., *Class, community and collective action: social change in two British coalfields, 1850–1926* (Oxford, 1992).

Giles, J. & Middleton, T. (eds.), *Writing Englishness, 1900–1950: an introductory sourcebook on national identity* (London, 1995).

Gloversmith, F. (ed.), *Class, culture and social change: a new view of the 1930s* (Brighton, 1980).

Grant, M., *Propaganda and the role of the state in inter-war Britain* (Oxford, 1994).

Green, E. H. H., *Crisis of Conservatism: the politics, economics and ideology of the British Conservative party, 1880–1914* (London, 1994).

Ideologies of Conservatism: Conservative political ideas in the twentieth century (Oxford, 2002).

Green, J. & Jennings, W., *The politics of competence: parties, public opinion and voters* (Cambridge, 2017).

Bibliography

Greenleaf, W. H., *The British political tradition, vol. ii: the ideological heritage* (London, 1983).

Gregory, A., *The last Great War: British society and the First World War* (Cambridge, 2008).

Griffiths, C., *Labour and the countryside: the politics of rural Britain, 1918–1939* (Oxford, 2007).

Griffiths, T., *The Lancashire working classes, c. 1880–1930* (Oxford, 2001).

Grimley, M., *Citizenship, community, and the Church of England: liberal Anglican theories of the state between the wars* (Oxford, 2004).

Hempton, D., *Religion and political culture in Britain and Ireland: from the Glorious Revolution to the decline of empire* (Cambridge, 1996).

Higson, A., *Waving the flag: constructing a national cinema in Britain* (Oxford, 1995).

Hilliard, C., *To exercise our talents: the democratization of writing in Britain* (Cambridge, MA, 2006).

Hilton, B., *The age of atonement: the influence of Evangelicalism on social and economic thought, 1785–1865* (Oxford, 1988).

Hinton, J., *Women, social leadership and the Second World War: continuities of class* (Oxford, 2002).

— *The Mass Observers: a history, 1937–1949* (Oxford, 2013).

Hodgkins, J. R., *Over the hills to glory: radicalism in Banburyshire, 1832–1945* (Southend, 1978).

Howe, A., *Free trade and Liberal England, 1846–1946* (Oxford, 1997).

Howell, D. W. (ed.), *Pembrokeshire county history, vol. iv: modern Pembrokeshire, 1815–1974* (Haverfordwest, 1993).

Howkins, A., *Poor labouring men: rural radicalism in Norfolk, 1872–1923* (London, 1985).

Howson, S., *Domestic monetary management in Britain, 1919–1938* (Cambridge, 1975).

Humble, N., *The feminine middlebrow novel, 1920s to 1950s: class, domesticity, and bohemianism* (Oxford, 2001).

Hynes, S., *The Auden generation: literature and politics in England in the 1930s* (New York, 1976).

Jackson, A., *Semi-detached London: suburban development, life and transport, 1900–1939* (London, 1973).

Jackson, A., *The two unions: Ireland, Scotland and the survival of the United Kingdom, 1707–2007* (Oxford, 2010).

James, L., *The middle class: a history* (London, 2006).

Jones, A., *Press, politics and society: a history of journalism in Wales* (Cardiff, 1993).

Kinnear, M., *The British voter: an atlas survey since 1885* (London, 1968).

— *The fall of Lloyd George: the political crisis of 1922* (London, 1973).

Kitson, M. & Solomou, S., *Protectionism and economic revival: the British interwar economy* (Cambridge, 1990).

Koss, S., *Nonconformity in modern British politics* (London, 1975).

Laity, P. (ed.), *Left Book Club anthology* (London, 2001).

Lawrence, J., *Speaking for the people: party, language and popular politics in England, 1867–1914* (Cambridge, 1998).

324   Bibliography

Electing our masters: the hustings in British politics from Hogarth to Blair (Oxford, 2009).

Lawrence, J. & Taylor, M. (eds.), *Party, state and society: electoral behaviour in Britain since 1820* (Aldershot, 1997).

Lee, R., *Rural society and the Anglican clergy, 1815–1914: encountering and managing the poor* (Woodbridge, 2006).

LeMahieu, D., *A culture for democracy: mass communication and the cultivated mind in Britain between the wars* (Oxford, 1988).

Light, A., *Forever England: femininity, literature and conservatism between the wars* (London, 1991).

Linehan, T., *British fascism, 1918–1939: parties, ideology and culture* (Manchester, 2004).

Lipset, S. M. & Rokkan, S., *Party systems and voter alignments: cross-national perspectives* (London, 1967).

Lowe, R., *Adjusting to democracy: the role of the Ministry of Labour in British politics, 1916–1939* (Oxford, 1986).

Lynch, P., *The Liberal party in rural England, 1885–1910: radicalism and community* (Oxford, 2003).

McCarthy, H., *The British people and the League of Nations: democracy, citizenship and internationalism, c.1918–1948* (Manchester, 2011).

Macintyre, S., *Little Moscows: Communism and working-class militancy in inter-war Britain* (London, 1980).

McKibbin, R., *Classes and cultures: England, 1918–1951* (Oxford, 1998).

Parties and people: England, 1914–1951 (Oxford, 2010).

McCrillis, N., *The British Conservative party in the age of universal suffrage: popular Conservatism, 1918–1929* (Columbus, OH, 1998).

Magnússon, S. & Szijártó, I., *What is microhistory? Theory and practice* (Abingdon, 2013).

Mandler, P., *The fall and rise of the stately home* (London, 1997).

The English national character: the history of an idea from Edmund Burke to Tony Blair (London, 2006).

Mansfield, N., *English farmworkers and local patriotism, 1900–1930* (Aldershot, 2001).

Marcus, L. & Nicholls, P. (eds.), *The Cambridge history of twentieth-century English literature* (Cambridge, 2004).

Marquand, D., *Ramsay MacDonald* (London, 1977).

Marriott, J., *The culture of Labourism: the East End between the wars* (Edinburgh, 1991).

Marrison, A., *British business and protection, 1903–1932* (Oxford, 1996).

Marsh, P., *The discipline of popular government: Lord Salisbury's domestic statecraft, 1881–1902* (Aldershot, 1978).

Martin, J., *The development of modern agriculture: British farming since 1931* (London, 2000).

Melman, B., *The culture of history: English uses of the past, 1800–1953* (Oxford, 2006).

Middlemas, K. & Barnes, J., *Baldwin: a biography* (London, 1969).

Bibliography

Middleton, R., *Towards the managed economy: Keynes, the Treasury and the fiscal debate of the 1930s* (London, 1985).

Miliband, R., *Parliamentary socialism: a study in the politics of Labour* (London, 1961).

Miller, W. L., *Electoral dynamics in Britain since 1918* (London, 1977).

Mitchell, J., *The Scottish question* (Oxford, 2014).

Montefiore, J., *Men and women writers of the thirties: the dangerous flood of history* (London, 1996).

Moore, J., *The transformation of urban Liberalism: party politics and urban government in late nineteenth-century England* (Aldershot, 2006).

Morgan, K. O., *Wales in British politics, 1868–1922* (Cardiff, 1963).

Consensus and disunity: the Lloyd George coalition government, 1918–1922 (Oxford 1979).

Rebirth of a nation: Wales, 1880–1980 (Oxford, 1981).

Morgan, P. (ed.), *Brad y Llyfrau Gleision: ysgrifau ar hanes Cymru* (Llandysul, 1991).

Muldoon, A., *Empire, politics and the creation of the 1935 India Act: last act of the Raj* (Farnham, 2009).

Nicholas, H. G., *The British general election of 1950* (London, 1951).

Nicholas, K., *The social effects of unemployment on Teesside* (Manchester, 1986).

Nuttall, J., *Psychological socialism: the Labour party and qualities of mind and character, 1931 to the present* (Manchester, 2006).

Olechnowicz, A., *Working-class housing in England between the wars: Becontree estate* (Oxford, 1997).

Overy, R., *The morbid age: Britain between the wars* (London, 2009).

Peden, G. C., *British rearmament and the Treasury, 1932–1939* (Edinburgh, 1979).

Pelling, H., *Social geography of British elections, 1885–1910* (London, 1967).

Perkin, H., *The rise of professional society: England since 1880* (London, 1989).

Perren, R., *Agriculture in depression, 1870–1940* (Cambridge, 1995).

Perry, M., *The Jarrow crusade: protest and legend* (Sunderland, 2005).

Pimlott, B., *Labour and the left in the 1930s* (Cambridge, 1977).

Pinto-Dushinsky, M., *British political finance, 1830–1980* (Washington, DC, 1981).

Poole, H. R., *The Liverpool Council of Social Service, 1909–1959* (Liverpool, 1960).

Pope, R., *Building Jerusalem: nonconformity, Labour and the social question in Wales, 1906–1939* (Cardiff, 1998).

Pope, R. (ed.), *Religion and national identity: Wales and Scotland, c.1700–2000* (Cardiff, 2001).

Pugh, M., *The Tories and the people, 1880–1935* (Oxford, 1985).

The making of modern British politics, 1867–1945 (3rd edn; Oxford, 2002).

'Hurrah for the Blackshirts!' Fascists and fascism in Britain between the wars (London, 2005).

Ramsden, J., *The age of Balfour and Baldwin, 1902–1940* (London, 1978).

Read, D., *The English provinces: a study in influence, 1760–1960* (London, 1964).

Readman, P., *Land and nation in England: patriotism, national identity, and the politics of land, 1880–1914* (Woodbridge, 2008).

326   Bibliography

Reynolds, D., *In command of history: Churchill fighting and writing the Second World War* (London, 2004).

Reynolds, J. & Laybourn, K., *Labour heartland: the history of the Labour party in West Yorkshire during the inter-war years, 1918–1939* (Bradford, 1987).

Richards, J., *The age of the dream palace: cinema and society in Britain, 1930–1939* (London, 1984).

Richardson, H. W., *Economic recovery in Britain, 1932–1939* (London, 1967).

Riddell, N., *Labour in crisis: the second Labour government, 1929–1931* (Manchester, 1999).

Rieger, B., *Technology and the culture of modernity in Britain and Germany, 1890–1945* (Cambridge, 2005).

Ritschel, D., *The politics of planning: the debate on economic planning in Britain in the 1930s* (Oxford, 1997).

Robbins, K., *History, religion and identity in modern Britain* (London, 1993).

Robertson, N., *The Co-operative movement and communities in Britain, 1914–1960* (Farnham, 2010).

Rooth, T., *British protectionism and the international economy: overseas commercial policy in the 1930s* (Cambridge, 1993).

Rush, M., *The role of the member of parliament since 1868* (Oxford, 2001).

Russell, D., *Looking north: northern England and the national imagination* (Manchester, 2004).

Saltzman, R., *A lark for the sake of their country: the 1926 general strike* (Manchester, 2012).

Sarvlick, B. & Crewe, I., *Decade of dealignment: the Conservative victory of 1979 and electoral trends in the 1970s* (Cambridge, 1983).

Savage, J., *Rural depopulation in England and Wales, 1851–1951* (London, 1957).

Savage, M. & Miles, A., *The remaking of the British working class, 1840–1940* (London, 1994).

Scotland, N., *Methodism and the revolt of the field: a study of the Methodist contribution to agricultural trade unionism in East Anglia, 1872–96* (Gloucester, 1981).

Scott, P., *Triumph of the south: a regional economic history of twentieth century Britain* (Aldershot, 2007).

Searle, G., *Country before party: coalition and the idea of 'National government' in modern Britain, 1885–1987* (London, 1995).

Self, R., *Tories and tariffs: the Conservative party and the politics of tariff reform, 1922–1933* (London, 1986).

    Neville Chamberlain: a biography (Aldershot, 2006).

    The evolution of the British party system, 1885–1940 (Harlow, 2014).

Skidelsky, R., *Politicians and the slump: the Labour government of 1929–1931* (London, 1967).

Sloman, P., *The Liberal party and the economy, 1929–1964* (Oxford, 2015).

Smart, N., *The National government, 1931–40* (Basingstoke, 1999).

Snell, K. D. M. & Ell, P. S., *Rival Jerusalems: the geography of Victorian religion* (Cambridge, 2000).

Stannage, T., *Baldwin thwarts the opposition: the British general election of 1935* (London, 1980).

Bibliography 327

Stapleton, J., *Englishness and the study of politics: the social and political thought of Ernest Barker* (Cambridge, 1994).

Sir Arthur Bryant and national history in twentieth century Britain (Lanham, 2005).

Stevenson, J. & Cook, C., *The slump: society and politics during the depression* (London, 1977).

Tanner, D., *Political change and the Labour party, 1900–1918* (Cambridge, 1990).

Taylor, J., *From self-help to glamour: the working men's club* (History Workshop Pamphlet, 7; Oxford, 1972).

Thackeray, D., *Conservatism for the democratic age: Conservative cultures and the challenge of mass politics in early twentieth-century England* (Manchester, 2013).

Thomas, D., *Churchill: the member for Woodford* (London, 1994).

Thompson, F. M. L., *Gentrification and the enterprise culture: Britain, 1780–1980* (Oxford, 2001).

Thompson, J., *British political culture and the idea of 'public opinion', 1867–1914* (Cambridge, 2013).

Thompson, N., *The anti-appeasers: Conservative opposition to appeasement in the 1930s* (Oxford, 1971).

Thompson, S., *Unemployment, poverty and health in interwar South Wales* (Cardiff, 2006).

Thorpe, A., *The British general election of 1931* (Oxford, 1991).

Todd, S., *Young women, work, and family in England, 1918–1950* (Oxford, 2005).

Tomlinson, J., *Public policy and the economy since 1900* (Oxford, 1990).

Dundee and the empire: 'Juteopolis', 1850–1939 (Edinburgh, 2014).

Managing the economy, managing the people: narratives of economic life in Britain from Beveridge to Brexit (Oxford, 2017).

Toye, R., *The Labour party and the planned economy, 1931–51* (Woodbridge, 2003).

Tregidga, G., *The Liberal party in south-west Britain since 1918: political decline, dormancy and rebirth* (Exeter, 2000).

Tremlett, G., *Clubmen: history of the Working Men's Club and Institute Union* (London, 1987).

Trentmann, R., *Free trade nation: commerce, consumption and civil society in modern Britain* (Oxford, 2008).

Turberfield, A. F., *John Scott Lidgett: archbishop of British Methodism?* (London, 2003).

Vernon, J., *Politics and the people: a study in England political culture, c.1815–1867* (Cambridge, 1993).

Hunger: a modern history (Cambridge, MA, 2007).

Wahrman, D., *Imagining the middle class: the political representation of class in Britain, c.1780–1840* (Cambridge, 1995).

Waller, P., *Democracy and sectarianism: a political and social history of Liverpool, 1868–1939* (Liverpool, 1981).

Ward, P., *Red flag and Union Jack: Englishness, patriotism and the British left, 1881–1924* (Woodbridge, 1998).

Whetham, E., *The Cambridge agrarian history of England and Wales, 1914–1939* (Cambridge, 1978).

328 Bibliography

Wiener, M., *English culture and the decline of the industrial spirit, 1850–1980* (Cambridge, 1981).
Williams, C., *Capitalism, community and conflict: the South Wales coalfield, 1898–1947* (Cardiff, 1998).
Williams, S., *The People's King: the true story of the abdication* (London, 2003).
Williamson, P., *National crisis and national government: British politics, the economy and empire, 1926–1932* (Cambridge, 1992).
Stanley Baldwin: Conservative leadership and national values (Cambridge, 1999).
Wilson, T., *The downfall of the Liberal party, 1914–1935* (London, 1966).
Wilt, A. F., *Food for war: agriculture and rearmament in Britain before the Second World War* (Oxford, 2001).
Windscheffel, A., *Popular Conservatism in imperial London, 1868–1906* (Woodbridge, 2007).
Worley, M., *Labour inside the gate: a history of the British Labour party between the wars* (London, 2005).
Wrigley, C., *Lloyd George and the challenge of Labour: the post-war coalition, 1918–1922* (Hemel Hempstead, 1990).
Young, K., *Local politics and the rise of party: the London Municipal Society and the Conservative intervention in local elections, 1894–1963* (Leicester, 1975).
Zweiniger-Bargielowska, I., *Managing the body: beauty, health and fitness, 1880–1939* (Oxford, 2010).

Articles and Essays

Aubel, F., 'The Conservatives in Wales, 1880–1935', in M. Francis & I. Zweiniger-Bargielowska (eds.), *The Conservatives and British society, 1880–1990* (Cardiff, 1996), 96–110.
Ball, S., 'The Conservative party and the formation of the National government: August, 1931', *Historical Journal*, 29 (1986), 159–82.
'The politics of appeasement: the fall of the Duchess of Atholl and the Kinross and West Perth by-election, December 1938', *Scottish Historical Review*, 69 (1990), 49–83.
'The National government, 1931: crisis and controversy', *Parliamentary History*, 12 (1993), 184–200.
Baxter, K. & Kenefick, W., 'Labour politics and the Dundee working class, c.1895–1936', in J. Tomlinson & C. Whatley (eds.), *Jute no more: transforming Dundee* (Dundee, 2011), 191–219.
Beers, L., 'Counter-Toryism: Labour's response to anti-socialist propaganda, 1918–1939', in M. Worley (ed.), *The foundation of the British Labour party: identities, cultures and perspectives, 1900–1939* (Farnham, 2009), 231–54.
'"Is this man an anarchist?" Industrial action and the battle for public opinion in interwar Britain', *Journal of Modern History*, 82 (2010), 30–60.
Bennett, G. H., '"Part of the puzzle": Northampton and other Midlands by-election defeats for the Conservatives, 1927–1929', *Midland History*, 20 (1995), 151–73.
Bernstein, G., 'Liberalism and the Progressive Alliance in the constituencies, 1900–1914: three case studies', *Historical Journal*, 26 (1983), 617–40.

Bibliography

'Yorkshire Liberalism during the First World War', *Historical Journal*, 32 (1989), 107–29.

Berthezene, C., 'Creating Conservative Fabians: the Conservative party, political education and the founding of Ashridge College', *Past & Present*, 182 (2004), 211–40.

Black, L., 'The lost world of young Conservatism', *Historical Journal*, 51 (2008), 991–1024.

Booth, A., 'Britain in the 1930s: a managed economy?', *Economic History Review*, 40 (1987), 499–522.

Blouet, O. M., 'Buxton, Sir Thomas Fowell, first baronet (1786–1845)', *Oxford Dictionary of National Biography* (Oxford, 2004).

Boyce, D. G., '"Rights of Citizenship": the Conservative party and the constitution, 1906–1914', in A. O'Day (ed.), *Government and institutions in the post-1832 United Kingdom* (Lampeter, 1995), 215–36.

Burchardt, J., 'Reconstructing the rural community: village halls and the National Council of Social Service, 1919 to 1939', *Rural History*, 10 (1999), 193–216.

Burness, C., 'The making of Scottish Unionism, 1886–1914', in S. Ball & I. Holliday (eds.), *Mass Conservatism: the Conservative party since the 1880s* (London, 2002), 16–35.

Campbell, R. H., 'The Scottish Office and the Special Areas in the 1930s', *Historical Journal*, 22 (1979), 167–83.

Cannadine, D., 'Apocalypse when? British politicians and British "decline" in the twentieth century', in P. Clarke & C. Trebilcock (eds.), *Understanding decline: perceptions and realities of British economic performance* (Cambridge, 1997), 261–84.

Cardiff, D. & Scannell, P., 'Broadcasting and national unity', in J. Curran, A. Smith & P. Wingate (eds.), *Impacts and influences: essays in media power in the twentieth century* (London, 1987), 157–73.

Ceadel, M., 'The first British referendum: the Peace Ballot, 1934–5', *English Historical Review*, 95 (1980), 810–39.

'Popular fiction and the next war, 1918–39', in F. Gloversmith (ed.), *Class, culture and social change: a new view of the 1930s* (Brighton, 1980), 161–84.

'Interpreting East Fulham', in C. Cook & J. Ramsden (eds.), *By-elections in British politics* (London, 1997), 94–111.

Cleaver, D., 'Labour and Liberals in the Gower constituency, 1885–1910', *Welsh History Review*, 12 (1985), 388–410.

Close, D., 'Conservatives and coalition after the First World War', *Journal of Modern History*, 45 (1973), 240–60.

'The realignment of the British electorate in 1931', *History*, 67 (1982), 393–404.

Coetzee, F., 'Villa Toryism reconsidered: Conservatism and suburban sensibilities in late-Victorian Croydon', in E. H. H. Green (ed.), *An age of transition: British politics, 1880–1914* (Edinburgh, 1997), 29–47.

Coleman, M., '"A terrible danger to the moral of the country": the Irish hospitals' sweepstake in Great Britain, 1930–1987', *Proceedings of the Royal Irish Academy*, 105 (2005), 197–220.

330 Bibliography

Cook, C., 'By-elections of the first Labour government', in Cook & J. Ramsden (eds.), *By-elections in British politics* (London, 1997), 37–58.

Cooper, T., 'London-over-the-border: politics in suburban Walthamstow, 1870–1914', in M. Cragoe & A. Taylor (eds.), *London politics, 1760–1914* (Basingstoke, 2005).

Cornford, J., 'The transformation of Conservatism in the late nineteenth century', *Victorian Studies*, 12 (1963), 35–66.

Cragoe, M., 'Welsh electioneering and the purpose of parliament: "from radicalism to nationalism" reconsidered', *Parliamentary History*, 17 (1998), 113–30.

'The anatomy of an eviction campaign: the general election of 1868 in Wales and its aftermath', *Rural History*, 9 (1998), 177–93.

'Conservatives, "Englishness" and "civic nationalism" between the wars', in D. Tanner, C. Williams, W. P. Griffith & A. Edwards (eds.), *Debating nationhood and governance in Britain, 1885–1939: perspectives from the four nations* (Manchester, 2006), 192–210.

'"We like local patriotism": the Conservative party and the discourse of decentralisation, 1947–51', *English Historical Review*, 122 (2007), 965–85.

'"Brimful of patriotism": Welsh Conservatives, the South African war and the "khaki" election of 1900', in Cragoe & C. Williams (eds.), *Wales and war: society, politics and religion in the nineteenth and twentieth centuries* (Cardiff, 2007), 101–25.

Crafts, N. & Mills, T. C., 'Rearmament to the rescue? New estimates of the impact of "Keynesian" policies in 1930s Britain', *Journal of Economic History*, 73 (2013), 1077–1104.

Craig, D., '"High politics" and the "new political history"', *Historical Journal*, 53 (2010), 453–75.

Dare, R., 'British Labour, the National government and the "national interest", 1931', *Historical Studies in the Physical Sciences*, 18 (1979), 345–64.

Darling, E., '"Enriching and enlarging the whole sphere of human activities": the work of the voluntary sector in housing reform in inter-war Britain', in C. Lawrence & A-K. Mayer (eds.), *Regenerating England: science, medicine and culture in inter-war Britain* (Amsterdam, 2000), 149–78.

Davies, S. & Morley, B., 'The reactions of municipal voters in Yorkshire to the second Labour government, 1929–32', in M. Worley (ed.), *Labour's grass roots: essays on the activities and experiences of local Labour parties and members, 1918–1945* (Aldershot, 2005), 124–46.

'Electoral turnout in county borough elections, 1919–1938', *Labour History Review*, 71 (2006), 167–86.

Davis, J. W., 'Working-class make-believe: the South Lambeth Parliament (1887–1890)', *Parliamentary History*, 12 (1993), 249–58.

Dawson, M., 'The Liberal land policy, 1924–1929: electoral strategy and internal division', *Twentieth Century British History*, 2 (1991), 272–90.

'Liberalism in Devon and Cornwall, 1910–1931: "the old-time religion"', *Historical Journal*, 38 (1995), 425–37.

Dearlove, P., 'Fen Drayton, Cambridgeshire: an estate of the Land Settlement Association', in J. Thirsk (ed.), *The English rural landscape* (Oxford, 2000), 323–35.

Bibliography

Digby, A., 'Changing welfare cultures in region and state', *Twentieth Century British History*, 17 (2006), 297–322.

Dimsdale, N. H., 'British monetary policy and the exchange rate, 1920–1939', *Oxford Economic Papers*, 33 (1981), 306–49.

Dorling, D., 'Distressed times and areas: poverty, polarisation and politics in England, 1918–1971', in A. Baker & M. Billinge (eds.), *Geographies of England: the north-south divide, imagined and material* (Cambridge, 2004), 44–63.

Doyle, B., 'Who paid the price of patriotism? The funding of Charles Stanton during the Merthyr Boroughs by-election of 1915', *English Historical Review*, 109 (1994), 1215–22.

'Urban Liberalism and the "lost generation": politics and middle class culture in Norwich, 1900–1935', *Historical Journal*, 38 (1995), 617–34.

Drake, P. '*The Town Crier*: Birmingham's Labour weekly, 1919–1951', in R. Shackleton & A. Wright (eds.), *Worlds of Labour: essays in Birmingham Labour history* (Birmingham, 1983), 103–26.

Dunbabin, J. P. D., 'British elections in the nineteenth and twentieth centuries, a regional approach', *English Historical Review*, 95 (1980), 241–67.

Dupree, M., 'The provision of social services', in M. Daunton (ed.), *The Cambridge urban history of Britain, vol. iii: 1840–1950* (Cambridge, 2000), 378–93.

Dutton, D., '1932: a neglected date in the history of the decline of the British Liberal party', *Twentieth Century British History*, 14 (2003), 43–60.

'Liberalism in crisis: Liberals, Liberal Nationals and the politics of North-east Wales, 1931–1935', *Welsh History Review*, 26 (2003), 106–23.

Eastwood, D., 'Contesting the politics of deference: the rural electorate, 1820–1860', in J. Lawrence & M. Taylor (eds.), *Party, state and society: electoral behaviour in Britain since 1820* (Aldershot, 1997), 27–49.

Eichengreen, B., 'The British economy between the wars', in R. C. Floyd & P. A. Johnson (eds.), *The Cambridge economic history of modern Britain, vol. 2: economic maturity, 1860–1939* (Cambridge, 2004), 314–43.

Ewen, S., 'Central government and the modernisation of the British Fire Service, 1900–1938', *Twentieth Century British History*, 14 (2003), 317–38.

Feldman, D., 'Migration', in M. Daunton (ed.), *The Cambridge urban history of Britain, vol. III: 1840–1950* (Cambridge, 2000), 185–206.

Fielding, S., 'Looking for the "New Political History"', *Journal of Contemporary History*, 42 (2007), 515–24.

Finnigan, R., 'Council housing in Leeds, 1919–1939: social policy and urban change', in M. Daunton (ed.), *Councillors and tenants: local authority housing in English cities, 1919–1939* (Leicester, 1984), 102–53.

Fisher, J. R., 'The limits of deference: agricultural communities in a mid-nineteenth century election campaign', *Journal of British Studies*, 21 (1981), 90–115.

Forgacs, D., 'National-popular: genealogy of a concept', in B. Schwarz & M. Langan, (eds.), *Formations of nation and people* (London, 1984).

Fry, G., 'A reconsideration of the general election of 1935 and the electoral revolution of 1945', *History*, 76 (1991), 43–55.

332   Bibliography

Garrard, J., 'Urban elites, 1850–1914: the rule and decline of a new squirearchy?', *Albion*, 27 (1995), 583–621.

Garside, W. R., 'Party politics, political economy and British protectionism, 1919–1932', *History*, 83 (1998), 47–65.

Ghosh, S. C., 'Decision-making and power in the British Conservative party: a case study of the Indian problem, 1929–1934', *Political Studies*, 13 (1965), 198–212.

Grant, M., 'The National Health Campaigns of 1937–1938', in D. Fraser (ed.), *Cities, class and communication: essays in honour of Asa Briggs* (London, 1990).

Green, E. H. H., 'Thatcherism: a historical perspective', *Transactions of the Royal Historical Society*, 9 (1999), 17–42.

'"No longer the farmers' friend?" The Conservative party and agricultural protection, 1880–1914', in J. R. Wordie (ed.), *Agriculture and politics in England, 1815–1939* (Basingstoke, 2000), 149–77.

'An intellectual in Conservative politics: the case of Arthur Steel-Maitland', in *Ideologies of Conservatism: Conservative political ideas in the twentieth century* (Oxford, 2002), 72–113.

'Conservatism, anti-socialism, and the end of the Lloyd George coalition', in *Ideologies of Conservatism: Conservative politics ideas in the twentieth century* (Oxford, 2002), 114–34.

'The battle of the books: book clubs and Conservatism in the 1930s', in *Ideologies of Conservatism: Conservative politics ideas in the twentieth century* (Oxford, 2002), 135–56.

'Searching for the middle-way: the political economy of Harold Macmillan', in *Ideologies of Conservatism: Conservative politics ideas in the twentieth century* (Oxford, 2002), 157–91.

'The Conservative party and Keynes', in Green and D. Tanner (eds.), *The strange survival of Liberal England: political leaders, moral values and the reception of economic debate* (Cambridge, 2007), 186–211.

Grieves, K., 'Huts, demobilisation and the quest for an associational life in rural communities in England after the Great War', in P. Purseigle (ed.), *Warfare and belligerence: perspective in First World War studies* (Leiden, 2005), 243–64.

Griffiths, C. V. J., 'Buxton, Noel Edward Noel-, first Baron Noel-Nuxton (1869–1948)', *Oxford Dictionary of National Biography* (Oxford, 2004).

Gruffudd, P., 'Back to the land: historiography, rurality and the nation in interwar Wales', *Transactions of the Institute of British Geographers*, 19 (1994), 61–77.

Gunn, S., 'Class, identity and the urban: the middle class in England, c.1790–1950', *Urban History*, 31 (2004), 29–47.

Hastings, R. P., 'The Birmingham Labour movement, 1918–1945', *Midland History*, 5 (1979–80), 78–92.

Hayburn, R. H. C., 'The Voluntary Occupational Centre movement, 1932–39', *Journal of Contemporary History*, 6 (1971), 156–71.

Heller, M., 'Suburbia, marketing and stakeholders: developing Ilford, Essex, 1880–1914', *Urban History*, 41 (2014), 62–80.

Bibliography

Hinton, J., 'Conservative women and voluntary social service, 1938–1951', in S. Ball & I. Holliday (eds.), *Mass Conservatism: the Conservatives and the public since the 1880s* (London, 2002), 100–19.

Hollins, T. J., 'The Conservative party and film history between the wars', *English Historical Review*, 96 (1981), 359–69.

Holton, S. S., 'British freewomen: national identity, constitutionalism and languages of race in early suffragist histories', in E. Yeo (ed.), *Radical femininity: women's self-representation in the public sphere* (Manchester, 1998), 149–71.

Hopkin, D., 'Llafur a'r diwylliant Cymreig, 1900–1940', *Transactions of the Honourable Society of Cymmrodorion*, 7 (2001), 149–63.

Howarth, J., 'The Liberal revival in Northamptonshire, 1880–1895: a case study in late nineteenth century elections', *Historical Journal*, 12 (1969), 78–118.

Howe, A., 'Towards the "hungry forties": free trade in Britain, c. 1880–1906', in E. Biagini (ed.), *Citizenship and community: Liberals, radicals and collective identities in the British Isles, 1865–1931* (Cambridge, 1996), 193–218.

Howell, D., 'A "less obtrusive and exacting" nationality: Welsh ethnic mobilisation in rural communities, 1850–1920', in Howell (ed.), *Roots of rural ethnic mobilisation* (Aldershot, 1993), 51–97.

Howkins, A., 'The discovery of rural England', in R. Colls & P. Dodd (eds.), *Englishness: politics and culture, 1880–1920* (London, 1988), 62–88.

  'From diggers to dongas: the land in English radicalism, 1649–2000', *History Workshop Journal*, 54 (2002), 1–23.

  'Qualifying the evidence: perceptions of rural change in Britain in the second half of the twentieth century', in D. Gilbert, D. Matless & B. Short (eds.), *Geographies of British modernity: space and society in the twentieth century* (Oxford, 2003), 97–112.

Huggins, M., 'Betting, sport and the British, 1919–1939', *Journal of Social History*, 41 (2007), 283–306.

Hulme, T., '"A nation of town criers": civic publicity and historical pageantry in inter-war Britain', *Urban History*, 44 (2017), 270–92.

Humphries, J., 'Inter-war house building, cheap money and building societies: the housing boom revisited', *Business History*, 29 (1987), 325–45.

Jaggard, E., 'Farmers and English county politics, 1832–80', *Rural History*, 16 (2005), 191–207.

Jarvis, D., 'Mrs. Maggs and Betty: the Conservative appeal to women voters in the 1920s', *Twentieth Century British History*, 5 (1994), 129–52.

  'British Conservatism and class politics in the 1920s', *English Historical Review*, 111 (1996), 59–84.

  'The shaping of the Conservative electoral hegemony, 1918–39', in J. Lawrence & M. Taylor (eds.), *Party, state and society: electoral behaviour in Britain since 1820* (Aldershot, 1997), 131–52.

Jeffery, T., 'The suburban nation: politics and class in Lewisham', in D. Feldman & G. S. Jones (eds.), *Metropolis London: histories and representations of London since 1800* (London, 1989), 189–216.

Jeffery, T. & McClelland, K., 'A world fit to live in: the Daily Mail and the middle classes, 1918–1939', in J. Curran, A. Smith & P. Wingate (eds.), *Impacts and influences: essays in media power in the twentieth century* (London, 1987), 27–52.

334 Bibliography

John, B. S., 'The linguistic significance of the Pembrokeshire Landsker', *Pembrokeshire Historian*, 4 (1972), 7–29.

Johnson, J. H., 'The suburban expansion of housing in London, 1918–1939', in J. T. Coppock & H. C. Prince (eds.), *Greater London* (London, 1964), 142–66.

Johnston, R. et al., 'The Conservative century? Geography and Conservative electoral success during the twentieth century', in D. Gilbert, D. Matless & B. Short (eds.), *Geographies of British modernity: space and society in the twentieth century* (Oxford, 2003), 54–79.

Jones, A., 'Sir John Gibson and the *Cambrian News*', *Ceredigion*, 12 (1994), 57–83.

Jones, J. G., 'Sir Rhys Hopkin Morris and Cardiganshire politics, 1922–1932', *Ceredigion*, 15 (2006), 73–104.

Jones, R. W., Scully, R. & Trystan, D., 'Why do the Conservatives always do (even) worse in Wales?', *Journal of Elections, Public Opinion and Parties*, 12 (2002), 229–45.

Joyce, P., 'What is the social in social history?', *Past &Present*, 206 (2010), 213–48.

Kennedy, T. C., 'The Next Five Years Group and the failure of the politics of agreement', *Canadian Journal of History*, 9 (1974), 45–68.

King., A., 'Remembering and forgetting in the public memorials of the Great War', in A. Forty & S. Küchler (eds.), *The art of forgetting* (Oxford, 1999), 147–70.

Kitson, M. 'Slump and recovery: the UK experience', in T. Balderston (ed.), *The world economy and national economies in the interwar slump* (Basingstoke, 2003), 88–104.

Knox., W. W. & Mackinlay, A., 'The re-making of Scottish Labour in the 1930s', *Twentieth Century British History*, 6 (1995), 174–93.

Koss, S., 'Lloyd George and nonconformity: the last rally', *English Historical Review*, 89 (1974), 77–108.

Lawrence, J., 'Class and gender in the making of urban Toryism, 1880–1914', *English Historical Review*, 108 (1993), 629–52.

'Labour – the myths it has lived by', in D. Tanner, P, Thane & N. Tiratsoo (eds.), *Labour's first century* (Cambridge, 2000), 341–66.

'The politics of place and the politics of nation', *Twentieth Century British History*, 11 (2000), 83–94.

'Forging a peaceable kingdom: war, violence and the fear of brutalization in post- First World War Britain', *Journal of Modern History*, 75 (2003), 557–89.

'The transformation of British public politics after the First World War', *Past & Present*, 190 (2006), 185–216.

'Labour and the politics of class, 1900–1940', in D. Feldman & Lawrence (eds.), *Structures and transformations in modern British history: papers for Gareth Stedman Jones* (Cambridge, 2011), 237–60.

'Paternalism, class and the British path to modernity', in S. Gunn & J. Vernon (eds.), *The peculiarities of liberal modernity in imperial Britain* (Berkeley, CA, 2011), 147–64.

Bibliography

Lawrence, J. & Taylor, M., 'Introduction: electoral sociology and the historians', in Lawrence & Taylor (eds.), *Party, state and society: electoral behaviour in Britain since 1820* (Aldershot, 1997), 1–26.

LeMahieu, D., 'John Reith, 1889–1971: entrepreneur of collectivism', in S. Pedersen & P. Mandler (eds.), *After the Victorians: private conscience and public duty in modern Britain* (London, 1994), 189–206.

Lewis, R., 'The Welsh radical tradition and the ideal of a democratic popular culture', in E. F. Biagini (ed.), *Citizenship and community: Liberals, radicals and collective identities in the British Isles, 1865–1931* (Cambridge, 1996), 325–40.

Linehan, D. & Pyrs, G., 'Unruly topographies: unemployment, citizenship and land settlement in inter-war Wales', *Transactions of the Institute of British Geographers*, 29 (2004), 46–63.

Linklater, M., 'Elliot, Katharine, Baroness Elliot of Harwood (1903–1994)', *Oxford Dictionary of National Biography* (Oxford, 2004)

Love, G., 'The periodical press and the intellectual culture of Conservatism in interwar Britain', *Historical Journal*, 57 (2014), 1027–56.

McCaffrey, J., 'The origins of Liberal Unionism in the west of Scotland', *Scottish Historical Review*, 50 (1971), 47–71.

McCarthy, H., 'Parties, voluntary associations, and democratic politics in inter-war Britain', *Historical Journal*, 50 (2007), 891–912.

'Democratizing British foreign policy: rethinking the Peace Ballot, 1934–5', *Journal of British Studies*, 49 (2010), 358–87.

McClelland, K., 'England's greatness, the working man', in C. Hall, McClelland & J. Rendall (eds.), *Defining the Victorian nation: class, race, gender and the reform act of 1867* (Cambridge, 2000), 71–118.

McClymont, G., 'Socialism, puritanism, hedonism: the parliamentary Labour party's attitude to gambling, 1923–31', *Twentieth Century British History*, 19 (2008), 288–313.

McDonald, G. W. & Gospel, H. F., 'The Mond-Turner talks, 1927–1933: a study in industrial co-operation', *Historical Journal*, 16 (1973), 807–29.

Macintyre, S., 'British Labour, Marxism, and working class apathy in the nineteen twenties', *Historical Journal*, 20 (1977), 479–96.

McKibbin, R., 'The economic policy of the second Labour government, 1929–1931', *Past & Present*, 68 (1975), 95–123.

'Working-class gambling in Britain, 1880–1939', *Past & Present*, 82 (1979), 147–78.

'Class and conventional wisdom: the Conservative party and the "Public" in inter-war Britain', in *The ideologies of class: social relations in Britain, 1880–1950* (Oxford, 1990), 259–93.

'Politics and the medical hero: A. J. Cronin's *The Citadel*', *English Historical Review*, 123 (2008), 651–78.

Mandler, P., 'Against "Englishness": English culture and the limits of rural nostalgia, 1850–1940', *Transactions of the Royal Historical Society*, 17 (1997), 155–75.

336   Bibliography

'The consciousness of modernity? Liberalism and the English "national character", 1870–1940', in B. Rieger & M. Daunton (eds.), *Meanings of modernity: Britain from the late-Victorian era to World War II* (Oxford, 2001), 119–44.

'What is "national identity"? Definitions and applications in modern British historiography', *Modern Intellectual History*, 3 (2006), 271–97.

Manton, K., 'Playing both sides against the middle: the Labour party and the wholesaling industry, 1919–1951', *Twentieth Century British History*, 18 (2007), 306–33.

Marwick, A., 'Middle opinion in the thirties: planning, progress and political "agreement"', *English Historical Review*, 79 (1964), 285–98.

Mathers, H., 'The city of Sheffield, 1893–1926', in C. Binfield, et al. (eds.), *The history of the city of Sheffield, 1843–1993, vol. 1: politics* (Sheffield, 1993), 53–83.

Matthews, I., 'Pembrokeshire county politics, 1860–1880', *Journal of the Pembrokeshire Historical Society*, 9 (2000), 39–55.

May, E., 'Charles Stanton and the limits of "patriotic labour"', *Welsh History Review*, 18 (1997), 483–508.

Moore, J., 'Liberalism and the politics of suburbia: electoral dynamics in late nineteenth-century South Manchester', *Urban History*, 30 (2003), 225–50.

Morgan, K., 'The Conservative party and mass housing, 1918–1939', in S. Ball & I. Holliday (eds.), *Mass Conservatism: the Conservatives and the public since the 1880s* (London, 2002), 58–77.

Morgan, K. O., 'The Merthyr of Keir Hardie', in G. Williams & G. A. Williams (eds.), *Merthyr politics: the making of a working-class tradition* (Cardiff, 1966).

'Twilight of Welsh Liberalism: Lloyd George and the "Wee Frees", 1918–35', *Bulletin of the Board of Celtic Studies*, 12 (1968), 389–405.

'The New Liberalism and the challenge of Labour: the Welsh experience, 1885–1929', in K. D. Brown (ed.), *Essays in anti-Labour history: responses to the rise of Labour in Britain* (London, 1974), 159–82.

'1902–1924', in D. Butler (ed.), *Coalitions in British politics* (London, 1978).

'Peace movements in Wales, 1899–1945', *Welsh History Review*, 10 (1981), 398–430.

Morgan, P., 'Wild Wales: civilising the Welsh from the sixteenth to the nineteenth centuries', in P. Burke, B. Harrison & P. Slack (eds.), *Civil histories: essays presented to Sir Keith Thomas* (Oxford, 2000), 265–83.

Morgan, S., 'Domestic economy and political agitation: women and the Anti-Corn Law League, 1839–1846', in K. Gleadle & S. Richardson (eds.), *Women in British politics, 1760–1860: the power of the petticoat* (Basingstoke, 2000), 115–33.

Mór-O-Brien, A., 'The Merthyr Boroughs election, November 1915', *Welsh History Review*, 12 (1985), 538–66.

Neill, E., 'Conceptions of citizenship in twentieth century Britain', *Twentieth Century British History*, 17 (2006), 424–38.

Nicholas, S., 'The construction of a national identity: Stanley Baldwin, "Englishness" and the mass media in inter-war Britain', in M. Francis & I. Zweiniger-Bargielowska (eds.), *The Conservatives and British society, 1880–1990* (Cardiff, 1996), 27–46.

Bibliography

Olechnowicz, A., 'Civic leadership and education for democracy: the Simons and the Wythenshawe estate', *Contemporary British History*, 14 (1999), 3–26.

'Unemployed workers, "enforced leisure" and education for "the right use of leisure" in Britain in the 1930s', *Labour History Review*, 70 (2005), 27–52.

Ottewill, R., 'Virgin territory?: researching the local political history of interwar Britain', *Local Historian*, 37 (2007), 45–50.

Owen, N., 'MacDonald's parties: the Labour party and the "aristocratic embrace", 1922–31', *Twentieth Century British History*, 18 (2007), 1–53.

Parkin, F., 'Working-class Conservatives: a theory of political deviance', *British Journal of Sociology*, 18 (1967), 278–89.

Parry, J. P., 'High and low politics in modern Britain', *Historical Journal*, 29 (1986), 753–70.

'The quest for leadership in Unionist politics, 1886–1956', *Parliamentary History*, 12 (1993), 296–311.

Pedersen, S., 'From national crisis to "national crisis": British politics, 1914–1931', *Journal of British Studies*, 33 (1994), 322–35.

'What is political history now?', in D. Cannadine (ed.), *What is history now?* (London, 2002), 36–56.

Peele, G., 'Revolt over India', in Peele & C. Cook (eds.), *The politics of reappraisal, 1918–1939* (London, 1975), 114–45.

Pocock, J. G. A., 'The politics of historiography', *Historical Research*, 78 (2005), 1–14.

Pronay, N., 'The newsreels: the illusion of actuality', in P. Smith (ed.), *The historian and film* (Cambridge, 1976), 95–119.

Pryce, W. T. R., 'Language zones, demographic changes, and the Welsh culture area, 1800–1911', in G. H. Jenkins (ed.), *The Welsh language and its social domains, 1801–1911* (Cardiff, 2000), 37–79.

Pugh, M., 'The *Daily Mirror* and the revival of Labour, 1935–45', *Twentieth Century British History*, 9 (1998), 420–38.

'Lancashire, cotton, and Indian reform: Conservative controversies in the 1930s', *Twentieth Century British History*, 15 (2004), 143–51.

'The Liberal party and the Popular Front', *English Historical Review*, 121 (2006), 1327–50.

Ramsden, J., '"A party for owners or a party for earners?" How far did the British Conservative party really change after 1945?', *Transactions of the Royal Historical Society*, 37 (1987), 49–63.

'The Newport by-election and the fall of the Coalition', in Ramsden & C. Cook (eds.), *By-elections in British politics* (Abingdon, 1997), 13–36.

Rasmussen, J. S., 'Government and intra-party opposition: dissent within the Conservative parliamentary party in the 1930s', *Political Studies*, 19 (1971), 172–83.

Readman, P., 'Conservatives and the politics of land: Lord Winchilsea's National Agricultural Union, 1893–1901', *English Historical Review*, 121 (2006), 25–69.

'Jesse Collings and land reform, 1886–1914', *Historical Research*, 81 (2008), 292–314.

338   Bibliography

Ridley, J., 'The Unionist Social Reform Committee, 1911–1914: wets before the deluge', *Historical Journal*, 30 (1987), 391–413.

Roberts, G. T., '"Under the hatches": English parliamentary commissioners' views of the people and language of mid-nineteenth-century Wales', in B. Schwarz (ed.),*The expansion of England: race, ethnicity and cultural history* (London, 1996), 169–94.

Roberts, M., '"Villa Toryism" and popular Conservatism in Leeds, 1885–1902', *Historical Journal*, 49 (2006), 217–46.

'Constructing a Tory world-view: popular politics and the Conservative press in late-Victorian Leeds', *Historical Research*, 79 (2006), 115–43.

'W. L. Jackson, exemplary manliness and late Victorian popular Conservatism', in M. McCormack (ed.), *Public men: masculinity and politics in modern Britain* (Basingstoke, 2007), 123–42.

Robson, B., 'Coming full circle: London versus the rest, 1890–1980', in G. Gordon (ed.), *Regional cities in the UK, 1890–1980* (London, 1986), 217–33.

Rolf, R., 'The politics of agriculture: farmers' organisations and parliamentary representation in Herefordshire, 1909–22', *Midland History*, 2 (1974), 168–86.

Rubinstein, W. D., 'Wealth, elites and the class structure of modern Britain', *Past & Present*, 76 (1977), 99–126.

Russell, D., 'The *Heaton Review*, 1927–1943: culture, class and a sense of place in inter-war Yorkshire', *Twentieth Century British History*, 17 (2006), 323–49.

Ryder, R., 'Council house building in County Durham, 1900–1939: the local implementation of national policy', in M. Daunton (ed.), *Councillors and tenants: local authority housing in English cities, 1919–1939* (Leicester, 1984), 40–100.

Saint, A., '"Spread the people": the LCC's dispersal policy, 1899–1965', in *Politics and the people of London: the London County Council, 1889–1965* (London, 1989), 215–35.

Scannell, P., 'Broadcasting and the politics of unemployment, 1930–1935', in R. Collins et al., *Media, culture and society: a critical reader* (London, 1986), 214–27.

Schwarz, B., 'The language of constitutionalism: Baldwinite Conservatism', in Schwarz & M. Langan (eds.), *Formations of nation and people* (London, 1984), 1–18.

'Conservatism and "caesarism", 1903–22', in Schwarz & M. Langan (eds.), *Crises in the British state, 1880–1930* (London, 1985), 33–62.

'Politics and rhetoric in the age of mass culture', *History Workshop Journal*, 46 (1998), 129–59.

Schwarz, B. & Hall, S., 'State and society, 1880–1930', in M. Langan & Schwarz (eds.), *Crises in the British state, 1880–1930* (London, 1985), 7–32.

Scott, P., 'The evolution of Britain's built environment', in M. Daunton (ed.), *The Cambridge urban history of Britain, vol. III: 1840–1950* (Cambridge, 2000), 495–523.

Searle, G., 'The Edwardian Liberal party and business', *English Historical Review*, 98 (1983), 28–60.

Bibliography 339

Sewell Jr., W., 'The concept(s) of culture', in V. E. Bonnell & L. Hunt (eds.), *Beyond the cultural turn: new directions in the study of society and culture* (Berkeley, 1999), 35–61.

Smyth, J., 'Resisting Labour: Unionists, Liberals, and moderates in Glasgow between the wars', *Historical Journal*, 42 (2003), 375–401.

St John, I., '*Writing to the defence of empire*: Winston Churchill's press campaign against constitutional reform in India, 1929–1935', in C. Kaul (ed.), *Media and the British empire* (Basingstoke, 2006), 104–24.

Stapleton, J., 'Citizenship versus patriotism in twentieth-century England', *Historical Journal*, 48 (2005), 151–78.

Stead, P., 'Working class leadership in South Wales, 1900–1920', *Welsh History Review*, 6 (1973), 329–53.

Stedman Jones, G., 'Working-class culture and working-class politics in London, 1870–1900: notes on the remaking of a working class', in *Languages of class: studies in English working class history, 1832–1982* (Cambridge, 1983), 179–238.

Stevens, C., 'The Conservative club movement in the industrial West Riding, 1880–1914', *Northern History*, 38 (1991), 121–43.

Tanner, D., 'Elections, statistics, and the rise of the Labour party, 1906–1931', *Historical Journal*, 34 (1991), 893–908.

'The Labour party and electoral politics in the coalfields', in A. Campbell, N. Fishman & D. Howell (eds.), *Miners, unions and politics, 1910–47* (Aldershot, 1996), 59–92.

'Class voting and radical politics: the Liberal and Labour parties, 1910–31', in J. Lawrence & M. Taylor (eds.), *Party, state and society: electoral behaviour in Britain since 1820* (Aldershot, 1997), 106–30.

'The pattern of Labour politics, 1918–1939', in Tanner, C. Williams & D. Hopkin (eds.), *The Labour party in Wales, 1900–2000* (Cardiff, 2000), 113–39.

'Gender, civic culture and politics in South Wales: explaining Labour municipal policy, 1918–1939', in M. Worley (ed.), *Labour's grass roots: essays on the activities and experiences of local Labour parties and members, 1918–1945* (Aldershot, 2005), 170–93.

'Political leadership, intellectual debate and economic policy during the second Labour government, 1929–1931', in E. H. H. Green & Tanner (eds.), *The strange survival of Liberal England: political leaders, moral values and the reception of economic debate* (Cambridge, 2007), 113–50.

Taylor, A., 'Speaking to democracy: the Conservative party and mass opinion from the 1920s to the 1950s', in S. Ball & I. Holliday (eds.), *Mass Conservatism: the Conservatives and the public since the 1880s* (London, 2002), 78–99.

Taylor, D., 'The English dairy industry, 1860–1930', *Economic History Review*, 29 (1976), 585–601.

Taylor, M., 'John Bull and the iconography of public opinion in England, c. 1712–1929', *Past & Present*, 134 (1992), 93–128.

Thane, P., 'The working class and state "welfare" in Britain, 1880–1914', *Historical Journal*, 27 (1984), 877–900.

340   Bibliography

'Women, liberalism and citizenship, 1918–1930', in E. F. Biagini (ed.), *Citizenship and community: Liberals, radicals and collective identities in the British Isles, 1865–1931* (Cambridge, 1996), 66–92.

Thomas, G., 'Political modernity and 'government' in the construction of interwar democracy: local and national encounters', in L. Beers & G. Thomas (eds.), *Brave new world: imperial and democratic nation-building in Britain between the wars* (London, 2011), 39–65.

'The Conservative party and Welsh politics in the inter-war years', *English Historical Review*, 128 (2013), 877–913.

Thomas, M., 'Rearmament and economic recovery in the late 1930s', *Economic History Review*, 36 (1983), 552–79.

Thompson, J., '"Pictorial lies"? Posters and politics in Britain, c.1880–1914', *Past & Present*, 197 (2007), 177–210.

Thorpe, A., 'Myth and counter-myth in Second World War British politics', in C. Williams, & A. Edwards (eds.), *The art of the possible: politics and governance in modern British history, 1885–1997: essays in memory of Duncan Tanner* (Manchester, 2015), 121–42.

Tiratsoo, N., '"New vistas": the Labour party, citizenship and the built environment in the 1940s', in R. Weight & A. Beach (eds.), *The right to belong: citizenship and national identity in Britain, 1930–1960* (London, 1998), 136–56.

Todd, S., 'Young women, work and family in interwar rural England', *Agricultural History Review*, 52 (2004), 83–98.

Tomlinson, J., 'The political economy of globalization: the genesis of Dundee's two "united fronts" in the 1930s', *Historical Journal*, 57 (2014), 225–45.

Trainor, R. H., 'Neither metropolitan nor provincial: the interwar middle class', in A. Kidd & D. Nicholls (eds.), *The making of the British middle class? Studies of regional and cultural diversity since the eighteenth century* (Stroud, 1998), 203–13.

'The "decline" of British urban governance since 1850: a reassessment', in R. J. Morris & Trainor (eds.), *Urban governance: Britain and beyond since 1750* (Aldershot, 2000), 28–46.

Trentmann, F., 'The transformation of fiscal reform: reciprocity, modernization and the fiscal debate within the business community in early twentieth-century Britain', *Historical Journal*, 39 (1996), 1005–48.

'Wealth versus welfare: the British left between free trade and national political economy before the First World War', *Historical Research*, 70 (1997), 70–98.

'Bread, milk and democracy: consumption and citizenship in twentieth-century Britain', in M. Daunton & M. Hilton (eds.), *The politics of consumption: material culture and citizenship in Europe and America* (Oxford, 2001), 129–63.

'Materiality in the future of history: things, practices, and politics', *Journal of British Studies*, 48 (2009), 283–307.

Turner, A. J., 'Stanley Baldwin, heresthetics and the realignment of British politics', *British Journal of Political Science*, 35 (2005), 429–63.

Turner, M. E. & Beckett, J. V., 'End of the old order? F. M. L. Thompson, the land question, and the burden of ownership in England, c.1880–c.1925', *Agricultural History Review*, 55 (2007), 265–84.

Verdery, K., 'Ethnicity and local systems: the religious organisation of Welshness', in C. A. Smith (ed.), *Regional analysis, vol. ii: social systems* (New York, 1976), 191–227.

Vernon, J., 'What is a cultural reading of politics?', *History Workshop Journal*, 52 (2001), 261–5.

Wahrman, D., 'The new political history: a review', *Social History*, 21 (1996), 343–54.

Waller, P., 'Altercation over civil society: the bitter cry of the Edwardian middle classes', in J. Harris (ed.), *Civil society in British history: ideas, identities, institutions* (Oxford, 2005), 115–34.

Waller, R., 'Conservative electoral support and social class', in A. Seldon & S. Ball (eds.), *Conservative century: the Conservative party since 1900* (Oxford, 1994), 579–610.

Ward, P., 'Preparing for the People's War: Labour and patriotism in the 1930s', *Labour History Review*, 67 (2002), 171–85.

Ward, S., 'The means test and the unemployed in south Wales and the north-east of England, 1931–1939', *Labour History Review*, 73 (2008), 113–32.

Ward-Smith, G., 'Baldwin and Scotland: more than Englishness', *Contemporary British History*, 15 (2001), 61–82.

Waters, C., 'Autobiography, nostalgia, and the changing practices of working-class selfhood', in G. K. Behlmer & F. M. Leventhal (eds.), *Singular continuities: tradition, nostalgia, and society in modern Britain* (Stanford, 2000), 178–95.

Whetham, E., 'The Agriculture Act, 1920 and its repeal – the "great betrayal"', *Agricultural History Review*, 22 (1974), 36–49.

Wilding, P. R., 'The genesis of the Ministry of Health', *Public Administration*, 45 (1967), 149–68.

Wildman, C., 'Urban transformation in Liverpool and Manchester, 1918–1939', *Historical Journal*, 55 (2012), 119–43.

Williams, C., 'Labour and the challenge of local government, 1918–1939', in D. Tanner, C. Williams & D. Hopkin (eds.), *The Labour party in Wales, 1900–2000* (Cardiff, 2000), 140–65.

Williamson, P., '"Safety First": Baldwin, the Conservative party, and the 1929 general election', *Historical Journal*, 25 (1982), 385–409.

'The doctrinal politics of Stanley Baldwin', in M. Bentley (ed.), *Public and private doctrine: essays in British history presented to Maurice Cowling* (Cambridge, 1993), 181–208.

'Christian Conservatives and the totalitarian challenge, 1933–1940', *English Historical Review*, 115 (2000), 607–42.

'The Conservative party, 1900–1939: from crisis to ascendancy', in C. Wrigley (ed.), *A companion to early twentieth-century Britain* (Oxford, 2003), 2–33.

'Baldwin's reputation: politics and history, 1937–67', *Historical Journal*, 47 (2004) 127–68.

'Stanley Baldwin's myth: the making of an historical myth', *The Historian*, 82 (2004), 18–23.

342   Bibliography

'The monarchy and public values, 1910–1953', in A. Olechnowicz (ed.), *The monarchy and the British nation, 1780 to the present* (Cambridge, 2007), 223–57.

Windscheffel, A., 'Men or measures? Conservative party politics, 1915–1951', *Historical Journal*, 45 (2002), 937–51.

Theses

Bates, J. W. B., '*The Conservative party in the constituencies, 1918–1939*', DPhil thesis, University of Oxford, 1994.

Beers, L., ' *"Selling Socialism": Labour, democracy and the mass media, 1900–1939*', PhD thesis, Harvard University, 2007.

Cooper, T., '*Politics and place in suburban Walthamstow, 1870–1914*', PhD thesis, University of Cambridge, 2005.

Dearling, J., '*The language of Conservatism in Lancashire between the wars: a study of Ashton-under-Lyne, Chorley, Clitheroe, Royton, and South Salford*', PhD thesis, University of Manchester, 2002.

Jarvis, D., '*Stanley Baldwin and the ideology of the Conservative response to Socialism, 1918–1931*', PhD thesis, University of Lancaster, 1991.

Moore, S., '*Reactions to agricultural depression: the agrarian Conservative party in England and Wales, 1920–1929*', DPhil thesis, University of Oxford, 1988.

Rolf, K. W. D., '*Tories, tariffs and elections: the West Midlands in English politics, 1918–1935*', PhD thesis, University of Cambridge, 1975.

Taylor, E. M. M., '*The politics of Walter Elliot, 1929–1936*', PhD thesis, University of Edinburgh, 1980.

Thackeray, D., '*Popular politics and the making of modern Conservatism, c.1906–1924*', PhD thesis, University of Cambridge, 2009.

Williams, T. W., '*The Conservative party in north-east Wales, 1906–1924*', PhD thesis, University of Liverpool, 2008.

Index

1918 election
  in Birmingham, 28, 103
  Conservative challenges in, 25, 27
  Conservative-Liberal alliance, 64
  defence, questions of, 96
  in Devizes, 171
  franchise, expansion of, 16
  new seats in, 29
  in Norfolk North, 174, 179
  vote share, 12, 15
1922 election
  Baldwin, role in, 25
  Conservative withdrawal from post-war
    coalition, 1, 4, 258
  Labour vote share, 33
  in Norfolk North, 174
  party identity in, 3, 254, 264
  in Stockton, 31
  three-party contests, 57
1923 election
  Baldwin, role in, 25, 42
  Conservative stagnation, 17
  dear food cry, 34
  in Devizes, 34, 169, 171
  in Ilford, 143
  Labour vote share, 39
  in Liverpool Edge Hill, 11
  protectionism in, 33, 72
  in Stockton, 33
  in Swindon, 17
  three-party contests, 57
1924 election
  anti-socialism in, 19, 55, 145
  as three-way contest, 17
  Baldwin, role in, 25, 39, 43, 61, 262
  in Birmingham, 39
  in Devizes, 171
  in Ilford, 30
  Labour party in, 17
  Liberal party in, 13, 52
  political education in, 35, 49, 53–4
  in Scotland, 199

  in Stockton, 40
  vote share, 12, 57
1929 election, 52–7
  Baldwin, role in, 52, 55, 61, 68
  Conservative response to, 59, 129
  Conservative stagnation, fears of, 17
  in Devizes, 14, 17
  in the industrial north, 108
  Labour party in, 17, 21, 46, 50, 103, 133
  Liberal party in, 54–7, 128
  in Norfolk North, 54, 60
  in Scotland, 199
  in Stockton, 57, 62
  in Wales, 204–5, 206, 221
1931 election, 65–72
  Baldwin, role in, 68, 70, 72
  broadcasting in, 111
  in the countryside, 168–79
  in Devizes, 71, 172–3
  in Dundee, 108, 199–200
  in Epping, 142
  in Ilford, 71, 139
  in the industrial north, 107–12
  in Liverpool, 140, 144
  in Norfolk North, 55, 169, 179
  in Scotland, 199–204
  in Stockton, 66, 107, 112
  in the suburbs, 138–44
  in Wales, 204–10
1935 election, 96–100
  Baldwin, role in, 98, 160
  broadcasting, 97–8, 159
  in the countryside, 191–6
  in Devizes, 193, 195–6
  in Dunbartonshire, 199, 226
  in Dundee, 119
  in Epping, 161
  in Ilford, 157, 161
  in the industrial north, 127–33
  in Liverpool, 119
  in Norfolk North, 195
  in Scotland, 224–9

343

344 Index

1935 election (cont.)
  in Stockton, 119, 129
  in the suburbs, 156–64
  in Wales, 222–4
39 Steps, The (film) 1935, 158

abdication crisis, 234
Abyssinian crisis, 96, 99, 160
Adams, Vyvyan
  1931 election, 108, 109
  1935 election, 127
  as anti-appeaser, 233, 238
  as centrist Conservative, 8
  on MacDonald, 68
  as maverick, 265
  on protectionism, 113
Addison, Christopher, 181, 186
agitprop, 84, 87
Agricultural Marketing Act of 1933, 181
Agricultural Party, 38, 179
Agricultural Wages Act of 1924, 189
Agricultural Wages Board, 39
agriculture
  depression in, 167–8
  Labour party on, 254
  Liberal party on, 52
  protection of, 34, 38, 60, 62, 171
  recovery, politics of, 20, 81–2, 166–7,
    168, 177–8, 179–87, 192, 265
  trade unionism in, 9, 34, 166, 174
  unemployment in, 53, 189–90
Ailesbury, George Brudenell-Bruce, 6th
    Marquess of, 37
Altrincham by-election 1933, 150, 151, 153
Amery, Leo, 26, 41, 179
Anglo-Celtic frontier, 198, 210
anti-socialism
  1929 election, 55, 56
  1931 election, 66–7
  1935 election, 128
  of Baldwin, 26, 42–3, 45, 49
  under Chamberlain, 235
  as Conservative strategy, 19, 50–1,
    83, 162
  Liberal voters, appeal to, 52, 56, 142
  middle-class, 37, 135
  National Government, culture of, 72,
    95, 261
  rural, 173
  sensationalist (1920s), 108, 223, 256
  suburban, 138–40, 163–4
  in Wales, 223
  working-class, 103, 106, 109,
    111, 112
Anti-Waste League, 37, 59

apathy
  among Conservative activists, 61
  of known Conservatives, 29, 35–6, 58,
    60, 116, 150, 246
  towards National Government, 240
  with party politics, 154
  among Scottish voters, 227
  of suburban voters, 145
  among Welsh liberals, 208
appeasement, 234–5, 238, 251
Argyll Works (Dunbartonshire), 219, 226
Ashford by-election 1933, 150
Ashridge College (Circles), 33, 255
Asquith, Herbert, 45
Association of Conservative Clubs (ACC),
    92, 123, 126
Attlee, Clement, 22, 97, 105, 157, 235,
    247–8, 251, 265

Baldwin, Stanley
  1922 election, 25
  1923 election, 25, 33, 42
  1924 election, 25, 39, 43, 61, 262
  1929 election, 52, 55, 61, 68
  1931 election, 68, 70, 72
  1935 election, 98, 160
  abdication crisis, 234
  Abyssinia crisis, 160, 233
  on active citizenship, 120
  anti-socialism, 26, 39, 42–3, 45, 49
  on beer duty, 115
  broadcasts, use of, 61, 62, 98, 159,
    160, 261
  Conservative criticism of, 58, 59–61, 65,
    68, 71, 137, 160, 262
  as electoral asset, 26, 68, 96, 263
  as enigma, 26, 44
  General Strike, 43–4, 45
  inaction, image of, 262
  Labour criticism of, 83
  leadership style, 25–7, 61–2
  on Lloyd George, 214
  national values of, 3, 91, 95, 131, 138,
    163, 197, 259
  as Prime Minister, 2, 65, 128
  protectionism, 33, 65, 72
  on rearmament, 97, 99, 236
  resignation, 234
  rhetorical tone, 42–4, 52, 64, 145
  on rural life, 166, 176
  Safety First campaigns, 53, 55
  Scotland, role in, 204
  suburban Conservative appeal, 164
  in USRC, 41
  on world peace, 159

Index

345

Ball, Stuart, 26, 61
Barron, Hester, 46
Bates, Jonathan, 106
Batley and Morley, 112
Bayford, Robert Sanders, 1st Baron
  Bayford, 44, 92, 122, 170
Beaverbrook, Max Aitken, 1st Baron
  Beaverbrook, 8, 57, 60, 62, 171
Beaverbrook press, 26, 118
Becontree estate, 9, 29, 50, 148, 151, 161
beer duty, 74, 115
Bell, Hewart, 171
Bennett, Sir Ernest, 212
Bernays, Robert, 242
Betterton, Sir Henry, 190, 263
Betting and Lotteries Bill of 1934, 125
Beveridge Report, 233
Beveridge, William, 190
Billingham, 31
Birkenhead, Frederick Edwin Smith, 1st
  Earl of, 39, 41
Birmingham
  1918 election, 28, 103
  1924 election, 40
  1929 election, 54
  1931 election, 111, 144
  1935 election, 161
  Neville Chamberlain as Mayor, 41
  Conservative activists in, 58, 92
  Conservative tradition in, 29
  Conservative vote share, 15, 240
  fascist activity in, 93
  Labour party in, 16, 28, 40, 46–7, 48,
    103, 249
  Liberal party in, 153, 157, 161
  middle-class political apathy, 35
  parliamentary constituencies, 27
  protectionist tradition, 73, 104, 108,
    113, 140
Birmingham City Council, 35
Birmingham Conservative and Unionist
  Association, 28, 29
Birmingham Edgbaston, 146
Birmingham Erdington, 94, 146
Birmingham King's Norton, 40, 162
Birmingham Ladywood, 40
Birmingham Moseley
  1921 by-election, 32, 37
  1924 election, 40
  1931 election, 144
  1935 election, 161
  black-coated workers in, 158
  Conservative non-party approach, 137,
    146, 163
  Labour vote, 162

as middle-class constituency, 8
new estates in, 243
as safe seat, 40
suburban expansion, 146
Birmingham Municipal Tenants'
  Association, 249
Birmingham Post, 142, 157
black-coated workers, 149, 158, 168, 191
Bleak House, Great Expectations speech
  (Chamberlain), 76
Branson, Noreen, 266
Bread (film) 1934, 84
Bridgeman, William, 1st Viscount
  Bridgeman, 53, 72
Brierley, Walter, 84
Britain's Industrial Future (Yellow Book)
  1928, 51, 52, 142
British Commercial Gas Association, 84
British Commonwealth Union, 8, 31
British Institute of Public Opinion, 253
broadcasting
  1931 election, 111
  1935 election, 97–8, 159
  Attlee, 97
  Baldwin, 61, 62, 98, 159, 160, 261
  Chamberlain, 76
  listening groups, 255
  Lloyd George, 205, 210
  National Government publicity, 88,
    184, 240
  political communication, role in, 25,
    260, 262
  Samuel, 161
  Snowden, 111, 160
  social change, 6, 20, 84
Brooke, Henry, 85–6
Brown, Ernest, 95, 219, 228
Burderop Park (Wiltshire), 186
Burton, Sir Montague, 130
Buxton, Captain Harry, 175
Buxton, Sir Thomas, 175
by-elections
  Aberdeen North 1928, 52
  Altrincham 1933, 150, 151, 153
  Ashford 1933, 150
  Birmingham Moseley 1921, 32, 37
  Cardiganshire 1932, 214
  Darlington 1926, 45
  Dartford 1937, 251
  Dunbartonshire 1926, 45, 52
  Dunbartonshire 1932, 113, 216, 227
  Dunbartonshire 1936, 227, 254
  East Fulham 1933, 153
  East Ham North 1926, 45
  Hitchin 1933, 150, 153

346　Index

by-elections (cont.)
  Ilford 1928, 50–1
  Ilford 1937, 235, 246
  Islington North 1937, 239, 250
  Liverpool East Toxteth 1929, 51
  Liverpool Exchange 1933, 150
  Merthyr 1934, 214
  Monmouth 1934, 215
  Norfolk North 1930, 60, 169, 171
  North Dorset 1937, 246
  North Lanarkshire 1929, 52
  Oxford 1937, 251
  Portsmouth North 1934, 152
  Stockport 1926, 45
  Swindon 1934, 186
  Wakefield 1932, 115

Cadogan, Sir Edward, 14
Caledon shipyard (Dundee), 218,
  221, 225
Calley, General, 186
Cambray, Philip, 55
Cambrian News, 204, 205
Campbell case, 41
Carr, Arthur Comyns, 51
Carroll, Madeleine, 158
Cassells, Thomas, 226
Ceadel, Martin, 156
Cecil, Robert, 1st Viscount Cecil of
  Chelwood, 130
Central Electricity Board, 147
Chamberlain, Austen, 39, 46, 72
Chamberlain, Hilda, 243
Chamberlain, Joseph, 8, 32, 73, 171, 185
Chamberlain, Mary, 186
Chamberlain, Neville
  1924 election, 40
  1929 election, 56
  on balanced budgets, 245
  Baldwin, relationship with, 26, 98, 160
  Birmingham, role in, 28, 41
  as Chancellor of the Exchequer, 19, 73
  construction boom under, 147, 235
  as CRD chairman, 58–9
  electoral popularity, 253
  health agenda, 239, 241
  Labour municipal policies, admiration
    for, 48
  on League of Nations Union (LNU), 155
  as man of the moment, 77
  as Minister of Health, 41
  Munich agreement, 251–2
  on National Government's record, 99
  as Prime Minister, 2, 235, 246
  rearmament under, 234, 236, 238

  reform agenda, 40–2, 43–4, 95, 118,
    179, 263
  restoration budget (1934), 76, 148
  on social relief, 83
  tariffs, introduction of, 72–3
  on unemployment, 85–6, 119
  Wales, policies on, 223
  on working-class Labour support, 103
Christian Brotherhood, 144
Churchill, Randolph, 151–2
Churchill, Winston
  anti-socialism of, 145, 157
  Baldwin, contrast with, 26, 62
  as Chancellor of the Exchequer, 41,
    43, 44
  on Indian home rule, 93, 150
  Liberal party, opposition from, 140, 154
  as MP for Epping, 9, 11, 60, 147
  on National Government, 139, 152
  on rearmament, 238
  on reform programme, 158
  resignation from shadow cabinet
    1931, 60
  super cinema, Woodford, 146, 147
  wartime coalition, 2, 19, 234
cinema, 10, 11, 77, 121, 134, 146, 147,
  237, 242
cinema-vans, 192, 220, 240
Citadel, The (Cronin) 1937, 252
Citizens' Advice Bureau, 88, 256
City of Back to Backs, A (1933), 252
civic amenities, 148–9
civic associations, 37
civic culture, 8, 16, 29, 36–7, 135, 146,
  156, 243
civic publicity movement, 106, 118
class, politics of, 32–3, *see also* middle-class
  voters; paternalism, rural; working-
  class voters
Classes and cultures (McKibbin), 136
Cleary, Mr (in East Toxteth), 51, 156
club movement, 120–7, 133
Clubs Bill of 1933, 122
Clynes, J.R., 97
coal dispute 1925, 44
Cochrane, Commander Archibald, 113,
  216–17, 219, 220, 226–7
Cockburn, Claude, 266
Collins, Sir Godfrey, 219, 227, 263
Colomb, Admiral Philip Howard, 92
Colville, John, 219, 225
Colvin, General Sir Richard, 154
Communist party, 199
Conservative activists
  1929 election, 53–4

Index

1931 election, 5, 66, 75, 138
agricultural reform, 181
anti-socialism, 49, 95
apathy among, 61
Baldwin, views on, 27, 43, 68, 98, 160, 262, 263
in Birmingham, 28
civic culture, role in, 37, 243, 256
club movement, 123–4
community interests, focus on, 260
Conservative stagnation, perception of, 14–17, 25, 137
co-operative movement, 47
in the countryside, 166
Empire Crusade, response to, 59
evaluative process, 12
health campaign, impact of, 242
Indian home rule, 92–3
in the industrial north, 104, 116, 132, 133
Liberal activists, relations with, 56, 142, 144, 152, 173
in local politics, 5–8, 11, 27, 28–9, 264
mass-media, influence of, 61, 260
National Government, support for, 4, 21, 64, 93, 254
National party, scepticism of, 92
National Publicity Bureau (NPB), enthusiasm for, 240
new estates, reluctance to visit, 106
non-party approach, 145, 154
party discipline, 89
party organisation, relationship with, 18, 34, 106
patriotism, appeal of, 112
philanthropy of, 121
political education, 255
political rhetoric, reception of, 262
positive politics, demand for, 57, 71, 261
post-war coalition, condemnation of, 1
on rearmament, 238
recovery, narratives of, 99–100, 263, 264, 267
on rural paternalism, 38–9, 174, 193
in Scotland, 202, 219
in the suburbs, 135, 138
target voters, 32, 259
on tariffs, 113, 169
in Wales, 213, 215
working-class, 58
Conservative agents, 11, 33, 256, 257
Conservative Agents' Journal, 38
Conservative and Unionist Film Association, 82
Conservative associations
on Baldwin, 26

club movement, 123
empire free trade, support for, 60
Indian home rule, 154
landed families, patronage by, 174
local government, 56
middle-class recruits, 36
National parties, relations with, 254
non-party membership, 145
party identity, reassertion of, 151
political education, 35
role of, 31
in Wales, 212, 214
Conservative Central Office
1929 election, 53
1931 election, 65, 67, 68
activists, relationship with, 106
broadcasts, use of, 261
Indian home rule, 154
newsreels, cooperation with, 79
political education, 233, 255
Welsh Conservatives, relationship with, 211
Conservative clubs, 122, 124
Conservative Research Department (CRD), 58–9, 65, 85
Conservative Teachers' Circles (Clubs), 163, 255
Contributory Pensions Act, 43
Cook, Ernest, 176
Cook, Thomas
1929 election, 56
1931 election, 69
1935 election, 191–4, 195
on agricultural reform, 181–2, 183
Baldwin, support for, 60
as Empire Free Trade candidate 1930, 171
farm-labourer vote, 177
firefighting scheme, 191, 193
on landed estates, 165, 178
Liberal National vote for, 94
paternalist appeal of, 173–4, 176, 178, 186, 191, 193, 195–6
as protectionist, 171–2
on rural welfare, 189–90
co-operative movement, 47
corn laws, 170
Corn Production Act of 1917, 189
Cornford, James, 135
Council of Action for Peace and Reconstruction, 97, 128, 130, 132, 161, 194, 195, 215
council-house building, 43, 117, 124, 203, 248, *see also* housing policy
Cowling, Maurice, 44, 97

348   Index

Cozens-Hardy, Archibald, 175
Cozens-Hardy, Herbert, 175
Cripps, Sir Stafford, 19, 157, 187
Cronin, A.J., 252
Crowson, Nick, 237
Cunliffe-Lister, Sir Philip, 41
Cunningham, Valentine, 104
Currie, Sir James, 169, 172
Cymru Fydd, 214

Daily Express, 234
Daily Herald, 252
Daily Mail, 150, 234
Daily Mirror, 234, 250
Daily Sketch, 234
Dalton, Hugh, 236, 249
Darlington & Stockton Times, 111
Darlington by-election 1926, 45
Dartford by-election 1937, 251
Davidson, J.C.C., 58–9
Davies, Rees, 209
Davies, Sam, 28
Day, Graham, 6
De La Warr, Herbrand Sackville, 9th Earl
    De La Warr, 90, 183
de Valera, Eamon, 126
dear food campaigns, 34, 75, 172
Deeds, Not Words (film) 1938, 241
deferential voting, 20, 166, 173, 174–5
Devizes
    1918 election, 171
    1923 election, 34, 169, 171
    1924 election, 171
    1929 election, 14, 17
    1931 election, 71, 172
    1935 election, 193, 195
    agricultural recovery in, 179, 184
    anti-socialism in, 67
    Conservative protectionists in, 171, 179
    Conservative vote share, 15, 57
    Conservative-Liberal competition, 14,
        74, 169–70, 262
    Conservative-Liberal National co-
        operation, 194
    farm labourers as voters, 32, 188
    Labour party in, 17, 188
    National Government, appeal of, 254
    national health campaign in, 243
    NPB film tour in, 240
    population, stability of, 15
    as rural constituency, 9, 10, 27
    rural paternalism in, 37, 168, 174
    as semi-rural constituency, 167
disarmament, 69, 96–7, 142, 154–5,
    195, 215

Disraeli, Benjamin, 32, 42, 135, 266
dole, the, 63, 105, 109, 110, 116, 141,
    189, 215
Duck, Alderman James, 169
Dumping Vans, 108, 140
Dunbartonshire
    1926 by-election, 45, 52
    1931 election, 199
    1932 by-election, 113, 216
    1935 election, 226
    1936 by-election, 227, 254
    Communist hooligans in, 199
    inter-party agreement in, 254
    Labour vote in, 203, 226, 268
    Liberal vote in, 119, 203
    as marginal seat, 198
    as mixed constituency, 9, 32
    National Government, support for, 228
    Scottish Special Area, inclusion in, 220
    SNP in, 217, 227
    Unionist vote share, 15, 98
Dundee
    1931 election, 108, 199–200
    1935 election, 119
    cinema vans in, 220
    economic recovery in, 225, 237
    Five Year Housing Plan, 117
    global considerations in, 10, 210
    jute industry, 113, 210, 218
    League of Nations Union (LNU), 219
    Liberal tradition, 118
    National Government, support for, 228
    Special Areas, exclusion from, 86
    tariffs 'betrayal', 218
    trade, decline of, 32
    Unionist vote share, 15
    Unionist-Liberal cooperation, 202
    as working-class constituency, 10
Dundee Courier, 225, 237
Dunnico, Harriet, 30
Dunnico, Reverend Herbert, 29
Durham Municipal and County
    Federation, 112
Durham, County
    club movement in, 122
    coalfields, 85
    coal-mining politics, 8
    council-house building, 117
    General Strike in, 46
    Labour party in, 16, 48, 109, 115, 116,
        119, 129
    Local government, 85
    National Government, support for, 21
    Special Area, 86
    unemployment in, 49

Index

Eales, J.F., 94
East Fulham by-election 1933, 153
East Ham North by-election
1926, 45
Eastern Daily Press, 175
Ebbw Vale steelworks, 223
Economy Act of 1926, 43
Eden, Anthony, 238, 267
Edgerton, David, 265
Education Act 1936, 239
Edward, Prince of Wales (Edward VIII), 87,
126, 234
Eichengreen, Barry, 236, 245
Electricity Supply Bill, 147
Elliott, Walter, 81, 168, 219, 222,
228, 263
Ellis, Geoffrey, 54
Empire Crusade, 57, 59–60
English Journey (Priestley) 1934, 10
Epping
1931 election, 142
1935 election, 161
Conservative non-party approach,
137, 144
Conservative vote share, 15, 57
Conservative-Liberal competition, 140,
154, 157
Conservative-Liberal cooperation, 143
Indian home rule controversy, 21,
93, 150
Labour party in, 158
middle-class interests, 32
National Government, scepticism of,
9, 86
political education in, 255
as safe seat, 11
as semi-rural constituency, 17
as suburban constituency, 9
super cinema, Woodford, 146, 147
voter apathy, 35, 58, 60
estates. *See* landed estates, new estates
Evans, R.T., 214
Evans, Victor, 214
Everton constituency, 40

farm labourers
1931 election, 170–1, 174, 178
1935 election, 192, 193
anti-Tory traditions, 168
Conservative appeal to, 32, 67, 165,
196
Labour appeal to, 187, 188, 189, 195
minimum wage, 34
nonconformist traditions, 38
paternalist appeal to, 37

unemployment insurance, 167, 188, 189,
190, 191
Farm Notes (*Norfolk Chronicle*), 192
farmers
agricultural protection, 38–9, 165
agricultural reform, 178, 180–1, 183–6,
192–3
discontent among, 246, 254
income, decline in, 187
Labour policy on, 168, 187
Noel-Buxton on, 194
rural intimidation, 171
in Scotland, 217
subsidies for, 34
tenant farmers, 52
in Wales, 222
fascism, 93
Fields, Gracie, 79
Films of Scotland Committee, 228
Firth, Sir William, 223
Fitzwilliams, Colonel, 214
flapper vote, 65
Foot, Dingle, 95, 202–3, 218, 225
For Socialism and Peace, 247
four year programme (Chamberlain), 41
Fourth Reform Act, 27
free-trade traditions
collective security, ideal of, 155
in the countryside, 169–70, 179
in Lancashire, 82
liberal, 73, 74, 75, 128, 138, 144, 205
middle-class, abandonment of, 144
in Scotland, 10, 202
in the suburbs, 141, 142
Victorian, 72
in Wales, 206
in Yorkshire, 34, 75, 113–14

Gallacher, Willie, 222
gambling, 125–6
Gardner, James, 54
Gas Light and Coke Company, 244
Gee, Stephen, 173
General Post Office, 80, 81
General Strike, 25, 44, 45–6, 49, 51,
52, 262
Geneva disarmament conference, 215
Gilmour, Sir John, 219, 228
Gislea, 186
Gladstone, William Ewart, 156, 201
Glasgow, 9, 56, 115, 198, 199, 202, 203,
222, 226, 227
Glasgow Empire Exhibition, 228
Glossop, Clifford, 181
gold standard, 43

350 Index

Gollancz, Victor, 84
Goulding, Edward, 171
Government of India Act of 1935, 150
Gower, 9, 207, 211, 223, 224
Gray, Robert, 217
great betrayal of 1921, 38, 189
Great Crusade, the story of a million homes
(film) 1937, 240
Great War, legacy of, 69–70, 155
Great Western Railway, 186
Green, E.H.H., 64, 245
Greenwood, Arthur, 115
Greenwood, Walter, 84
Grey, Edward, 1st Viscount Grey of
Fallodon, 68, 143, 172
Griffith-Boscawen, Sir Arthur, 38
Griffiths, C., 174
Guilty Men (Cato) 1940, 162
Guinness, Walter, 41

Haden-Guest, Leslie, 250
Hamilton, Sir George, 71, 141, 143,
147, 152
Hannon, Patrick
on black-coated workers, 158
on economic decline, 71
as far-right Conservative, 8
on industrial policy, 58
on League of Nations Union (LNU), 160
on Liberal party, 143, 159, 161
on middle-class interests, 31–2, 36
on policy-based appeal, 40
on post-war reconstruction, 31
Ratepayer's Association, opposition
from, 37
on tariffs, 141
Hawkey, Sir James, 5, 146
Headlam, Cuthbert
1931 election, 63
on Baldwin, 44
independence of, 132
on Labour strength, 129, 247
on political education, 233, 257
on unemployment, 4
on working-class voters, 119
Headlam, Mrs, 121
Health of the People, The (USRC), 42
Henderson, Arthur, 105, 111, 209
Hewins, W.A.S., 171
Hilliard, Chris, 105
Hinton, James, 243
historiography
Conservatives and the National
Government, 1–5
local political culture, 6–8

middle-class politics, 3, 13, 134–8
National Government, 2–4, 22
working-class politics, 103–7
Hitchcock, Alfred, 158
Hitchin by-election, 150, 153
Hoare, Sir Samuel, 41, 197, 233
Holidays with Pay Act 1938, 239
Homecraft Training Centres, 121
homes fit for heroes, 31
Hopkinson, Tom, 233
Hore-Belisha, Leslie, 90–1, 94, 184
Horsbrugh, Florence
1931 election campaign, 108, 110, 199
1935 election campaign, 225
cinema vans, use of, 221
jute industry, champion of, 113, 210, 218
League of Nations Assembly, role in, 218
on Liberal-Unionist cooperation, 202
on MacDonald, 204
Simon, support from, 219
spirit of war, evocation of, 111
on tariffs, 109, 200, 202
housebuilding, 53, 75, 99, 117, 125, 190,
237, 267
housewife consumers, 34, 250
housing policy. *See also* council-house
building
Baldwin's 2nd administration, 43
Hannon on, 31
in reformist culture, 40, 131
as National Government priority, 19,
118, 188, 240, 244, 267
in National government publicity, 240
under Labour councils, 117, 157, 247
Housing Problems (film) 1935, 84
Hurd, Percy
1923 election, 17
1931 election, 71, 169
1935 election, 191, 193, 195–6
on agricultural reform, 182, 183, 184–6
Beaverbrook and Rothermere, support
for, 171
on economic recovery, 72
on farm wages, 188
liberal voters, appeal to, 68, 193
on rural welfare, 165, 171–2, 179, 189, 190
Hutchinson, Geoffrey, 224
Hutchison, David, 151
Hydrocarbon Oil Production Act of
1934, 77

Ilford
1923 election, 143
1924 election, 30
1928 by-election, 50–1

Index

351

1931 election, 71, 139
1935 election, 157, 161
1937 by-election, 235, 246
anti-waste campaigns, 74, 148–9
Baldwin speech, 95
Conservative non-party approach, 137, 146, 163
Conservative publicity in, 157
Conservative vote share, 14, 15, 57, 161
Conservative-Liberal competition, 51–2
Conservative-Liberal cooperation, 143
creation of, 27, 29
independent conservatism in, 151
Labour vote, 16
League of Nations Union in, 157
Liberal vote, 51, 52, 134, 152, 262
middle-class interests, 32
political education in, 255
politics of place, 29–30
population growth, 15, 148
as semi-rural constituency, 17
as suburban constituency, 9
suburban growth, 147, 163
wage cuts, impact of, 141
Ilford and District Railway Users' Association, 147
Ilford Football Club, 30
Ilford Maternity and Child Welfare Association, 30
Ilford Monthly, the, 30, 51
Ilford Peace Council, 162
Ilford Ratepayers Association, 148
Ilford Recorder, 140, 148, 151
Ilford Women's Liberal Association, 142
Illustrated London News (ILN), 76–7, 82, 85, 237
Import Duties Act of 1932, 72, 113, 179, 181, 217
income tax, 43, 76, 148, 176
India Defence League (IDL), 150, 154
Indian home rule, 1, 21, 60, 89, 91, 92–3, 118, 138, 150–2
Industrial Transference Act of 1928, 86
Industrial Transference Board, 49
intimidation, of voters, 116, 171, 196
Irish Free State, 126

Jarrow, 85, 88
Jarrow Crusade, 266
Jarvis, Sir John, 88
Jeffery, Tom, 137
John Bull (poster), 138
Johnston, Tom, 216
Jones, Llewellyn, 214
Jones, Sir Edgar, 207

Joseph, Sir Keith, 267
Josephy, Frances, 193, 195
Joynson-Hicks, Sir William, 41
Junior Imperial League (JIL), 151
jute industry, 113, 199, 210, 218, 221
Juvenile Instruction Centres, 121

Keyes, Admiral Sir Roger, 152
Keynes, John Maynard, 62, 72, 143, 236, 265, 267
Kino Production Group, 84
Kirkintilloch Unemployed Workers' Union, 226
Knightswood estate (Dunbartonshire), 203
known Conservatives, 35, 36, 58, 60, 137, 150, 246

Labour and the Nation (1929 manifesto), 49
Labour party
1918 election, 12
1922 election, 33
1923 election, 34
1924 election, 39–40
1926 by-elections, 45
1929 election, 50, 52, 54, 55, 57
1931 election, 18–19, 62, 65–7, 68–9, 70, 107–11, 140, 169–78, 199–200, 203, 207–9, 263
1935 election, 97–8, 104, 105, 119, 127–30, 133, 161–2, 194–6, 221–2, 223–8
Abyssinian crisis, 160
agricultural policy, 254
Baldwin, response to, 42
in Birmingham, 35, 40, 46, 54, 244
in Conservative strategy, 25–6, 33, 39, 157–8, 259
in the countryside, 9, 38, 165–6, 168–79, 181, 182–3, 187–90, 194–6
in Dunbartonshire, 203–4, 216–17
in Dundee, 199–200
electoral recovery, post-1931, 21–2
General Strike, response to, 45, 49, 52
in government 1929–31, 57
government, cultures of, 246–53, 264
in Ilford, 50–1, 235
in the industrial north, 8, 105–6, 112–18, 119, 124–5, 127–30, 133
in Leeds, 40, 124
Liberal party, co-operation with, 15, 156
in Liverpool, 40, 51
in London, 94, 149, 239, 256
in municipal politics, 28, 35, 47–8, 58, 75, 83, 93–4, 124–5, 149, 151–3, 215–16, 239, 247–9, 254, 259, 262

352 Index

Labour party (cont.)
 National Government, critique of, 87,
  133, 234–5, 245, 262
 in Norfolk North, 56, 170–8
 post-war (1918) betrayal, rhetoric of, 70
 post-war (1945) politics, 265, 268
 rearmament, 236, 237
 rise of (in the interwar years),
  16–17, 18
 rural campaign 1934, 187–90
 in Scotland, 10, 197–8, 199–200, 201,
  203–4, 222, 224–8
 socialist planning, 87
 in Stockton, 40
 in the suburbs, 137–8, 140, 142, 149,
  161–2
 trade-union subscriptions, 44
 in Wales, 9, 197–8, 207–9, 213–16,
  221–2, 223–4, 229
Labour's Immediate Programme, 247
Lancashire Evening Post, 246
Land Settlement Association, 186
landed estates
 Baldwin on, 176
 break-up of, 37–8, 39, 165
 Cook on, 178
 labour relations in, 173
 modernisation in, 182, 186, 191
 role of, 165, 176, 194
Lansbury, George, 19
Laval, Pierre, 233
Lawrence, Jon, 27, 245
League of Nations, 96–7, 129, 159, 160,
  161, 162, 233, 238
League of Nations Assembly, 218
League of Nations Union (LNU)
 Adams, role in, 8
 Cecil as president, 130
 Conservative suspicion of, 114, 154–7
 Hannon on, 160
 Horsburgh, praise of, 218
 Labour co-operation with, 253
 national appeal of, 144
 Peace Ballot, 96, 163
 progressive appeal of, 162
 Simon on, 159
Leeds
 1935 election, 115, 119, 127–8
 Conservative propaganda campaigns, 48
 Conservative vote share, 15
 housing policy, 117, 124
 Labour party in, 16, 47, 48
 Liberal radicalism in, 262
 municipal politics, 124, 125, 130
 philanthropy in, 121

 post-war (1945) politics, 268
 slums in, 252
 Special Areas, exclusion from, 86
 tariff reform, 34
 unemployment in, 116
Leeds West
 1931 election, 108
 1935 election, 98, 127
 appeasement, opposition to, 238
 club movement in, 122
 cross-party appeals, 129, 130
 Labour threat, 40
 national appeal in, 68
 working-class Conservatism, 104
 as working-class constituency, 8
Left Book Club (LBC), 105, 252–3,
  255, 265
Let Us Face the Future (Labour manifesto,
  1945), 265
Leven, Vale of, 10
Liberal Nationals. *See also* Simonite
  Liberals
 1935 election, 99
 1937 by-elections, 235
 Conservative activists, relations with, 90
 Conservative domination of, 258
 in National ticket constituencies, 4, 8
 in Scotland, 216
 in Wales, 212
 National party, proposals for, 90
 seats contested by, 13
 Simon as leader, 158
Liberal party. *See also* Liberal Nationals;
  National Liberals; New Liberals;
  Samuelite Liberals; Simonite Liberals
 1923 election, 34
 1924 election, 43
 1929 election, 54–7, 128
 1931 election, 19, 68, 140–4, 169–76,
  200–10
 1935 election, 98, 128, 161–2, 193–4,
  195–6, 221, 222–3, 226
 in Birmingham, 40, 92, 157
 in Conservative strategy, 143–4, 152, 159
 Conservative activists, relations with, 56,
  142, 144, 152, 173
 in the countryside, 168, 169–76
 in Devizes, 14, 34, 37, 74, 168, 169, 170,
  172–3, 179, 193, 195
 on disarmament, 97
 in Dunbartonshire, 119, 228, 254
 in Dundee, 10, 95, 225
 in Epping, 140, 142, 157
 on gambling, 125
 in Glasgow, 202

Index

housewife consumers, interests of, 250
in Ilford, 14, 51, 134, 140, 142, 152, 157
Labour party, co-operation with, 156
League of nations Union, relationship with, 155
in Leeds West, 130
in Liverpool East Toxteth, 51, 140, 142, 156
Lloyd George as leader, 45, 51–2
in municipal politics, 56–7
National candidates, Conservative support for, 21
nineteenth century heritage, 265
in Norfolk North, 169, 174–6, 179, 187, 194
in opposition to National Government, 21–2
on protectionism, 73, 113–14, 172
radicalism in, 262
Samuelite-Simonite split, 74–5, 153–4
in Scotland, 200–4, 217–19
seats contested by, 13
in Southampton, 90
in Stockton, 30–1, 40, 90, 132
in the suburbs, 140–4
in Wakefield by-election, 115
in Wales, 204–10, 211–12, 213–15, 222–3
West Country tradition, 9
Liberal Unionists, 198, 199, 201
Lidgett, Reverend Scott, 194, 196
Lightman, Harold, 130
Lindsay & Low Ltd, 221
Listening Groups, 255
Liverpool
1931 election, 144
1935 election, 119
Baldwin, appeal of, 96
club movement in, 122, 126
Conservative vote share, 15, 240
fascist activity in, 93
Labour challenge, 16, 40, 48
Liberal party in, 143, 156
Liverpool City Council, 117, 118
Liverpool East Toxteth
1931 election, 140
Conservative non-party approach, 137
Conservative vote share, 57, 98, 161
Labour challenge, 40, 51, 156
Liberal vote, 142, 153
as middle-class constituency, 8
Liverpool Edge Hill, 11
Liverpool Exchange by-election, 150
Liverpool Post, 140, 142, 153
Liverpool Wavertree, 99, 151, 152, 153, 156

Liverpool West Derby, 98
Liverpool West Toxteth, 40
Lloyd George, David
1929 election, 55–7
1931 election, 68
1935 election, 159
agricultural reform, 189
Baldwin, contrast with, 25–6, 42
Conservative activists, response to, 31–2, 90, 130
Council of Action, 97, 128
electoral strategy, 52
as Liberal leader, 45
MacDonald, support for, 57
National Government agriculture portfolio, 180
post-war coalition, 1, 4, 64, 258
on protectionism, 172
reform agenda, 31, 99
Scotland, role in, 201
Wales, role in, 204–10, 211, 214–15, 229
Lloyd George, Gwilym, 205, 208–10, 222
Lloyd George, Megan, 205
Local Government Act of 1929, 43
London County Council (LCC), 21, 29, 42, 56, 94, 149, 239
London Municipal Society, 48
London Passenger Transport Board, 81
London Transport, 99
Londonderry, Edith Vane-Tempest-Stewart, Marchioness of, 112
Lothian, Philip Kerr, 11th Marquess of Lothian, 176

M'Gonigle, George, 184
MacDonald, James Ramsay
1929 election, 57
1931 election, 21, 68, 107, 110–12, 208, 258
1935 election, 99
as Conservative electoral asset, 1, 100, 110–11
Conservative support for, 64, 68
farm labourers, support from, 171
General strike, response to, 49
Labour opposition to, 18, 107
Lloyd George, relationship with, 205, 209
municipal agenda, 47
as National Labour leader, 2
national identity of, 96
as Prime Minister, 57, 95, 128, 258
Scotland, popularity in, 203
Welsh politics, role in, 208

354   Index

MacDonald, Malcolm, 228
Macmillan Lodge, 122
Macmillan, Harold
  1924 election, 40
  1929 election, 57, 62
  1931 election, 66, 69, 107
  1935 election, 103, 129
  as anti-appeaser, 238
  on Baldwin, 33
  club movement, support from, 123
  as Conservative progressive, 106, 265
  on economic reform, 71, 116, 263
  independence of, 131
  on Labour mismanagement, 109
  as MP for Stockton, 8, 11
  Next Five Years manifesto, 131–2
  on protectionism, 73
  on Ramsay MacDonald, 68, 110
  on slum clearances, 117
  on Special Areas, 86
  as target for demonstrations, 116
  on trade unionist rights, 31, 40
Macquisten, Frederick, 44
Mais, Peter, 87
Majestic Theatre, Woodford, 146
Manchuria, 160
Mandler, Peter, 162
Maternal Mortality Committee, 83
Maxton, James, 165
McCaffrey, John, 202
McCarthy, Helen, 37
McKenna Duties, 43
McKibbin, Ross
  1931 as pivotal accident, 5, 13
  middle-class Conservatism, 51, 134, 137,
    144, 147, 149
  on Conservative conventional wis-
    dom, 43
  working-class Conservatism, 3, 110
means test
  Communist opposition to, 199
  as financial orthodox policy, 19
  in the industrial north, 104
  Labour opposition to, 114, 115, 116, 216
  popular disquiet on, 74, 84, 118
  in Scotland, 203, 217
  women, role in, 123
media technology
  Labour use of mass-media, 105
  political communication, role in, 7, 18,
    25, 61, 95, 260
  social change, role in, 6
Mersey tunnel, 77
Middle Class Union, 36
middle-class voters

anti-socialism, 111, 116
anti-waste campaigns, 32, 50
civic leadership role, 36–7
Conservative strategy towards, 45
economic recovery, 147
historiography, 3, 13, 134–8
political apathy, 35–6
political culture, 50, 138, 253
protectionism, 140, 144
stereotypes of, 32
in the suburbs, 8, 9
Midlothian campaign, 156
Midwives Act of 1936, 239, 244
Milk Marketing Board, 181, 183
minimum wage, 34
mining communities
  in County Durham, 8, 119
  as Labour strongholds, 109, 133, 248
  in Scotland, 226
  unemployment in, 48
  in Wales, 9, 206, 216, 223, 244
ministry of all the Conservative talents, 39
Moderate party (Dundee council), 117
modernity, culture of, 77, 81, 168, 171,
  188, 244
Molden, J.W., 170
Molson, Hugh, 106
Montrose, James Graham, 6th Duke of
  Montrose, 218
More, Thomas, 95
Morgan, Evan, 212
Morley, Bob, 28
Morrison, Herbert, 149, 157, 247–8
Morton, H.V., 84, 252
Mosley, Oswald, 46
Movietone, 79
Munich agreement, 252
municipal politics
  1931 crisis, role in, 62, 107
  Chamberlain tradition in, 35, 42
  Conservative-Liberal alliances, 30
  in Glasgow, 202
  in the industrial north, 114
  Labour party, 16, 28, 47–8, 75, 115–16,
    117–18, 149, 151–2, 216, 235, 247–9,
    251, 253, 262
  Liberal party, 56–7
  in London, 240
  in Wales, 215
  in West Yorkshire, 125, 127
Municipal Reform Party, 56
Mussolini, Benito, 96

National alliance, 90, 217, 219, 226, 227
National Conservative League, 122

Index

National Council of Social Service (NCSS), 87–8, 120, 121, 186, 242, 244, 249
National Farmers Union (NFU), 38, 182
National Government
  1931 election, 68–9, 70–2, 107–12, 138–44, 168–79, 199–210
  1935 election, 99–100, 127–33, 194–6, 221–9
  agricultural reform, 20, 179
  Conservative activists on, 61, 63, 64–5, 66
  Conservative support for, 12
  countryside, electoral appeal in, 167–79, 194–6
  economic recovery, 19, 72–82, 112–19, 211–16
  historiography, 1–5, 22, 103–7
  industrial north, electoral appeal in, 107–12, 127–33
  Labour critique of, 87, 133, 234–5, 245, 262
  party identity in, 89–96, 150–64
  publicity campaigns, 48, 81–2, 85–6
  relief, politics of, 87–9
  Scotland, electoral appeal in, 9, 199–204, 216–21, 224–9
  suburban appeal of, 9, 21, 138–44
  under Chamberlain, 235–46
  Wales, electoral failure in, 9, 21, 204–10, 222–4
National Labour
  1935 election, 99, 127, 128
  Baldwin on, 67
  Conservative activists, relationship with, 4
  Conservative domination of, 153, 258
  in National Government, 2
  National party, proposals for, 90
  National ticket constituencies, 4, 8, 254
  seats contested by, 13
  in Wales, 212
National Liberals, 2, 121, 206, 207, *see also* Samuelite Liberals
National party, proposals for, 2, 90, 91–3, 94–5, 113
National Publicity Bureau (NPB), 79, 82, 119, 220, 240, 263
National Trust, 176
National Unemployed Workers Movement, 116
National Union of Agricultural Workers (NUAW), 174
National Union of Teachers, 141
Navy League, 8
new estates, 106, 127, 146–7, 162, 163, 242–3, 247

New Liberals, 22, 41, 43, 95, 104, 106, 264
New London Pictorial, 82
new towns, 116, 167
Newbury, 54
News Chronicle, 234
newsreels, 77–9, 81
Noel-Buxton, Lucy Edith, Baroness Noel-Buxton
  1930 by-election, 171
  1935 election, 187, 190, 195, 196
  deferential vote for, 174–5
  on intimidation of rural voters, 196
  Liberal voters, loss of, 176, 196
  National Government as Tory trick, 170
  on national recovery, 194
  on tariffs, 169–70
nonconformism
  in the countryside, 38, 165–6, 195
  disarmament, appeal of, 97
  League of Nations, support for, 155, 162
  Liberal tradition, 200
  middle-class, 137, 147
  National Government, support for, 194, 196
  in urban areas, 56
  in Wales, 9, 209
Norfolk
  1929 election, 54
  agricultural recovery, 182
  Conservative vote share, 15, 167
Norfolk and Norwich Hospital, 173
Norfolk Chronicle, 1, 55, 62, 182, 188, 191, 192–3
Norfolk North
  1918 election, 174, 179
  1922 election, 174
  1929 election, 60
  1930 by-election, 171
  1931 election, 55, 169, 179
  1935 election, 195
  agricultural recovery in, 179, 192
  anti-socialism, in 67
  Baldwin, crisis of confidence in, 60, 62
  Conservative-Liberal competition, 56
  Conservative-Liberal co-operation, 194
  farm labourers as voters, 32
  Indian home rule controversy in, 1, 92
  Labour party in, 170, 268
  Liberal party in, 175
  National Government, appeal of, 254
  National Government, scepticism of, 1
  nonconformist vote, 196
  population, stability of, 15
  protectionism, role of, 171
  as rural constituency, 9

356   Index

Norfolk North (cont.)
  rural paternalism in, 165, 173–5, 191
  women voters, 170
North Dorset by-election, 246
North Norfolk Elector, 194
North Norfolk hunt, 173
North Pembrokeshire and South
  Cardiganshire Tithepayers'
  Association, 222
north-south divide, 22, 116–17

Organisation for the Maintenance of
  Supplies, 44
Orwell, George, 84, 104, 252
Ottawa tariff agreements, 72, 73, 75, 89,
  113, 179, 218
Owen, Goronwy, 205
Oxford by-election, 251

Parker, Mrs, 47
party identity, 89, 150, 151, 154
party organisation (Conservative), 34
paternalism, rural, 37, 173–9, 191,
  193, 196
Pathé, 240
Peace Ballot, 9, 96, 99, 156, 163, 215, 236
Pease family, 45
Peat, Charles, 109
Pedersen, Susan, 70
Pelling, Henry, 9, 37
Pembroke Dockyard, 223
Pembrokeshire
  1931 election, 198, 208–10
  1935 election, 222–3
  Conservative vote share, 15, 21
  Conservative weakness in, 211
  Labour vote in, 268
  Liberal party in, 205
  as mixed constituency, 9, 32
  national appeal in, 198
  Special Areas, exclusion from, 86, 212
  Welsh language in, 213
Pembrokeshire Telegraph, The, 208
Peto, Basil, 171
Philip Stott College, 33
Physical Training and Recreation Act of
  1937, 241–2
Picture Post, 233, 252, 253
Pilgrim Trust, 85, 122
Pimlott, Ben, 105
Places without a future (Brooke, *Times* art-
  icles, 1934), 85, 184
Poor Law, abolition of, 43
Popular Illustrated, 79, 82, 157, 158,
  192, 220

Portrack Conservative Club, 123
poster campaigns
  1929 election, 53
  1931 crisis, use of, 18
  1931 election, 79, 111, 138–9,
    177–8, 192
  1935 election, 82, 119
  1950 election, 266
  Chamberlain in, 76, 77
  recovery, politics of, 184
  relief, politics of, 82
  in Scotland, 217
poverty
  1929 election, role in, 53
  1931 election, role in, 263
  in the countryside, 167, 169,
    173, 184
  in the industrial north, 85, 117
  Labour narrative of, 252, 266
  National Government, response to, 264
  in Scotland, 217
  in Wales, 215
Poverty in Plenty (BBC, 1934), 252
price guarantees, 32, 38
Price, Major Charles, 208–10
Priestley, J.B., 10, 84, 103, 134, 166
Primrose League, 15
Programme of Action (Cripps), 187
Progressive Party (in LCC), 56
Pronay, Nicholas, 79
property-owners, 32, 36, 110, 124, 138,
  147, 267
protectionism (tariffs)
  1923 election, 26, 33, 34, 43, 72
  1931 election, 65, 66, 138
  Baldwin on, 62
  Birmingham, tradition in, 104,
    108, 140
  Conservative appeal to liberalism,
    143–4
  Conservative distancing from,
    post-war, 267
  Conservative publicity on, 82
  in the countryside, 38, 60, 168, 169–73,
    179–80
  in Dundee, 108–9, 200, 202
  empire free trade, 60
  Keynes on, 143
  in Leeds, 34
  Liberal split over, 142, 205, 206–7,
    217, 218
  National Government policies, 72–3,
    218, 264, 265, 266
  Ottawa agreements, 72, 75, 89, 218
  revenues from, 117

Index

as scientific policy, 108, 113, 143, 179
Pugh, Martin, 162
Purdy, Colonel Thomas, 1, 3, 92

Ramsden, John, 267
ratepayers
  1931 election, 138
  anti-socialism of, 116
  anti-waste campaigns, 74
  civic amenities, 148–9
  in the countryside, 191, 196
  in municipal politics, 152, 157
  unemployment assistance, 120
  wage cuts, impact of, 141
  in Wales, 215
Ratepayers Associations, 36, 249
rearmament, 98, 215, 228, 234–5, 236–9, 251
recovery, politics of, 72–82
  in the countryside, 179–87
  in the industrial north, 119
  in Scotland, 216–21
  in the suburbs, 144–50
  in Wales, 211–16
Redistribution Act of 1918, 15, 27
relief, politics of, 82–9
  in the countryside, 187–91
  in the industrial north, 119–27
Restoration budget 1934, 76, 85, 118
Rhondda Infectious Diseases Hospital, 223
Right Book Club, 255
road construction, 19, 77, 100, 134, 182, 188, 190
Romford, 29
Rothermere press, 26, 118, 150
Rothermere, Harold Harmsworth, 1st Viscount Rothermere, 57, 59, 172
Roundway, Edward Murray Colston, 2nd Baron Roundway, 174, 194
Rowntree, Seebohm, 184, 241
Rowse, A.L., 194
Royal British Legion, 37, 144, 154, 173
Royal Norfolk Agricultural Society, 173
Runciman, Walter, 73, 220, 263
Rural District Councils' Association, 190

Safety First campaigns, 53, 55, 72, 129
Salisbury, Robert Gascoyne-Cecil, 3rd Marquess of Salisbury, 135
Samuel, Herbert
  1935 election, 159, 161
  as Conservative electoral asset, 68, 75, 172, 175
  on Conservative dominance, 153
  free-trade principles, 73, 179, 205

legitimating National Government, 96
  Lloyd George, split with, 205
  as National Liberal leader, 2
  resignation from National Government, 74, 153
  on Scottish home rule, 218
  Wales, importance in, 207, 209
Samuelite Liberals. *See also* National Liberals
  resignation 1932, 2, 74, 89, 218
  seats contested by, 13
  Simon, attacks on, 75
  tariffs, opposition to, 119, 153, 205
  in Wales, 206, 207, 214
Sandringham estate, 191
Sankey, John, 1st Viscount Sankey, 68
Scotland
  1924 election, 199
  1929 election, 199
  1931 election, 199–204
  1935 election, 224–9
  free-trade traditions, 10, 202
  home rule, 10, 200–1, 217–19
  Labour party in, 10, 197–8, 199–200, 201, 203–4, 222, 224–8
  Liberal party in, 200–4, 217–19
  municipal politics, 202
  National Government, electoral appeal of, 9, 199–204, 216–21, 225–9
  poverty in, 217
  recovery, politics of, 216–21
  trade unionism, 10
  unemployment in, 225
  Unionist activists, 202, 219
  voter apathy, 227
Scotsman, The, 201, 203, 217
Scott, Peter, 237
Scottish Development Council, 228
Scottish Illustrated, 82, 220
Scottish Liberal Federation, 218
Scottish National party (SNP), 217, 226–7
Scrymgeour-Wedderburn, Henry, 219
Seaham, 99
Sennowe Park, 165, 173, 178
Shamrock Football Club, 123
Sharp, Granville, 142
Sheppard, Frank, 31
Simon, John
  1935 election, 99
  as Conservative electoral asset, 68, 94, 100, 143, 161, 172, 175, 193–4, 264
  as Liberal National leader, 2
  Lloyd George, split with, 205
  as national figure, 96

358 Index

Simon, John (cont.)
  in *Popular Illustrated*, 158
  Samuelite split, 74, 205
  Scotland, importance in, 204, 219
  as tarnished Liberal, 159
  Wales, importance in, 207, 209
Simonite Liberals, 13, 153, 205, 206, 214,
    see also Liberal Nationals
Simpson, Mrs Wallis, 234
Sinclair, Sir Archibald, 217
Sing As We Go (film) 1934, 79
Skelton, Noel, 219
slum clearance
  in civic culture, 242
  Conservative activists on, 40, 117, 126
  in the countryside, 190
  in Labour councils, 124–5, 127
  as National Government priority, 19, 48,
    118, 264
  publicity campaigns, 77, 241
Smith, Alfred (of Peckham), 253
Snowden, Philip, 68, 89, 110, 128, 160,
    171, 258
Socialist League, 19, 157
something must be done (Prince of
    Wales), 87
South Wales Daily News, 206
South Wales Evening Post, 224
South Wales Miners' Federation, 224
Southampton, 90
Special Areas, 86–7, 118, 212–13, 215,
    219, 225, 227, 237, 249, 264
Special Areas (Development and
    Improvement) Act of 1934, 86
St Andrew's House, 228
Stanley, Oliver, 57, 237, 263
Stannage, T., 91
Steel-Maitland, Arthur, 41
Stockport, 45
Stockton-on-Tees
  1922 election, 31
  1923 election, 33
  1924 election, 40
  1929 election, 57, 62
  1931 election, 66, 107, 112
  1935 election, 119, 129
  club movement in, 121–2, 123
  Conservative challenge in, 30–1, 104
  Conservative propaganda campaigns, 48
  Conservative vote share, 15, 98
  Conservative-Liberal cooperation, 30,
    90, 113
  council-house building, 117
  economic reform, 117
  Labour party in, 47, 114, 268

national appeal in, 68
Next Five Years manifesto, 131–2
Priestley on, 103
as Special Area, 86
unemployment in, 103, 114
women voters in, 123
as working-class constituency, 8, 32
Stonehaven, John Baird, 1st Viscount
    Stonehaven, 4, 89–90, 91
Straightforward, the, 28, 46
Stuart, James, 219
suburbs
  1931 election, 138–44
  Conservative activists in, 135, 138
  National Government, appeal of, 9, 21,
    138–44
  politics of recovery, 144–50
  working-class voters in, 17, 136
Surrey Fund, 88
Swansea, 48, 207, 212, 224
Swindon, 17, 186

Tanner, Duncan, 18, 216, 245,
    248
Tariff Commission, 171
Tariff Reform League, 15, 171
tariffs. *See* protectionism (tariffs)
Tawney, R.H., 49
Tay bridge, 225
telephone exchange, 81
television, 81
Tennant, Katharine, 180
Thatcherism, 267
Therm, Mr, 244
Thom, Colonel, 200, 204
Thomas, Dr. Russell, 134
Thomas, J.H., 68, 110
Thompson, James, 77
Thorpe, Andrew, 65, 69
Times, The, 85, 184, 235, 253
Today We Live (film) 1937, 88, 244
Tomlinson, Jim, 210, 261
Town Crier, 28, 47
Townswomen's Guild, 114, 243
Toye, Richard, 247
Trade Disputes Act of 1927, 48,
    49, 195
trade unionism
  club movement, friction with, 123
  in the countryside, 9, 165, 174
  in the industrial north, 40, 66
  Labour party, co-operation with, 253
  in Scotland, 10
  in Wales, 216
  working-class Conservatism, 110

Index

Trades Union Congress (TUC), 45, 47, 49, 149, 252
transport, 50, 190, 250, 251
Tredegar, Courtenay Charles Evan Morgan, 1st Viscount, 212
Trentmann, Frank, 67, 144, 183, 260

unemployment
  1929 election, role in, 54, 55, 61
  1931 election, role in, 63, 66, 108
  Baldwin on, 62
  betting culture, 126
  black-coated workers, 149, 158
  Neville Chamberlain on, 41, 119
  club movement, role of, 120–2, 123
  Conservative publicity campaigns, 77
  in the countryside, 178, 186, 189–91
  in Dundee, 200, 221
  in the industrial north, 8, 48, 117
  Labour response to, 49, 105, 117, 247, 250, 266
  Macmillan on, 263
  National Government policies on, 73, 118–19, 210, 236, 239, 244, 263
  protectionism, role in, 33, 200
  public response to, 83–6, 87–9, 253
  in Scotland, 225
  in Stockton, 114
  in Wales, 215, 223
Unemployment Assistance Boards, 88
unemployment benefit, 76, 110, 118, 131, 199
unemployment insurance, 81, 88, 189–91, 261, 264
Union of Britain and India (UBI), 154
Unionist Propaganda Society, 29
Unionist Social Reform Committee (USRC), 41–2, 189
United Methodist Church, 194
Utopia (More), 95

Vernon, James, 266
Villa Tories, 35, 135

Wakefield, 54, 115
Wales
  1929 election, 204, 206, 221
  1931 election, 204–10
  1935 election, 222–4
  Conservative activists in, 212, 213, 215
  farmers, interests of, 222
  free-trade traditions, 206
  Labour party in, 9, 197–8, 207–9, 213–16, 221–2, 223–4, 229

Liberal party in, 204–10, 211–12, 213–15, 222–3
  municipal politics, 215
  National Government electoral failure, 9, 21, 204–10, 222–4
  National Labour in, 212
  nonconformist tradition, 9, 209
  poverty in, 215
  recovery, politics of, 211–16
  trade unionism, 216
  unemployment in, 215, 223
  working-class Conservatism in, 216
Walthamstow, 51
Watson, Bertrand, 30, 31
We can conquer unemployment (Liberal 1929 manifesto), 55
Wealth of a Nation (film) 1938, 228
Webb, Beatrice, 39
Welsh language, 9, 206, 208, 213, 214
West Yorkshire
  1929 election, 54
  1935 election, 98, 119
  free-trade traditions, 75, 113
  rearmament, impact on, 237
  unemployment in, 118
Western Mail, 206–7, 208, 213, 223
What I Saw in the Slums (Morton) 1933, 252
Wheat Act of 1932, 181
Wheatley Act, 43
Williams, Raymond, 197
Williamson, Philip, 26, 43, 71, 74, 95, 262
Wise, Sir Frederic, 11, 30, 50
Withers, Hartley, 237
women
  1929 election, 54, 57
  1931 election, 170
  as Conservative challenge, 25
  in Conservative organisations, 31, 123, 244
  in Dundee, 10
  enfranchisement of, 25
  Labour party policies, 216
  organisations, 146
  in Stockton, 123
  unemployment, 121
Women's Co-operative Guild, 83, 183
Women's Institute (WI), 36, 38, 144, 154, 243, 244, 255
Wood, Edward, 41
Wood, Sir Kingsley, 42, 81, 184, 240, 246, 263
Workers' Educational Association (WEA), 255
working-class Conservatism
  1931 election, 107–12

360   Index

working-class Conservatism (cont.)
  activists, recruitment of, 36, 58
  Chamberlain as embodiment of, 42, 58
  club movement, role in, 124, 125
  in Darlington, 45
  in Liverpool, 117
  in Stockton, 45
  in the industrial north, 103–4
  McKibbin on, 110
  strongholds of, 133
  Wales, challenges in, 216
working-class Unionism, 10, 226
working-class voters
  1931 election, 107–12
  1935 election, 119, 127, 133
  Conservative appeal to, 4, 15, 25, 29,
    33, 112
  in Dundee, 10, 199–200
  General Strike, 46, 49
  historiography, 3, 13, 103–7, 136
  Labour appeal to, 48, 117,
    119, 262

media image of, 79, 84
recovery, politics of, 114–15, 118
reformist culture, 40, 43
slum clearance, 124
stereotypes of, 32
in Stockton, 31, 66, 114
in the suburbs, 17, 136
in Wales, 224
World Disarmament Conference,
  155
World War I, legacy of, 69, 70, 155

Yellow Book (Britain's Industrial Future)
  1928, 51, 52, 142
Yorkshire Evening News, 55, 130
Yorkshire Evening Post, 110, 111, 130
Yorkshire Post, 115, 123, 130, 242
Young Conservatives' Guild, 151
Young Farmers' Clubs, 38
Young, Sir Hilton, 85, 118, 263

Zinoviev letter, 41

Lightning Source UK Ltd.
Milton Keynes UK
UKHW031016101120
373118UK00006B/53